Rumiko Takahashi

The spotlight on Rumiko Takahashi's career began in 1978 when she won an honorable mention in Shogakukan's annual New Comic Artist Contest for *Those Selfish Aliens*. Later that same year, her boy-meets-alien comedy series, *Urusei Yatsura*, was serialized in *Weekly Shonen Sunday*. This phenomenally successful manga series was adapted into anime format and spawned a TV series and half a dozen theatrical-release movies, all incredibly popular in their own right. Takahashi followed up the success of her debut series with one blockbuster hit after another—*Maison Ikkoku* ran from 1980 to 1987, *Ranma ½* from 1987 to 1996, and *Inuyasha* from 1996 to 2008. Other notable works include *Mermaid Saga*, *Rumic Theater*, and *One-Pound Gospel*.

Takahashi won the prestigious Shogakukan Manga Award twice in her career, once for *Urusei Yatsura* in 1981 and the second time for *Inuyasha* in 2002. A majority of the Takahashi canon has been adapted into other media such as anime, live-action TV series, and film. Takahashi's manga, as well as the other formats her work has been adapted into, have continued to delight generations of fans around the world. Distinguished by her wonderfully endearing characters, Takahashi's work adeptly incorporates a wide variety of elements such as comedy, romance, fantasy, and martial arts. While her series are difficult to pin down into one simple genre, the signature style she has created has come to be known as the "Rumic World." Rumiko Takahashi is an artist who truly represents the very best from the world of manga.

RIN-NE
VOLUME 7
Shonen Sunday Edition

STORY AND ART BY
RUMIKO TAKAHASHI

© 2009 Rumiko TAKAHASHI/Shogakukan
All rights reserved.
Original Japanese edition "KYOUKAI NO RINNE"
published by SHOGAKUKAN Inc.

Translation/Christine Dashiell
Touch-up Art & Lettering/Evan Waldinger
Design/Yukiko Whitley
Editor/Mike Montesa

Printed in the U.S.A.

Published by VIZ Media, LLC
P.O. Box 77010
San Francisco, CA 94107

10 9 8 7 6 5 4 3 2 1
First printing, November 2011

www.viz.com   WWW.SHONENSUNDAY.COM

Story and Art by
Rumiko Takahashi

RIN-NE

Characters

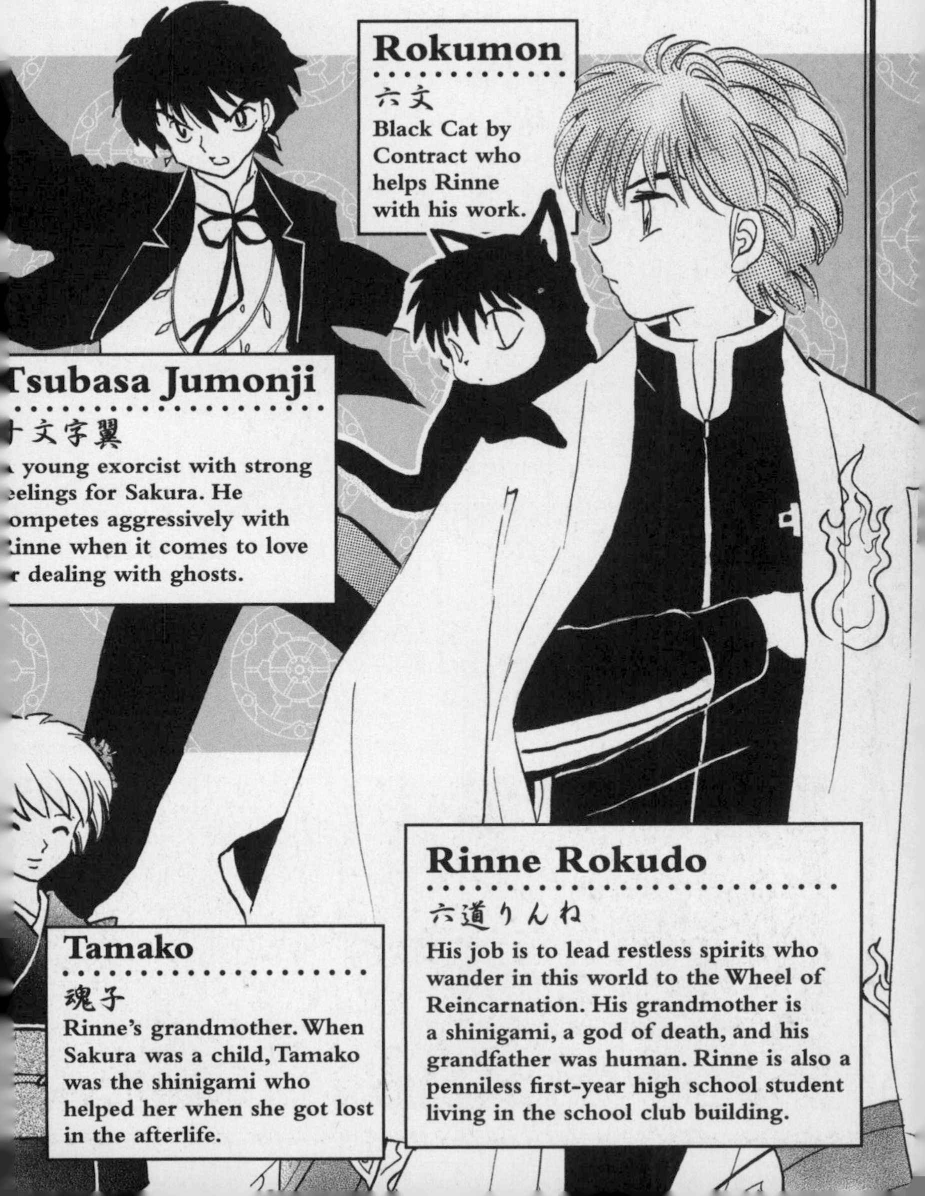

Rokumon

六文

Black Cat by Contract who helps Rinne with his work.

Tsubasa Jumonji

十文字翼

A young exorcist with strong feelings for Sakura. He competes aggressively with Rinne when it comes to love or dealing with ghosts.

Tamako

魂子

Rinne's grandmother. When Sakura was a child, Tamako was the shinigami who helped her when she got lost in the afterlife.

Rinne Rokudo

六道りんね

His job is to lead restless spirits who wander in this world to the Wheel of Reincarnation. His grandmother is a shinigami, a god of death, and his grandfather was human. Rinne is also a penniless first-year high school student living in the school club building.

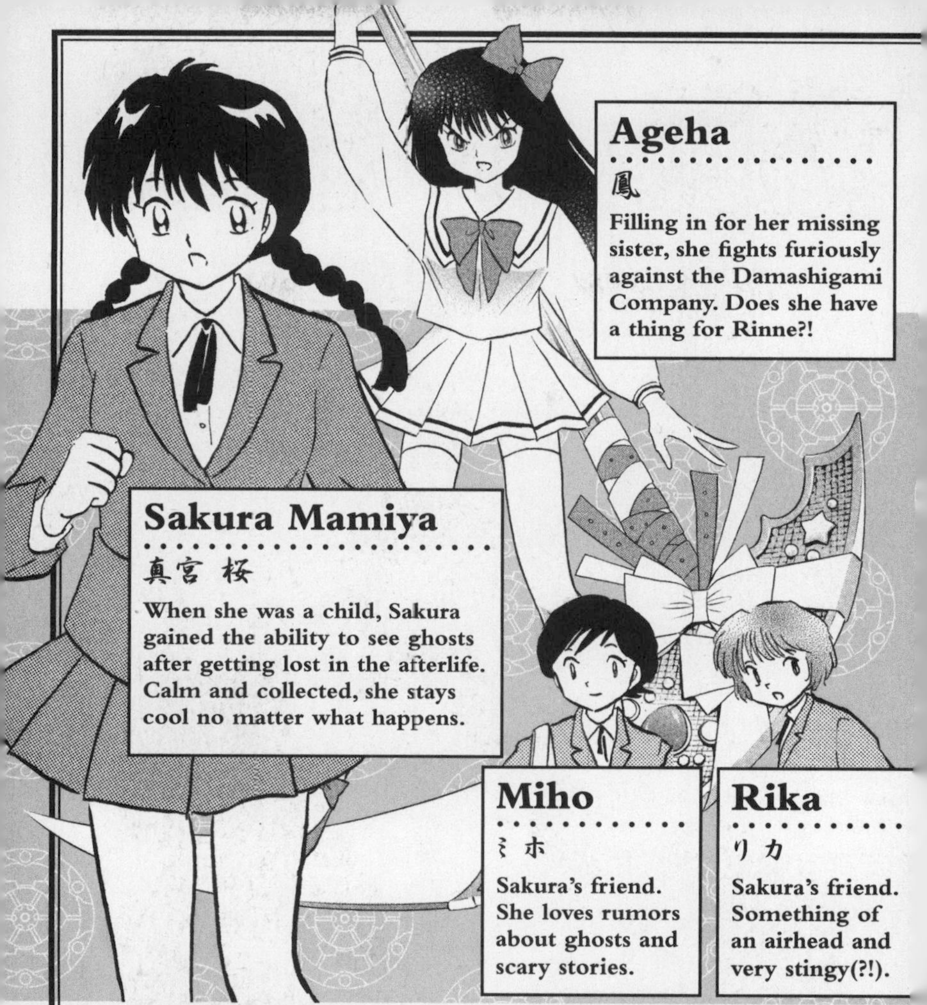

Ageha

鳳

Filling in for her missing sister, she fights furiously against the Damashigami Company. Does she have a thing for Rinne?!

Sakura Mamiya

真宮 桜

When she was a child, Sakura gained the ability to see ghosts after getting lost in the afterlife. Calm and collected, she stays cool no matter what happens.

Miho

ミホ

Sakura's friend. She loves rumors about ghosts and scary stories.

Rika

リカ

Sakura's friend. Something of an airhead and very stingy(?!).

The Story So Far

Together, Sakura, the girl who can see ghosts, and Rinne the shinigami (sort of) spend their days helping spirits that can't pass on reach the afterlife, and deal with all kinds of strange phenomena at their school.

One day, Rinne is suddenly attacked by Kain, a Shinigami Clerk from the afterlife who is responsible for keeping track of life spans. Rinne's father, Sabato, made Rinne the guarantor of his debts, and in exchange for the money, Kain makes off with Rinne's life flame! In disembodied form, Rinne desperately makes use of the legendary Shinigami tool the Ring of Judgment, and just barely manages to recover his life flame before it's too late!

Contents

CHAPTER 59: THE SUMMER FESTIVAL MYSTERY

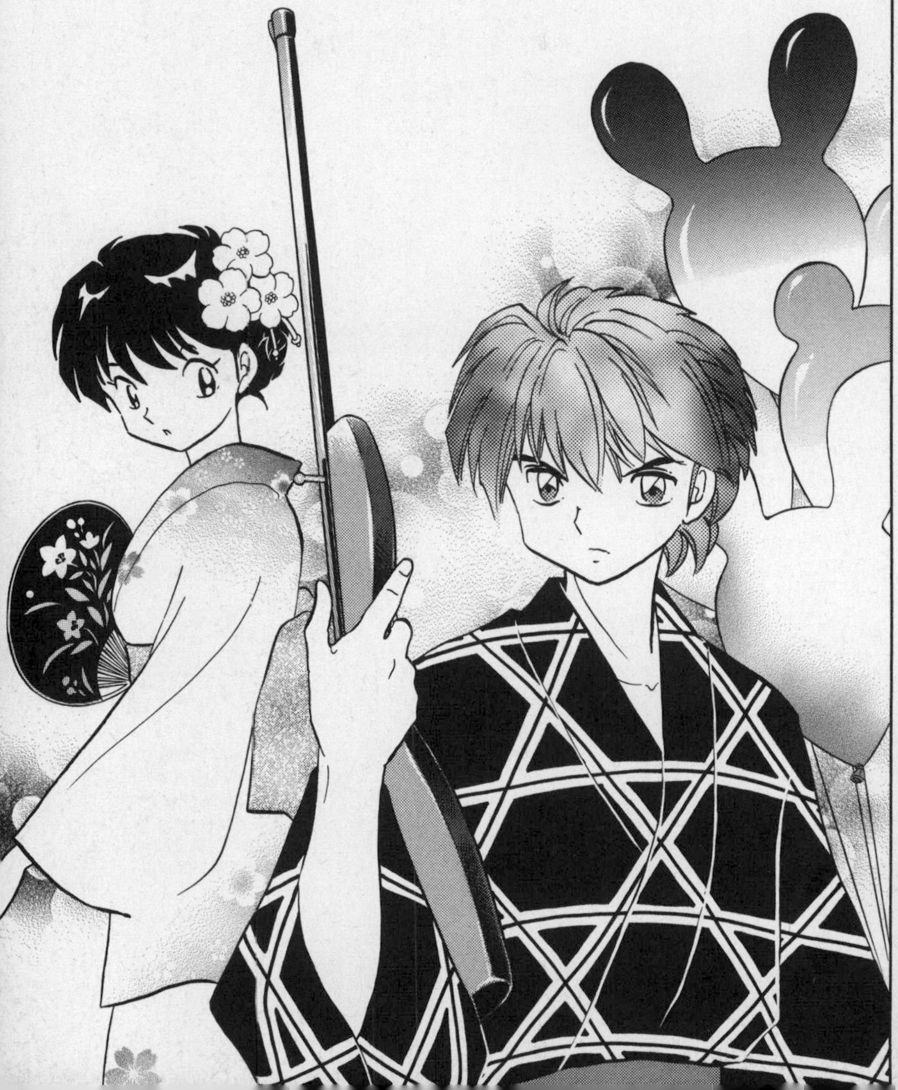

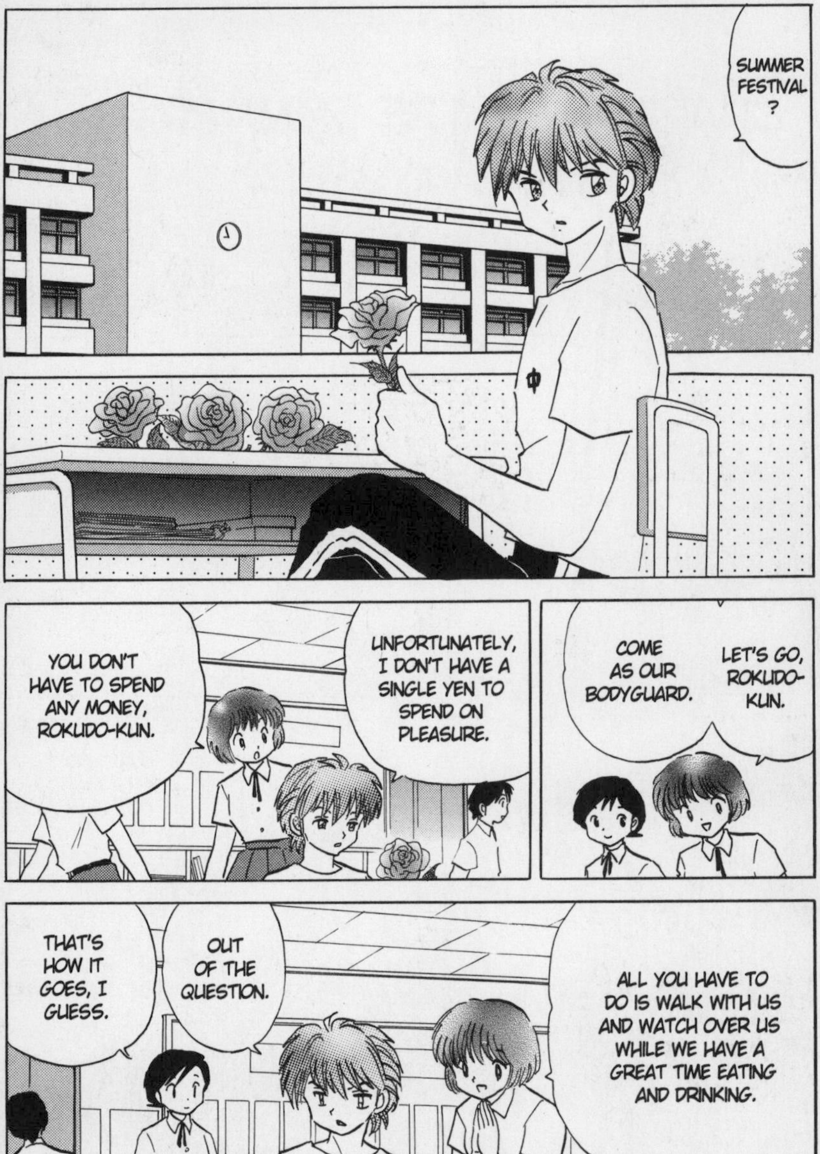
SUMMER FESTIVAL ?
LET'S GO, ROKUDO-KUN.
COME AS OUR BODYGUARD.
UNFORTUNATELY, I DON'T HAVE A SINGLE YEN TO SPEND ON PLEASURE.
YOU DON'T HAVE TO SPEND ANY MONEY, ROKUDO-KUN.
ALL YOU HAVE TO DO IS WALK WITH US AND WATCH OVER US WHILE WE HAVE A GREAT TIME EATING AND DRINKING.
OUT OF THE QUESTION.
THAT'S HOW IT GOES, I GUESS.

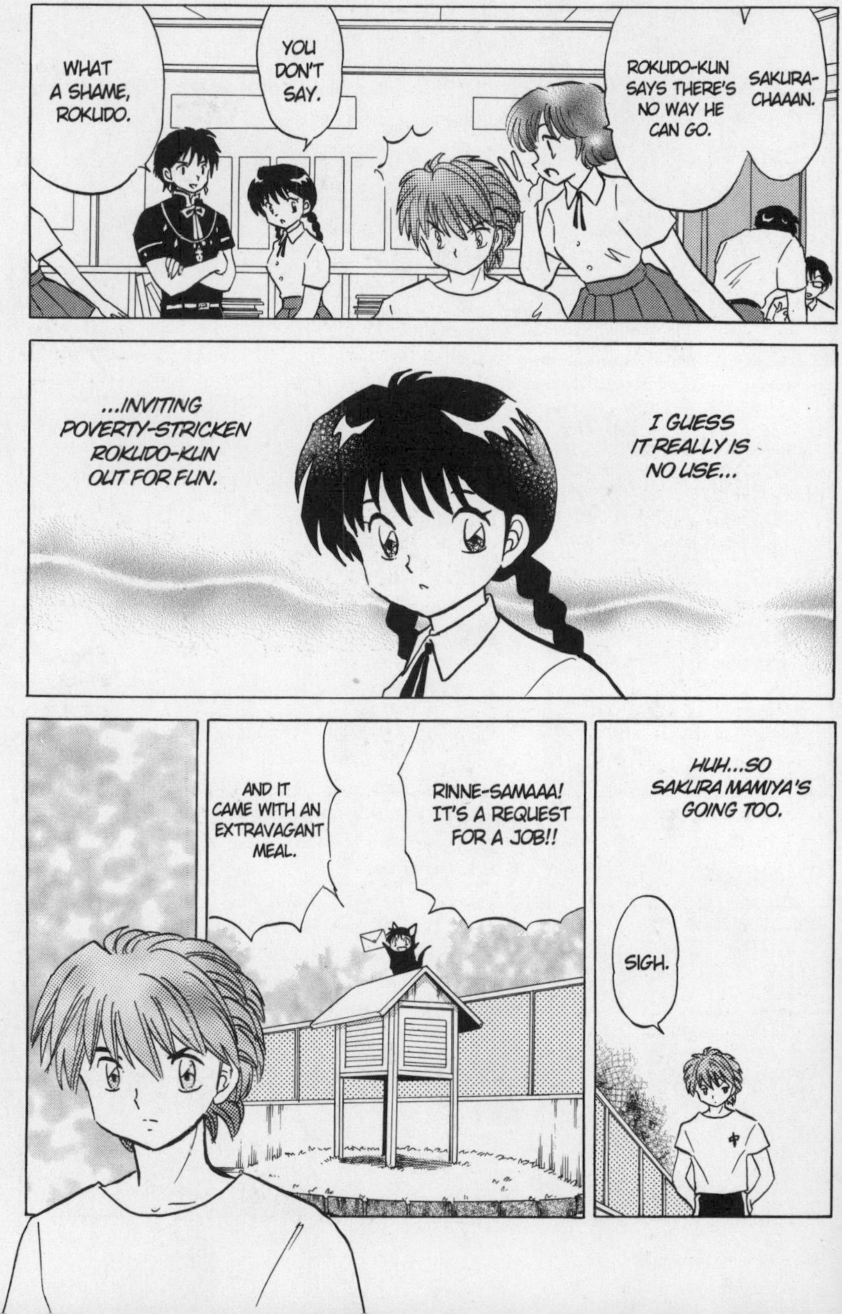
SAKURA-CHAAAN.
ROKUDO-KUN SAYS THERE'S NO WAY HE CAN GO.
YOU DON'T SAY.
WHAT A SHAME, ROKUDO.
I GUESS IT REALLY IS NO USE...
...INVITING POVERTY-STRICKEN ROKUDO-KUN OUT FOR FUN.
HUH...SO SAKURA MAMIYA'S GOING TOO.
SIGH.
RINNE-SAMAAA! IT'S A REQUEST FOR A JOB!!
AND IT CAME WITH AN EXTRAVAGANT MEAL.

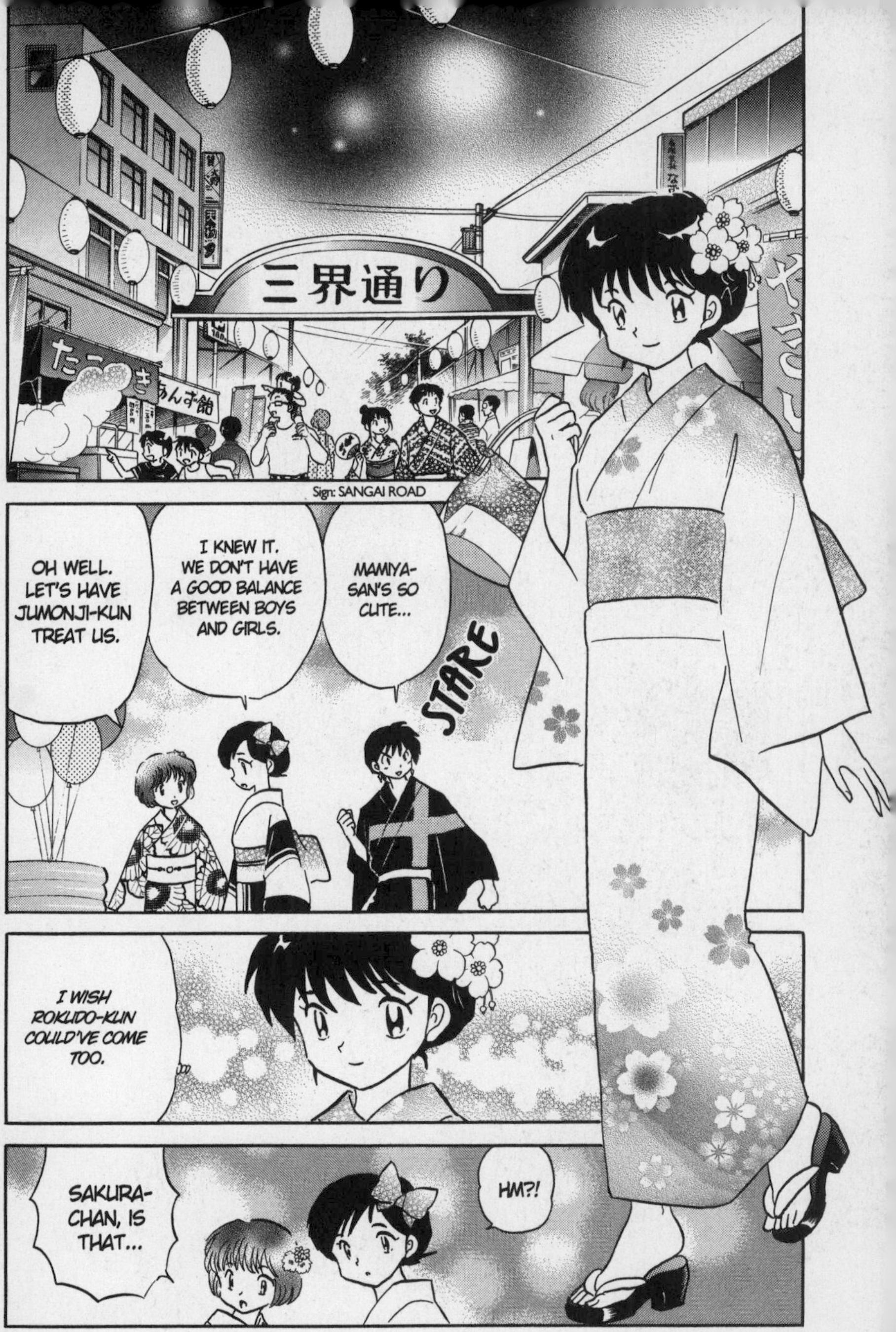
三界通り
あんず飴
Sign: SANGAI ROAD
MAMIYA-SAN'S SO CUTE...
STARE
I KNEW IT. WE DON'T HAVE A GOOD BALANCE BETWEEN BOYS AND GIRLS.
OH WELL. LET'S HAVE JUMONJI-KUN TREAT US.
I WISH ROKUDO-KUN COULD'VE COME TOO.
HM?!
SAKURA-CHAN, IS THAT...

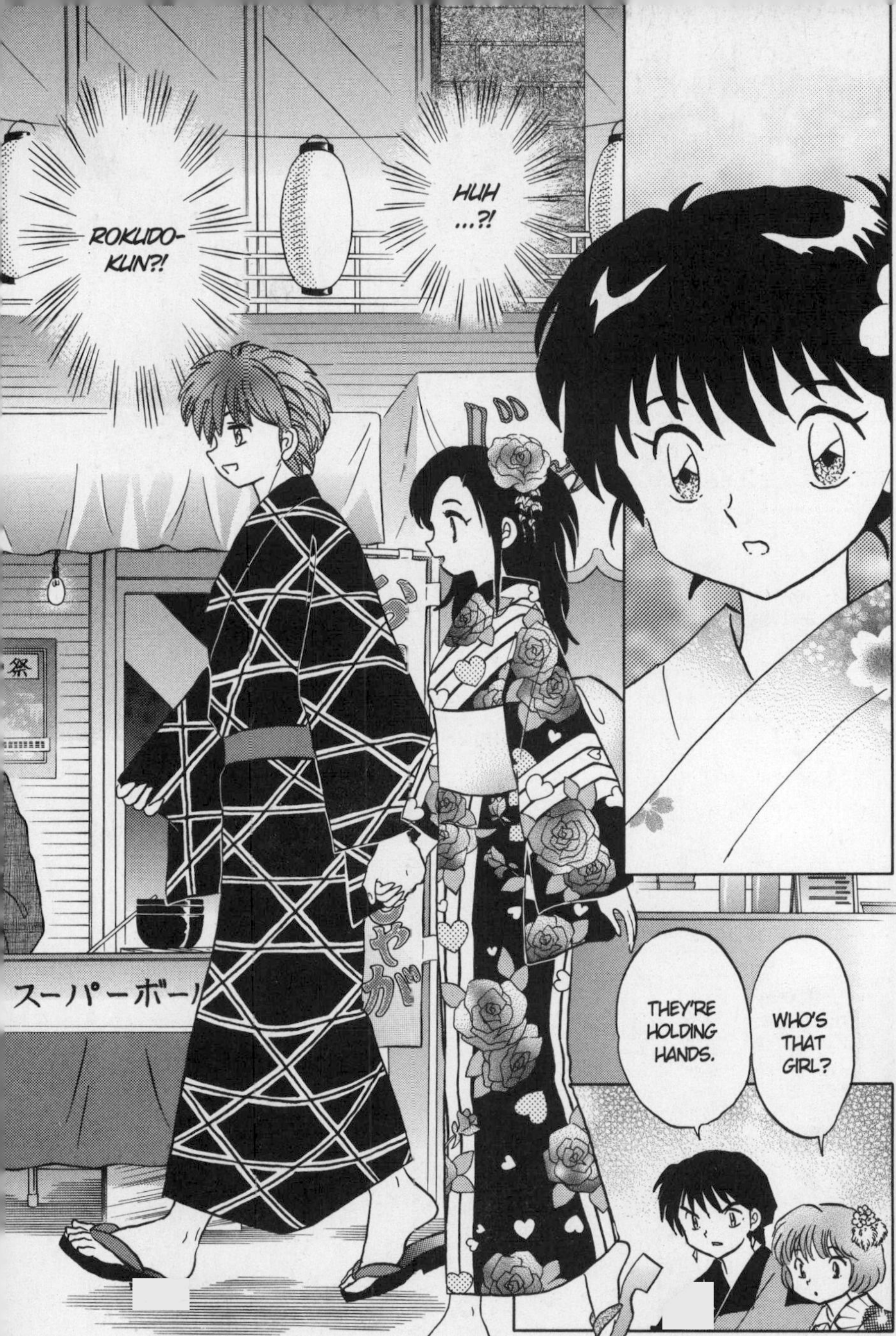
WHO'S THAT GIRL?
THEY'RE HOLDING HANDS.
HUH ...?!
ROKUDO-KUN?!
祭

Banner: SUPER BOWL

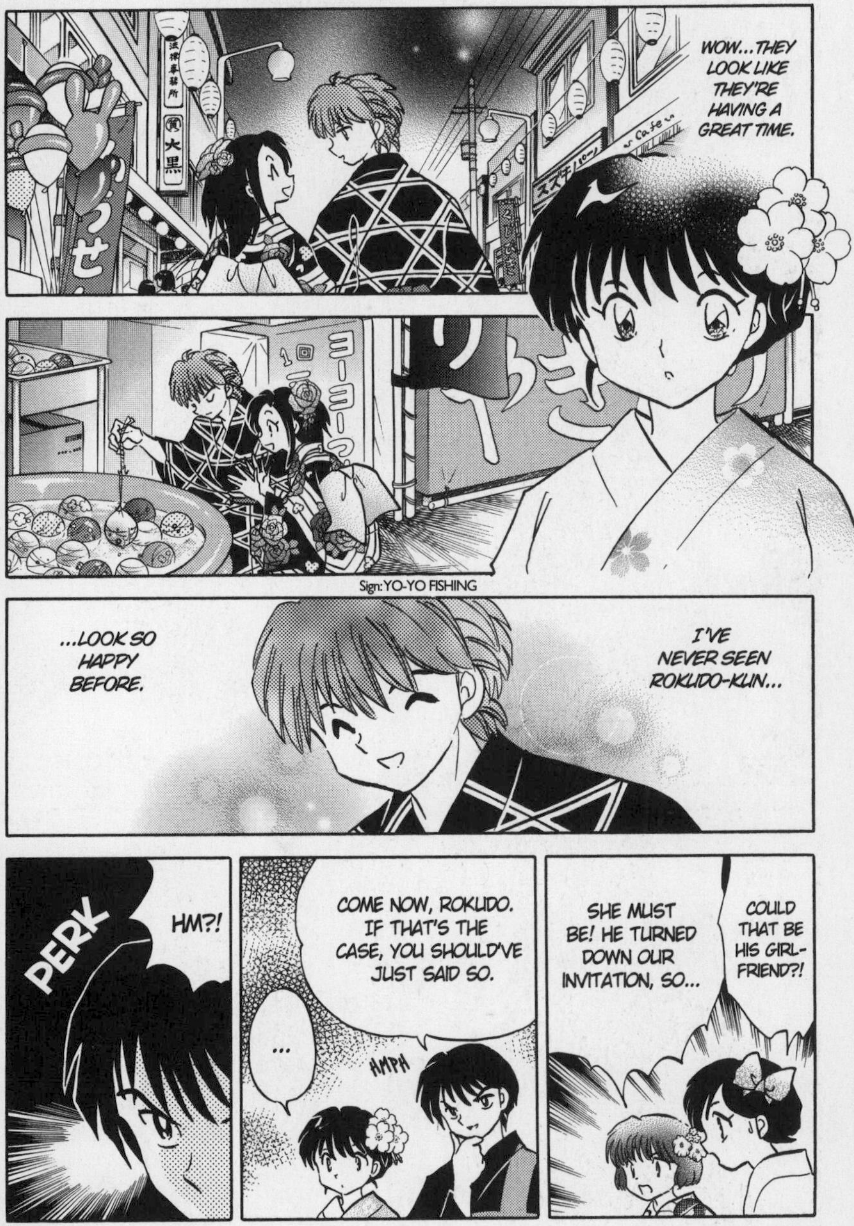
WOW...THEY LOOK LIKE THEY'RE HAVING A GREAT TIME.
Sign: YO-YO FISHING
I'VE NEVER SEEN ROKUDO-KUN...
...LOOK SO HAPPY BEFORE.
COULD THAT BE HIS GIRL-FRIEND?!
SHE MUST BE! HE TURNED DOWN OUR INVITATION, SO...
COME NOW, ROKUDO. IF THAT'S THE CASE, YOU SHOULD'VE JUST SAID SO.
HMPH
...
HM?!
PERK

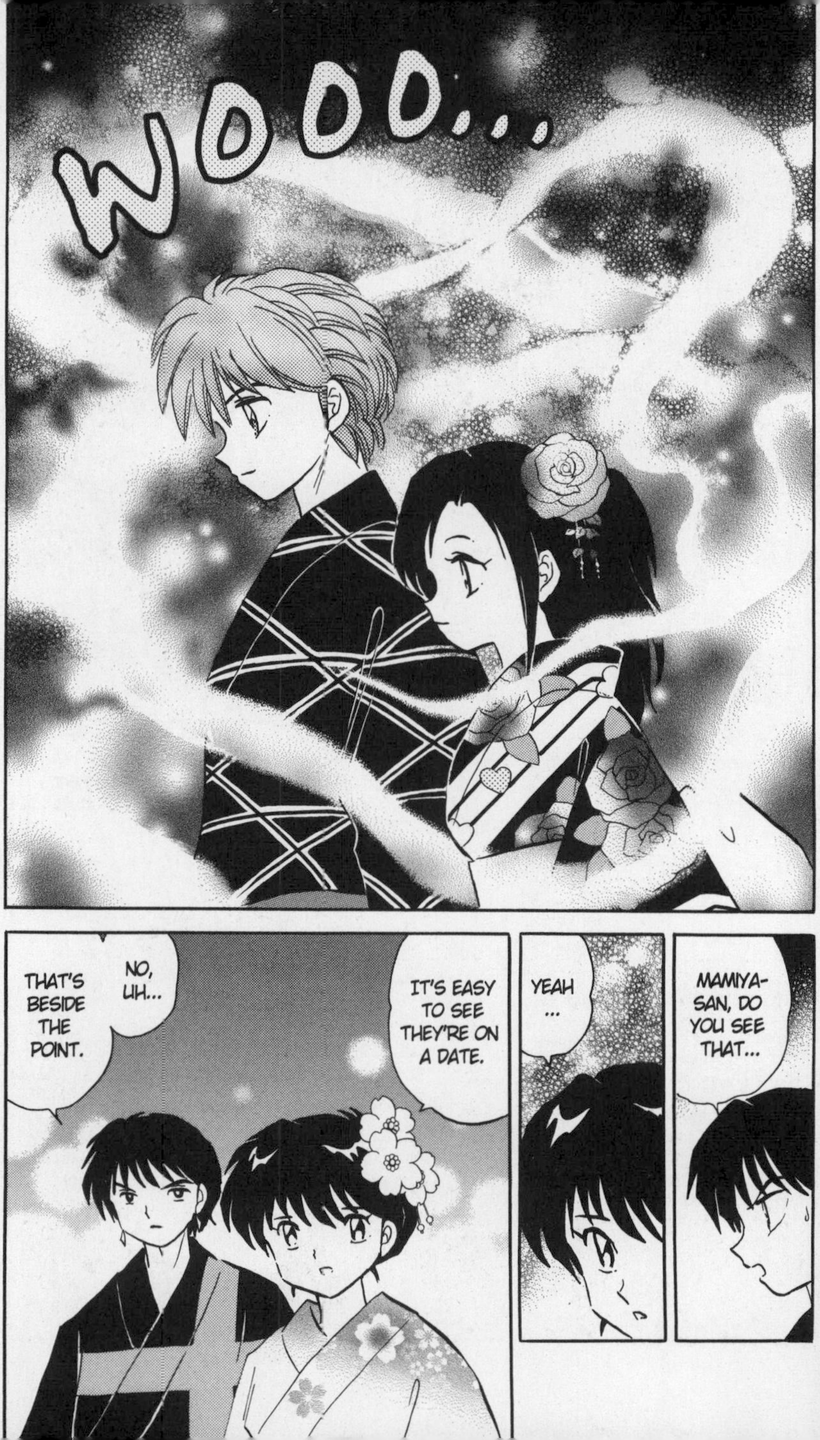
WOOO...
MAMIYA-SAN, DO YOU SEE THAT...
YEAH ...
IT'S EASY TO SEE THEY'RE ON A DATE.
NO, UH...
THAT'S BESIDE THE POINT.

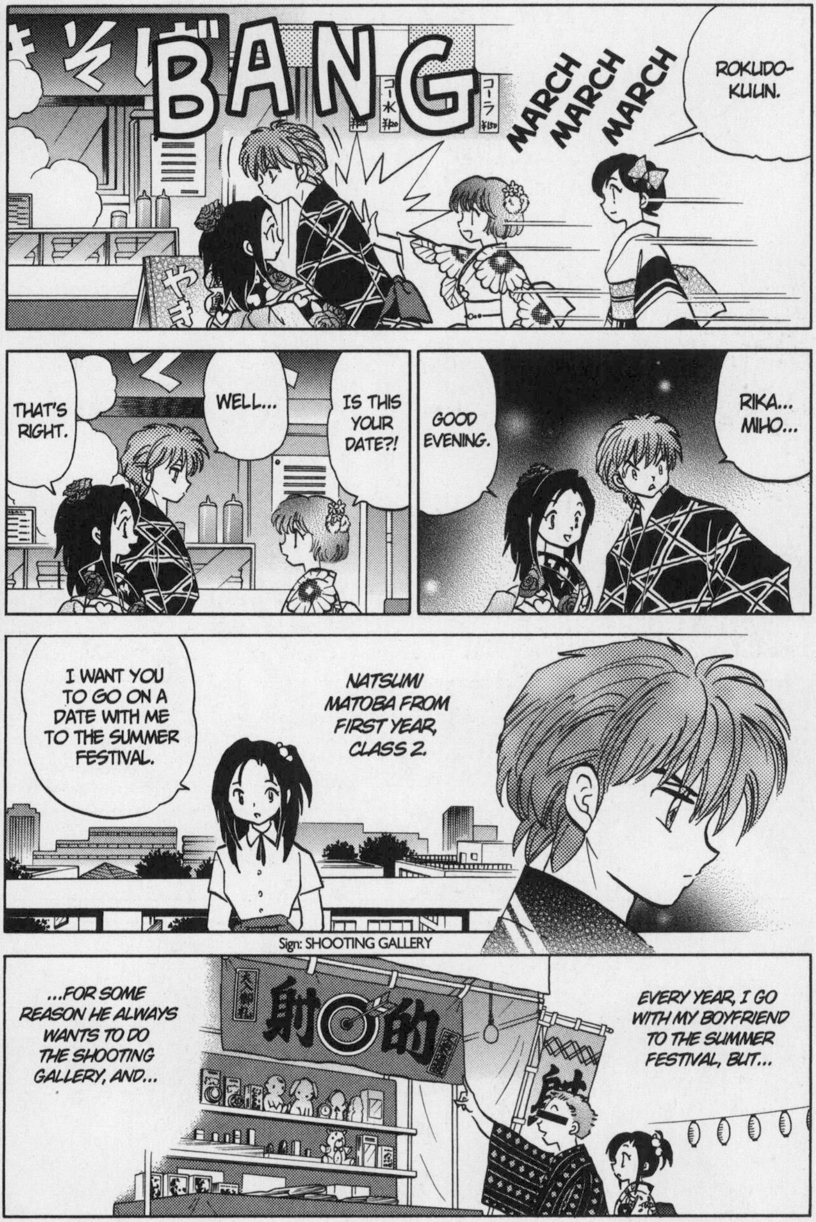
ROKUDO-KUUN.
MARCH MARCH MARCH
BANG
RIKA... MIHO...
GOOD EVENING.
IS THIS YOUR DATE?!
WELL...
THAT'S RIGHT.
NATSUMI MATOBA FROM FIRST YEAR, CLASS 2.
I WANT YOU TO GO ON A DATE WITH ME TO THE SUMMER FESTIVAL.
Sign: SHOOTING GALLERY
EVERY YEAR, I GO WITH MY BOYFRIEND TO THE SUMMER FESTIVAL, BUT...
...FOR SOME REASON HE ALWAYS WANTS TO DO THE SHOOTING GALLERY, AND...

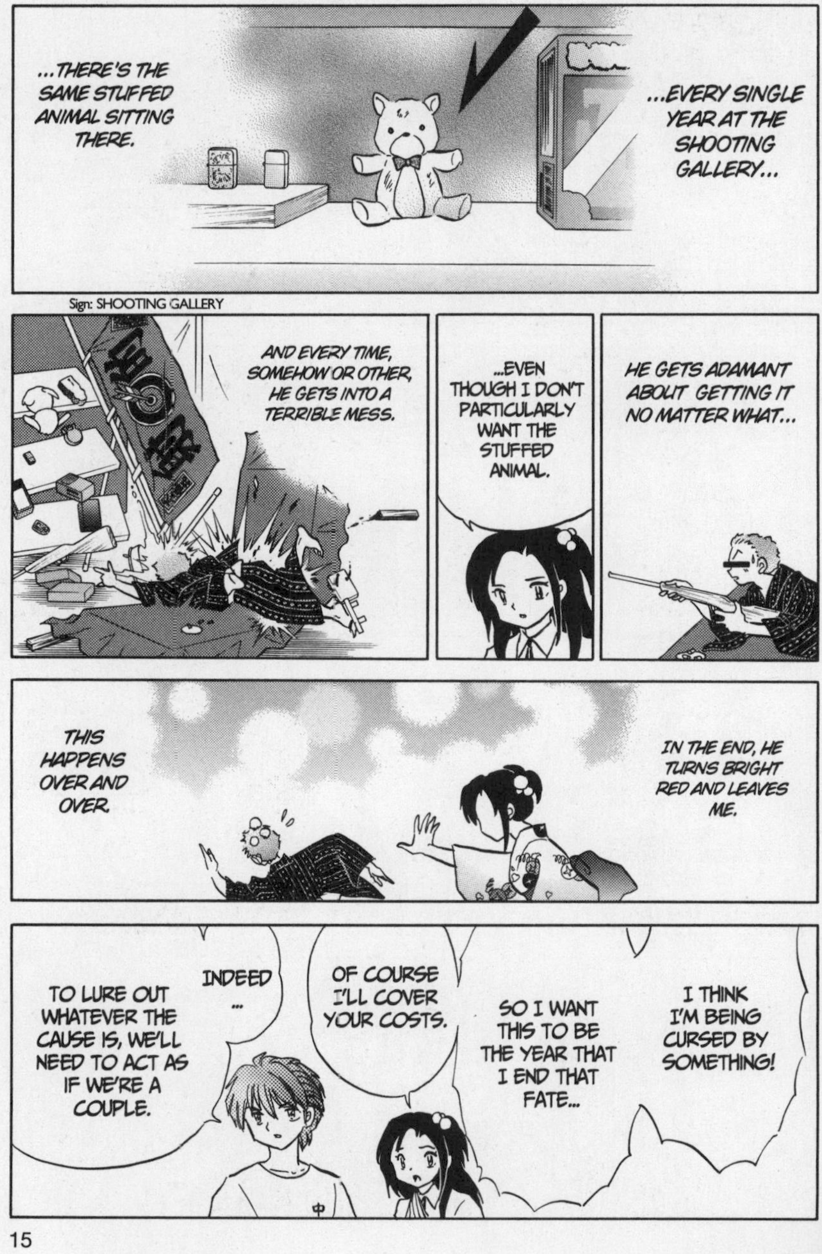

...EVERY SINGLE YEAR AT THE SHOOTING GALLERY...
...THERE'S THE SAME STUFFED ANIMAL SITTING THERE.
HE GETS ADAMANT ABOUT GETTING IT NO MATTER WHAT...
...EVEN THOUGH I DON'T PARTICULARLY WANT THE STUFFED ANIMAL.
AND EVERY TIME, SOMEHOW OR OTHER, HE GETS INTO A TERRIBLE MESS.
Sign: SHOOTING GALLERY
IN THE END, HE TURNS BRIGHT RED AND LEAVES ME.
THIS HAPPENS OVER AND OVER.
I THINK I'M BEING CURSED BY SOMETHING!
SO I WANT THIS TO BE THE YEAR THAT I END THAT FATE...
OF COURSE I'LL COVER YOUR COSTS.
INDEED...
TO LURE OUT WHATEVER THE CAUSE IS, WE'LL NEED TO ACT AS IF WE'RE A COUPLE.

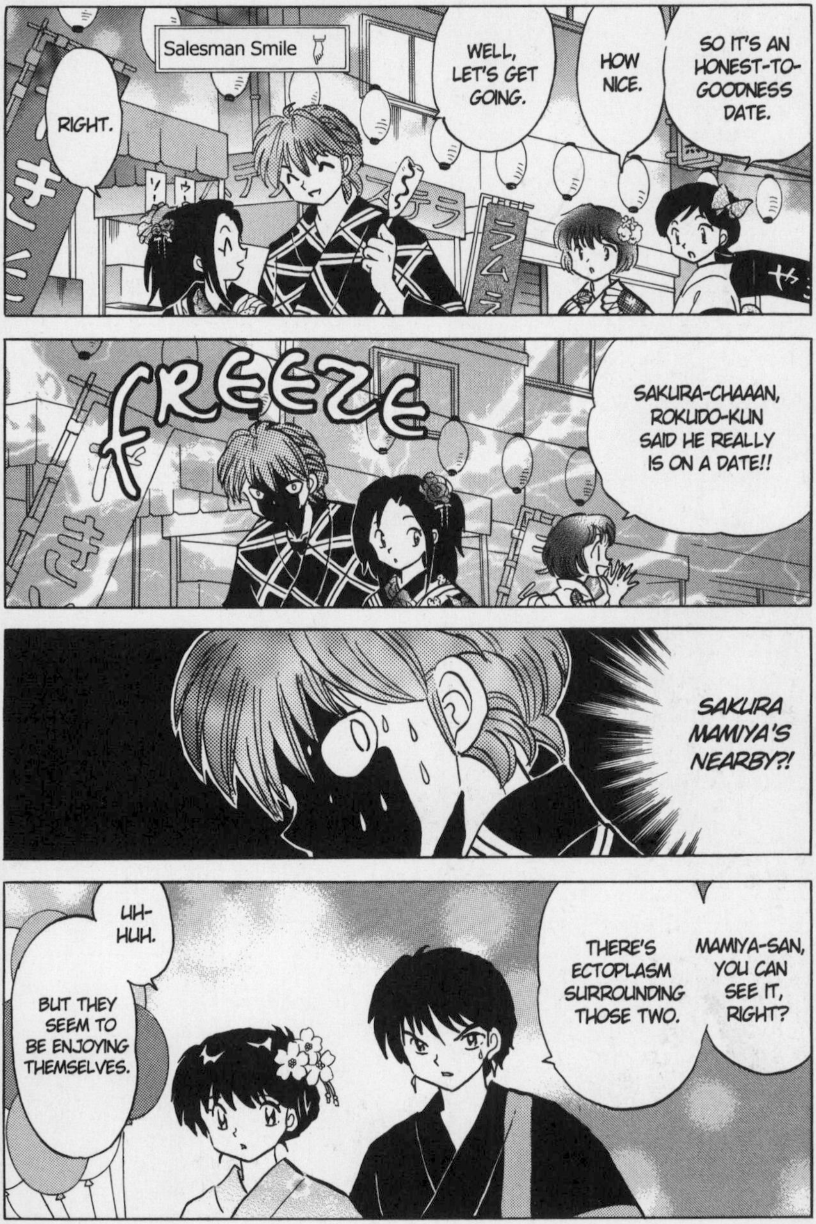
SO IT'S AN HONEST-TO-GOODNESS DATE.
HOW NICE.
WELL, LET'S GET GOING.
Salesman Smile
RIGHT.
SAKURA-CHAAAN, ROKUDO-KUN SAID HE REALLY IS ON A DATE!!
FREEZE
SAKURA MAMIYA'S NEARBY?!
MAMIYA-SAN, YOU CAN SEE IT, RIGHT?
THERE'S ECTOPLASM SURROUNDING THOSE TWO.
UH-HUH.
BUT THEY SEEM TO BE ENJOYING THEMSELVES.

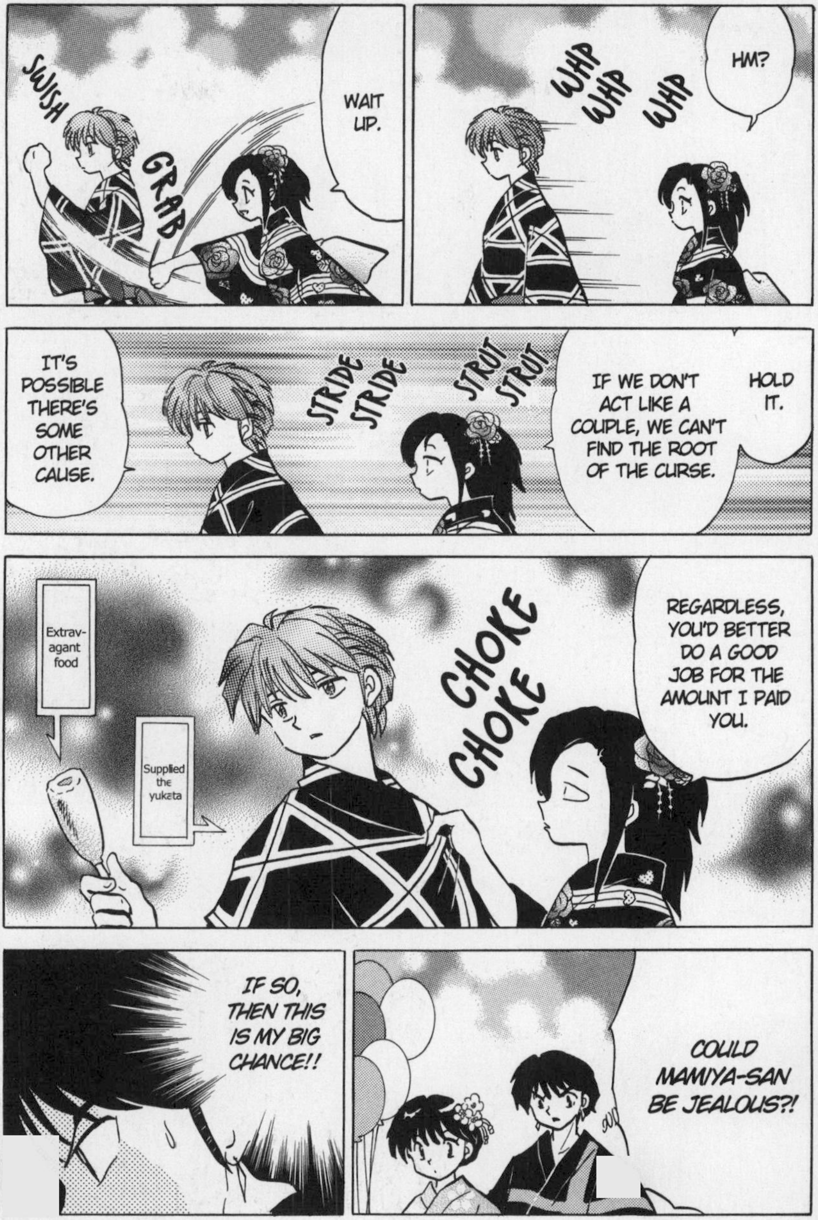
HM?
WHP WHP
WHP
WAIT UP.
SWISH
GRAB
HOLD IT.
IF WE DON'T ACT LIKE A COUPLE, WE CAN'T FIND THE ROOT OF THE CURSE.
STRUT STRUT
STRIDE STRIDE
IT'S POSSIBLE THERE'S SOME OTHER CAUSE.
REGARDLESS, YOU'D BETTER DO A GOOD JOB FOR THE AMOUNT I PAID YOU.
CHOKE CHOKE
Supplied the yukata
Extrav-agant food
COULD MAMIYA-SAN BE JEALOUS?!
IF SO, THEN THIS IS MY BIG CHANCE!!

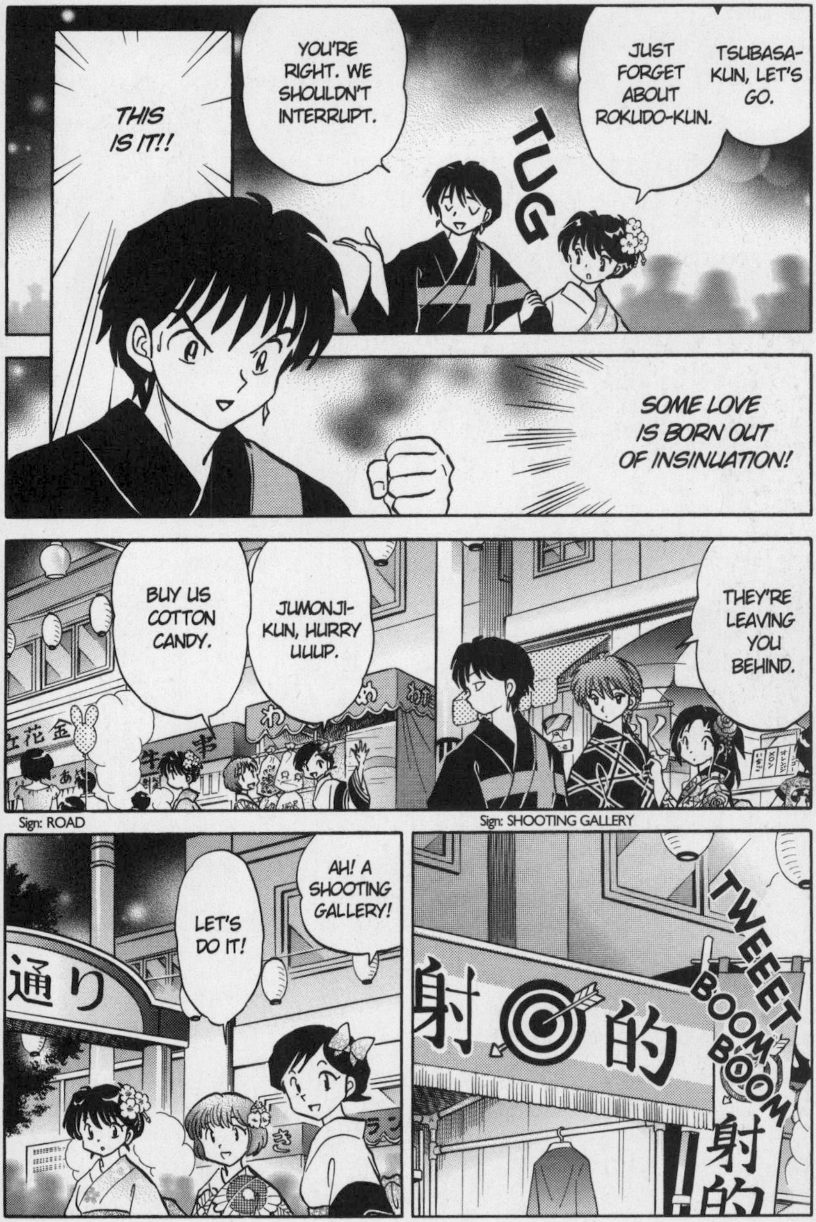
TSUBASA-KUN, LET'S GO.
JUST FORGET ABOUT ROKUDO-KUN.
TUG
YOU'RE RIGHT. WE SHOULDN'T INTERRUPT.
THIS IS IT!!
SOME LOVE IS BORN OUT OF INSINUATION!
THEY'RE LEAVING YOU BEHIND.
JUMONJI-KUN, HURRY UUUP.
BUY US COTTON CANDY.
TWEEET
BOOM
BOOM
射的
射的
AH! A SHOOTING GALLERY!
LET'S DO IT!
通り
Sign: SHOOTING GALLERY
Sign: ROAD

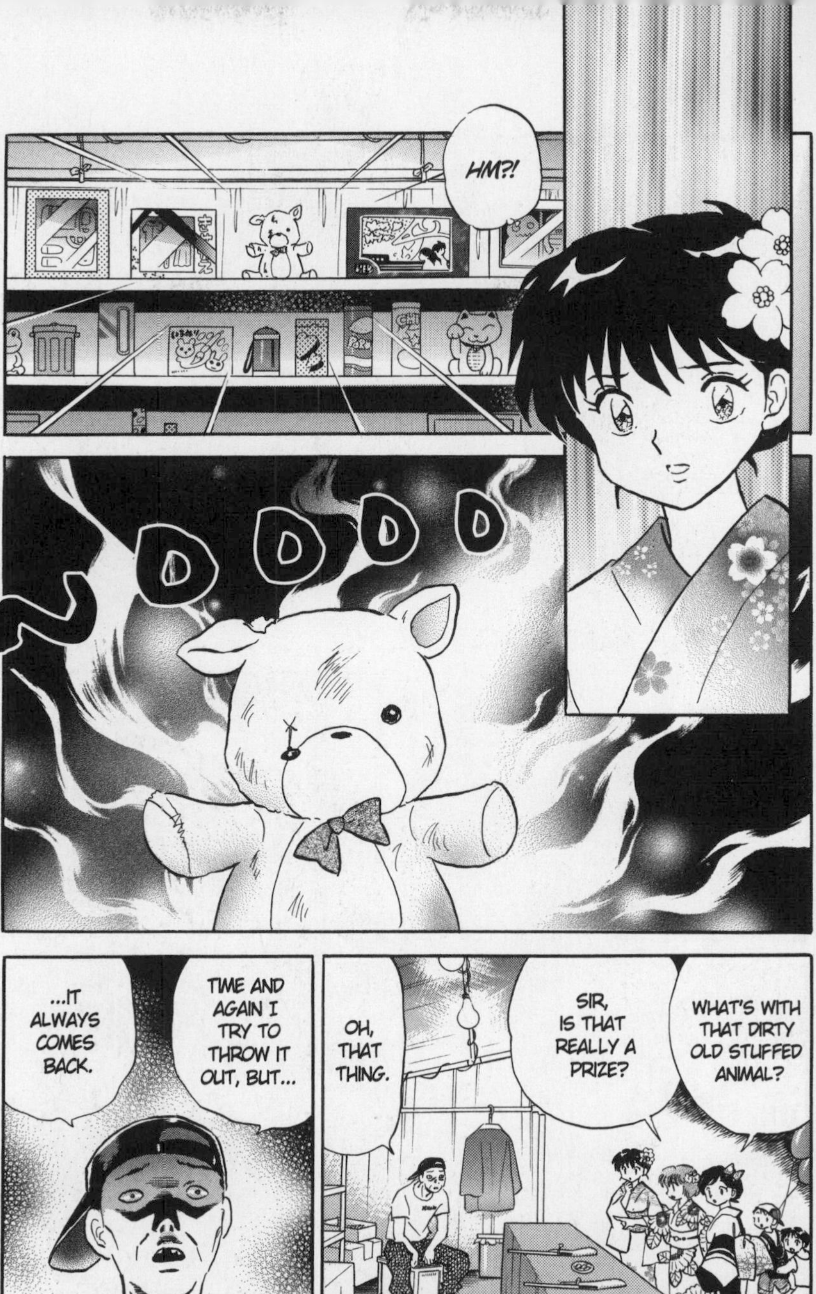
HM?!
WDDDD
WHAT'S WITH THAT DIRTY OLD STUFFED ANIMAL?
SIR, IS THAT REALLY A PRIZE?
OH, THAT THING.
TIME AND AGAIN I TRY TO THROW IT OUT, BUT...
...IT ALWAYS COMES BACK.

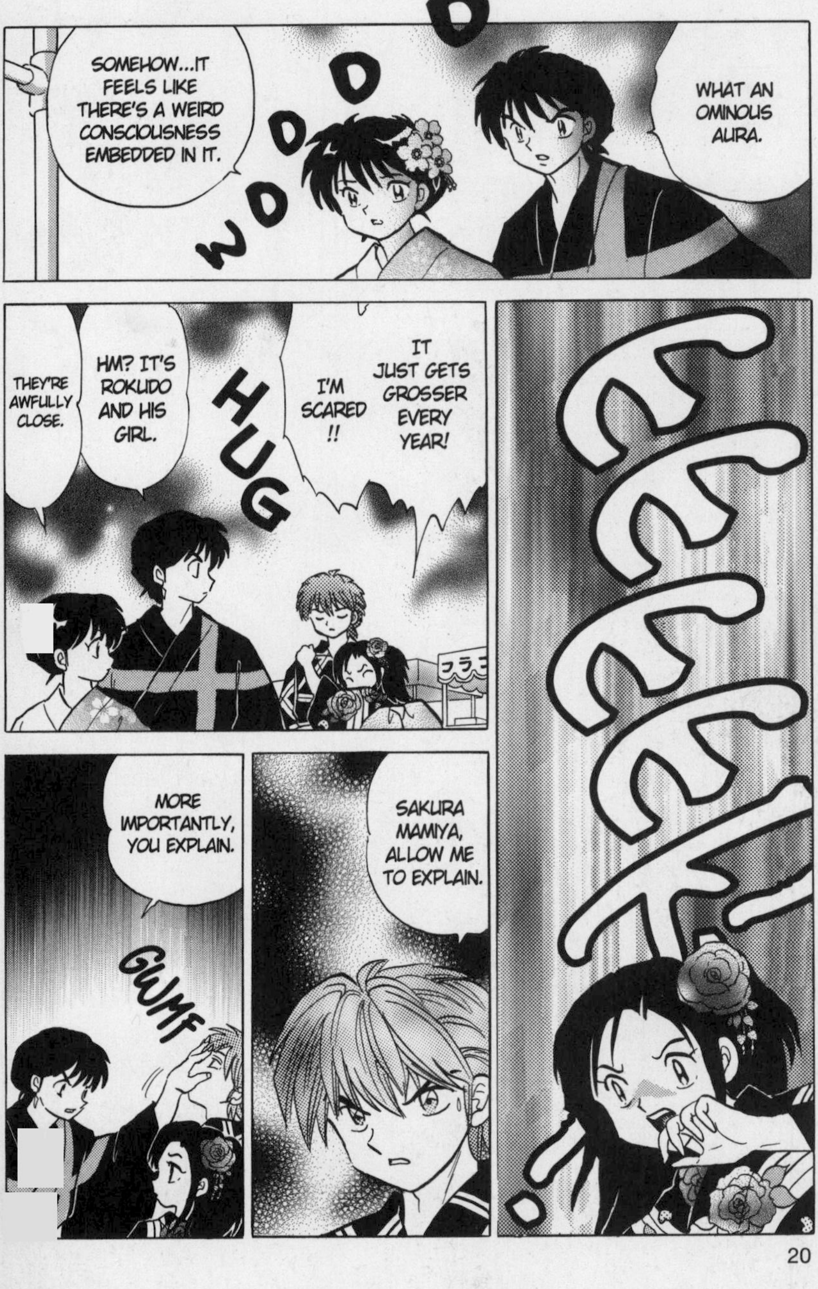
WHAT AN OMINOUS AURA.
WODDDD
SOMEHOW...IT FEELS LIKE THERE'S A WEIRD CONSCIOUSNESS EMBEDDED IN IT.
EEEEEK!
IT JUST GETS GROSSER EVERY YEAR!
I'M SCARED !!
HUG
HM? IT'S ROKUDO AND HIS GIRL.
THEY'RE AWFULLY CLOSE.
SAKURA MAMIYA, ALLOW ME TO EXPLAIN.
MORE IMPORTANTLY, YOU EXPLAIN.
GWMF

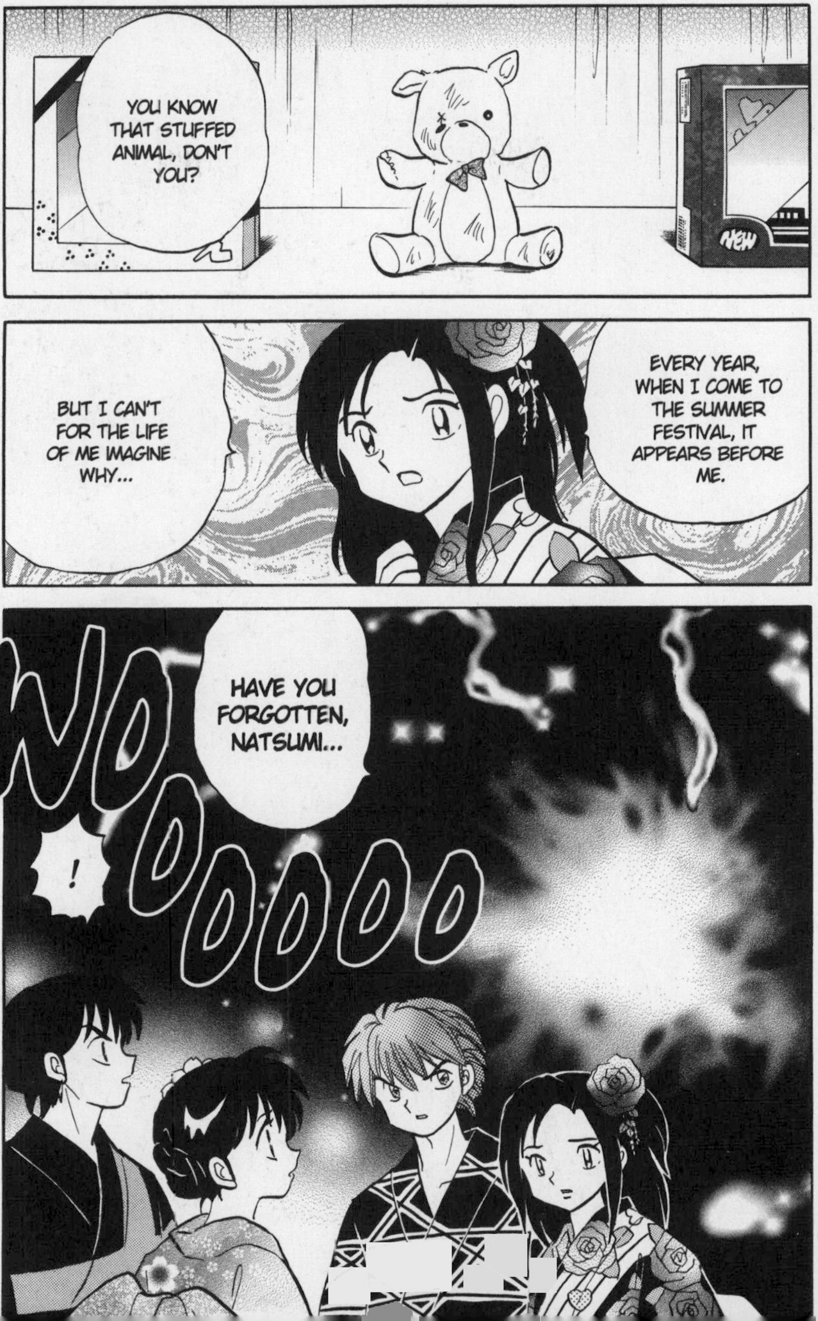
YOU KNOW THAT STUFFED ANIMAL, DON'T YOU?
EVERY YEAR, WHEN I COME TO THE SUMMER FESTIVAL, IT APPEARS BEFORE ME.
BUT I CAN'T FOR THE LIFE OF ME IMAGINE WHY...
HAVE YOU FORGOTTEN, NATSUMI...
WOOOOOOO
!

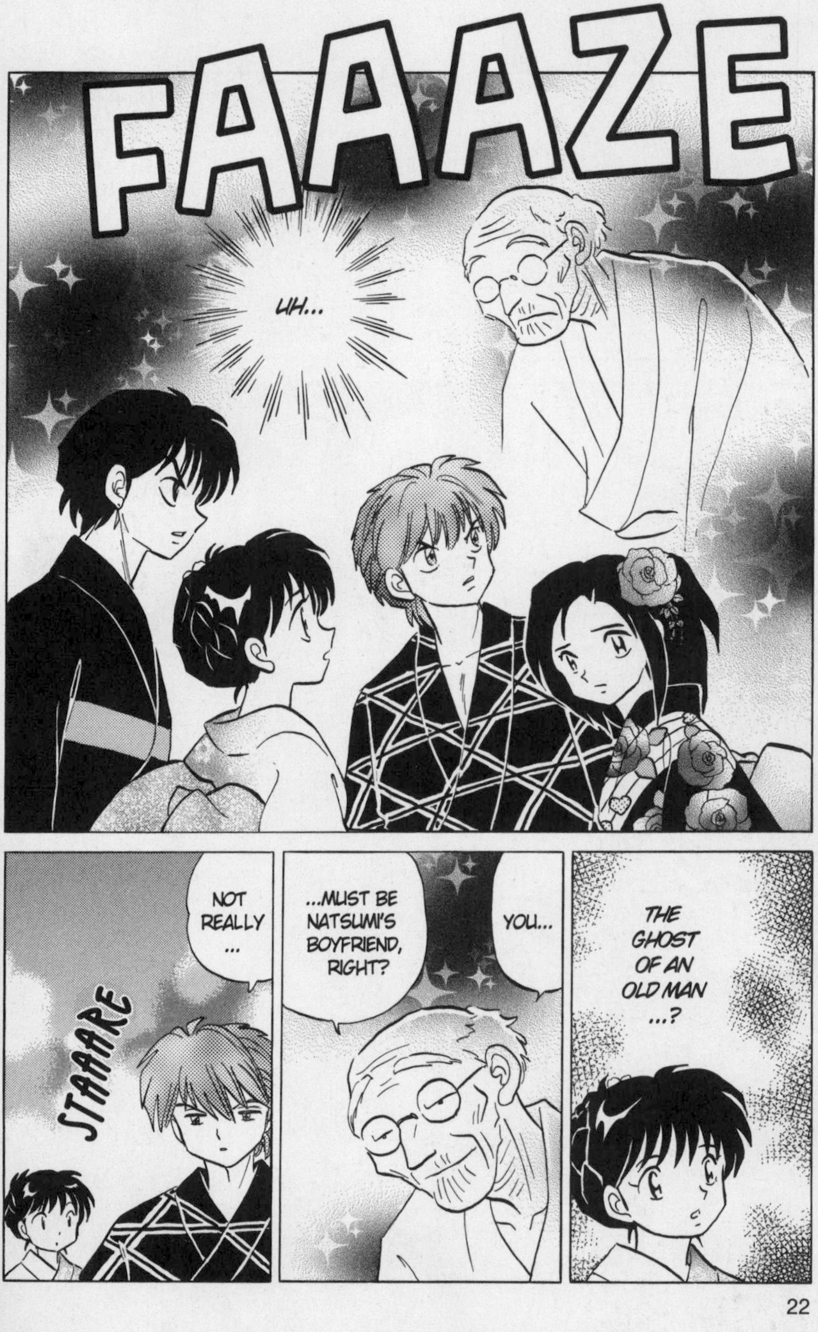
FAAAZE
UH...
THE GHOST OF AN OLD MAN ...?
YOU...
...MUST BE NATSUMI'S BOYFRIEND, RIGHT?
NOT REALLY ...
STAAARE

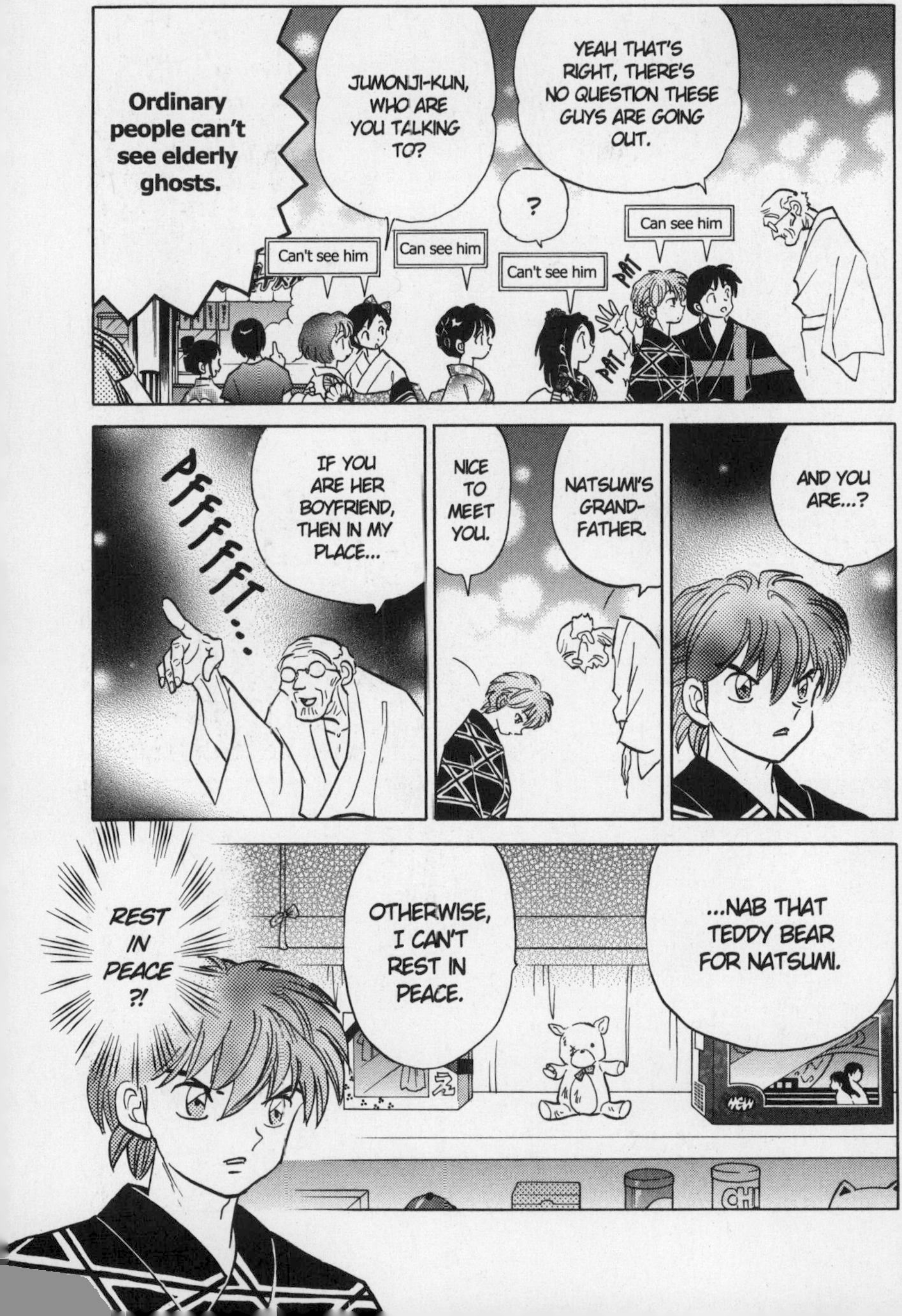
YEAH THAT'S RIGHT, THERE'S NO QUESTION THESE GUYS ARE GOING OUT.
JUMONJI-KUN, WHO ARE YOU TALKING TO?
Ordinary people can't see elderly ghosts.
Can see him
?
Can't see him
PAT
PAT
Can see him
Can't see him
AND YOU ARE...?
NATSUMI'S GRAND-FATHER.
NICE TO MEET YOU.
IF YOU ARE HER BOYFRIEND, THEN IN MY PLACE...
PFFFFFT...
...NAB THAT TEDDY BEAR FOR NATSUMI.
OTHERWISE, I CAN'T REST IN PEACE.
REST IN PEACE?!

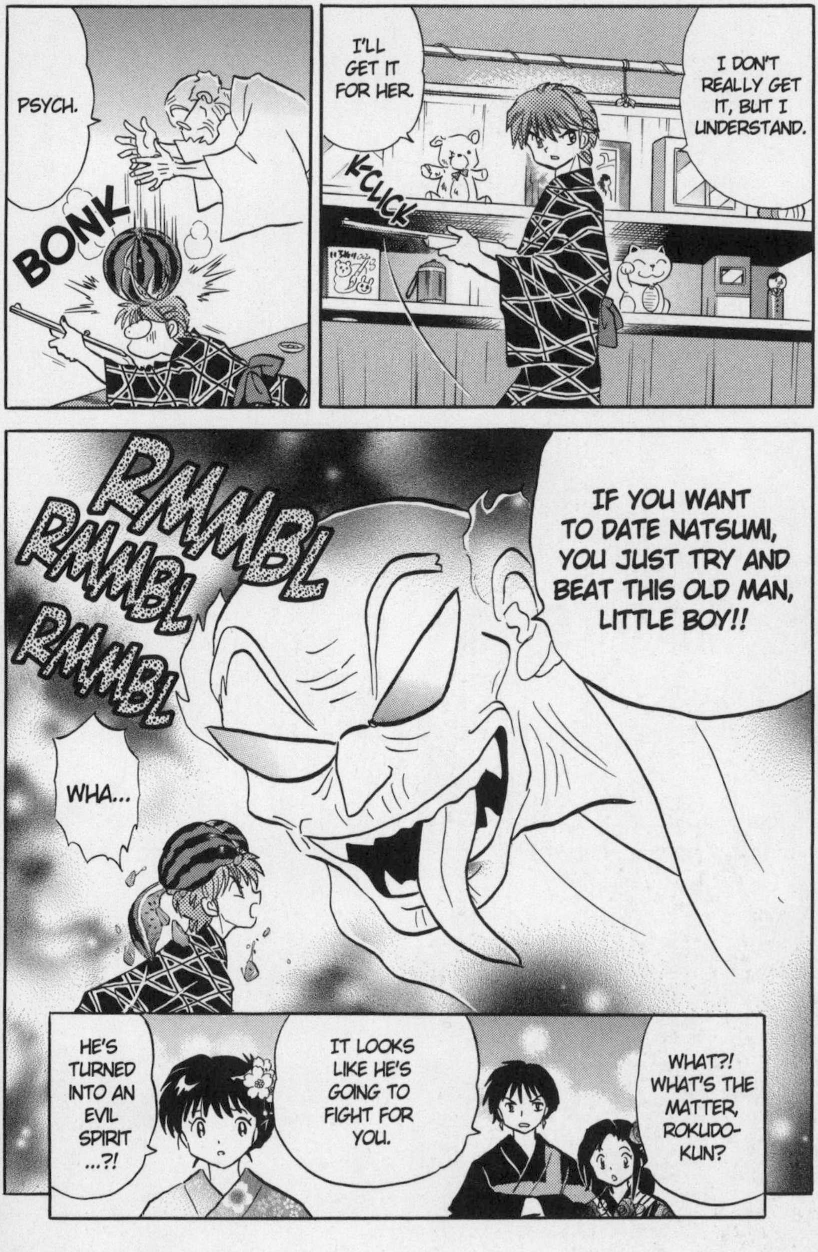
I DON'T REALLY GET IT, BUT I UNDERSTAND.
I'LL GET IT FOR HER.
K-CLICK
PSYCH.
BONK
IF YOU WANT TO DATE NATSUMI, YOU JUST TRY AND BEAT THIS OLD MAN, LITTLE BOY!!
RMMBL RMMBL RMMBL
WHA...
WHAT?! WHAT'S THE MATTER, ROKUDO-KUN?
IT LOOKS LIKE HE'S GOING TO FIGHT FOR YOU.
HE'S TURNED INTO AN EVIL SPIRIT ...?!

CHAPTER 60: THE TEDDY BEAR MEMORY

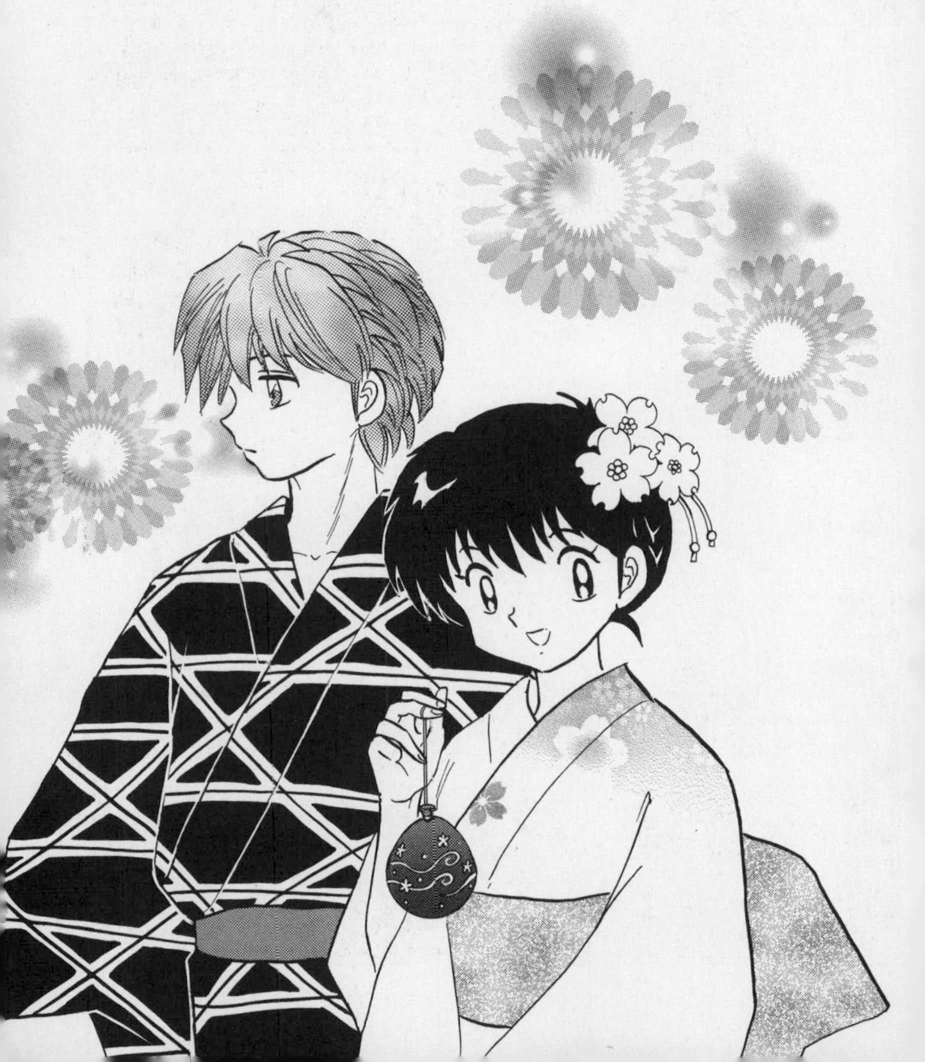

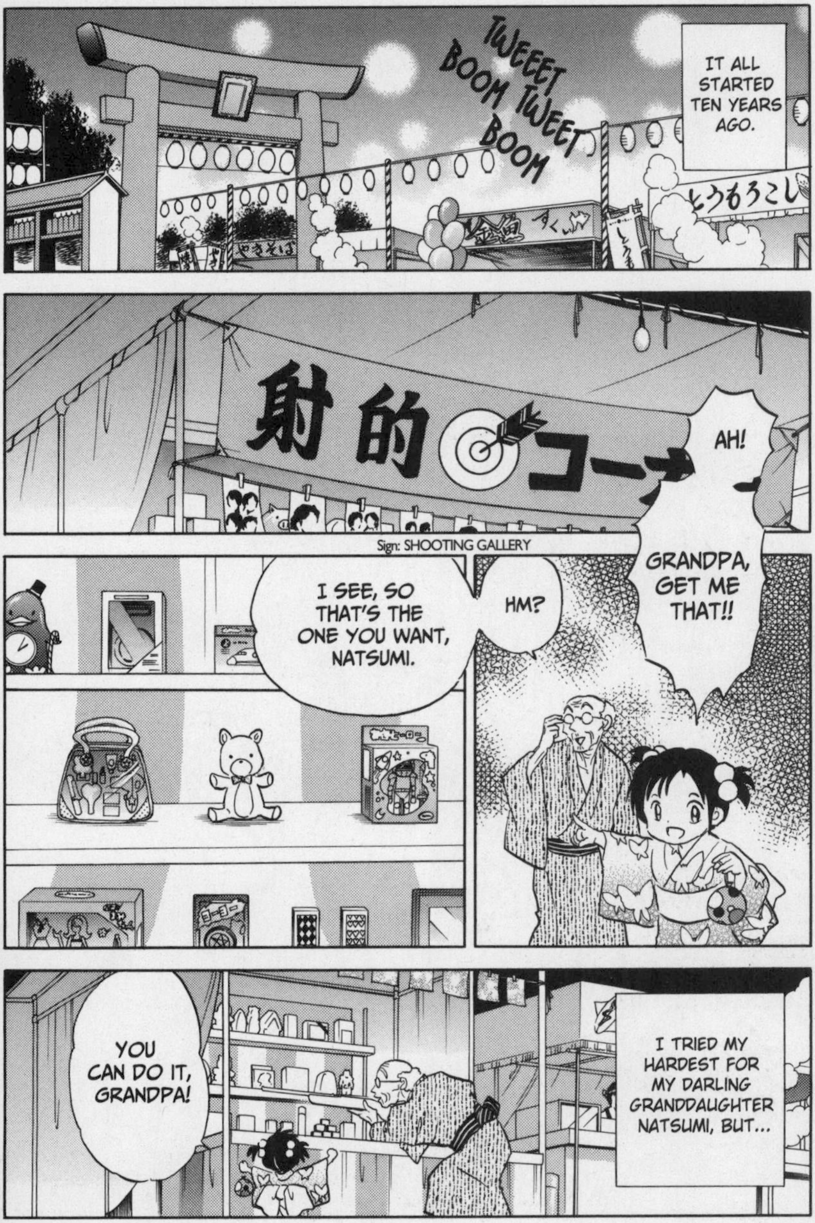
IT ALL STARTED TEN YEARS AGO.
TWEEEET BOOM TWEEET BOOM
とうもろこし
金魚すくい
やきそば
射的コーナー
AH!
Sign: SHOOTING GALLERY
GRANDPA, GET ME THAT!!
HM?
I SEE, SO THAT'S THE ONE YOU WANT, NATSUMI.
I TRIED MY HARDEST FOR MY DARLING GRANDDAUGHTER NATSUMI, BUT...
YOU CAN DO IT, GRANDPA!

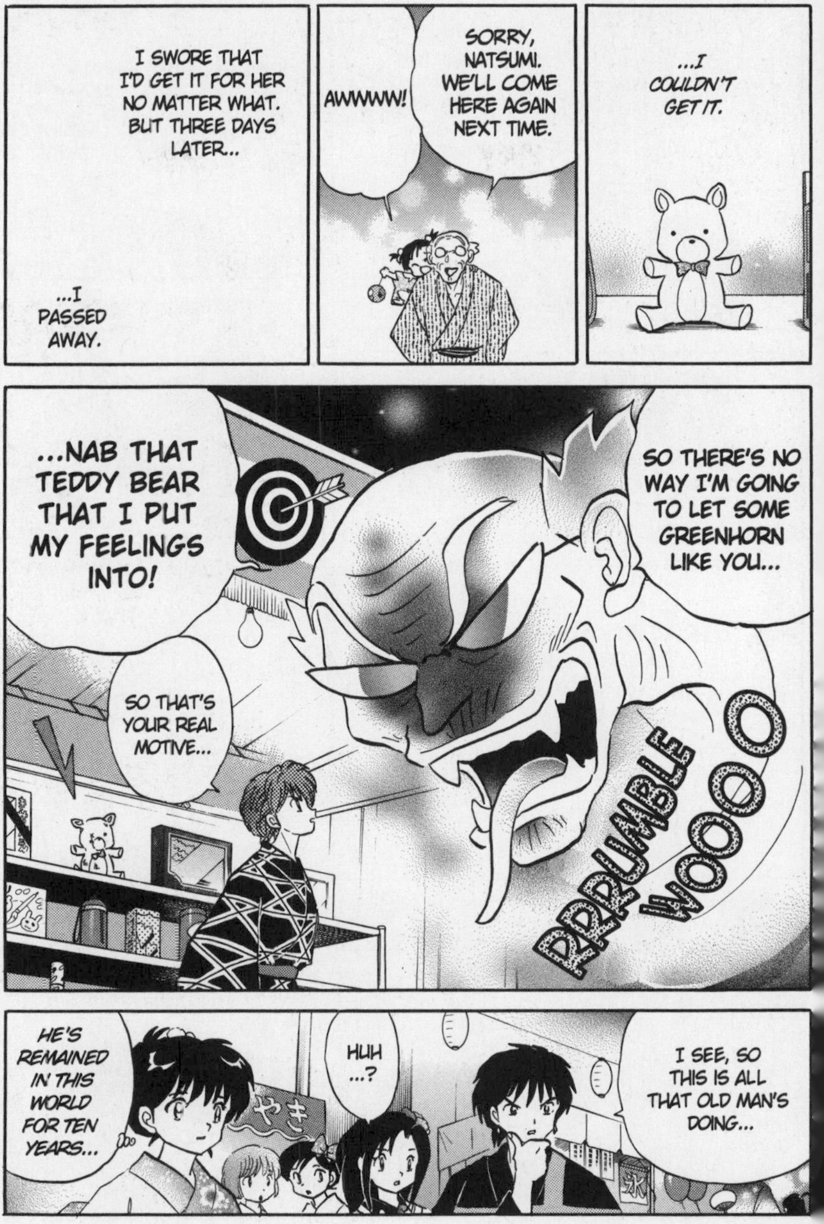
...I COULDN'T GET IT.
SORRY, NATSUMI. WE'LL COME HERE AGAIN NEXT TIME.
AWWWW!
I SWORE THAT I'D GET IT FOR HER NO MATTER WHAT. BUT THREE DAYS LATER...
...I PASSED AWAY.
SO THERE'S NO WAY I'M GOING TO LET SOME GREENHORN LIKE YOU...
...NAB THAT TEDDY BEAR THAT I PUT MY FEELINGS INTO!
RRRUMBLE WOOOOO
SO THAT'S YOUR REAL MOTIVE...
I SEE, SO THIS IS ALL THAT OLD MAN'S DOING...
HUH ...?
HE'S REMAINED IN THIS WORLD FOR TEN YEARS...

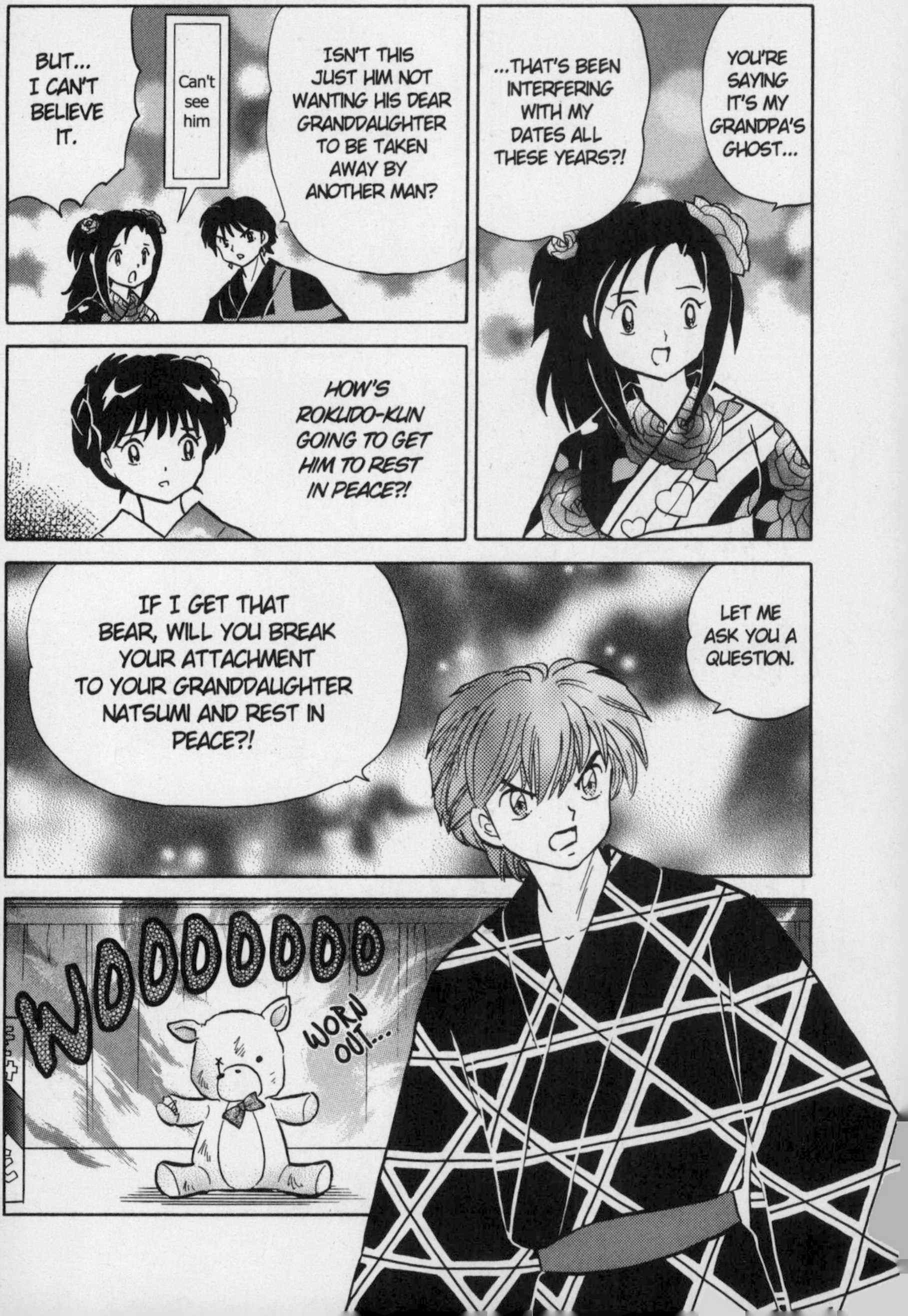
YOU'RE SAYING IT'S MY GRANDPA'S GHOST...
...THAT'S BEEN INTERFERING WITH MY DATES ALL THESE YEARS?!
ISN'T THIS JUST HIM NOT WANTING HIS DEAR GRANDDAUGHTER TO BE TAKEN AWAY BY ANOTHER MAN?
Can't see him
BUT... I CAN'T BELIEVE IT.
HOW'S ROKUDO-KUN GOING TO GET HIM TO REST IN PEACE?!
LET ME ASK YOU A QUESTION.
IF I GET THAT BEAR, WILL YOU BREAK YOUR ATTACHMENT TO YOUR GRANDDAUGHTER NATSUMI AND REST IN PEACE?!
WOOOOOOO
WORN OUT...

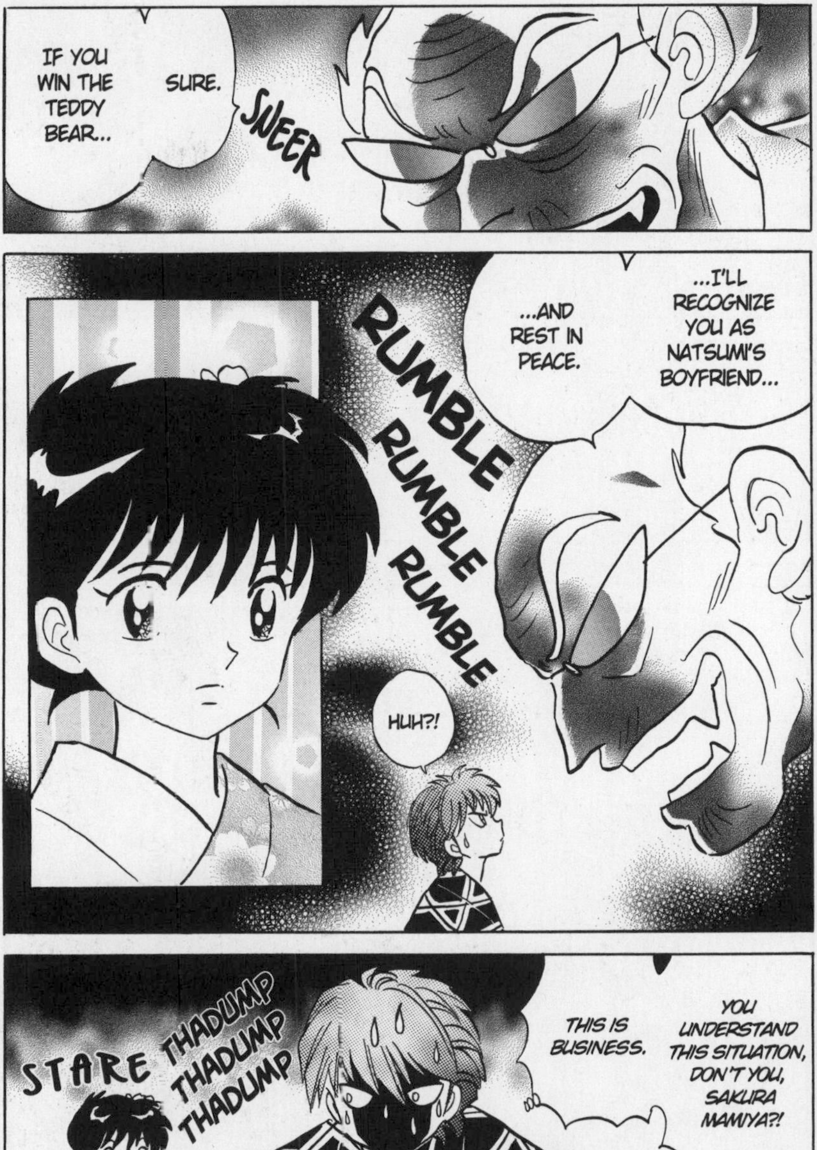
SURE.
IF YOU WIN THE TEDDY BEAR...
SWEER
...I'LL RECOGNIZE YOU AS NATSUMI'S BOYFRIEND...
...AND REST IN PEACE.
RUMBLE RUMBLE RUMBLE
HUH?!
YOU UNDERSTAND THIS SITUATION, DON'T YOU, SAKURA MAMIYA?!
THIS IS BUSINESS.
THADUMP THADUMP THADUMP
STARE

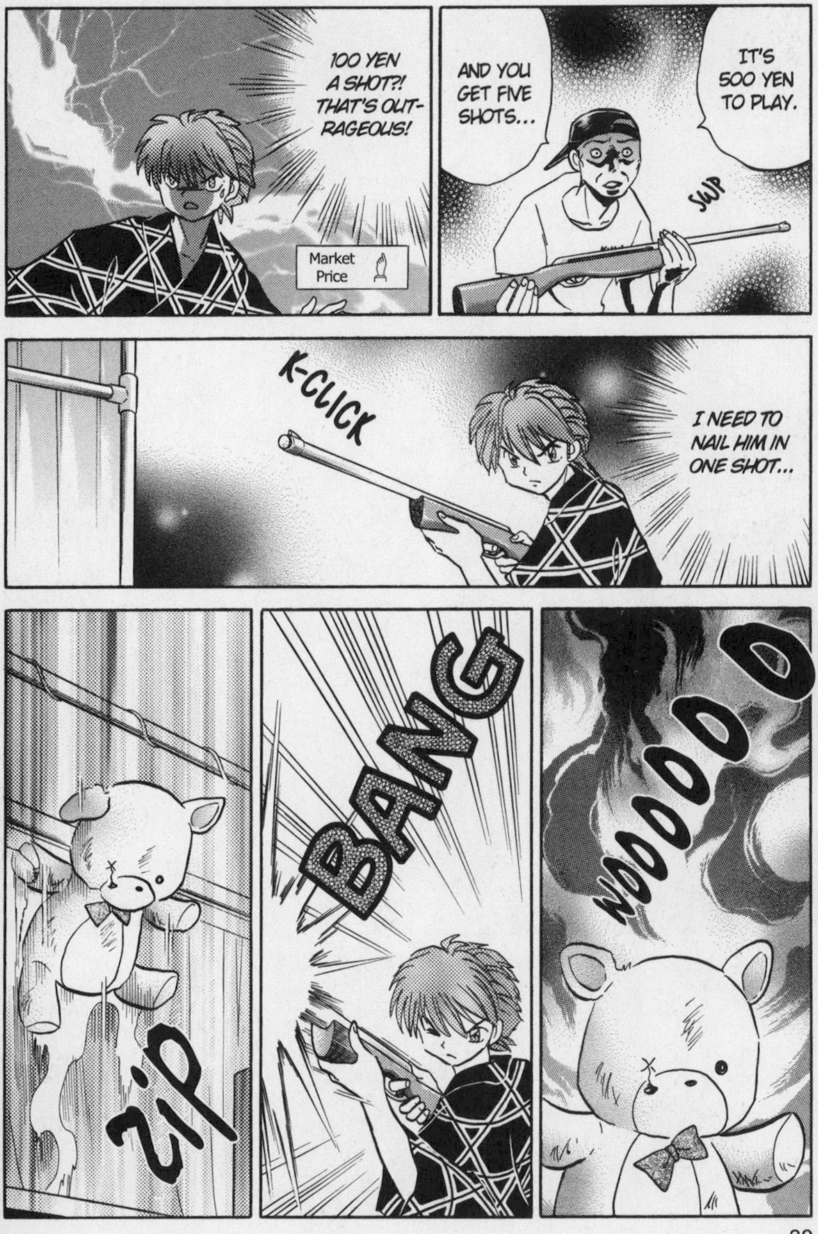
IT'S 500 YEN TO PLAY.
AND YOU GET FIVE SHOTS...
SWIP
100 YEN A SHOT?! THAT'S OUT-RAGEOUS!
Market Price
I NEED TO NAIL HIM IN ONE SHOT...
K-CLICK
NOOOOOO
BANG
zip

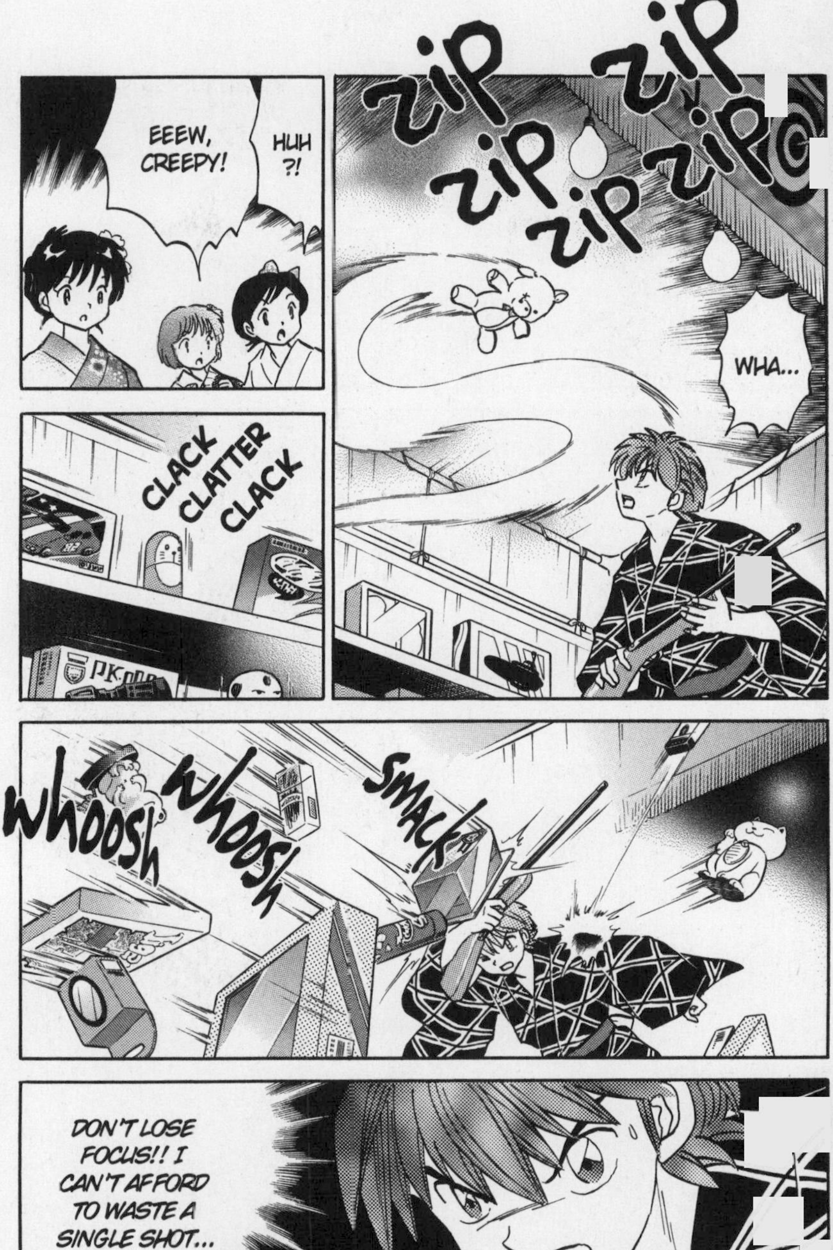
ZIP ZIP ZIP ZIP ZIP ZIP
WHA...
HUH ?!
EEEW, CREEPY!
CLACK CLATTER CLACK
SMACK
WHOOSH
WHOOSH
DON'T LOSE FOCUS!! I CAN'T AFFORD TO WASTE A SINGLE SHOT...

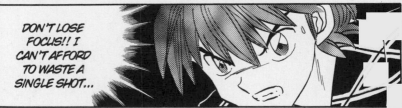

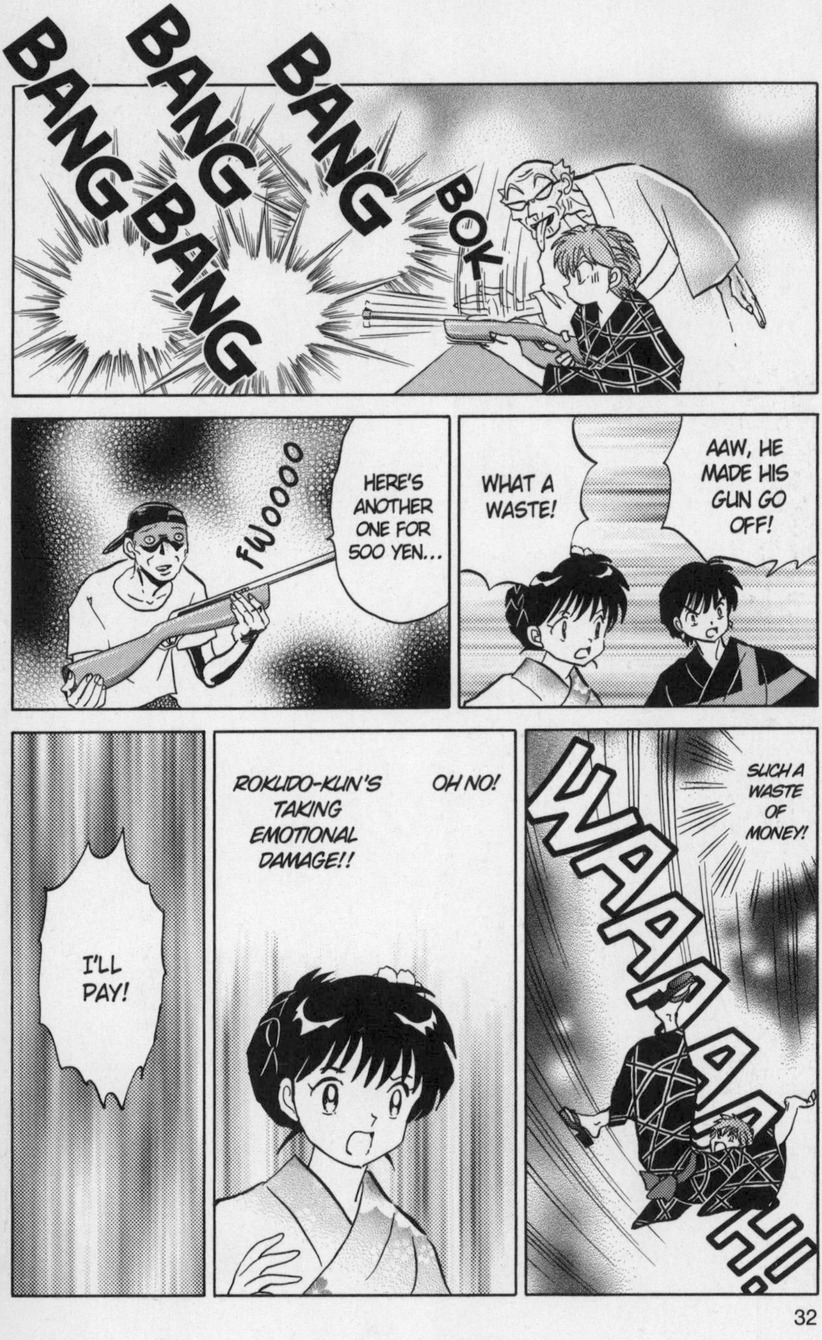
BOK
BANG
BANG
BANG
BANG
AAW, HE MADE HIS GUN GO OFF!
WHAT A WASTE!
HERE'S ANOTHER ONE FOR 500 YEN...
FWOOOO
SUCH A WASTE OF MONEY!
WAAAAAH!
OH NO!
ROKUDO-KUN'S TAKING EMOTIONAL DAMAGE!!
I'LL PAY!

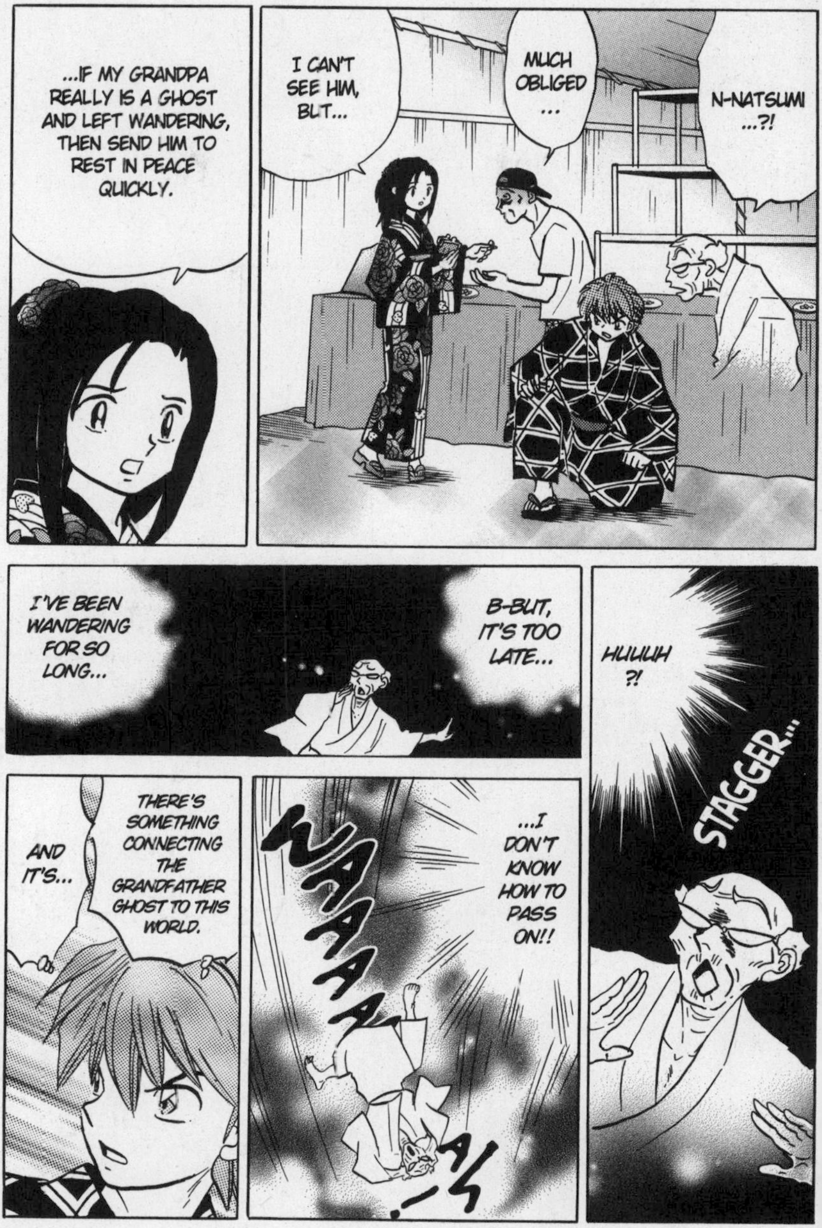
N-NATSUMI ...?!
MUCH OBLIGED ...
I CAN'T SEE HIM, BUT...
...IF MY GRANDPA REALLY IS A GHOST AND LEFT WANDERING, THEN SEND HIM TO REST IN PEACE QUICKLY.
HUUUH ?!
STAGGER...
B-BUT, IT'S TOO LATE...
I'VE BEEN WANDERING FOR SO LONG...
...I DON'T KNOW HOW TO PASS ON!!
WAAAAAAAH!
THERE'S SOMETHING CONNECTING THE GRANDFATHER GHOST TO THIS WORLD.
AND IT'S...

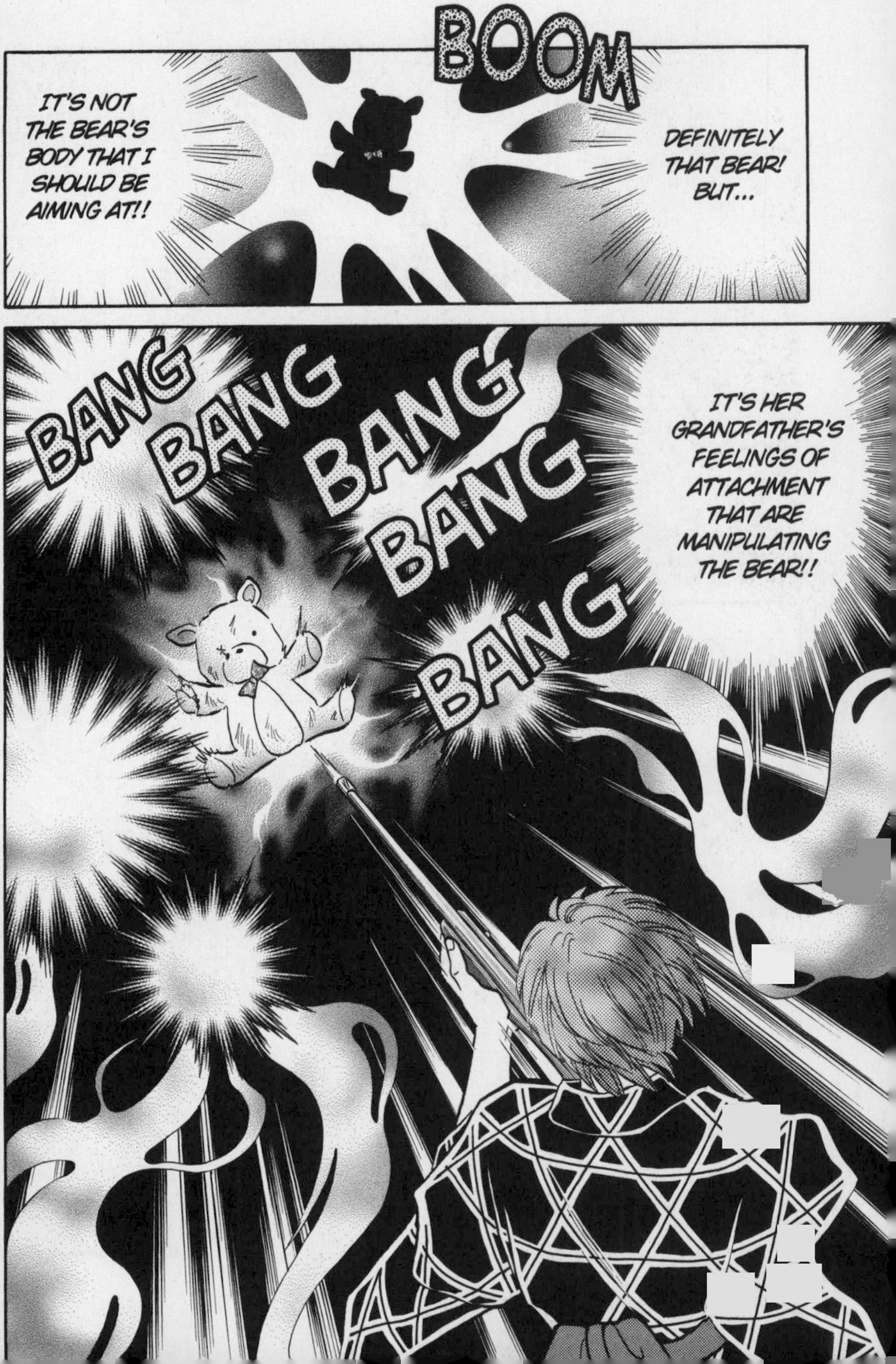
BOOM
DEFINITELY THAT BEAR! BUT...
IT'S NOT THE BEAR'S BODY THAT I SHOULD BE AIMING AT!!
IT'S HER GRANDFATHER'S FEELINGS OF ATTACHMENT THAT ARE MANIPULATING THE BEAR!!
BANG BANG BANG BANG BANG

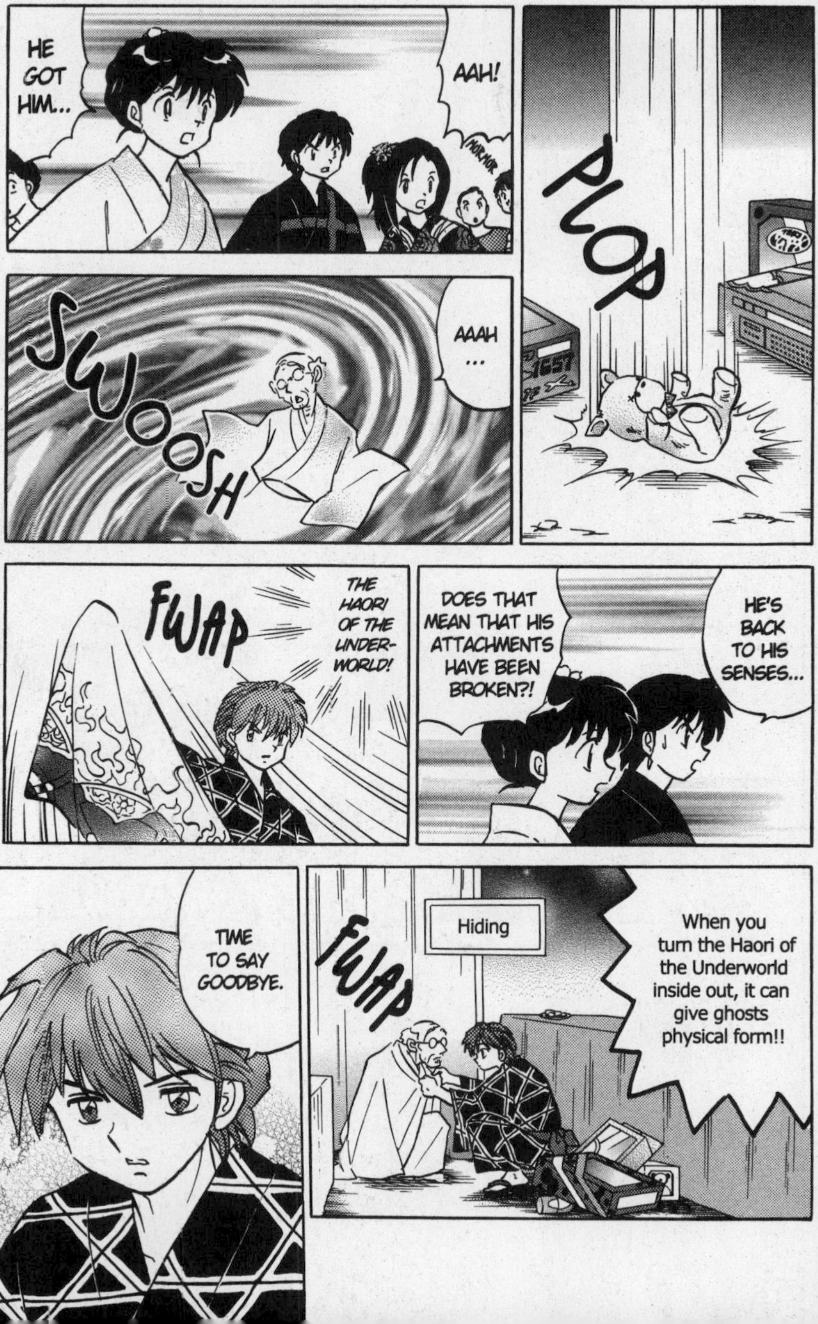
PLOP
AAH!
HE GOT HIM...
MUR MUR
AAAH ...
SWOOSH
HE'S BACK TO HIS SENSES...
DOES THAT MEAN THAT HIS ATTACHMENTS HAVE BEEN BROKEN?!
THE HAORI OF THE UNDER-WORLD!
FWAP
When you turn the Haori of the Underworld inside out, it can give ghosts physical form!!
Hiding
FWAP
TIME TO SAY GOODBYE.

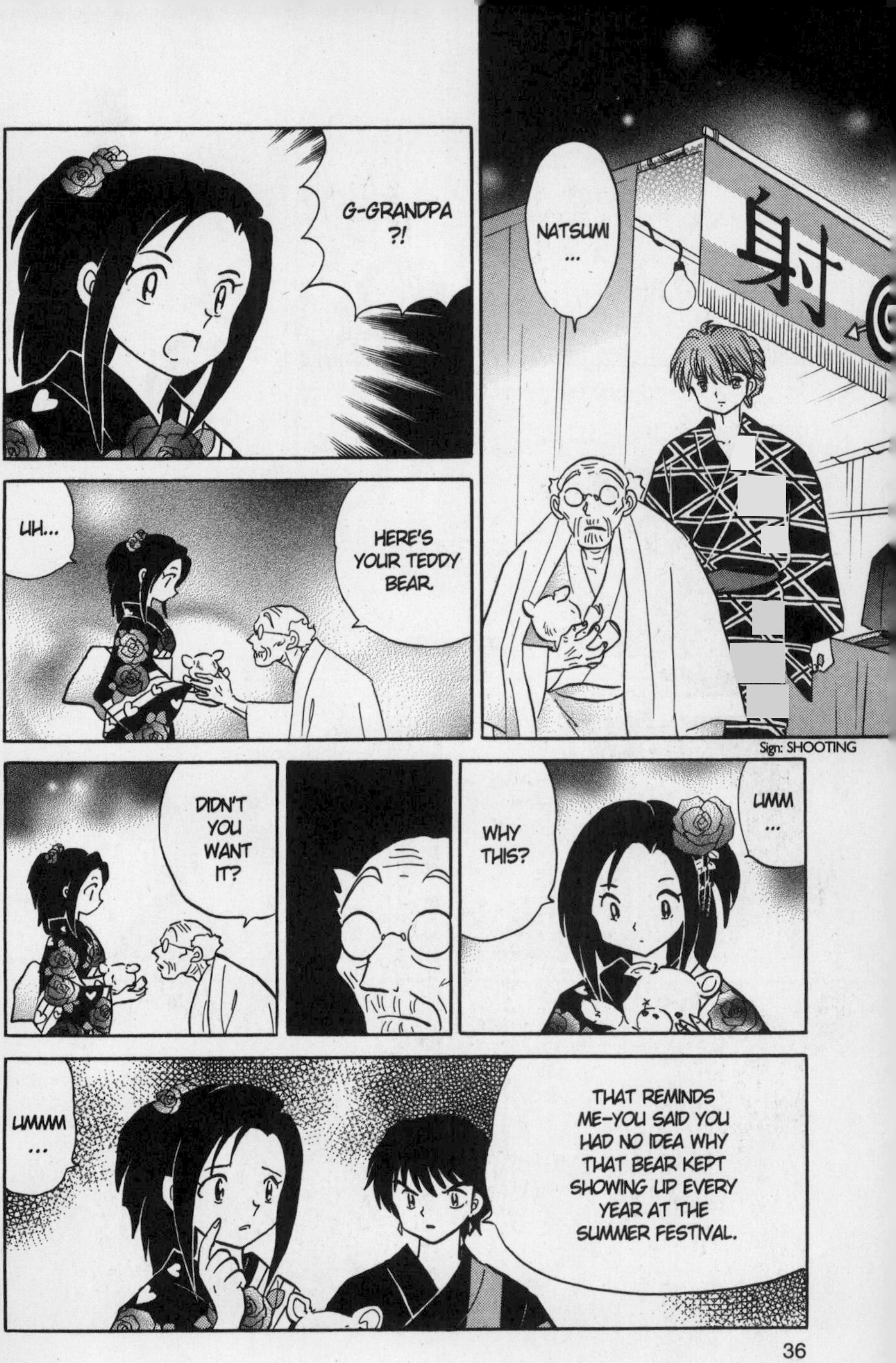
NATSUMI ...
G-GRANDPA ?!
HERE'S YOUR TEDDY BEAR.
UH...
UMM ...
WHY THIS?
DIDN'T YOU WANT IT?
THAT REMINDS ME—YOU SAID YOU HAD NO IDEA WHY THAT BEAR KEPT SHOWING UP EVERY YEAR AT THE SUMMER FESTIVAL.
UMMM ...
Sign: SHOOTING

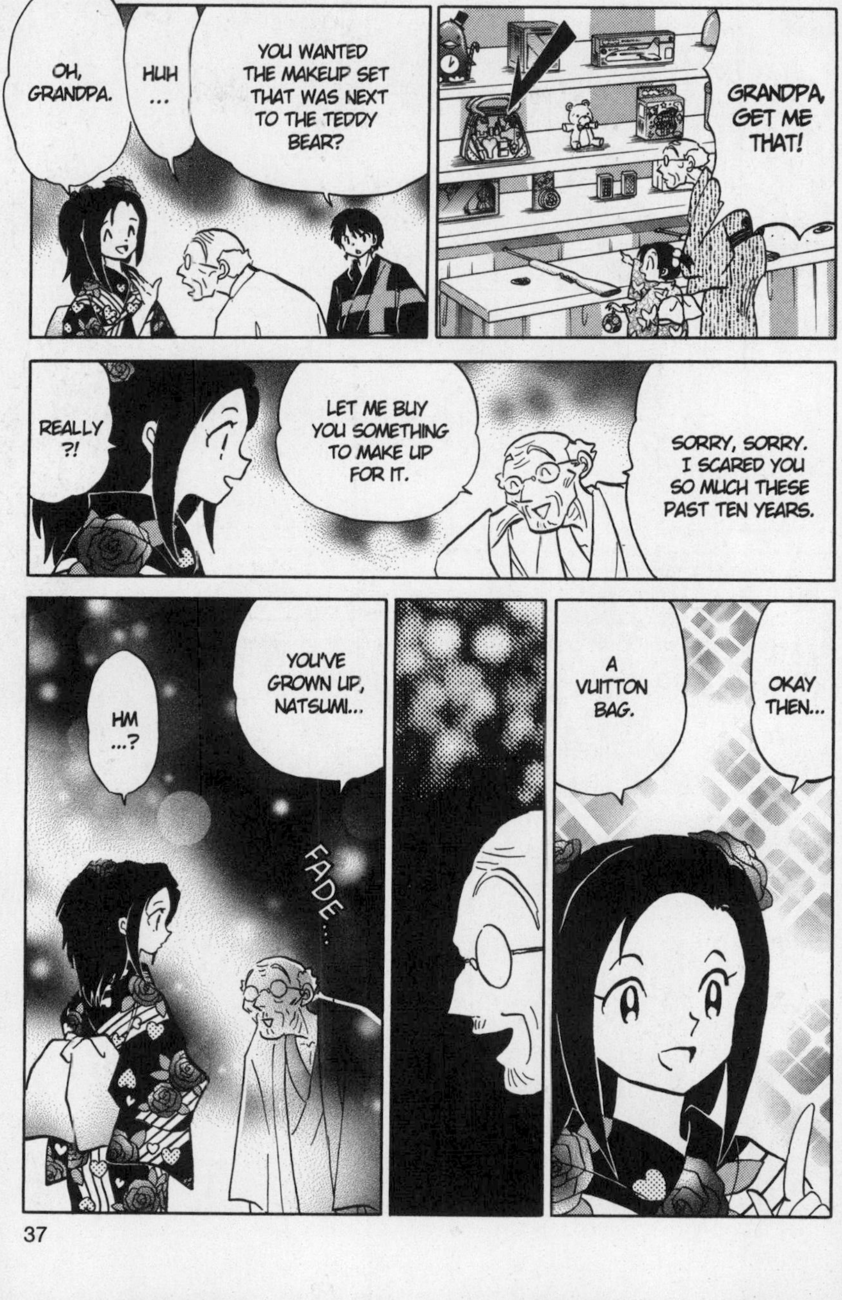
GRANDPA, GET ME THAT!
YOU WANTED THE MAKEUP SET THAT WAS NEXT TO THE TEDDY BEAR?
HUH ...
OH, GRANDPA.
SORRY, SORRY. I SCARED YOU SO MUCH THESE PAST TEN YEARS.
LET ME BUY YOU SOMETHING TO MAKE UP FOR IT.
REALLY ?!
OKAY THEN...
A VUITTON BAG.
YOU'VE GROWN UP, NATSUMI...
HM ...?
FADE...

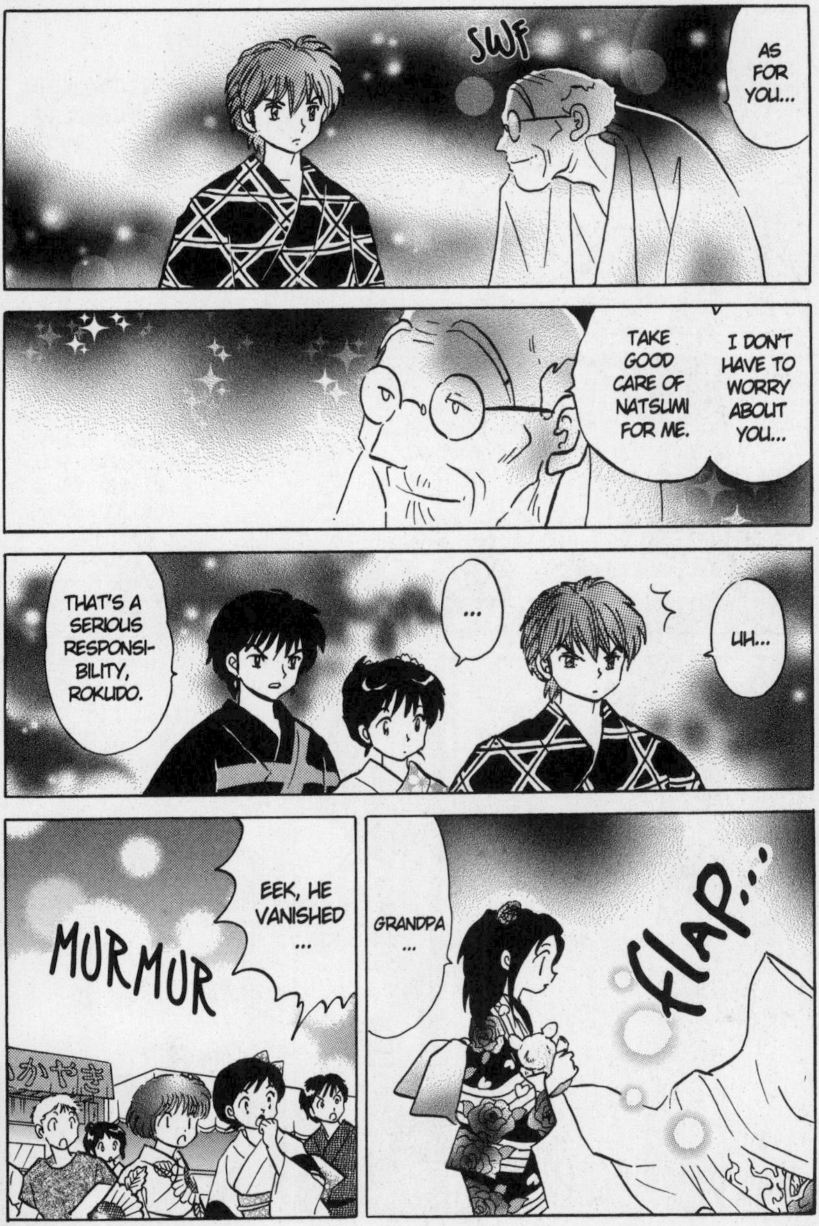

AS FOR YOU...
SWF
I DON'T HAVE TO WORRY ABOUT YOU...
TAKE GOOD CARE OF NATSUMI FOR ME.
UH...
...
THAT'S A SERIOUS RESPONSI-BILITY, ROKUDO.
FLAP...
GRANDPA ...
EEK, HE VANISHED ...
MURMUR

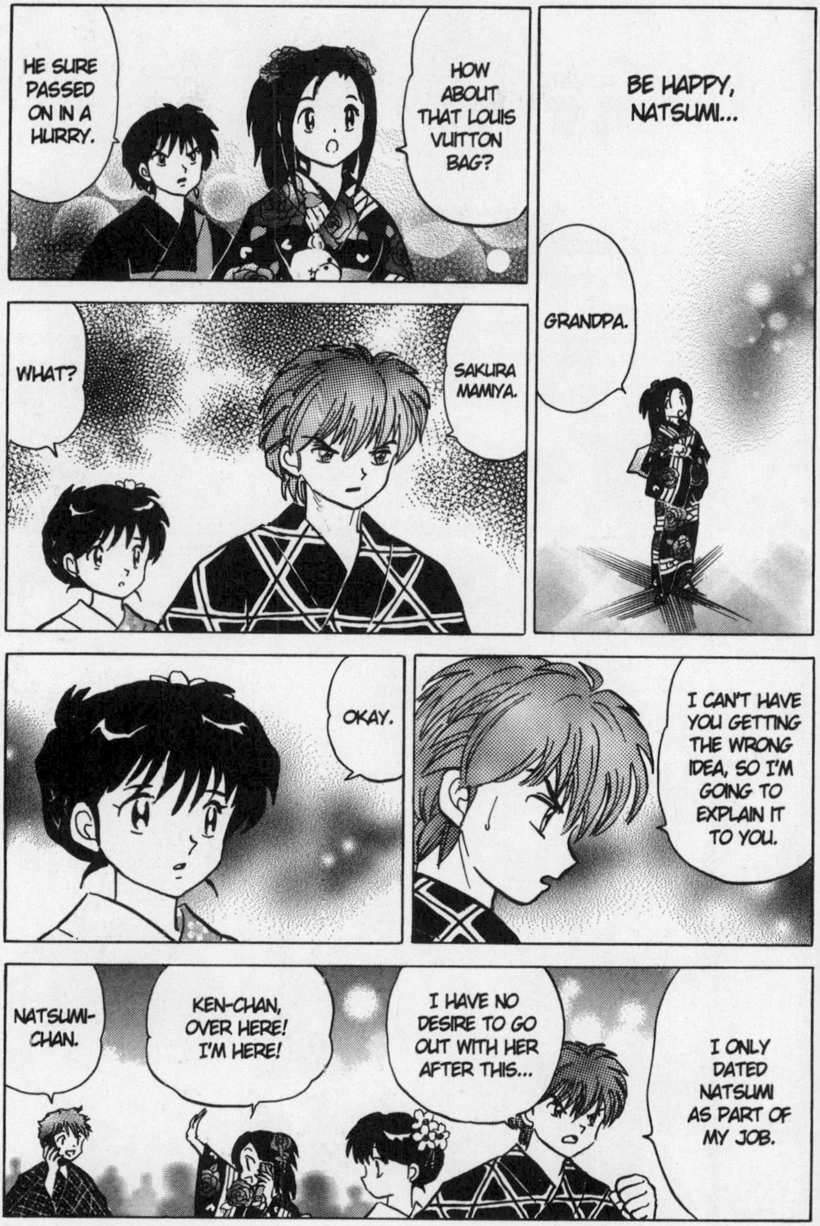
BE HAPPY, NATSUMI...
GRANDPA.
HOW ABOUT THAT LOUIS VUITTON BAG?
HE SURE PASSED ON IN A HURRY.
SAKURA MAMIYA.
WHAT?
I CAN'T HAVE YOU GETTING THE WRONG IDEA, SO I'M GOING TO EXPLAIN IT TO YOU.
OKAY.
I ONLY DATED NATSUMI AS PART OF MY JOB.
I HAVE NO DESIRE TO GO OUT WITH HER AFTER THIS...
KEN-CHAN, OVER HERE! I'M HERE!
NATSUMI-CHAN.

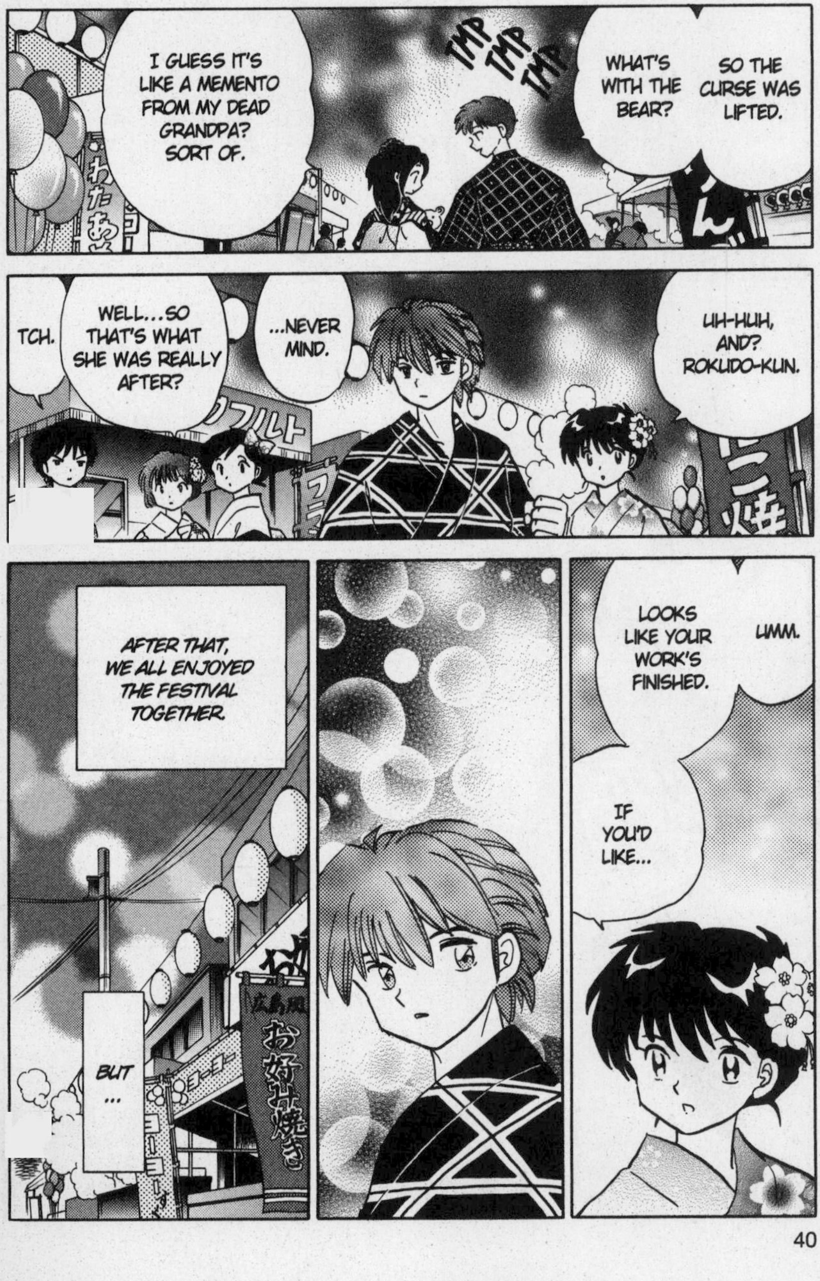
SO THE CURSE WAS LIFTED.
WHAT'S WITH THE BEAR?
TMP TMP TMP
I GUESS IT'S LIKE A MEMENTO FROM MY DEAD GRANDPA? SORT OF.
UH-HUH, AND? ROKUDO-KUN.
...NEVER MIND.
WELL...SO THAT'S WHAT SHE WAS REALLY AFTER?
TCH.
UMM.
LOOKS LIKE YOUR WORK'S FINISHED.
IF YOU'D LIKE...
AFTER THAT, WE ALL ENJOYED THE FESTIVAL TOGETHER.
BUT ...

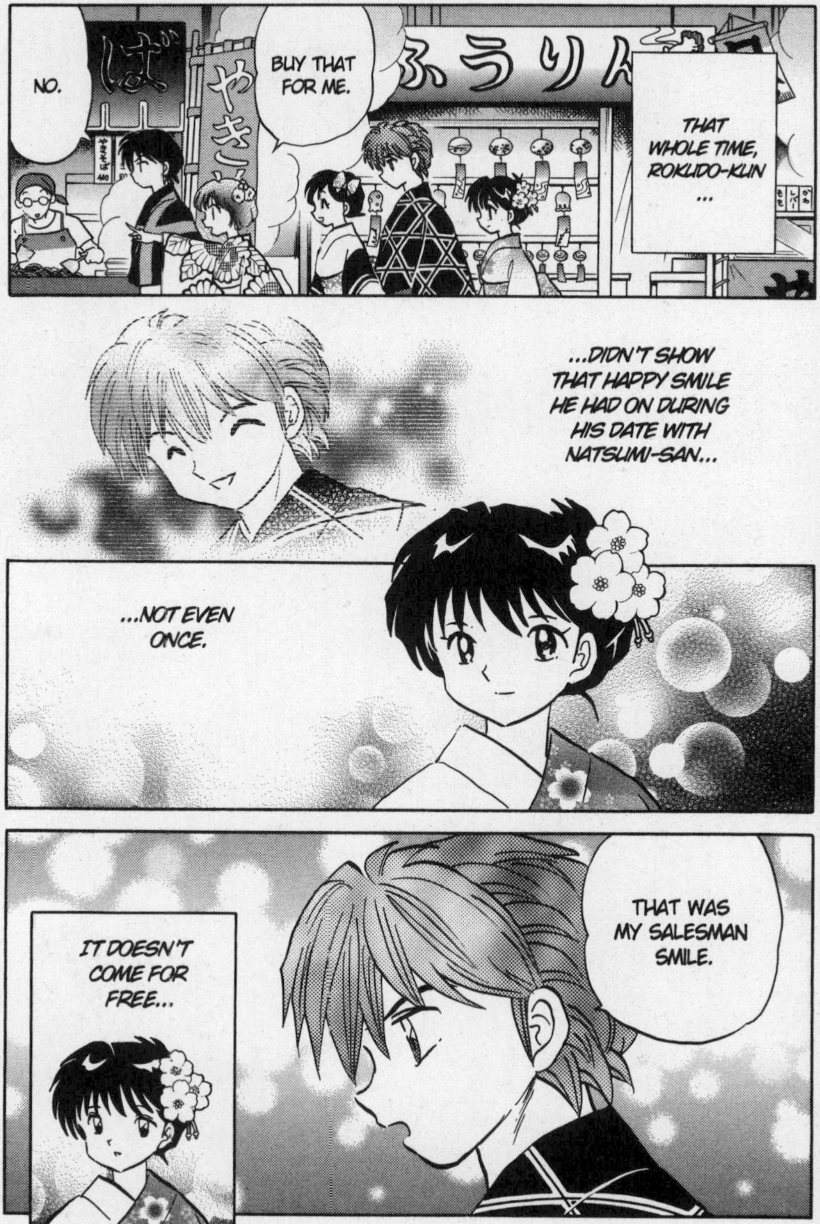
THAT WHOLE TIME, ROKUDO-KUN ...
BUY THAT FOR ME.
NO.
...DIDN'T SHOW THAT HAPPY SMILE HE HAD ON DURING HIS DATE WITH NATSUMI-SAN...
...NOT EVEN ONCE.
THAT WAS MY SALESMAN SMILE.
IT DOESN'T COME FOR FREE...

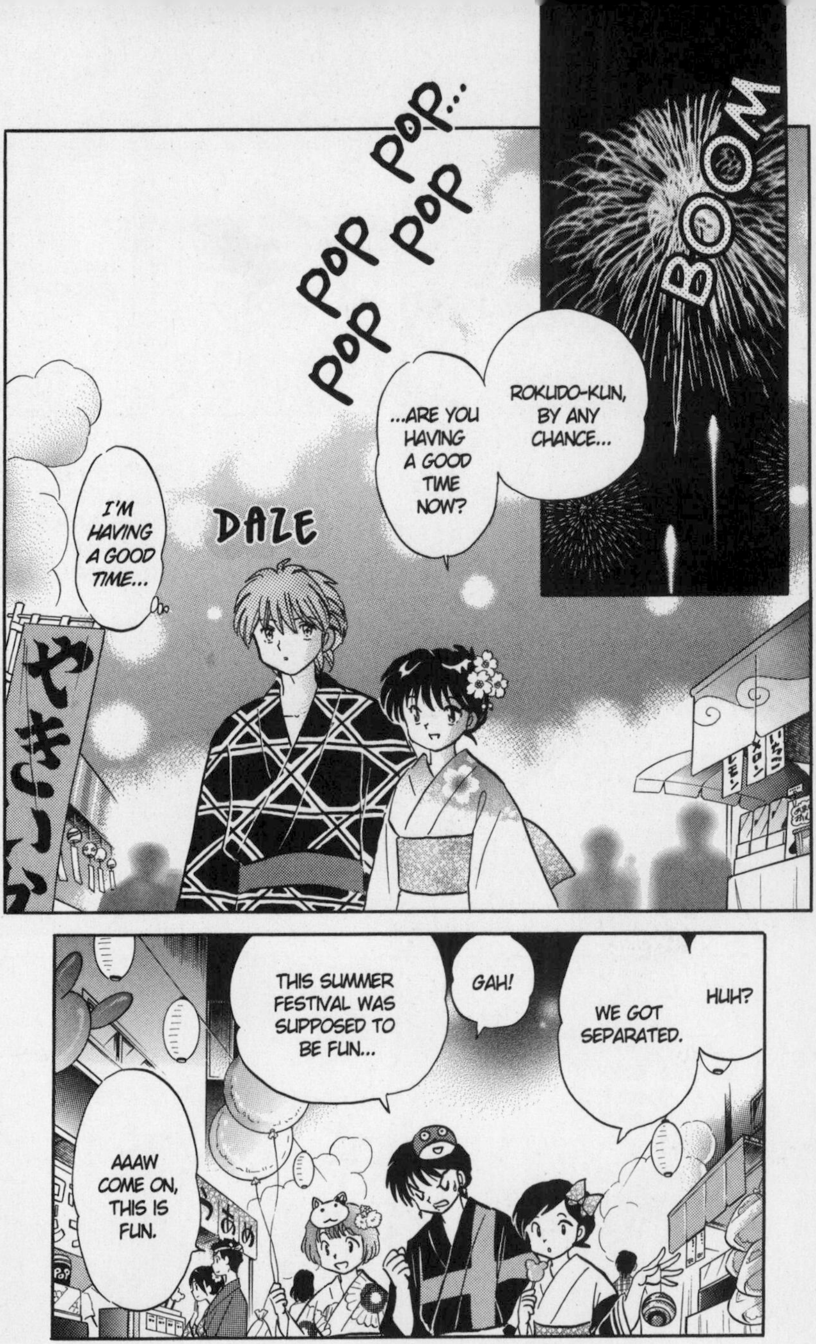
BOOM
ROKUDO-KUN, BY ANY CHANCE...
...ARE YOU HAVING A GOOD TIME NOW?
POP POP POP POP POP...
DAZE
I'M HAVING A GOOD TIME...
HUH?
WE GOT SEPARATED.
GAH!
THIS SUMMER FESTIVAL WAS SUPPOSED TO BE FUN...
AAAW COME ON, THIS IS FUN.

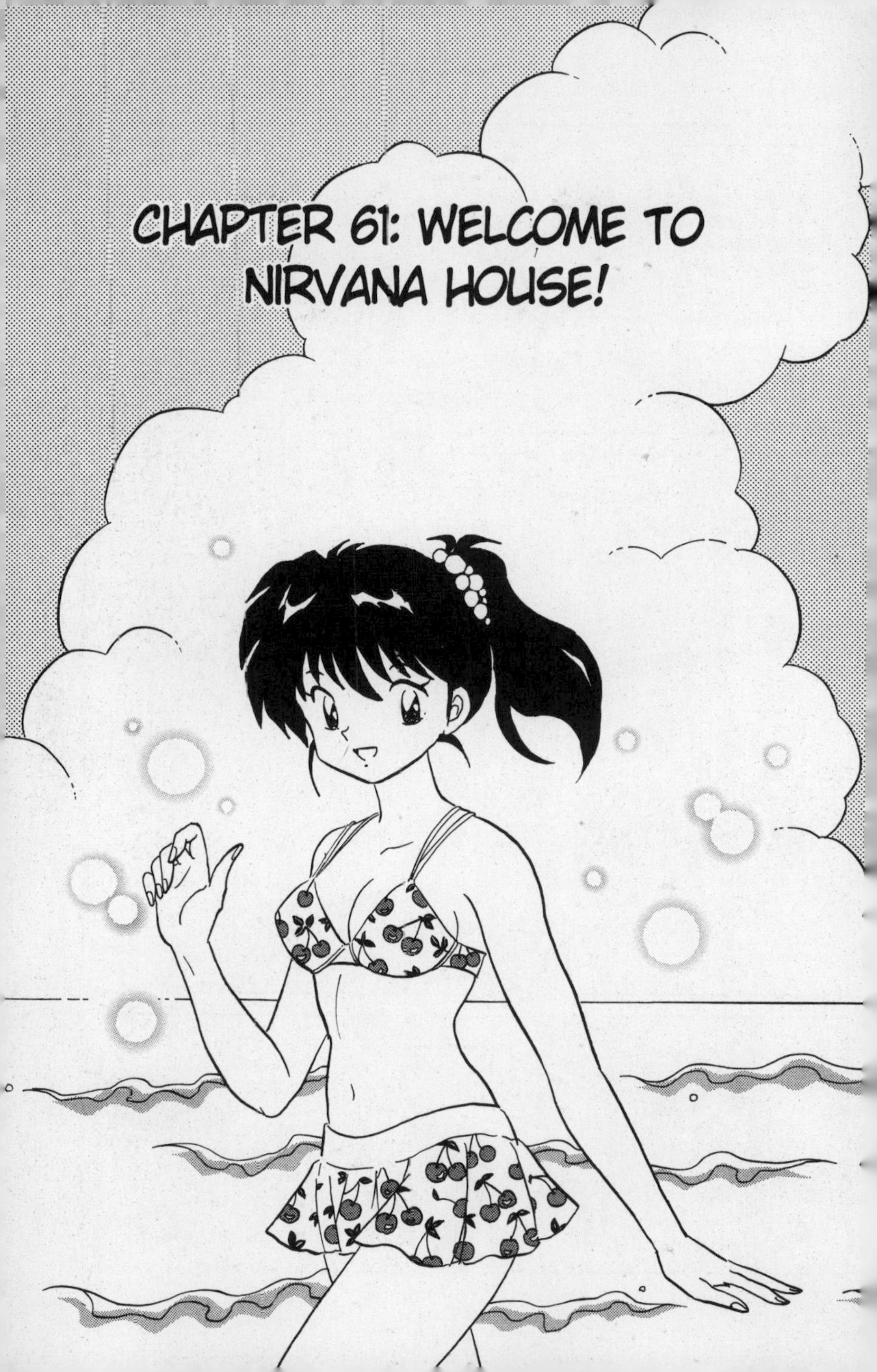
CHAPTER 61: WELCOME TO NIRVANA HOUSE!

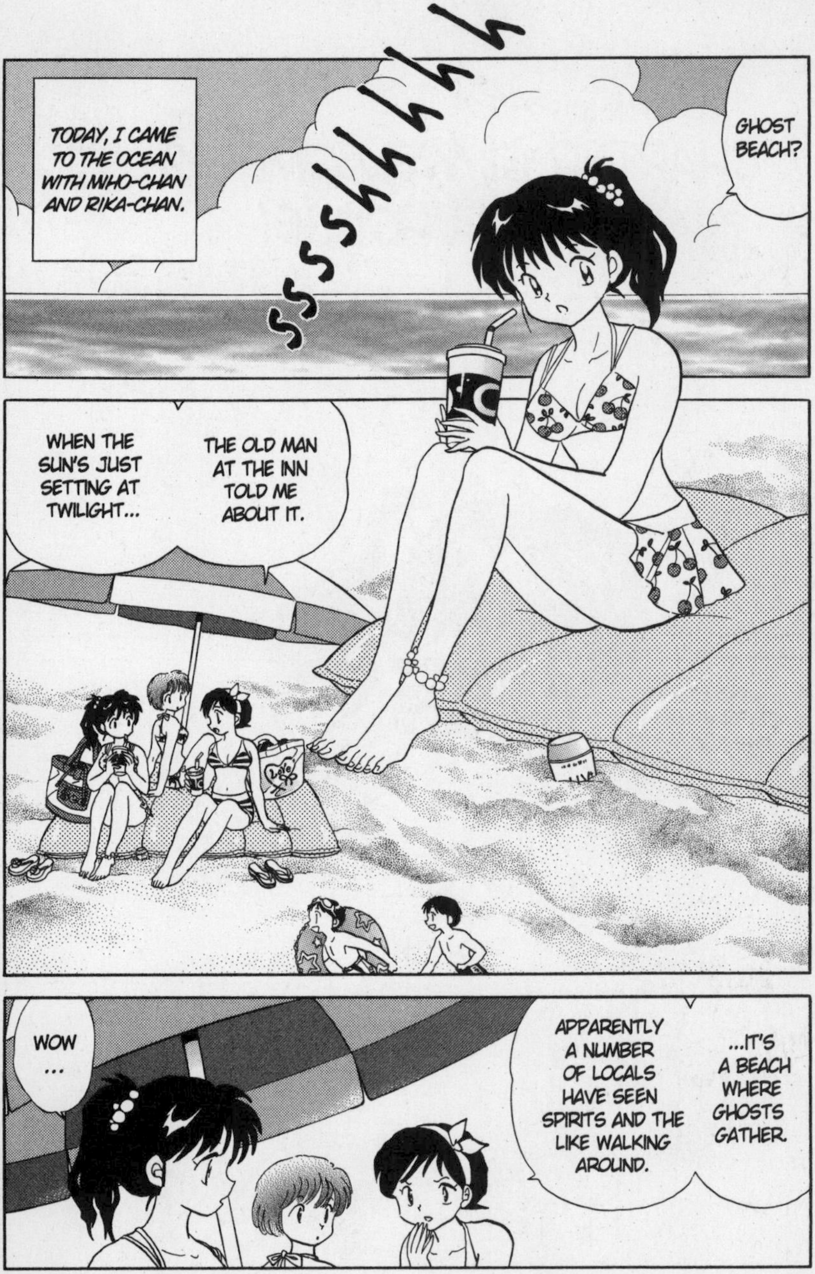
GHOST BEACH?
TODAY, I CAME TO THE OCEAN WITH MIHO-CHAN AND RIKA-CHAN.
SSSHHHHH
THE OLD MAN AT THE INN TOLD ME ABOUT IT.
WHEN THE SUN'S JUST SETTING AT TWILIGHT...
...IT'S A BEACH WHERE GHOSTS GATHER.
APPARENTLY A NUMBER OF LOCALS HAVE SEEN SPIRITS AND THE LIKE WALKING AROUND.
WOW ...

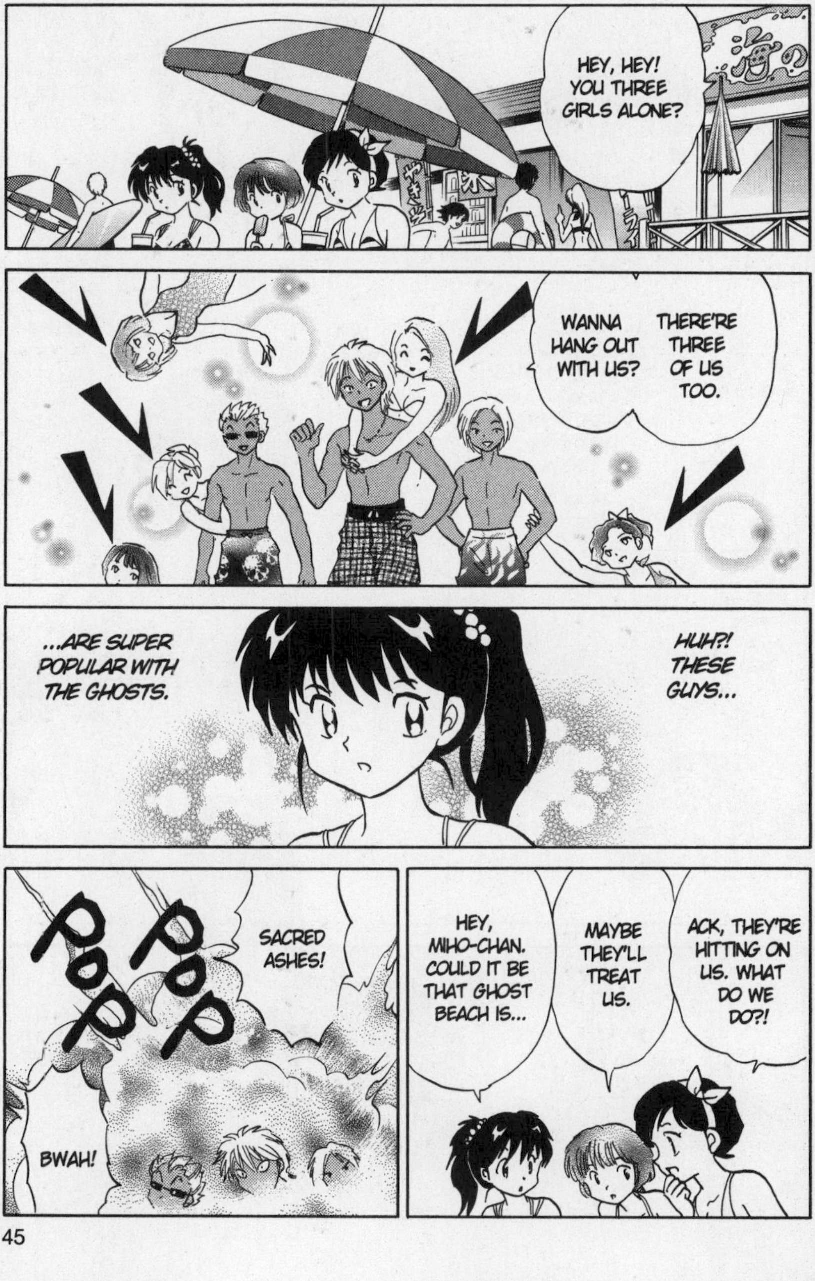
HEY, HEY! YOU THREE GIRLS ALONE?
THERE'RE THREE OF US TOO.
WANNA HANG OUT WITH US?
HUH?! THESE GUYS...
...ARE SUPER POPULAR WITH THE GHOSTS.
ACK, THEY'RE HITTING ON US. WHAT DO WE DO?!
MAYBE THEY'LL TREAT US.
HEY, MIHO-CHAN. COULD IT BE THAT GHOST BEACH IS...
SACRED ASHES!
POP POP
BWAH!

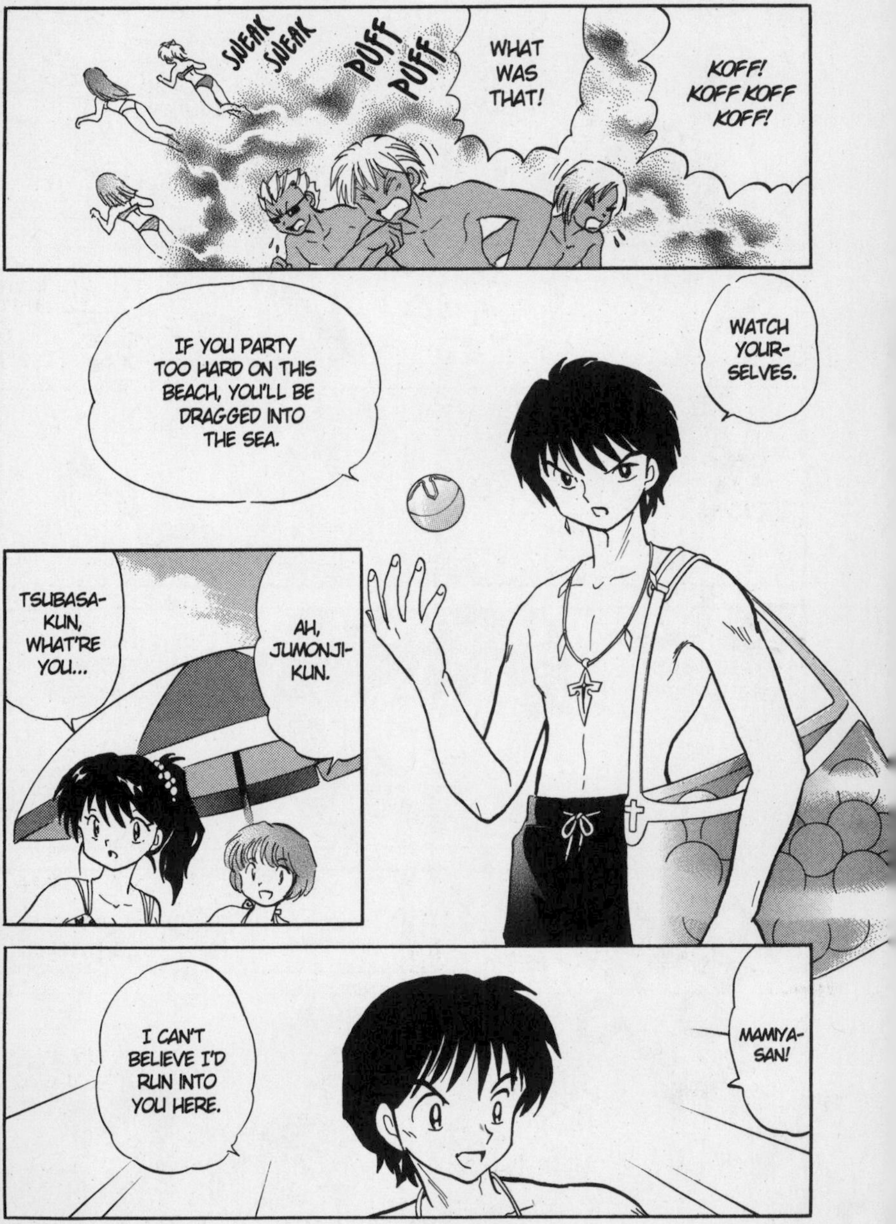
KOFF! KOFF KOFF KOFF!
WHAT WAS THAT!
PUFF PUFF
SNEAK SNEAK
WATCH YOURSELVES.
IF YOU PARTY TOO HARD ON THIS BEACH, YOU'LL BE DRAGGED INTO THE SEA.
AH, JUMONJI-KUN.
TSUBASA-KUN, WHAT'RE YOU...
MAMIYA-SAN!
I CAN'T BELIEVE I'D RUN INTO YOU HERE.

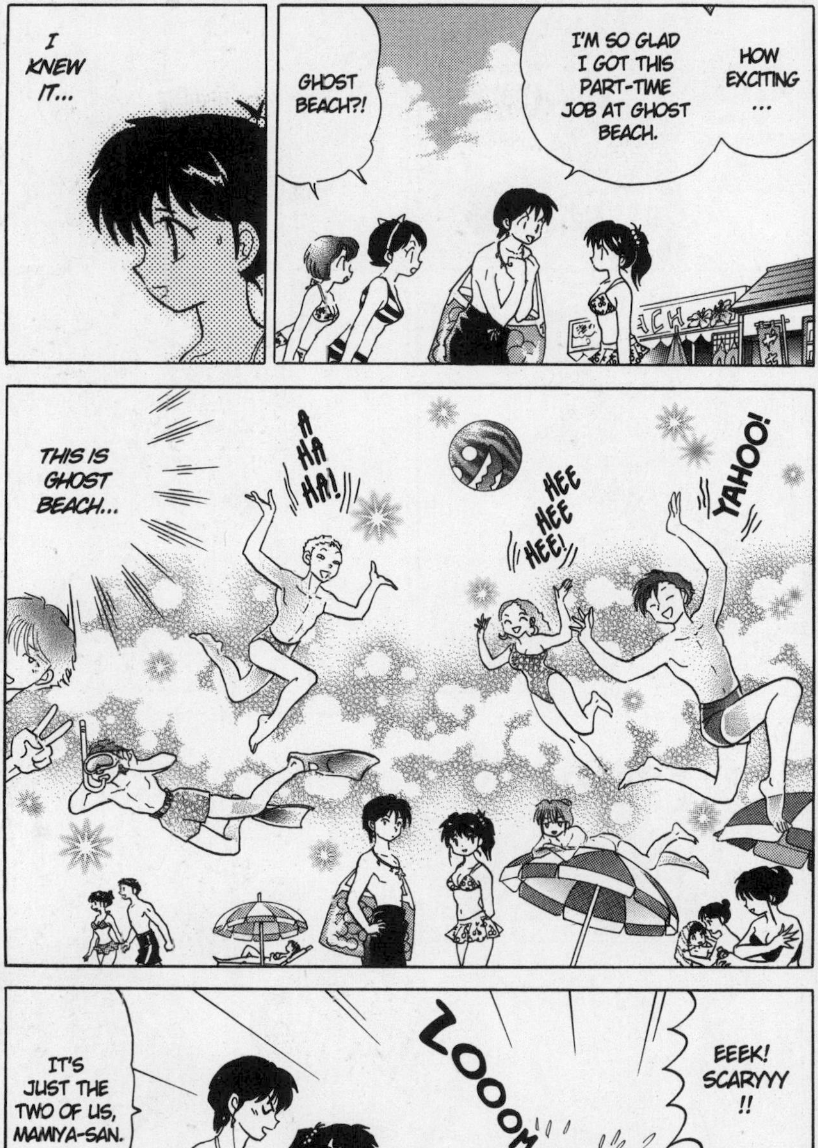
HOW EXCITING ...
I'M SO GLAD I GOT THIS PART-TIME JOB AT GHOST BEACH.
GHOST BEACH?!
I KNEW IT...
YAHOO!
HEE HEE HEE!
A HA HA!
THIS IS GHOST BEACH...
EEEK! SCARYYY !!
ZOOOM
IT'S JUST THE TWO OF US, MAMIYA-SAN.

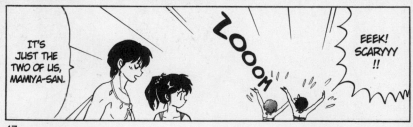

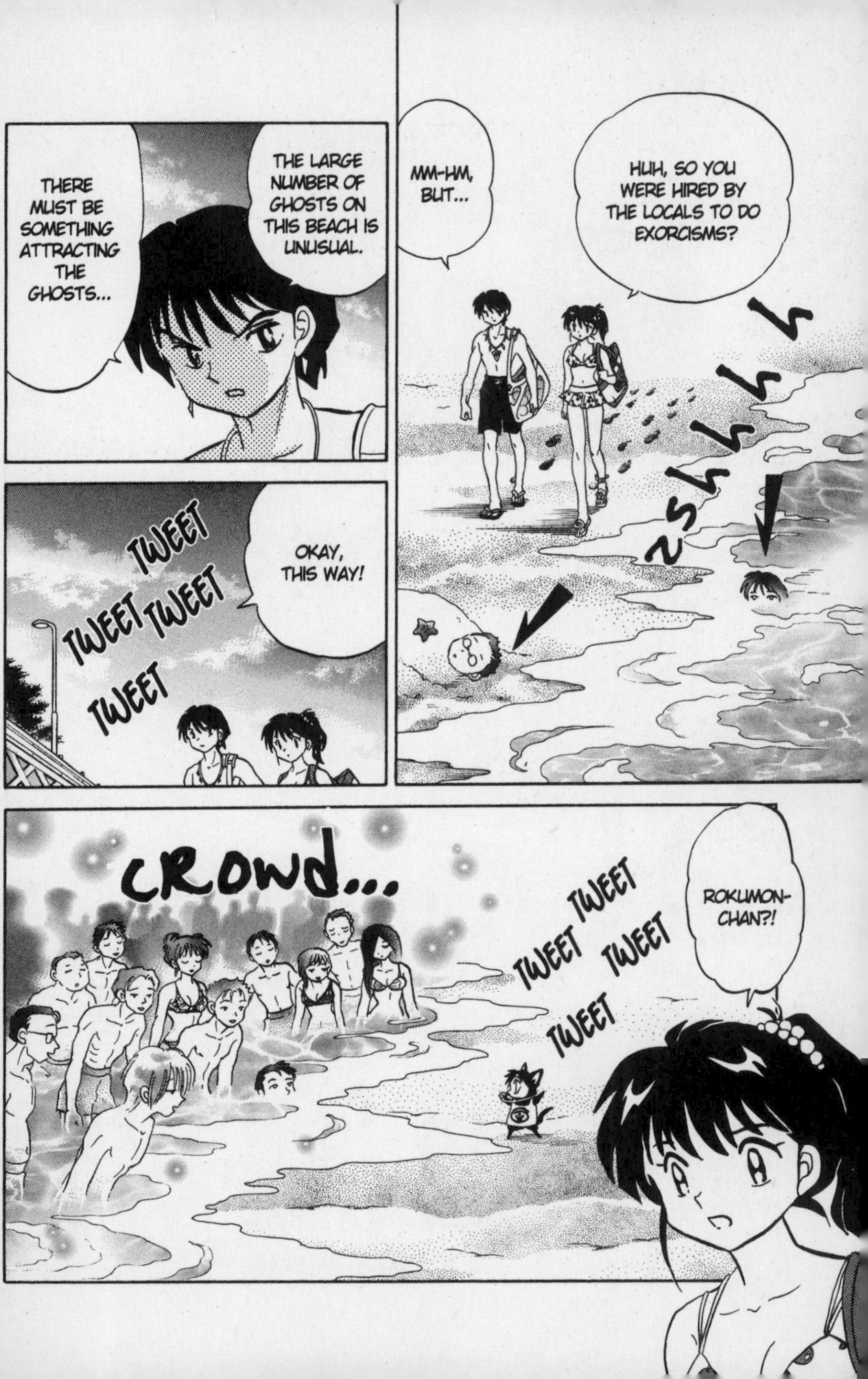
HUH, SO YOU WERE HIRED BY THE LOCALS TO DO EXORCISMS?
MM-HM, BUT...
THE LARGE NUMBER OF GHOSTS ON THIS BEACH IS UNUSUAL.
THERE MUST BE SOMETHING ATTRACTING THE GHOSTS...
OKAY, THIS WAY!
TWEET TWEET TWEET TWEET
ROKUMON-CHAN?!
TWEET TWEET TWEET TWEET
CROWD...

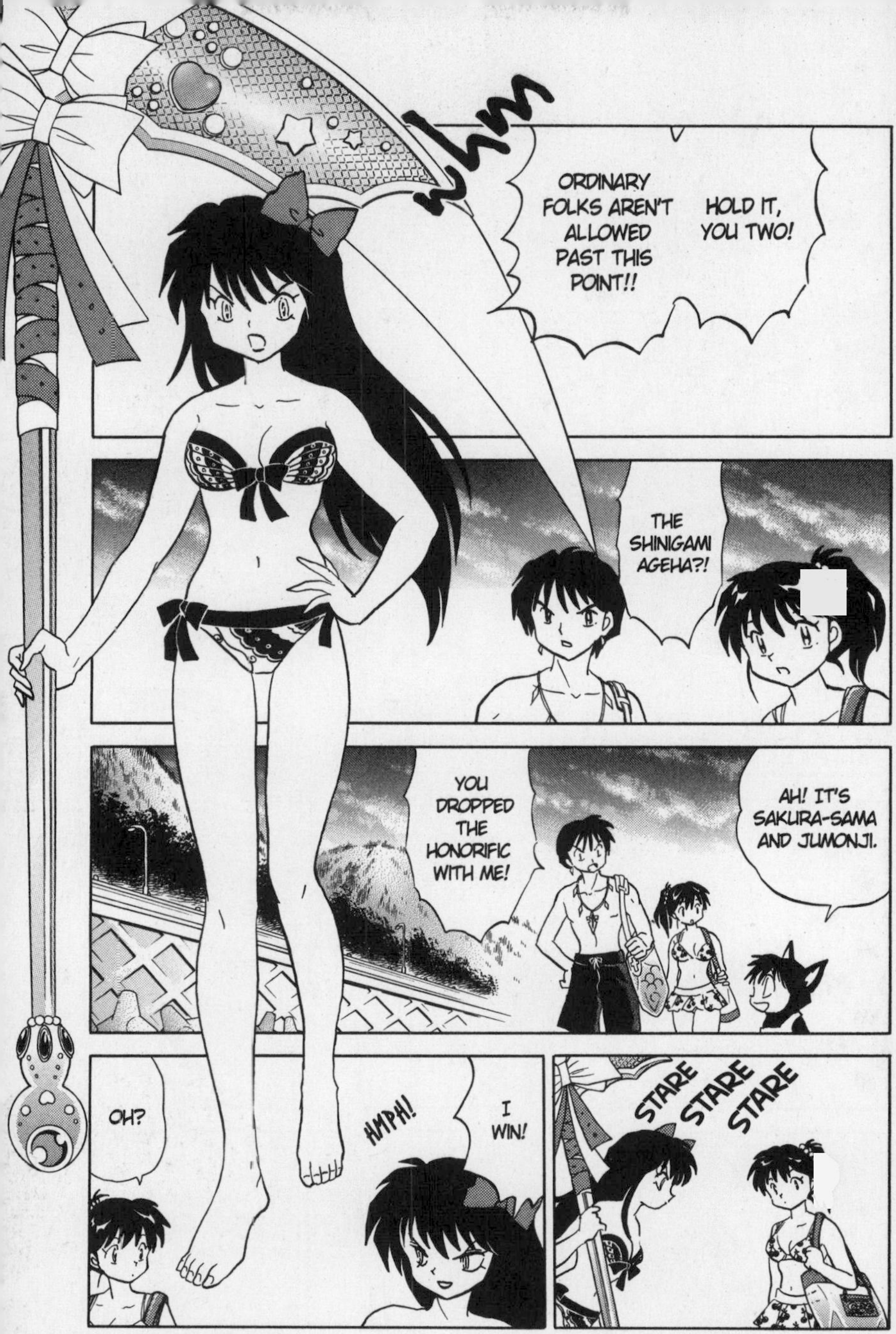
WHM
HOLD IT, YOU TWO!
ORDINARY FOLKS AREN'T ALLOWED PAST THIS POINT!!
THE SHINIGAMI AGEHA?!
AH! IT'S SAKURA-SAMA AND JUMONJI.
YOU DROPPED THE HONORIFIC WITH ME!
STARE STARE STARE
I WIN!
HMPH!
OH?

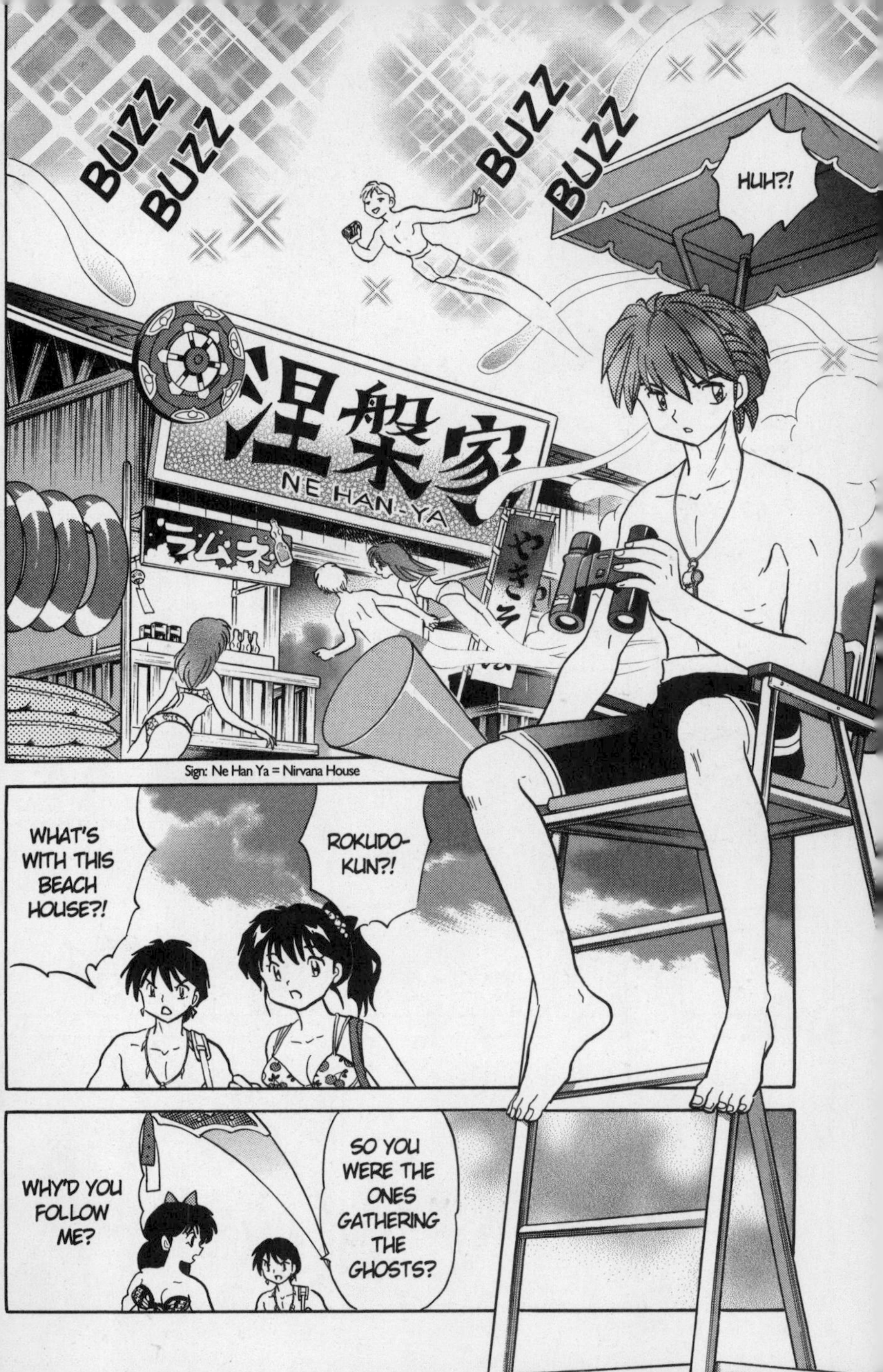
HUH?!
BUZZ BUZZ
BUZZ BUZZ
涅槃家
NE HAN-YA
ラムネ
ROKUDO-KUN?!
WHAT'S WITH THIS BEACH HOUSE?!
SO YOU WERE THE ONES GATHERING THE GHOSTS?
WHY'D YOU FOLLOW ME?
Sign: Ne Han Ya = Nirvana House

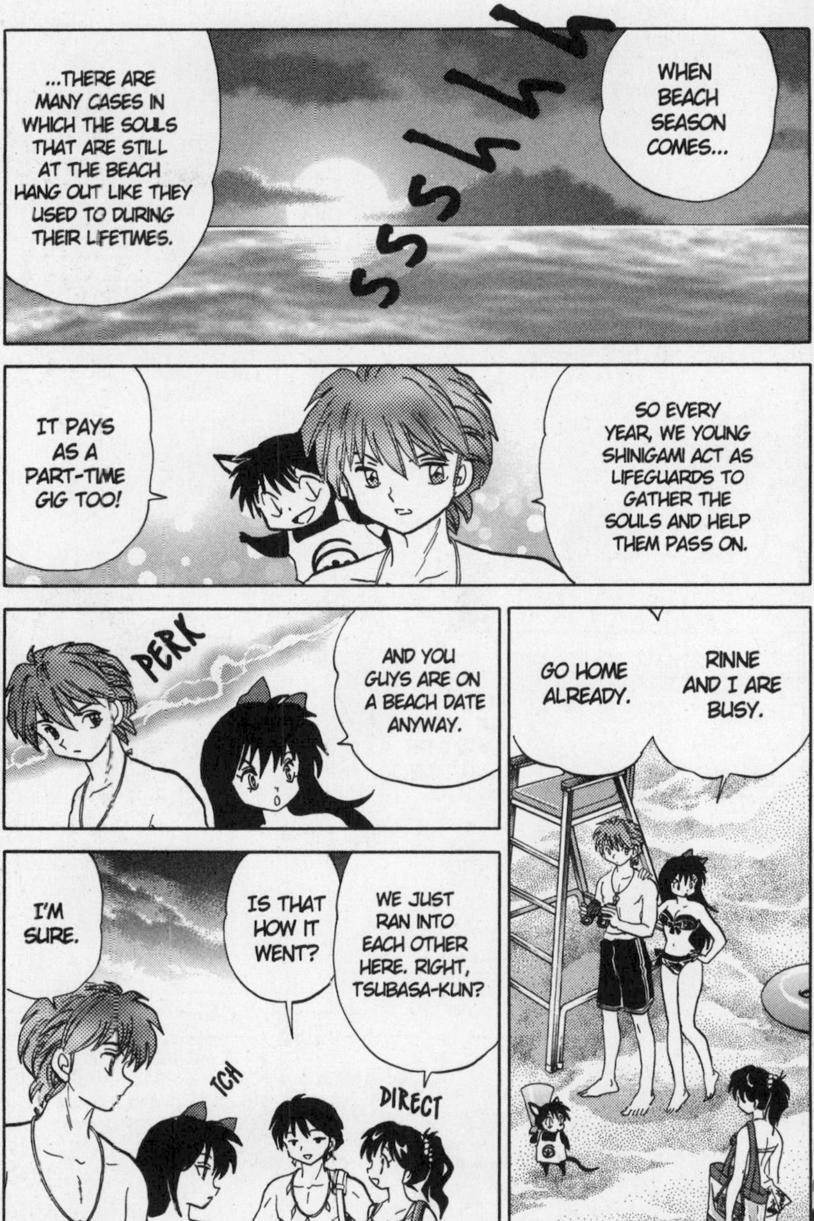
WHEN BEACH SEASON COMES...
...THERE ARE MANY CASES IN WHICH THE SOULS THAT ARE STILL AT THE BEACH HANG OUT LIKE THEY USED TO DURING THEIR LIFETIMES.
SO EVERY YEAR, WE YOUNG SHINIGAMI ACT AS LIFEGUARDS TO GATHER THE SOULS AND HELP THEM PASS ON.
IT PAYS AS A PART-TIME GIG TOO!
RINNE AND I ARE BUSY.
GO HOME ALREADY.
AND YOU GUYS ARE ON A BEACH DATE ANYWAY.
PERK
WE JUST RAN INTO EACH OTHER HERE. RIGHT, TSUBASA-KUN?
IS THAT HOW IT WENT?
I'M SURE.
TCH
DIRECT

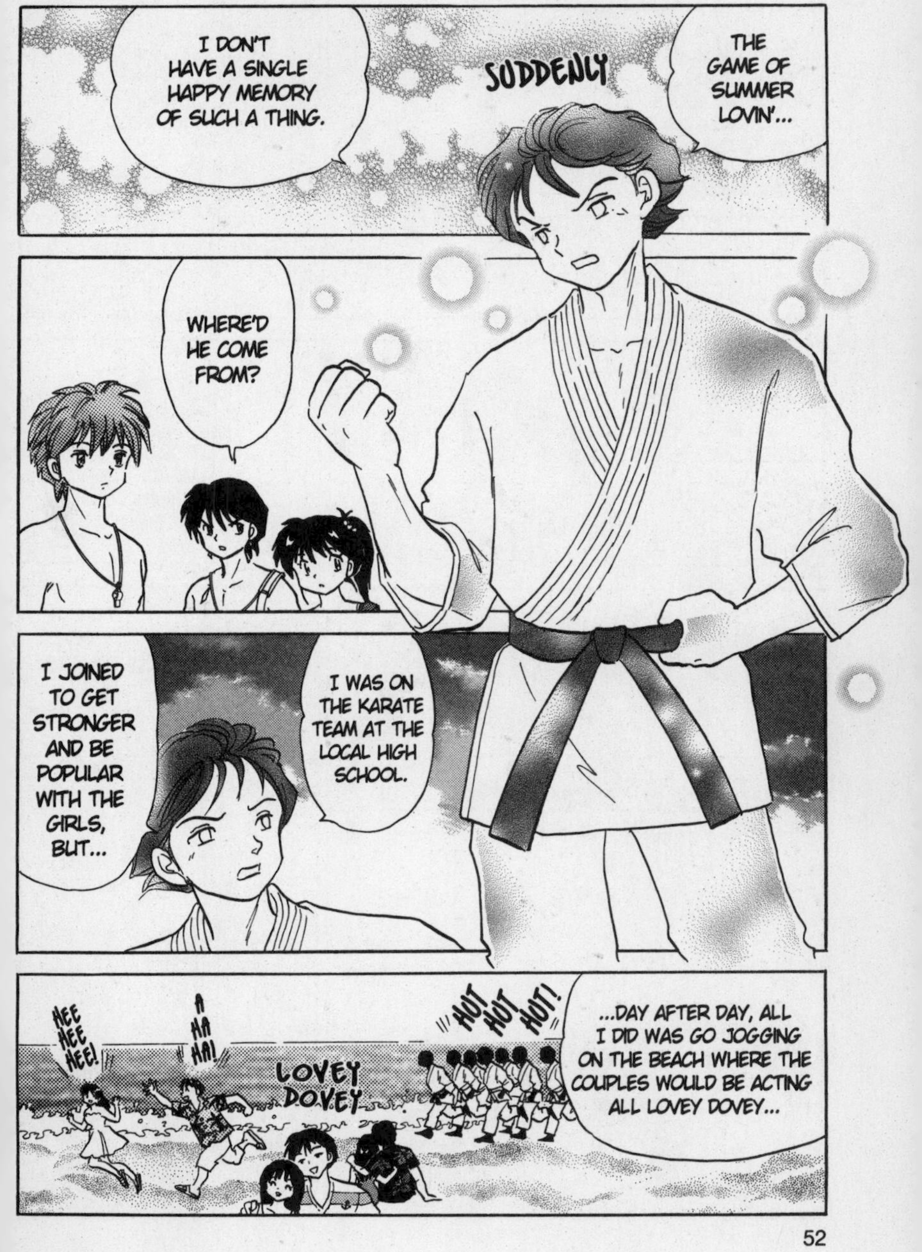
THE GAME OF SUMMER LOVIN'...
SUDDENLY
I DON'T HAVE A SINGLE HAPPY MEMORY OF SUCH A THING.
WHERE'D HE COME FROM?
I WAS ON THE KARATE TEAM AT THE LOCAL HIGH SCHOOL.
I JOINED TO GET STRONGER AND BE POPULAR WITH THE GIRLS, BUT...
...DAY AFTER DAY, ALL I DID WAS GO JOGGING ON THE BEACH WHERE THE COUPLES WOULD BE ACTING ALL LOVEY DOVEY...
HUT HUT HUT!
LOVEY DOVEY
A HA HA!
HEE HEE HEE!

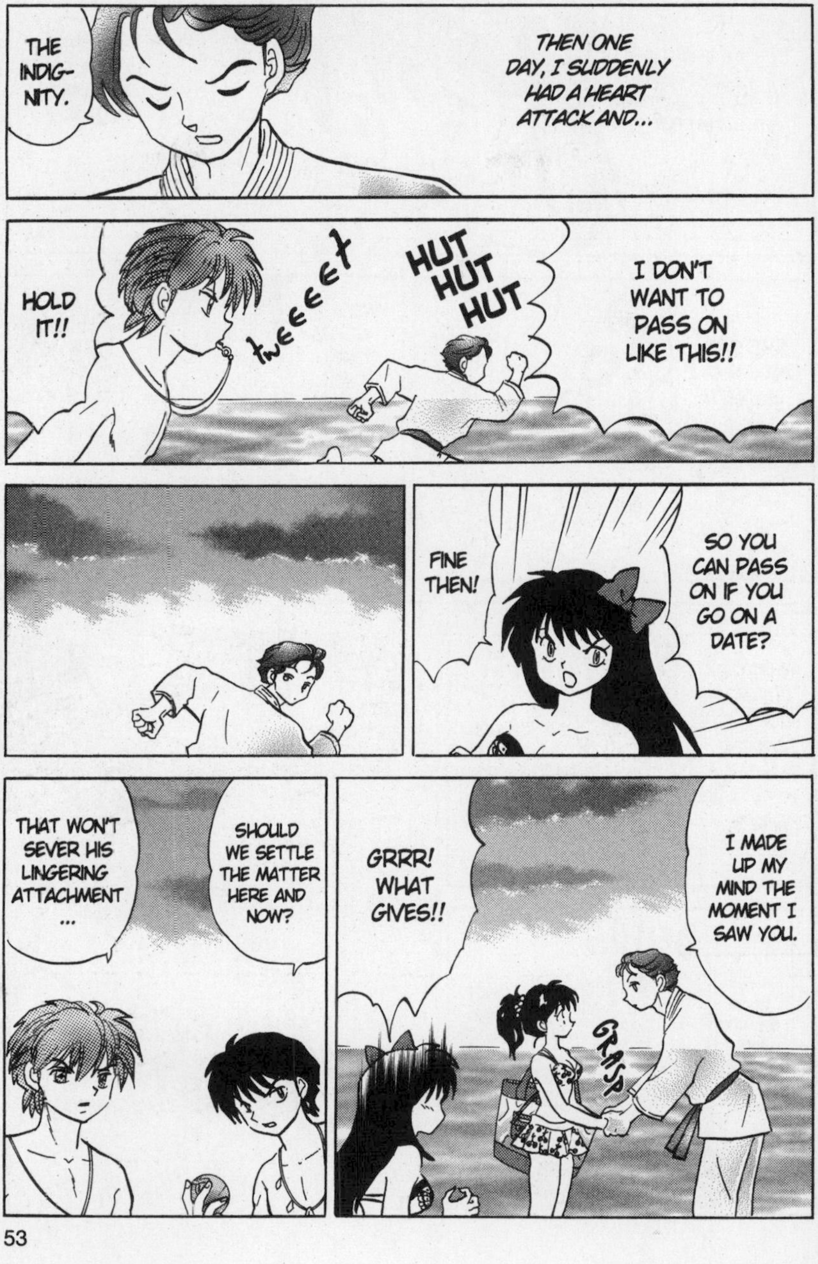
THEN ONE DAY, I SUDDENLY HAD A HEART ATTACK AND...
THE INDIG-NITY.
I DON'T WANT TO PASS ON LIKE THIS!!
HUT HUT HUT
tweeeet
HOLD IT!!
SO YOU CAN PASS ON IF YOU GO ON A DATE?
FINE THEN!
I MADE UP MY MIND THE MOMENT I SAW YOU.
GRASP
GRRR! WHAT GIVES!!
SHOULD WE SETTLE THE MATTER HERE AND NOW?
THAT WON'T SEVER HIS LINGERING ATTACHMENT ...

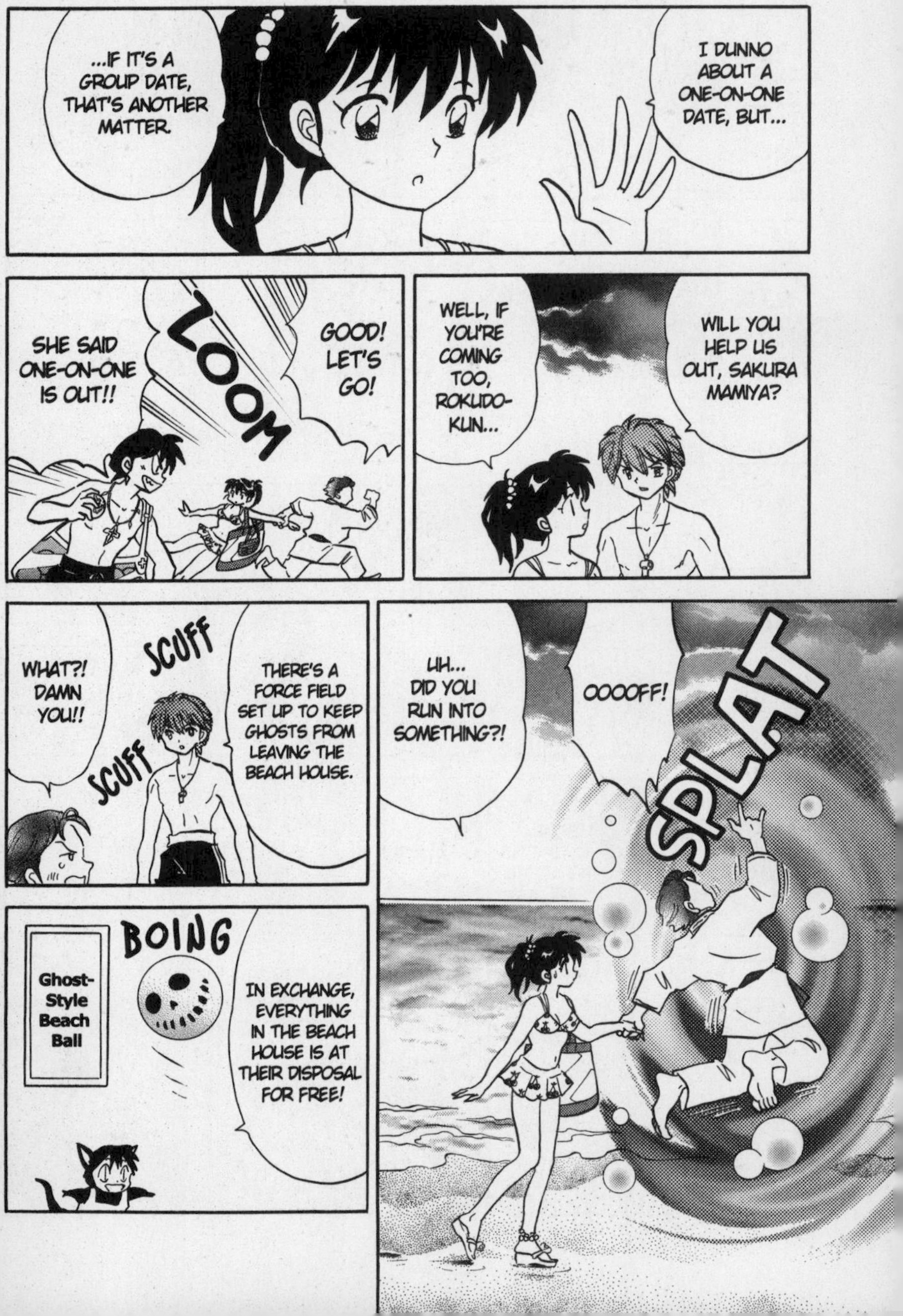
I DUNNO ABOUT A ONE-ON-ONE DATE, BUT...
...IF IT'S A GROUP DATE, THAT'S ANOTHER MATTER.
WILL YOU HELP US OUT, SAKURA MAMIYA?
WELL, IF YOU'RE COMING TOO, ROKUDO-KUN...
GOOD! LET'S GO!
ZOOM
SHE SAID ONE-ON-ONE IS OUT!!
SPLAT
OOOOFF!
UH... DID YOU RUN INTO SOMETHING?!
THERE'S A FORCE FIELD SET UP TO KEEP GHOSTS FROM LEAVING THE BEACH HOUSE.
SCUFF
SCUFF
WHAT?! DAMN YOU!!
IN EXCHANGE, EVERYTHING IN THE BEACH HOUSE IS AT THEIR DISPOSAL FOR FREE!
BOING
Ghost-Style Beach Ball

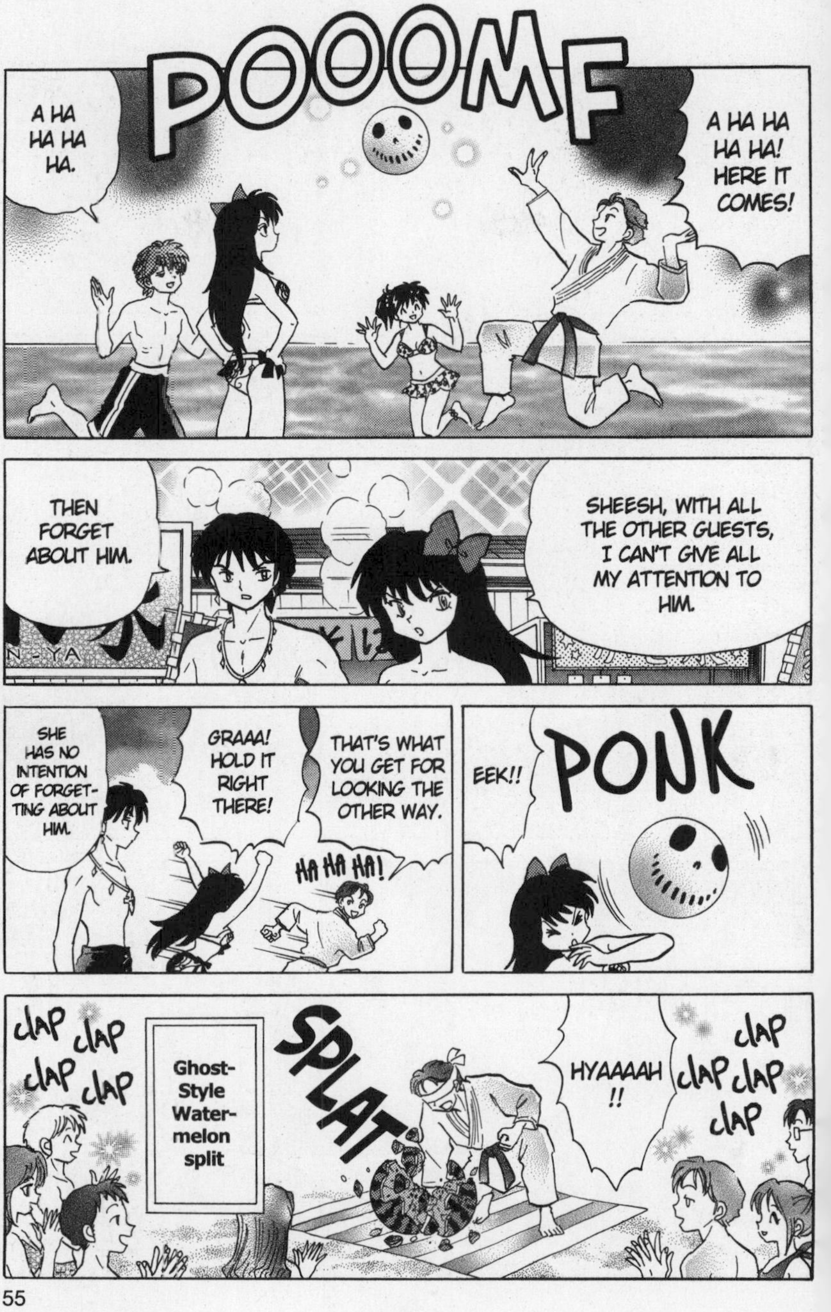
POOOMF
A HA HA HA HA! HERE IT COMES!
A HA HA HA HA.
SHEESH, WITH ALL THE OTHER GUESTS, I CAN'T GIVE ALL MY ATTENTION TO HIM.
THEN FORGET ABOUT HIM.
PONK
EEK!!
THAT'S WHAT YOU GET FOR LOOKING THE OTHER WAY.
HA HA HA!
GRAAA! HOLD IT RIGHT THERE!
SHE HAS NO INTENTION OF FORGETTING ABOUT HIM.
clap clap clap clap
HYAAAAH!!
SPLAT
Ghost-Style Watermelon split
clap clap clap clap

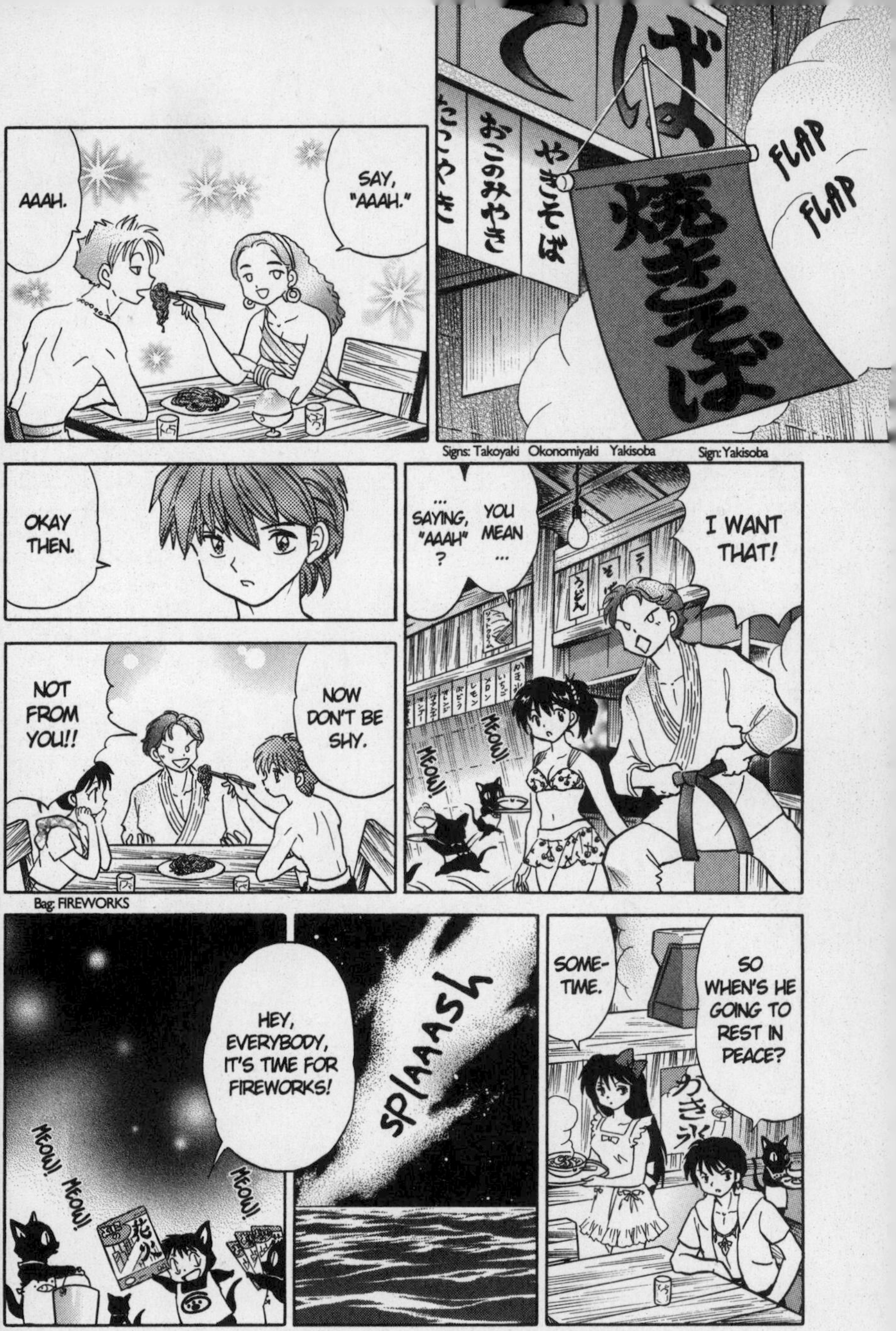
やきそば
おこのみやき
たこやき
焼きそば
FLAP
FLAP
Signs: Takoyaki Okonomiyaki Yakisoba
Sign: Yakisoba
SAY, "AAAH."
AAAH.
I WANT THAT!
YOU MEAN ...
... SAYING, "AAAH"?
MEOW!
MEOW!
OKAY THEN.
NOW DON'T BE SHY.
NOT FROM YOU!!
Bag: FIREWORKS
SO WHEN'S HE GOING TO REST IN PEACE?
SOME-TIME.
SPLAAASH
HEY, EVERYBODY, IT'S TIME FOR FIREWORKS!
MEOW!
MEOW!
MEOW!

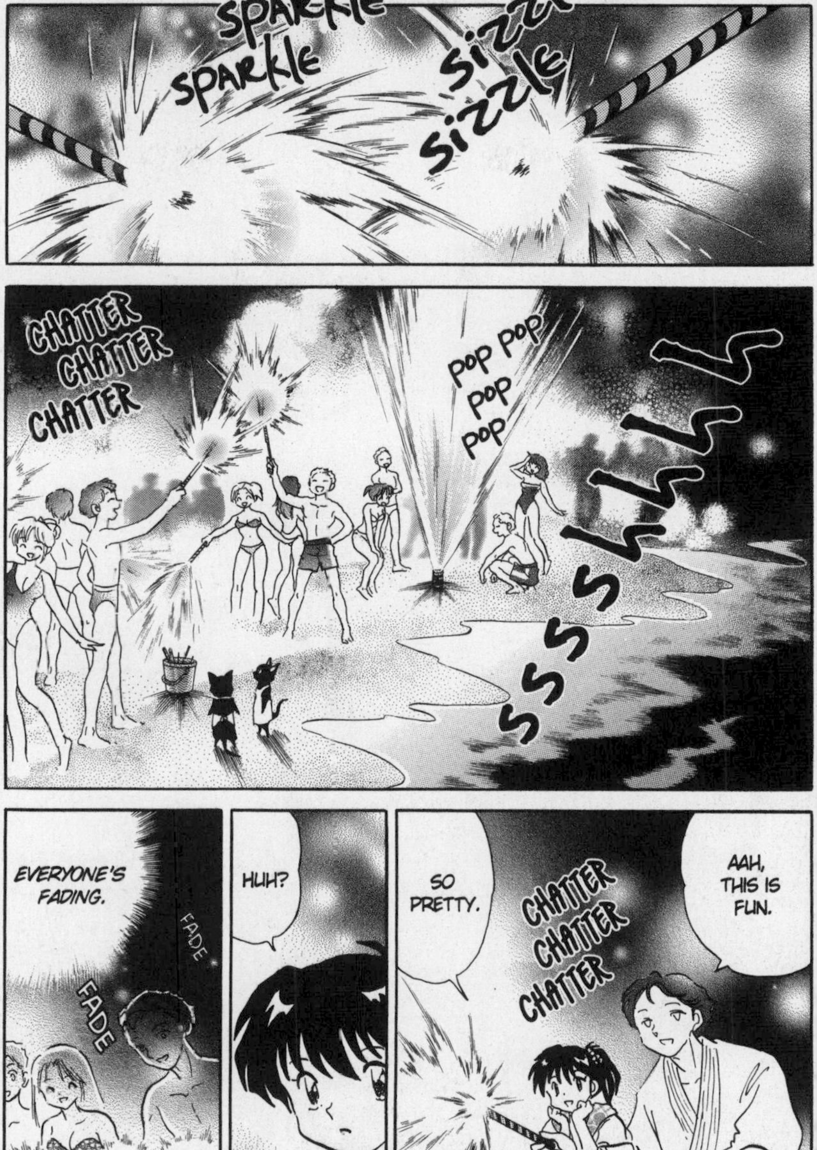
SIZZLE SIZZLE
SPARKLE SPARKLE
SSSSHHHH
POP POP POP POP
CHATTER CHATTER CHATTER
AAH, THIS IS FUN.
SO PRETTY.
CHATTER CHATTER CHATTER
HUH?
EVERYONE'S FADING.
FADE
FADE

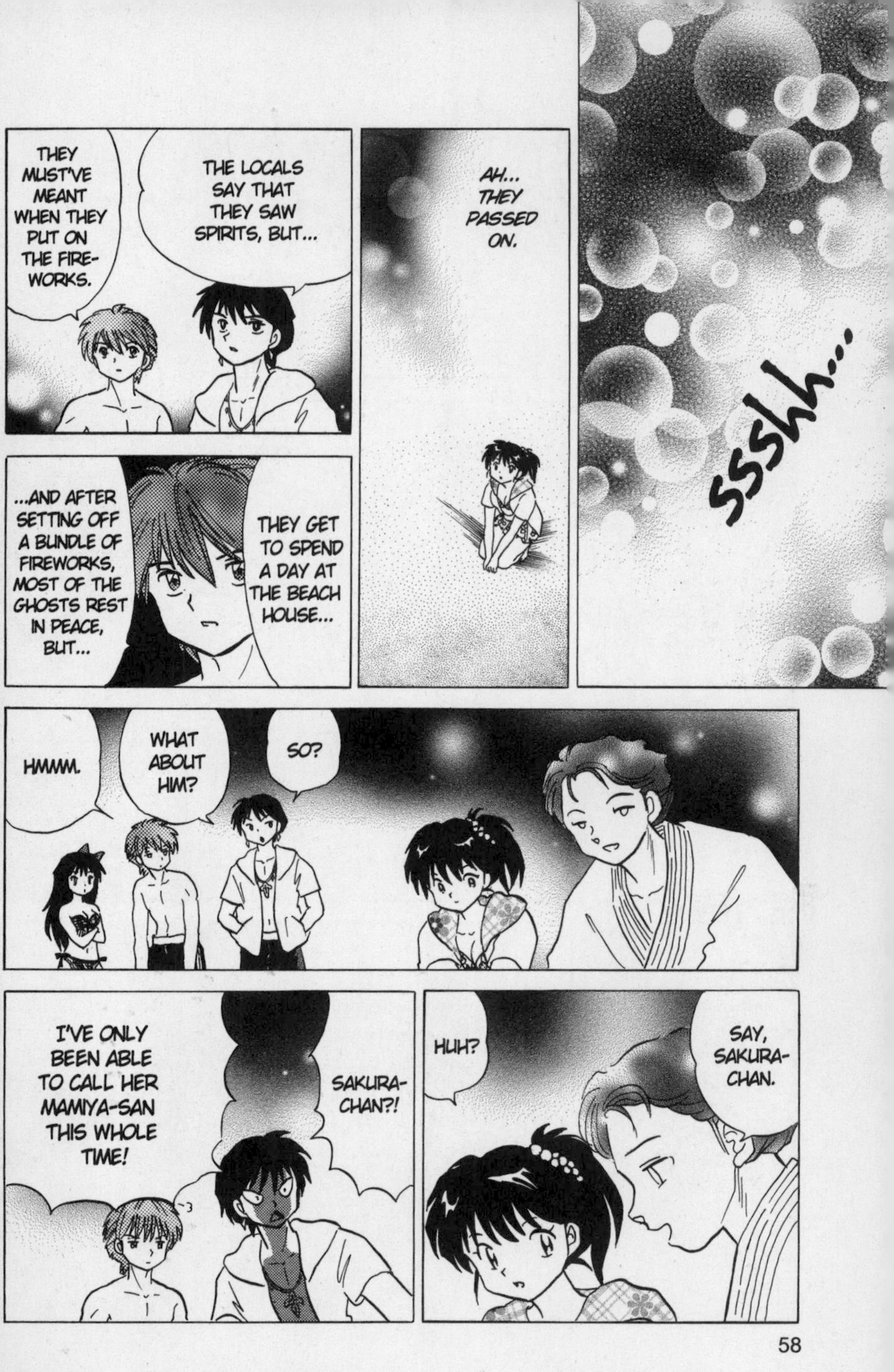
sssh...
AH... THEY PASSED ON.
THE LOCALS SAY THAT THEY SAW SPIRITS, BUT...
THEY MUST'VE MEANT WHEN THEY PUT ON THE FIRE-WORKS.
THEY GET TO SPEND A DAY AT THE BEACH HOUSE...
...AND AFTER SETTING OFF A BUNDLE OF FIREWORKS, MOST OF THE GHOSTS REST IN PEACE, BUT...
SO?
WHAT ABOUT HIM?
HMMM.
SAY, SAKURA-CHAN.
HUH?
SAKURA-CHAN?!
I'VE ONLY BEEN ABLE TO CALL HER MAMIYA-SAN THIS WHOLE TIME!

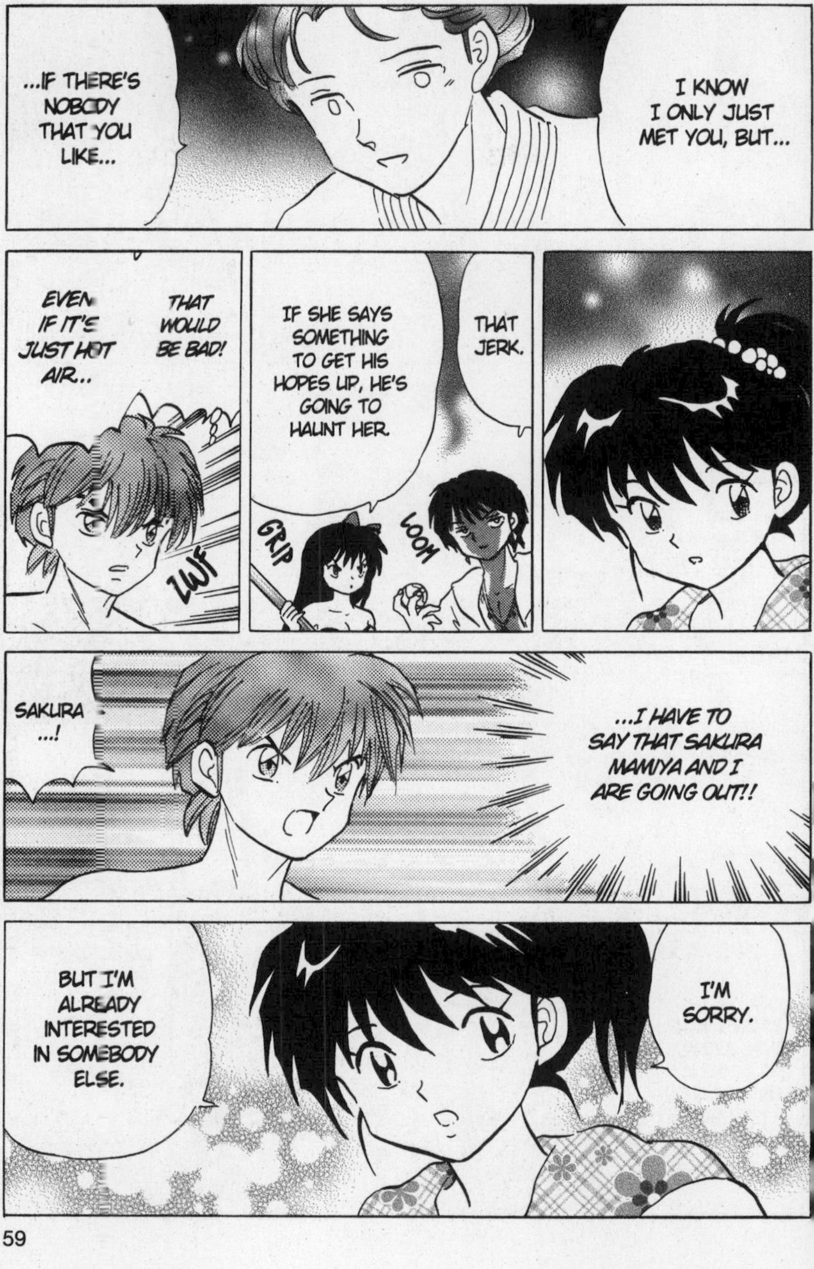
I KNOW I ONLY JUST MET YOU, BUT...
...IF THERE'S NOBODY THAT YOU LIKE...
THAT JERK.
IF SHE SAYS SOMETHING TO GET HIS HOPES UP, HE'S GOING TO HAUNT HER.
LOOM
GRIP
THAT WOULD BE BAD!
EVEN IF IT'S JUST HOT AIR...
ZWF
...I HAVE TO SAY THAT SAKURA MAMIYA AND I ARE GOING OUT!!
SAKURA ...!
I'M SORRY.
BUT I'M ALREADY INTERESTED IN SOMEBODY ELSE.

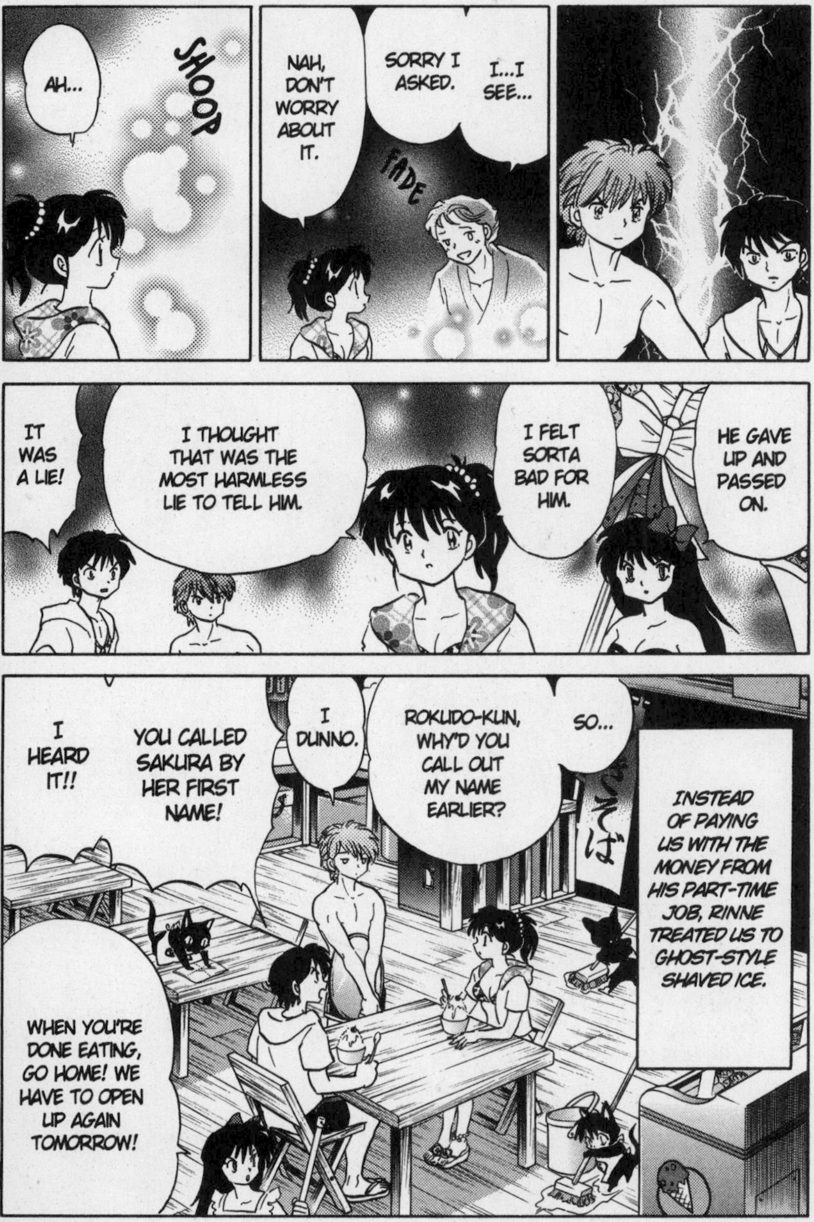
I...I SEE...
SORRY I ASKED.
NAH, DON'T WORRY ABOUT IT.
FADE
SHOOP
AH...
HE GAVE UP AND PASSED ON.
I FELT SORTA BAD FOR HIM.
I THOUGHT THAT WAS THE MOST HARMLESS LIE TO TELL HIM.
IT WAS A LIE!
INSTEAD OF PAYING US WITH THE MONEY FROM HIS PART-TIME JOB, RINNE TREATED US TO GHOST-STYLE SHAVED ICE.
SO...
ROKUDO-KUN, WHY'D YOU CALL OUT MY NAME EARLIER?
I DUNNO.
YOU CALLED SAKURA BY HER FIRST NAME!
I HEARD IT!!
WHEN YOU'RE DONE EATING, GO HOME! WE HAVE TO OPEN UP AGAIN TOMORROW!

CHAPTER 62: THE SPIRIT WAY STONE

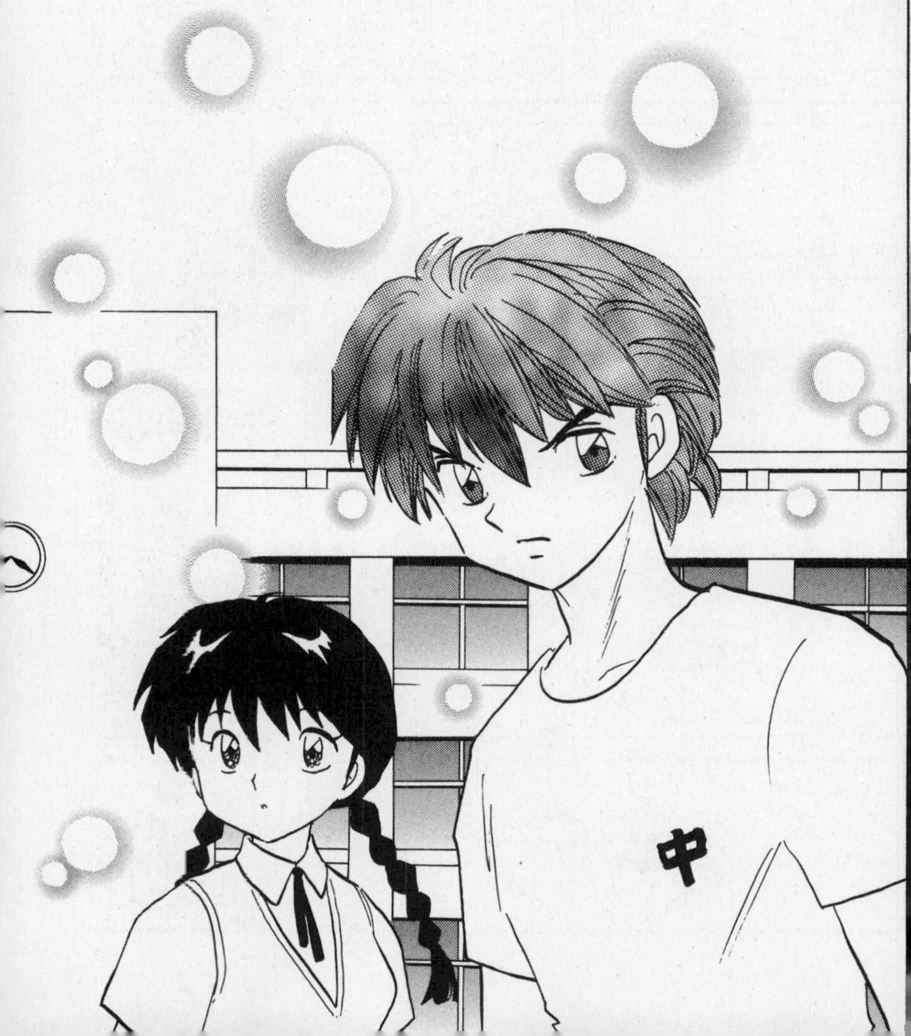
中

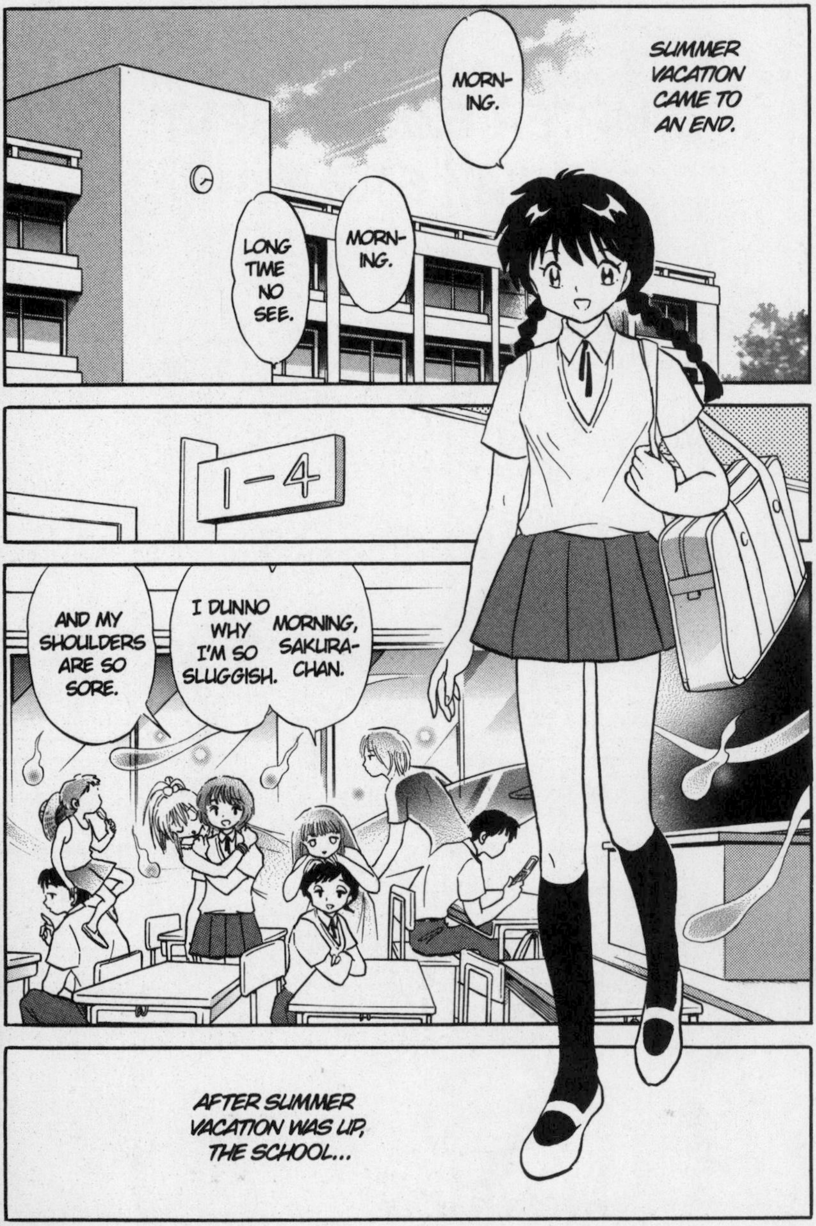
SUMMER VACATION CAME TO AN END.
MORN-ING.
MORN-ING.
LONG TIME NO SEE.
1-4
MORNING, SAKURA-CHAN.
I DUNNO WHY I'M SO SLUGGISH.
AND MY SHOULDERS ARE SO SORE.
AFTER SUMMER VACATION WAS UP, THE SCHOOL...

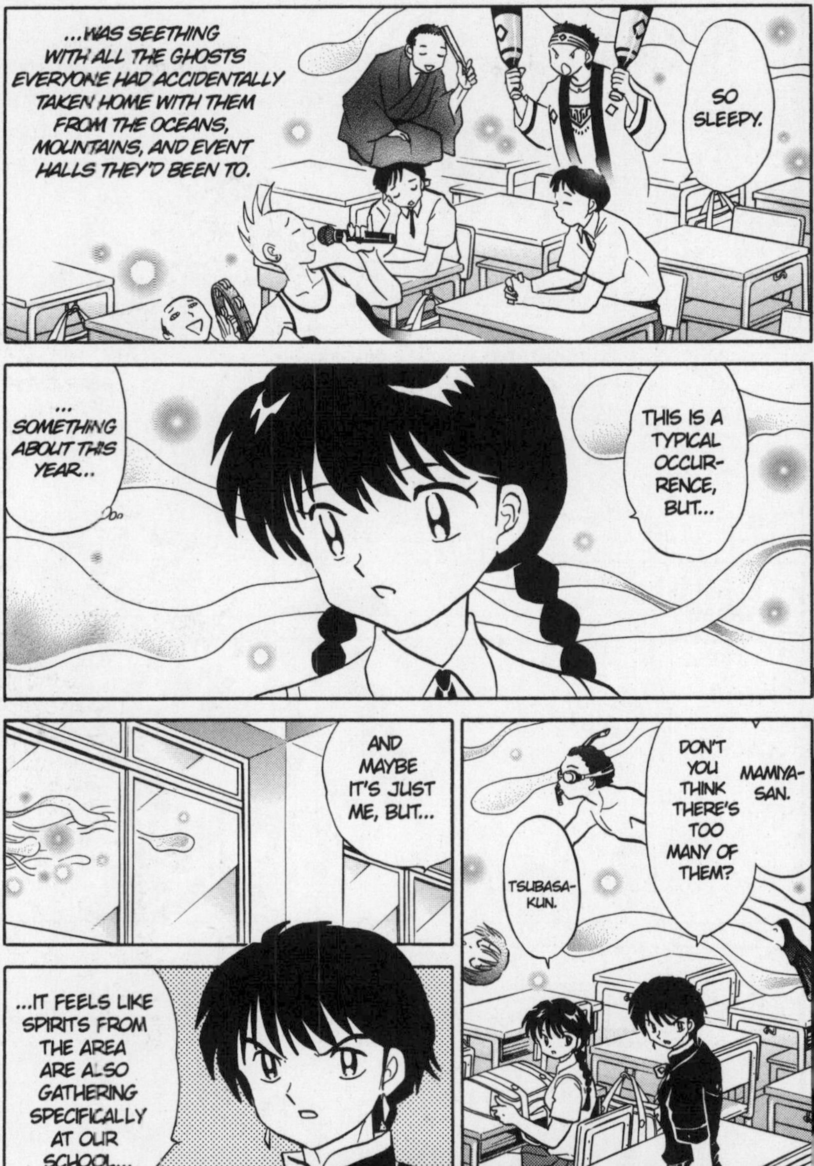
SO SLEEPY.
...WAS SEETHING WITH ALL THE GHOSTS EVERYONE HAD ACCIDENTALLY TAKEN HOME WITH THEM FROM THE OCEANS, MOUNTAINS, AND EVENT HALLS THEY'D BEEN TO.
THIS IS A TYPICAL OCCURRENCE, BUT...
...SOMETHING ABOUT THIS YEAR...
MAMIYA-SAN.
DON'T YOU THINK THERE'S TOO MANY OF THEM?
TSUBASA-KUN.
AND MAYBE IT'S JUST ME, BUT...
...IT FEELS LIKE SPIRITS FROM THE AREA ARE ALSO GATHERING SPECIFICALLY AT OUR SCHOOL...

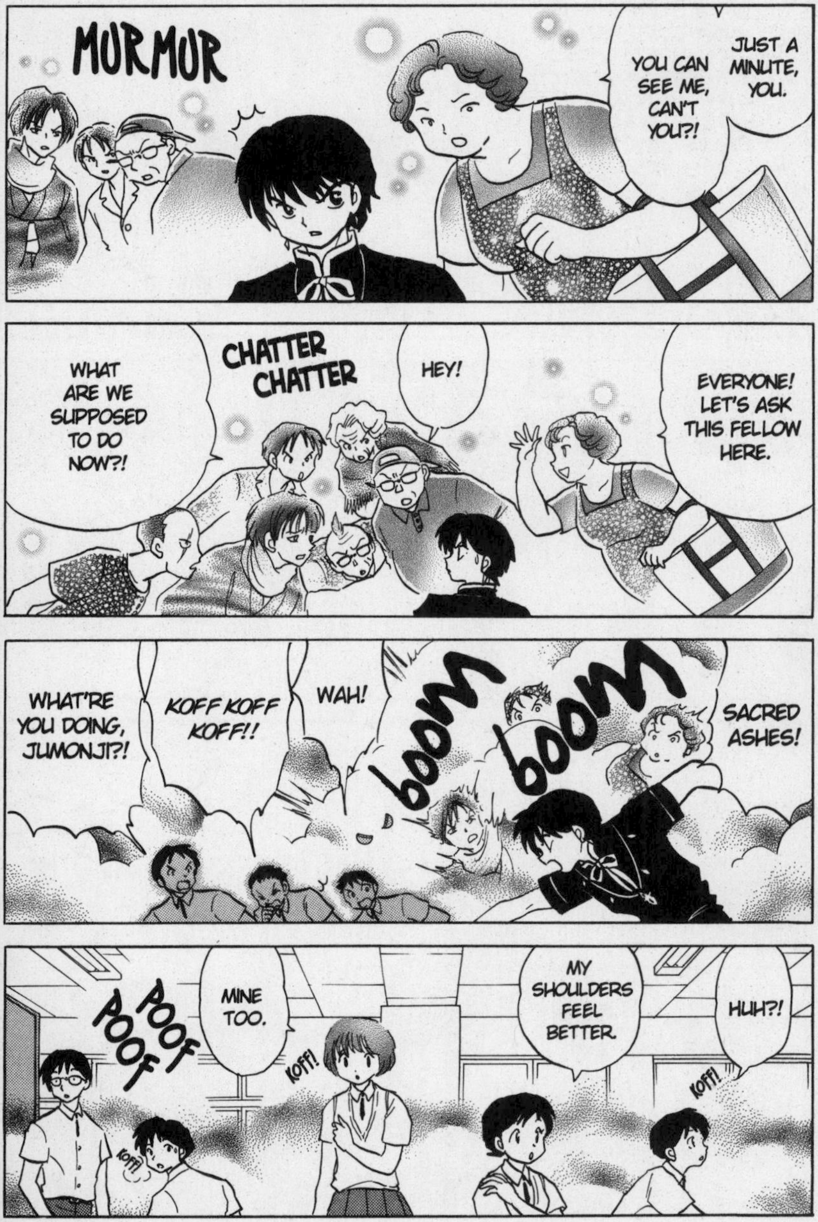
JUST A MINUTE, YOU.
YOU CAN SEE ME, CAN'T YOU?!
MURMUR
EVERYONE! LET'S ASK THIS FELLOW HERE.
HEY!
CHATTER CHATTER
WHAT ARE WE SUPPOSED TO DO NOW?!
SACRED ASHES!
boom boom
WAH!
KOFF KOFF KOFF!!
WHAT'RE YOU DOING, JUMONJI?!
HUH?!
KOFF!
MY SHOULDERS FEEL BETTER.
KOFF!
MINE TOO.
POOF POOF
KOFF!

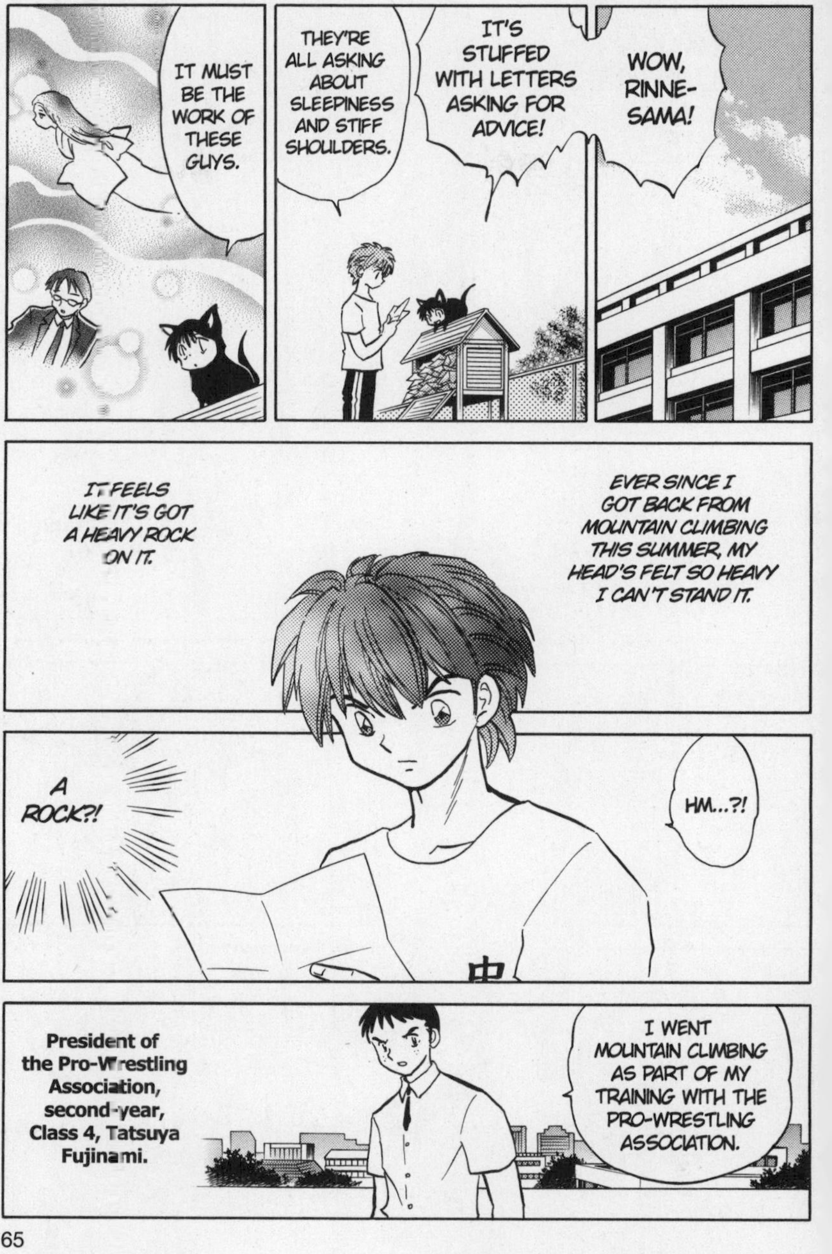
WOW, RINNE-SAMA!
IT'S STUFFED WITH LETTERS ASKING FOR ADVICE!
THEY'RE ALL ASKING ABOUT SLEEPINESS AND STIFF SHOULDERS.
IT MUST BE THE WORK OF THESE GUYS.
EVER SINCE I GOT BACK FROM MOUNTAIN CLIMBING THIS SUMMER, MY HEAD'S FELT SO HEAVY I CAN'T STAND IT.
IT FEELS LIKE IT'S GOT A HEAVY ROCK ON IT.
HM...?!
A ROCK?!
I WENT MOUNTAIN CLIMBING AS PART OF MY TRAINING WITH THE PRO-WRESTLING ASSOCIATION.
President of the Pro-Wrestling Association, second-year, Class 4, Tatsuya Fujinami.

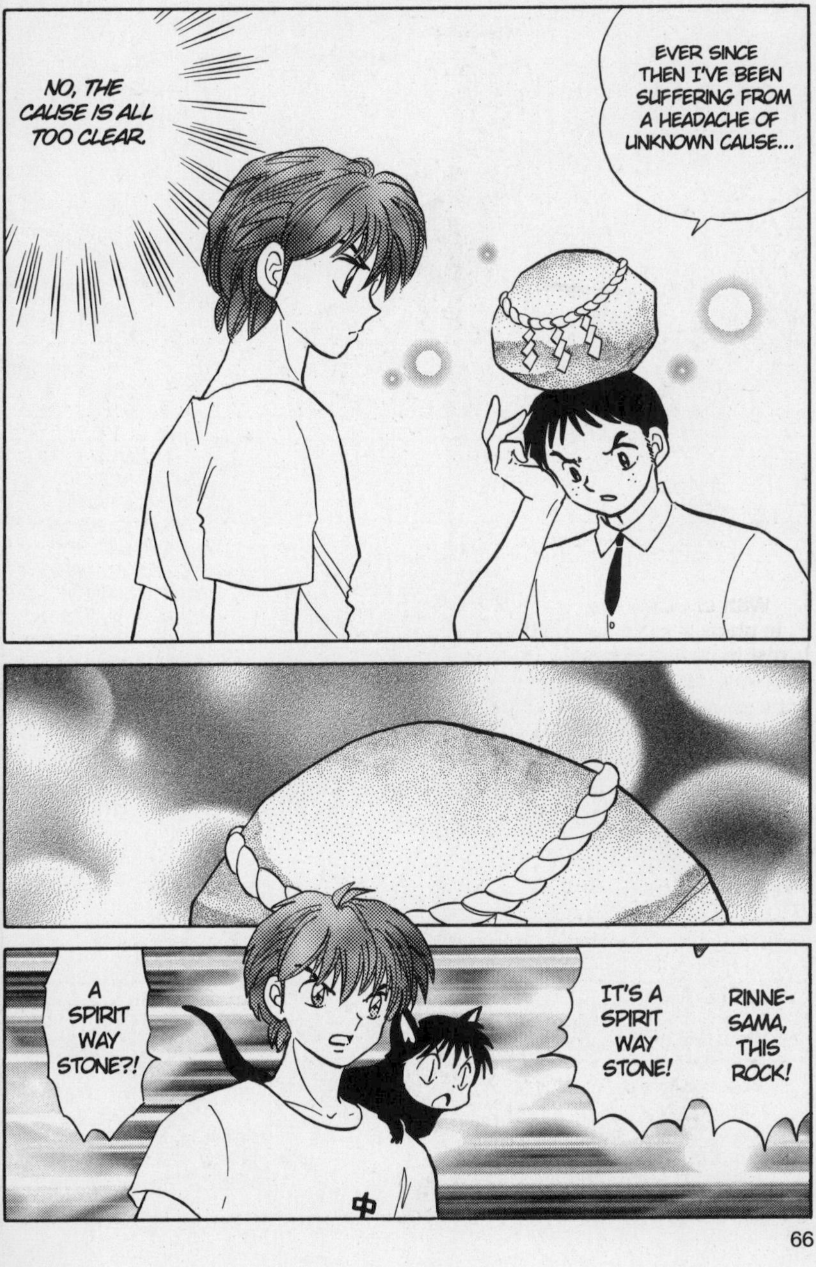
EVER SINCE THEN I'VE BEEN SUFFERING FROM A HEADACHE OF UNKNOWN CAUSE...
NO, THE CAUSE IS ALL TOO CLEAR.
RINNE-SAMA, THIS ROCK!
IT'S A SPIRIT WAY STONE!
A SPIRIT WAY STONE?!

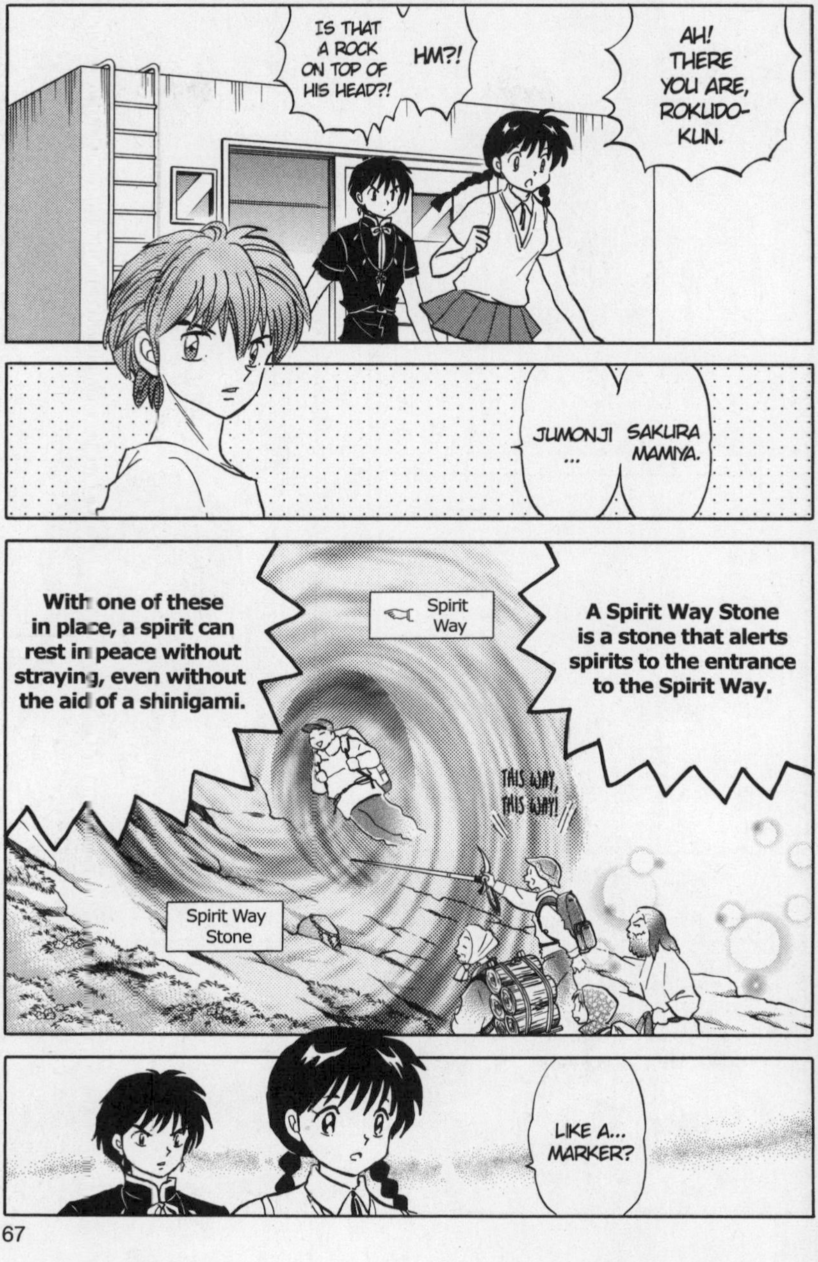
AH! THERE YOU ARE, ROKUDO-KUN.
HM?!
IS THAT A ROCK ON TOP OF HIS HEAD?!
SAKURA MAMIYA.
JUMONJI ...
A Spirit Way Stone is a stone that alerts spirits to the entrance to the Spirit Way.
Spirit Way
With one of these in place, a spirit can rest in peace without straying, even without the aid of a shinigami.
THIS WAY, THIS WAY!
Spirit Way Stone
LIKE A... MARKER?

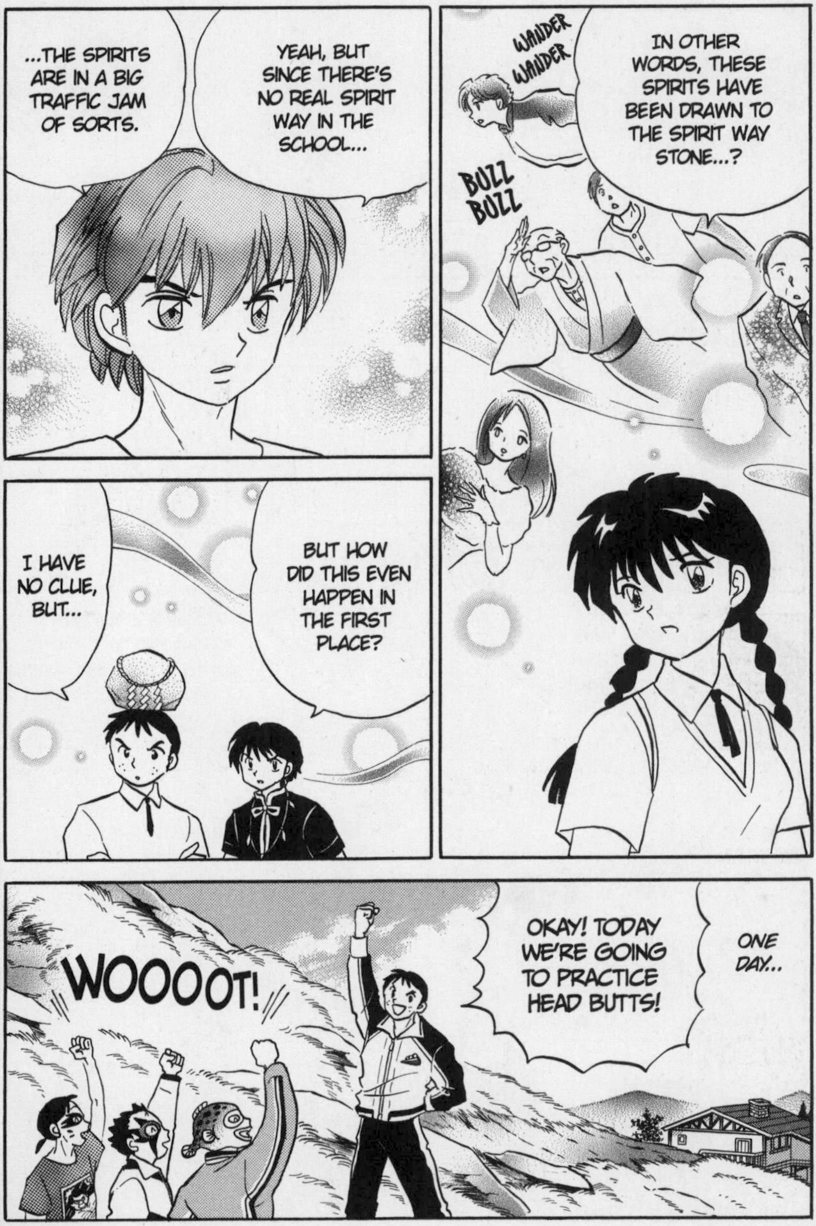

IN OTHER WORDS, THESE SPIRITS HAVE BEEN DRAWN TO THE SPIRIT WAY STONE...?
WANDER WANDER
BUZZ BUZZ
YEAH, BUT SINCE THERE'S NO REAL SPIRIT WAY IN THE SCHOOL...
...THE SPIRITS ARE IN A BIG TRAFFIC JAM OF SORTS.
BUT HOW DID THIS EVEN HAPPEN IN THE FIRST PLACE?
I HAVE NO CLUE, BUT...
ONE DAY...
OKAY! TODAY WE'RE GOING TO PRACTICE HEAD BUTTS!
WOOOOT!

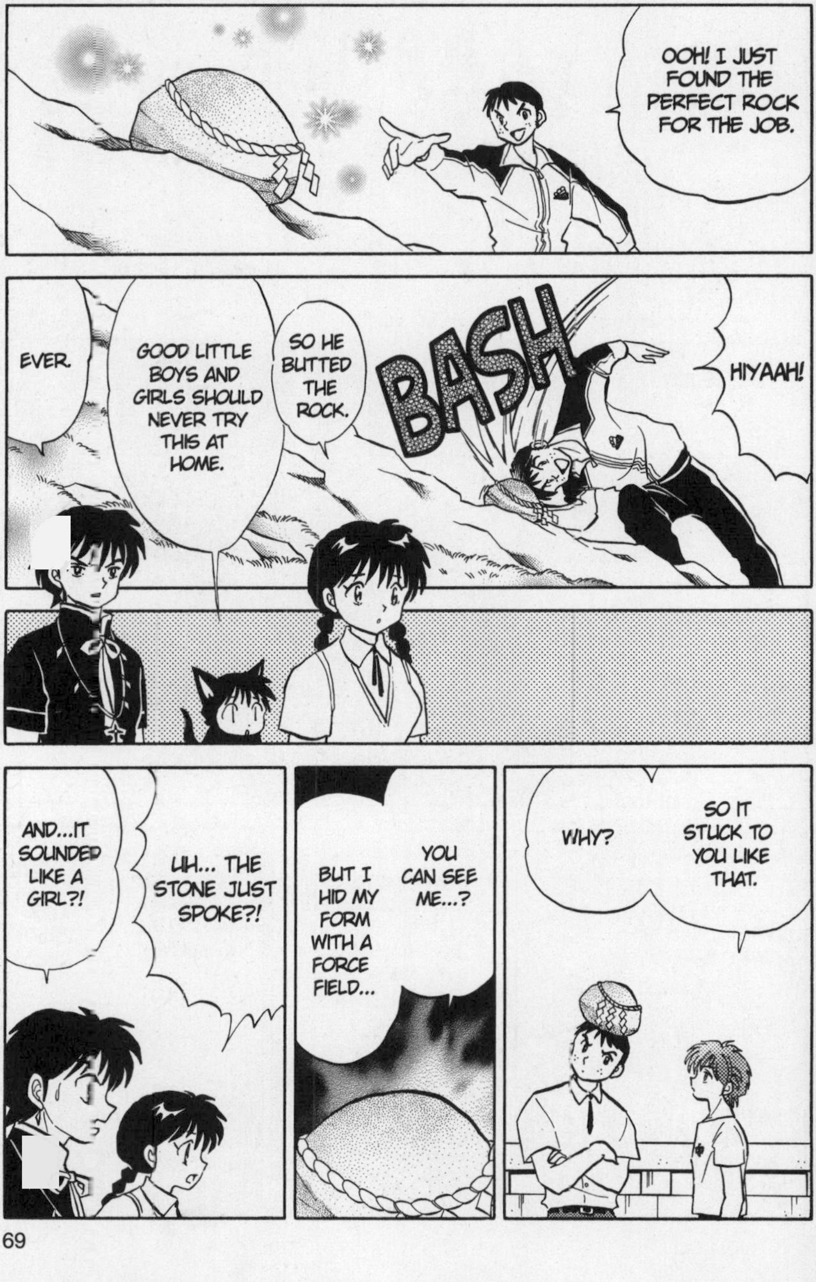
OOH! I JUST FOUND THE PERFECT ROCK FOR THE JOB.
HIYAAH!
BASH
SO HE BUTTED THE ROCK.
GOOD LITTLE BOYS AND GIRLS SHOULD NEVER TRY THIS AT HOME.
EVER.
SO IT STUCK TO YOU LIKE THAT.
WHY?
YOU CAN SEE ME...?
BUT I HID MY FORM WITH A FORCE FIELD...
UH... THE STONE JUST SPOKE?!
AND...IT SOUNDED LIKE A GIRL?!

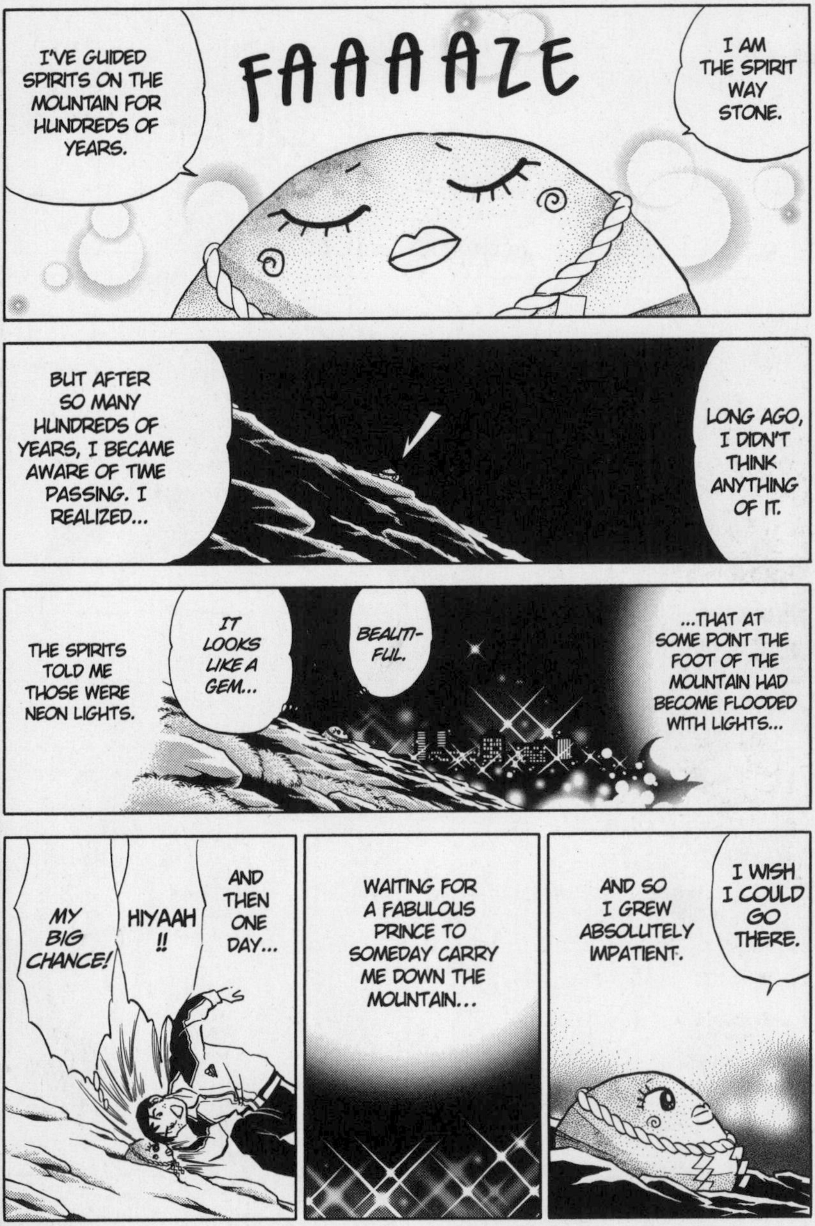
I AM THE SPIRIT WAY STONE.
FAAAAZE
I'VE GUIDED SPIRITS ON THE MOUNTAIN FOR HUNDREDS OF YEARS.
LONG AGO, I DIDN'T THINK ANYTHING OF IT.
BUT AFTER SO MANY HUNDREDS OF YEARS, I BECAME AWARE OF TIME PASSING. I REALIZED...
...THAT AT SOME POINT THE FOOT OF THE MOUNTAIN HAD BECOME FLOODED WITH LIGHTS...
BEAUTI-FUL.
IT LOOKS LIKE A GEM...
THE SPIRITS TOLD ME THOSE WERE NEON LIGHTS.
I WISH I COULD GO THERE.
AND SO I GREW ABSOLUTELY IMPATIENT.
WAITING FOR A FABULOUS PRINCE TO SOMEDAY CARRY ME DOWN THE MOUNTAIN...
AND THEN ONE DAY...
HIYAAH!!
MY BIG CHANCE!

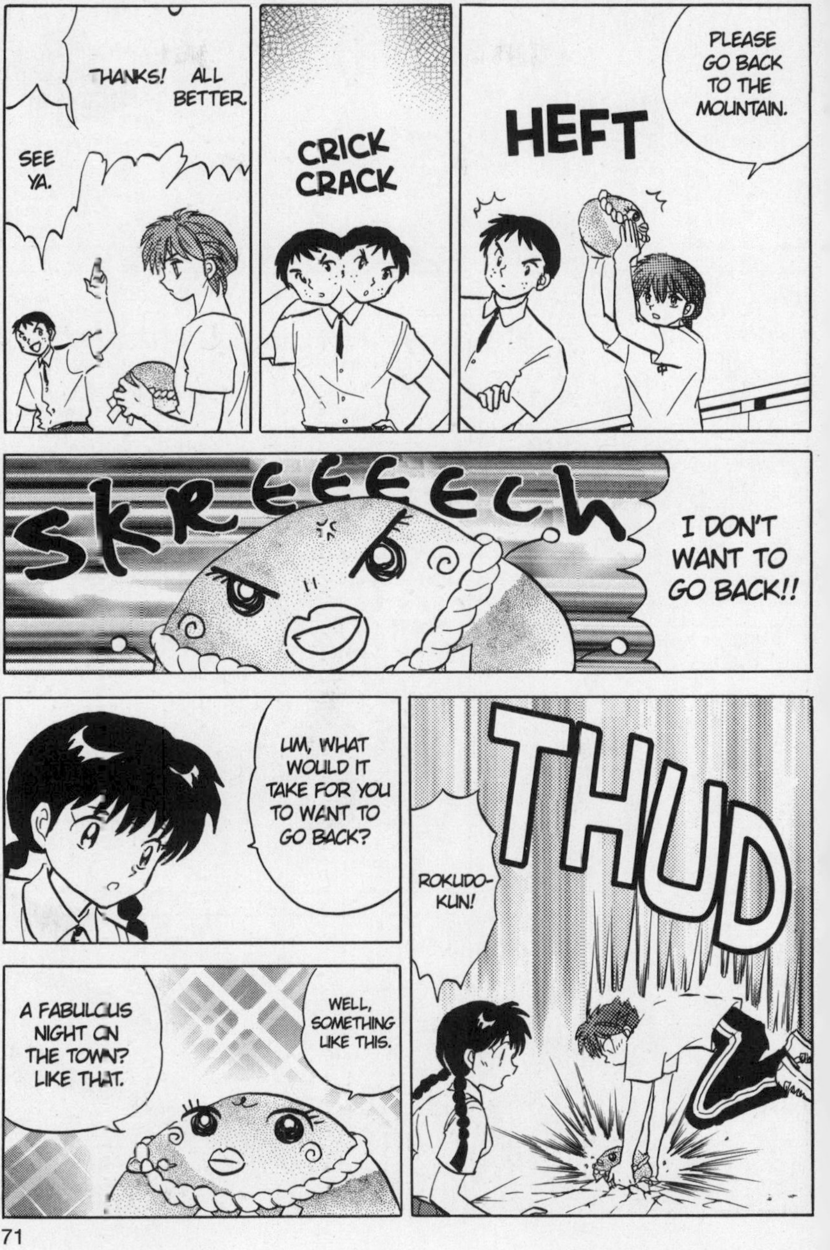
PLEASE GO BACK TO THE MOUNTAIN.
HEFT
CRICK CRACK
THANKS! ALL BETTER.
SEE YA.
I DON'T WANT TO GO BACK!!
SKREEEECH
THUD
ROKUDO-KUN!
UM, WHAT WOULD IT TAKE FOR YOU TO WANT TO GO BACK?
WELL, SOMETHING LIKE THIS.
A FABULOUS NIGHT ON THE TOWN? LIKE THAT.

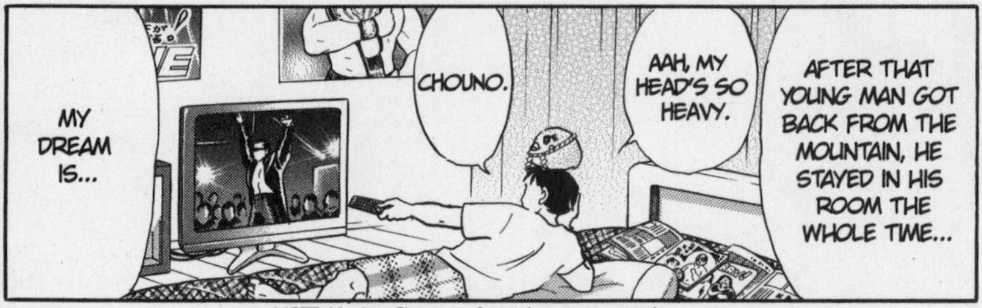
AFTER THAT YOUNG MAN GOT BACK FROM THE MOUNTAIN, HE STAYED IN HIS ROOM THE WHOLE TIME...
AAH, MY HEAD'S SO HEAVY.
CHOUNO.
MY DREAM IS...

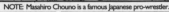

NOTE: Masahiro Chouno is a famous Japanese pro-wrestler.

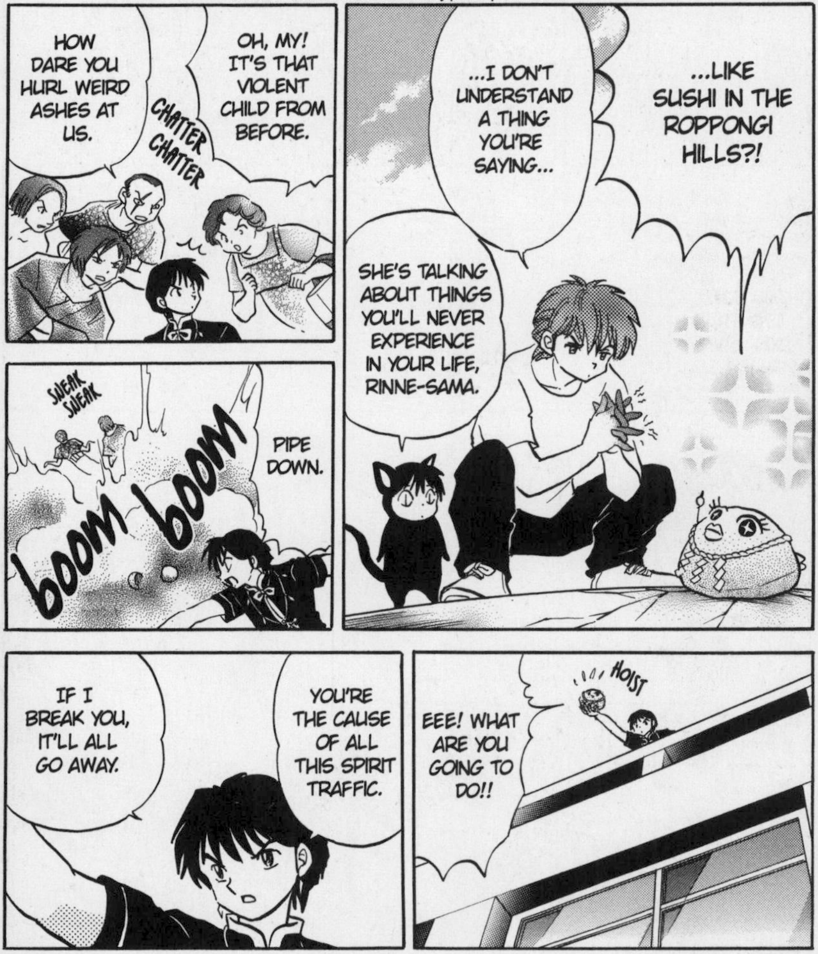
...LIKE SUSHI IN THE ROPPONGI HILLS?!
...I DON'T UNDERSTAND A THING YOU'RE SAYING...
SHE'S TALKING ABOUT THINGS YOU'LL NEVER EXPERIENCE IN YOUR LIFE, RINNE-SAMA.
OH, MY! IT'S THAT VIOLENT CHILD FROM BEFORE.
CHATTER CHATTER
HOW DARE YOU HURL WEIRD ASHES AT US.
PIPE DOWN.
boom boom
SNEAK SNEAK
HOIST
EEE! WHAT ARE YOU GOING TO DO!!
YOU'RE THE CAUSE OF ALL THIS SPIRIT TRAFFIC.
IF I BREAK YOU, IT'LL ALL GO AWAY.

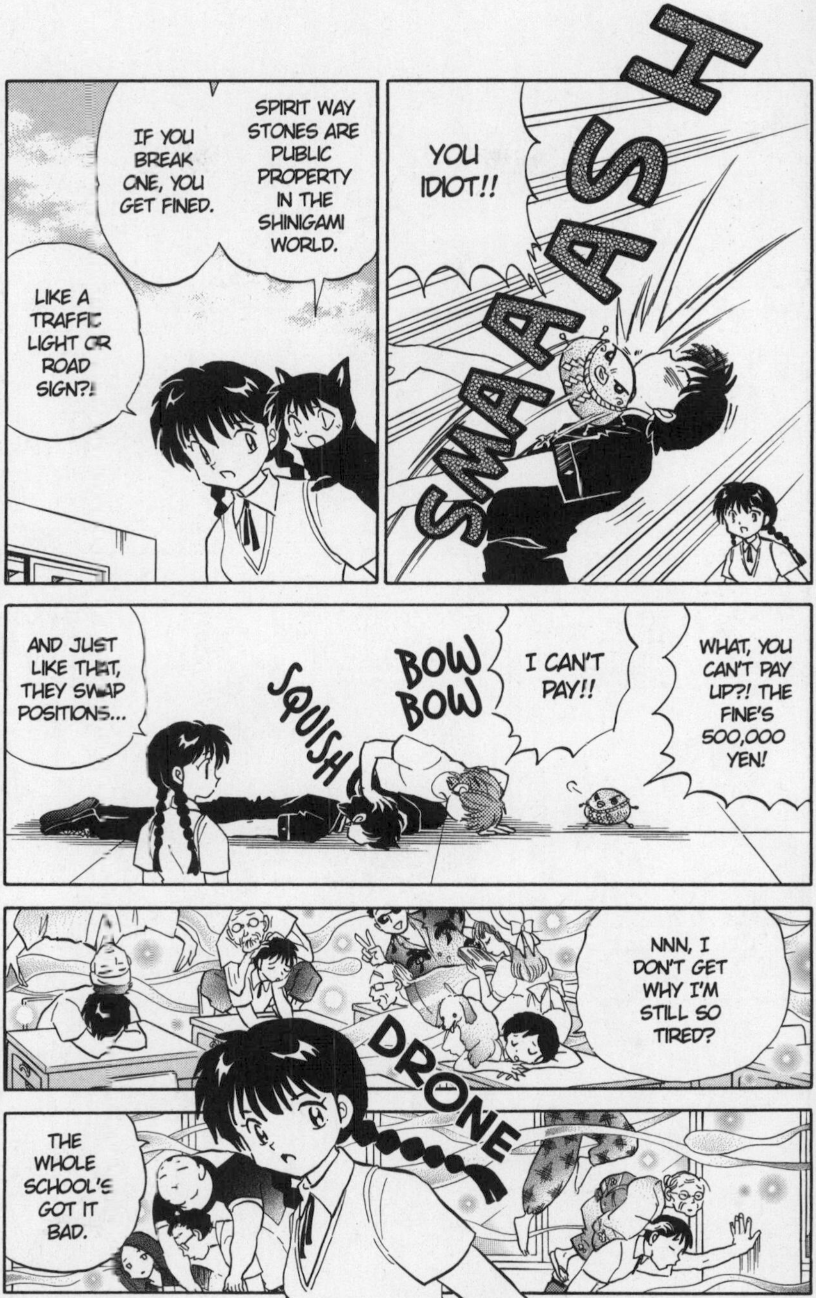
YOU IDIOT!!
SMAAASH
SPIRIT WAY STONES ARE PUBLIC PROPERTY IN THE SHINIGAMI WORLD.
IF YOU BREAK ONE, YOU GET FINED.
LIKE A TRAFFIC LIGHT OR ROAD SIGN?!
WHAT, YOU CAN'T PAY UP?! THE FINE'S 500,000 YEN!
I CAN'T PAY!!
BOW BOW
SQUISH
AND JUST LIKE THAT, THEY SWAP POSITIONS...
NNN, I DON'T GET WHY I'M STILL SO TIRED?
DRONE
THE WHOLE SCHOOL'S GOT IT BAD.

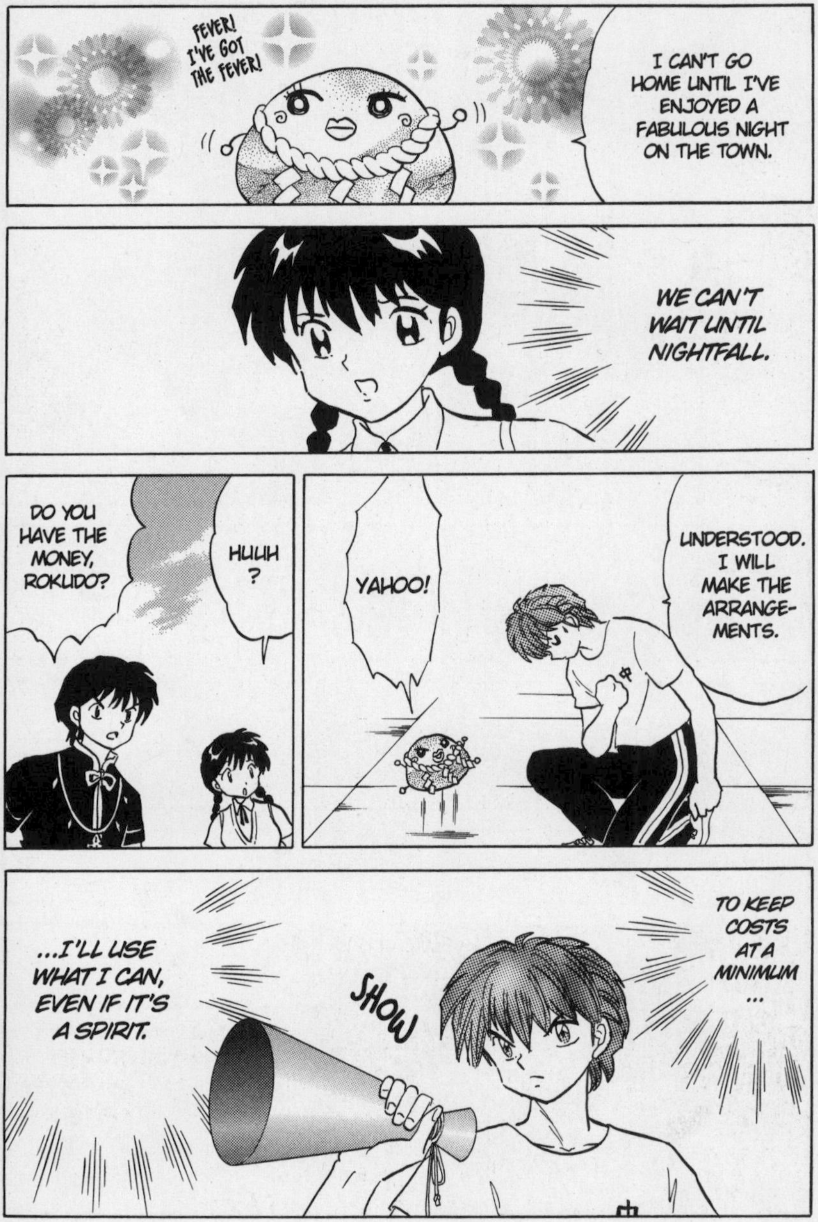
I CAN'T GO HOME UNTIL I'VE ENJOYED A FABULOUS NIGHT ON THE TOWN.
FEVER! I'VE GOT THE FEVER!
WE CAN'T WAIT UNTIL NIGHTFALL.
UNDERSTOOD. I WILL MAKE THE ARRANGE-MENTS.
YAHOO!
HUUH?
DO YOU HAVE THE MONEY, ROKUDO?
TO KEEP COSTS AT A MINIMUM...
SHOW
...I'LL USE WHAT I CAN, EVEN IF IT'S A SPIRIT.

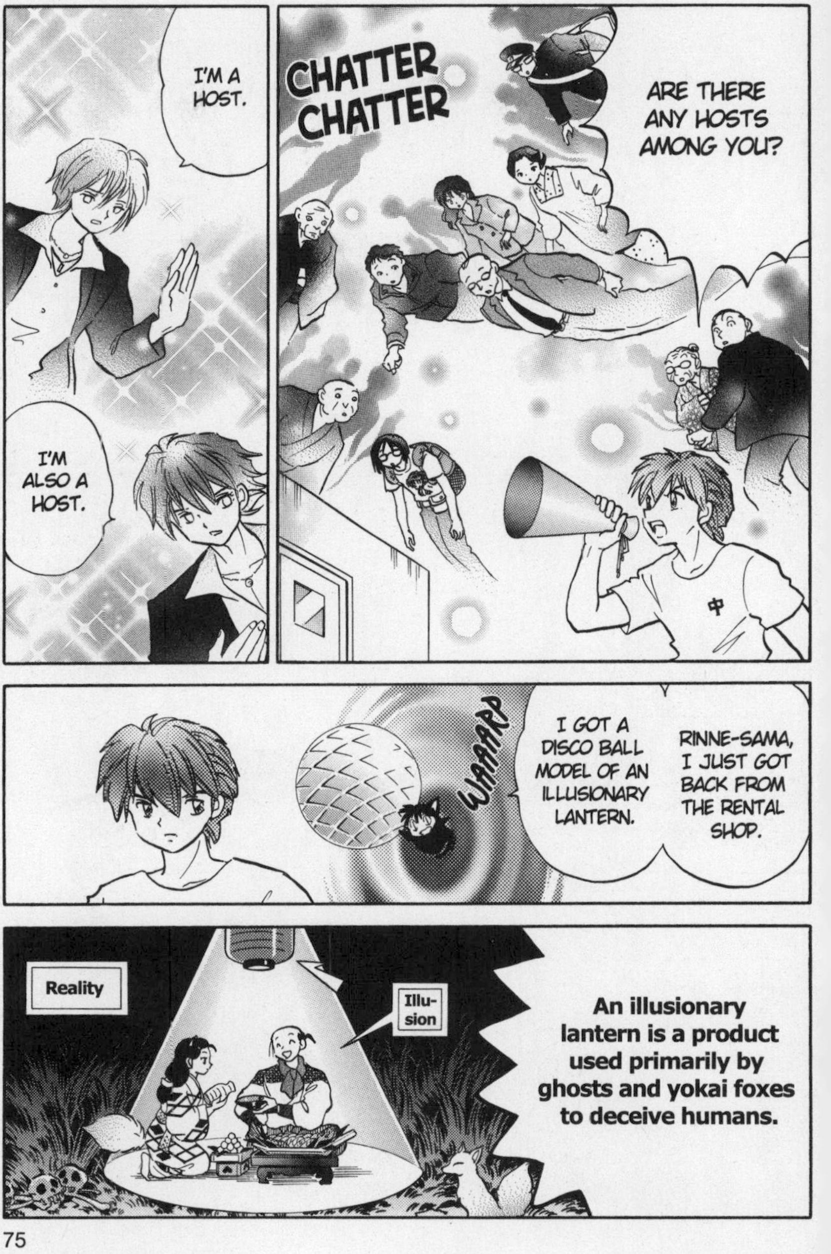
ARE THERE ANY HOSTS AMONG YOU?
CHATTER CHATTER
I'M A HOST.
I'M ALSO A HOST.
RINNE-SAMA, I JUST GOT BACK FROM THE RENTAL SHOP.
I GOT A DISCO BALL MODEL OF AN ILLUSIONARY LANTERN.
WAAARP
An illusionary lantern is a product used primarily by ghosts and yokai foxes to deceive humans.
Illu-sion
Reality

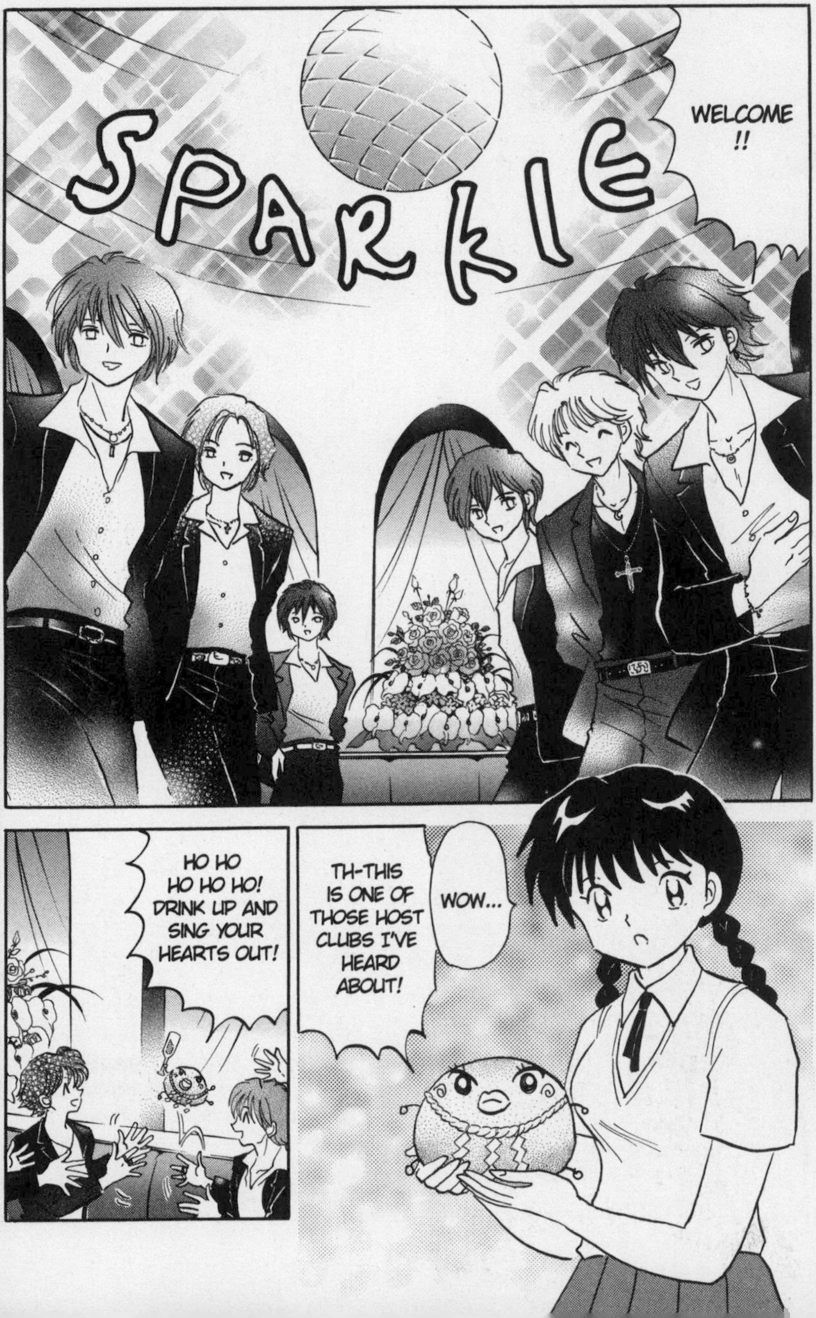
SPARKLE
WELCOME !!
WOW...
TH-THIS IS ONE OF THOSE HOST CLUBS I'VE HEARD ABOUT!
HO HO HO HO HO! DRINK UP AND SING YOUR HEARTS OUT!

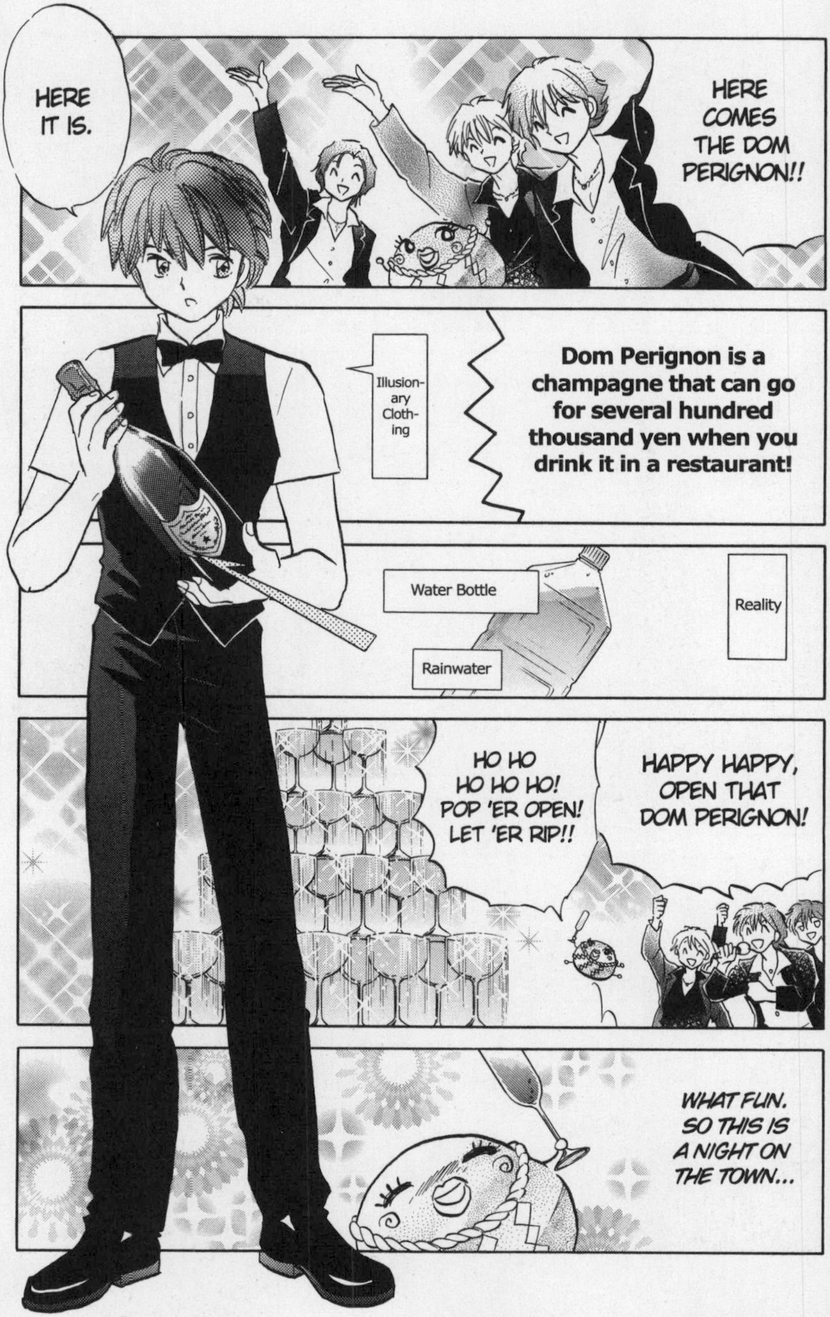
HERE COMES THE DOM PERIGNON!!
HERE IT IS.
Dom Perignon is a champagne that can go for several hundred thousand yen when you drink it in a restaurant!
Illusion-ary Cloth-ing
Reality
Water Bottle
Rainwater
HAPPY HAPPY, OPEN THAT DOM PERIGNON!
HO HO HO HO HO! POP 'ER OPEN! LET 'ER RIP!!
WHAT FUN. SO THIS IS A NIGHT ON THE TOWN...

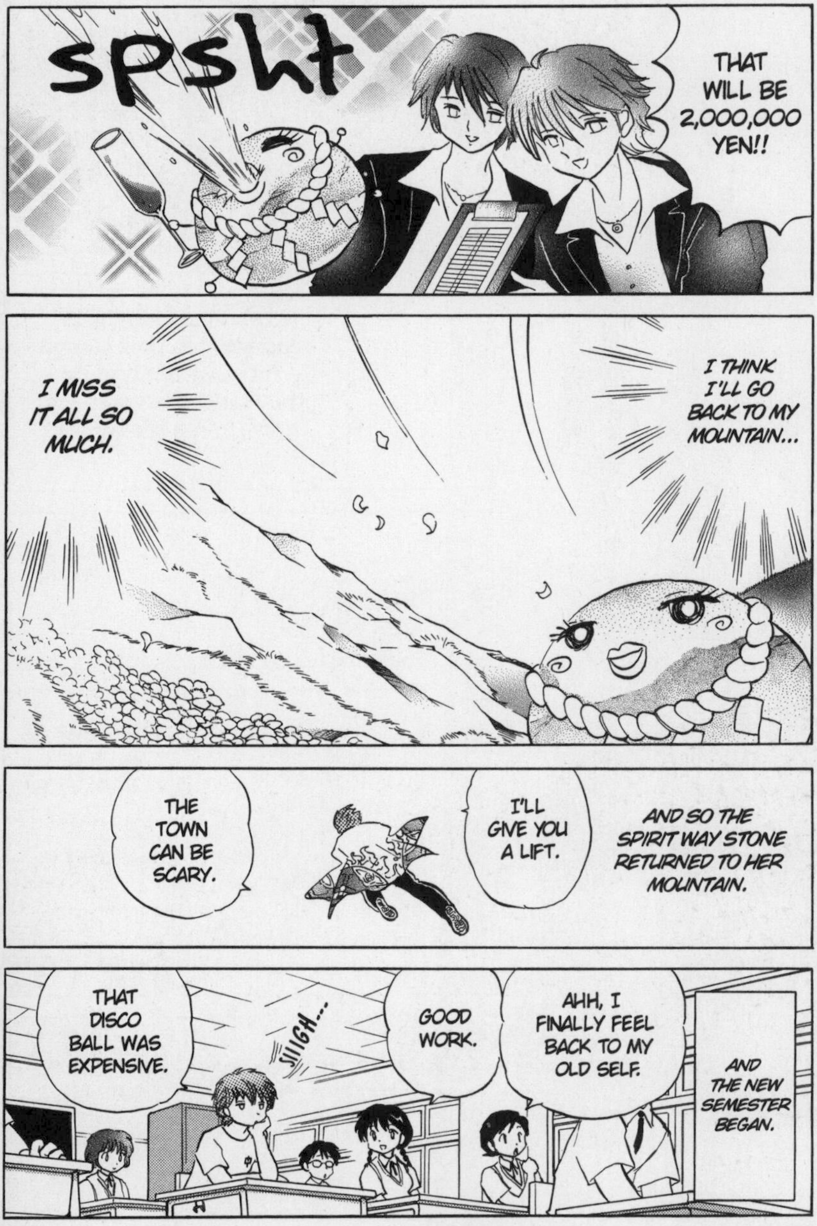
THAT WILL BE 2,000,000 YEN!!
SPSHT
I THINK I'LL GO BACK TO MY MOUNTAIN...
I MISS IT ALL SO MUCH.
AND SO THE SPIRIT WAY STONE RETURNED TO HER MOUNTAIN.
I'LL GIVE YOU A LIFT.
THE TOWN CAN BE SCARY.
AND THE NEW SEMESTER BEGAN.
AHH, I FINALLY FEEL BACK TO MY OLD SELF.
GOOD WORK.
SIIIGH...
THAT DISCO BALL WAS EXPENSIVE.

CHAPTER 63: THE VOICES FROM THE SHRINE

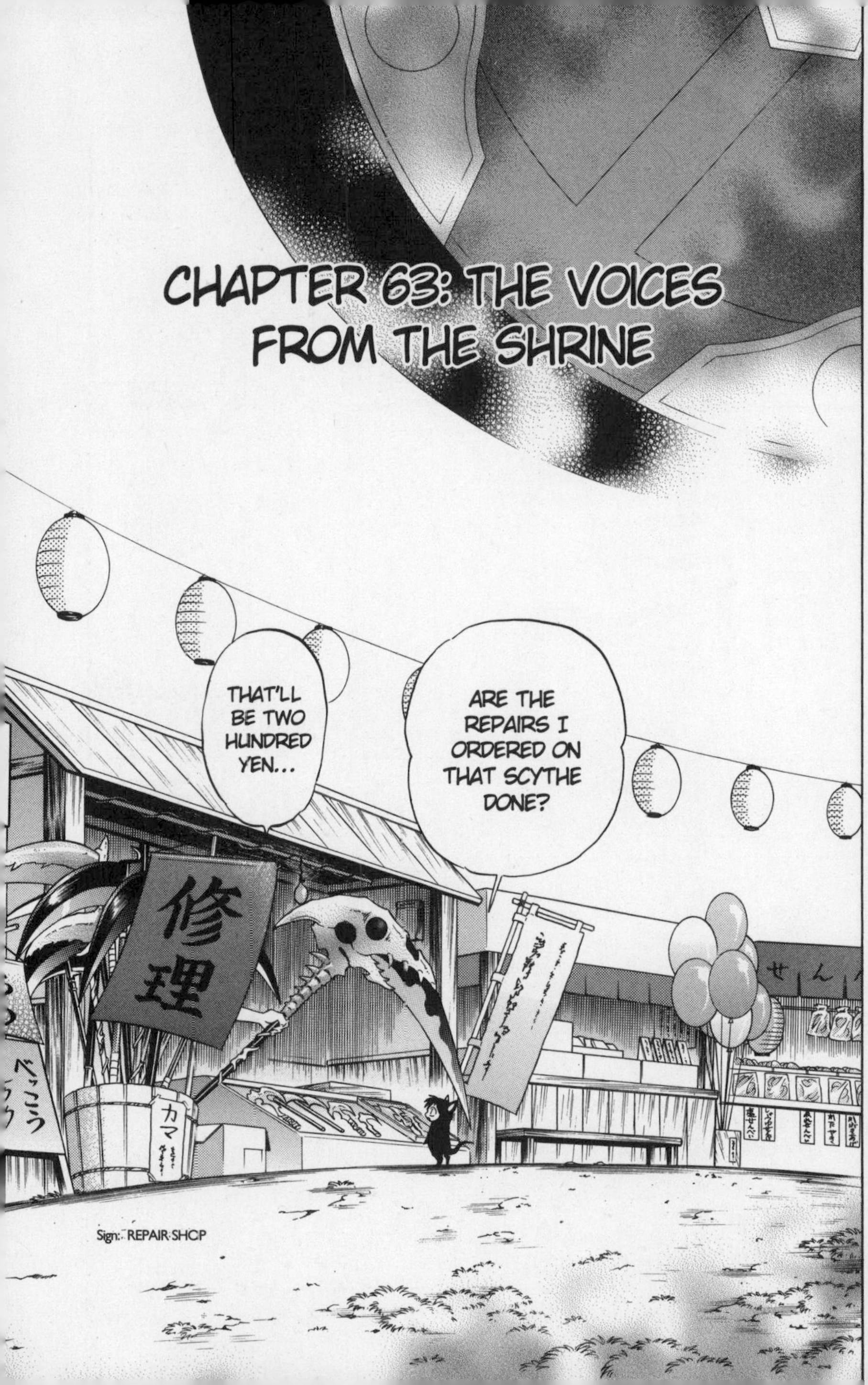
ARE THE REPAIRS I ORDERED ON THAT SCYTHE DONE?
THAT'LL BE TWO HUNDRED YEN...
修理
カマ

Sign: REPAIR SHCP

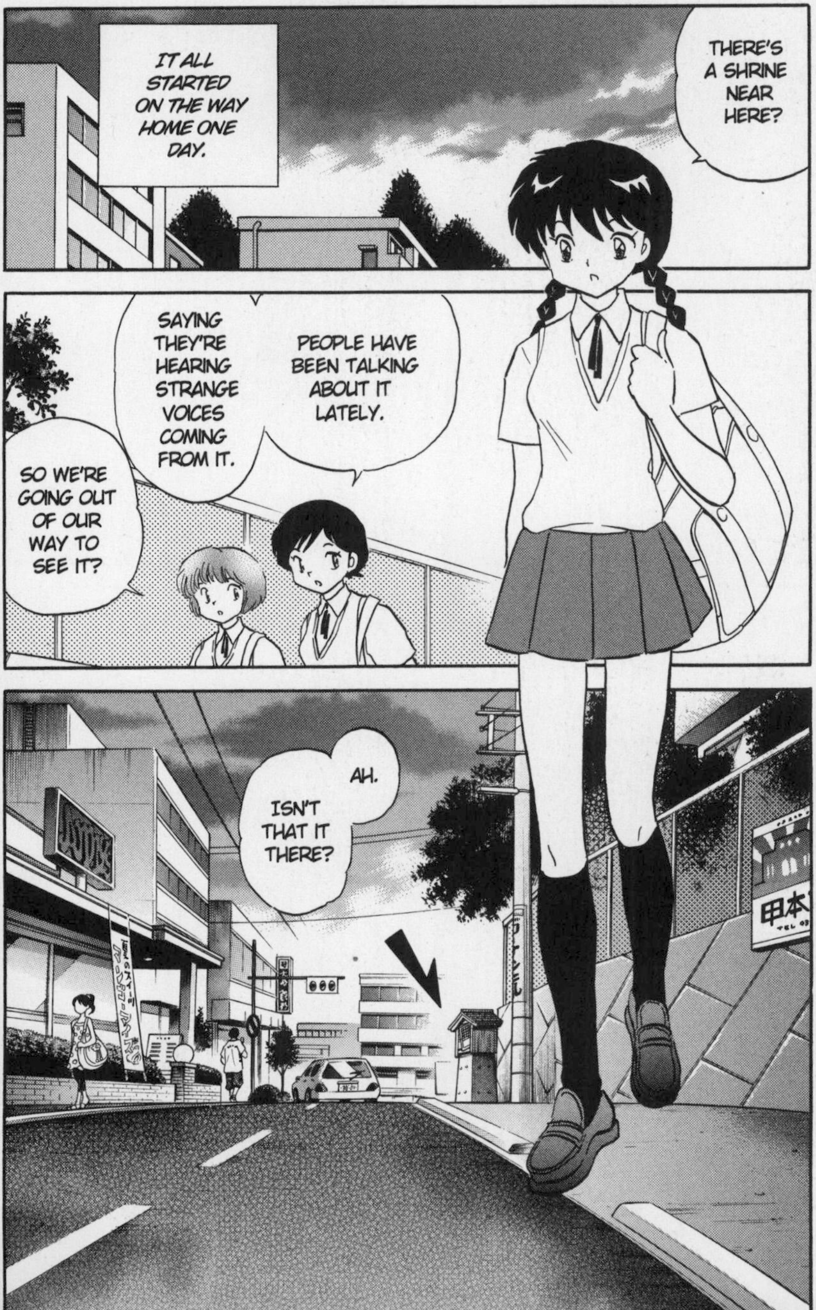
THERE'S A SHRINE NEAR HERE?
IT ALL STARTED ON THE WAY HOME ONE DAY.
PEOPLE HAVE BEEN TALKING ABOUT IT LATELY.
SAYING THEY'RE HEARING STRANGE VOICES COMING FROM IT.
SO WE'RE GOING OUT OF OUR WAY TO SEE IT?
AH.
ISN'T THAT IT THERE?

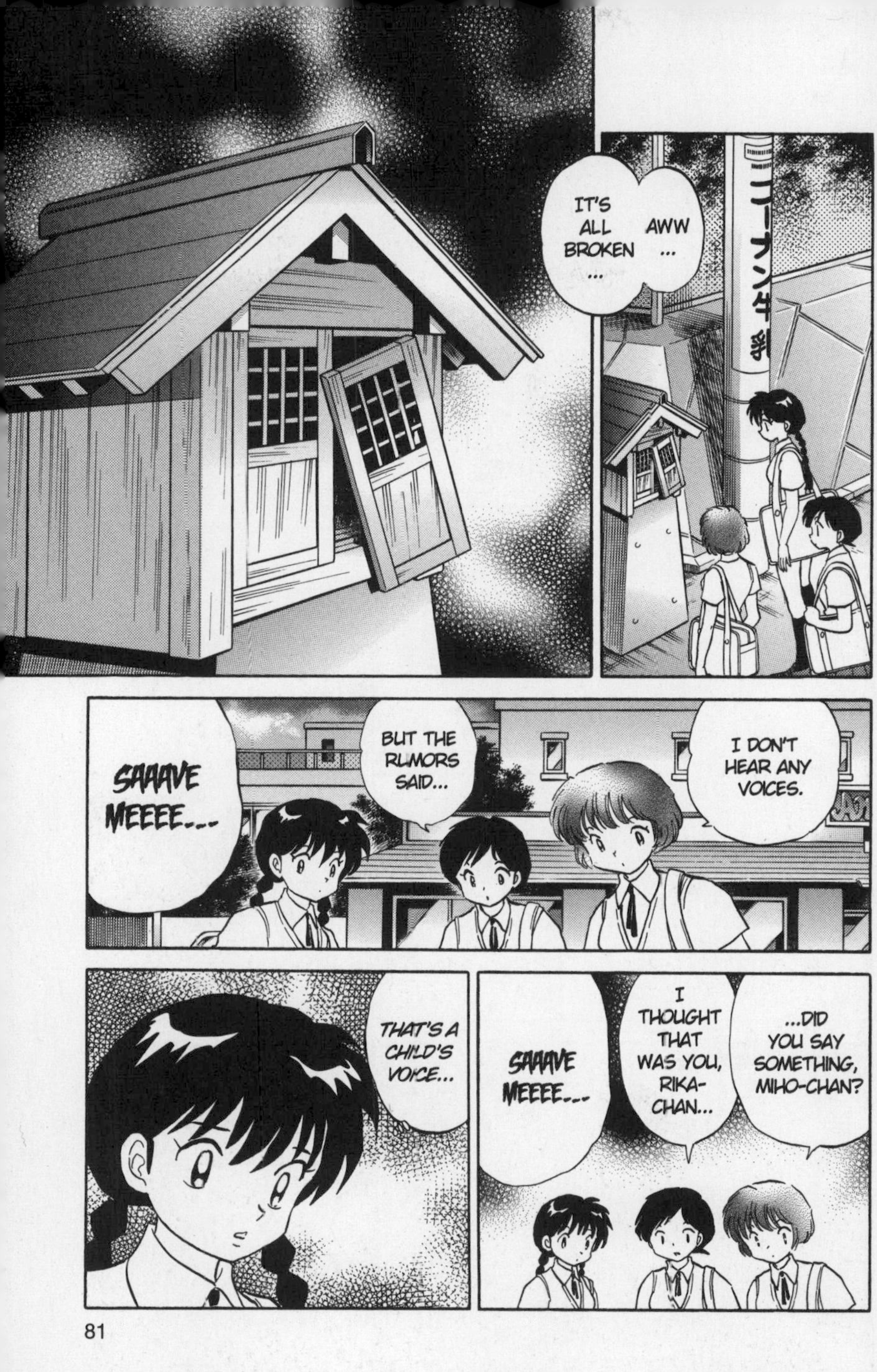
AWW ...
IT'S ALL BROKEN ...
I DON'T HEAR ANY VOICES.
BUT THE RUMORS SAID...
SAAAVE MEEEE...
...DID YOU SAY SOMETHING, MIHO-CHAN?
I THOUGHT THAT WAS YOU, RIKA-CHAN...
SAAAVE MEEEE...
THAT'S A CHILD'S VOICE...

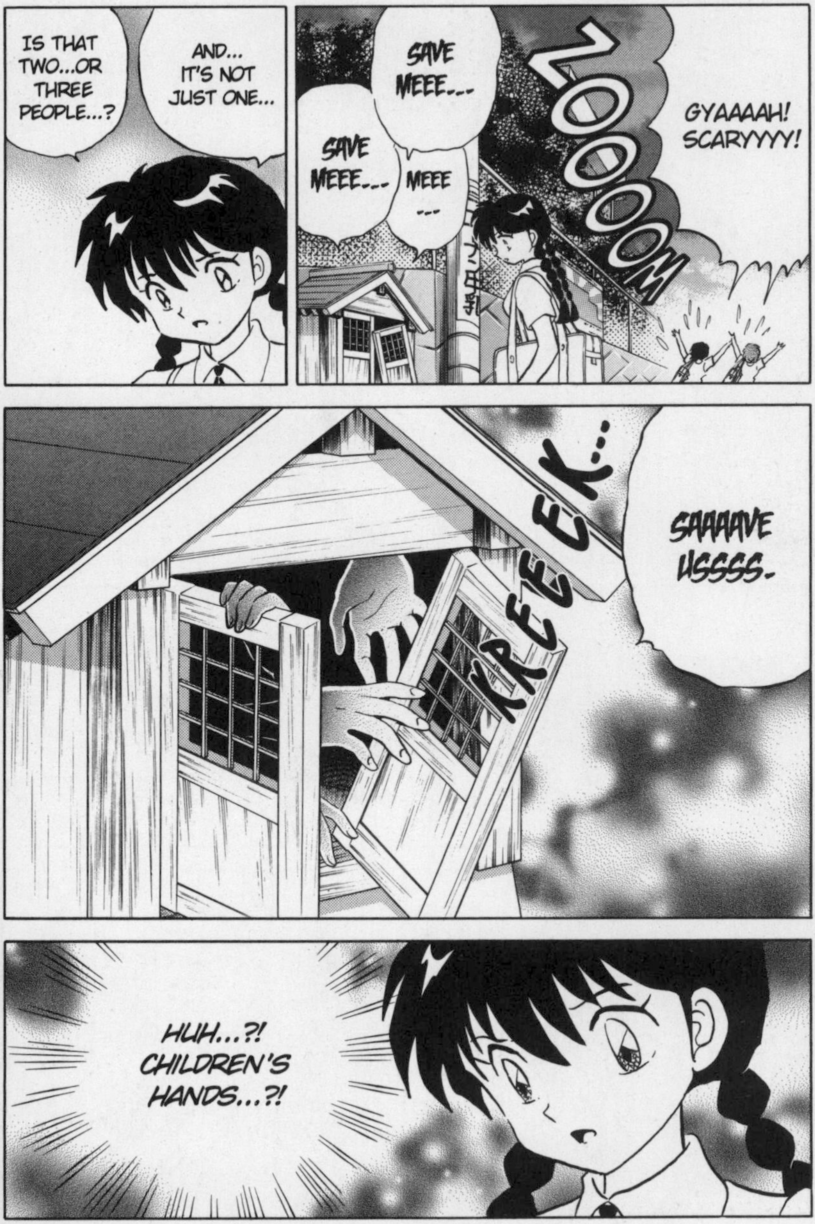
GYAAAAH! SCARYYYY!
ZOOOOOM
SAVE MEEE...
SAVE MEEE...
MEEE ...
AND... IT'S NOT JUST ONE...
IS THAT TWO...OR THREE PEOPLE...?
SAAAAVE USSSS-
KREEEK...
HUH...?! CHILDREN'S HANDS...?!

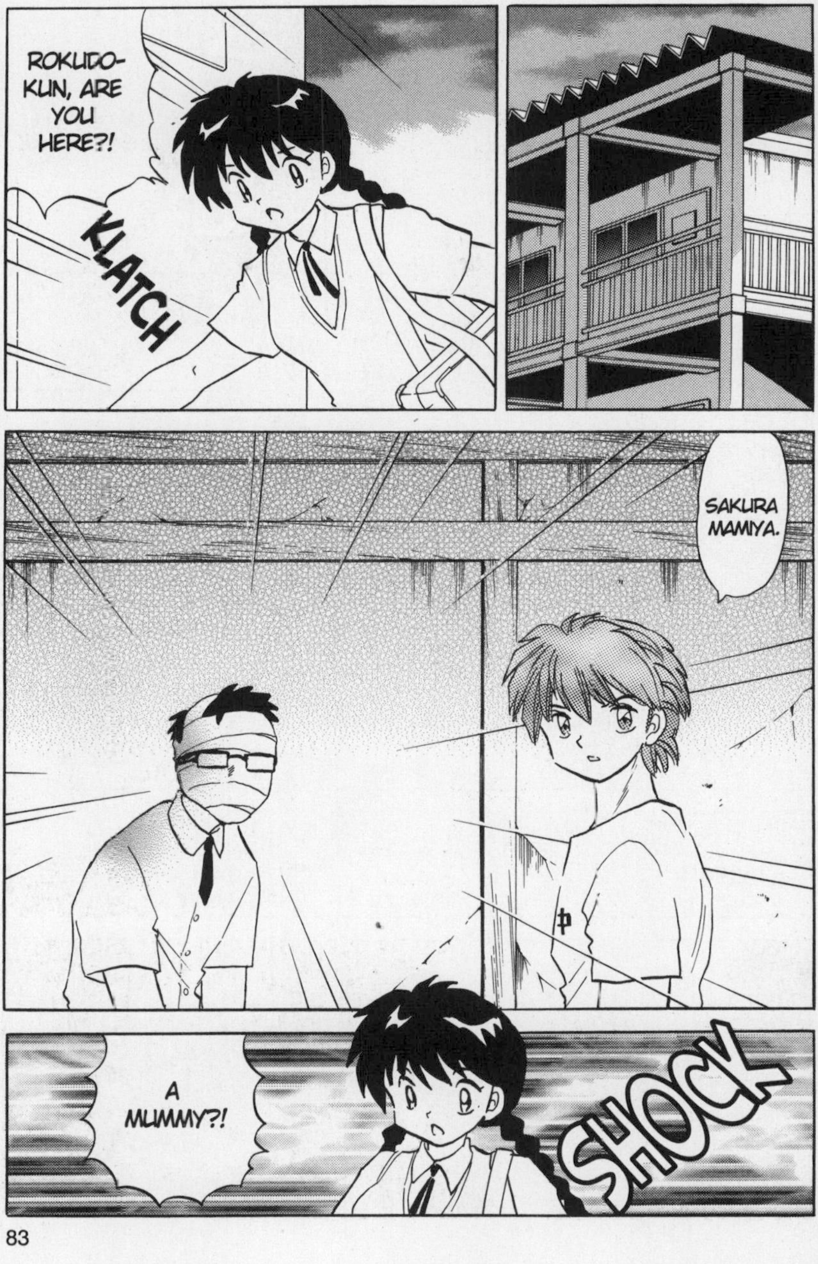
ROKUDO-KUN, ARE YOU HERE?!
KLATCH
SAKURA MAMIYA.
SHOCK
A MUMMY?!

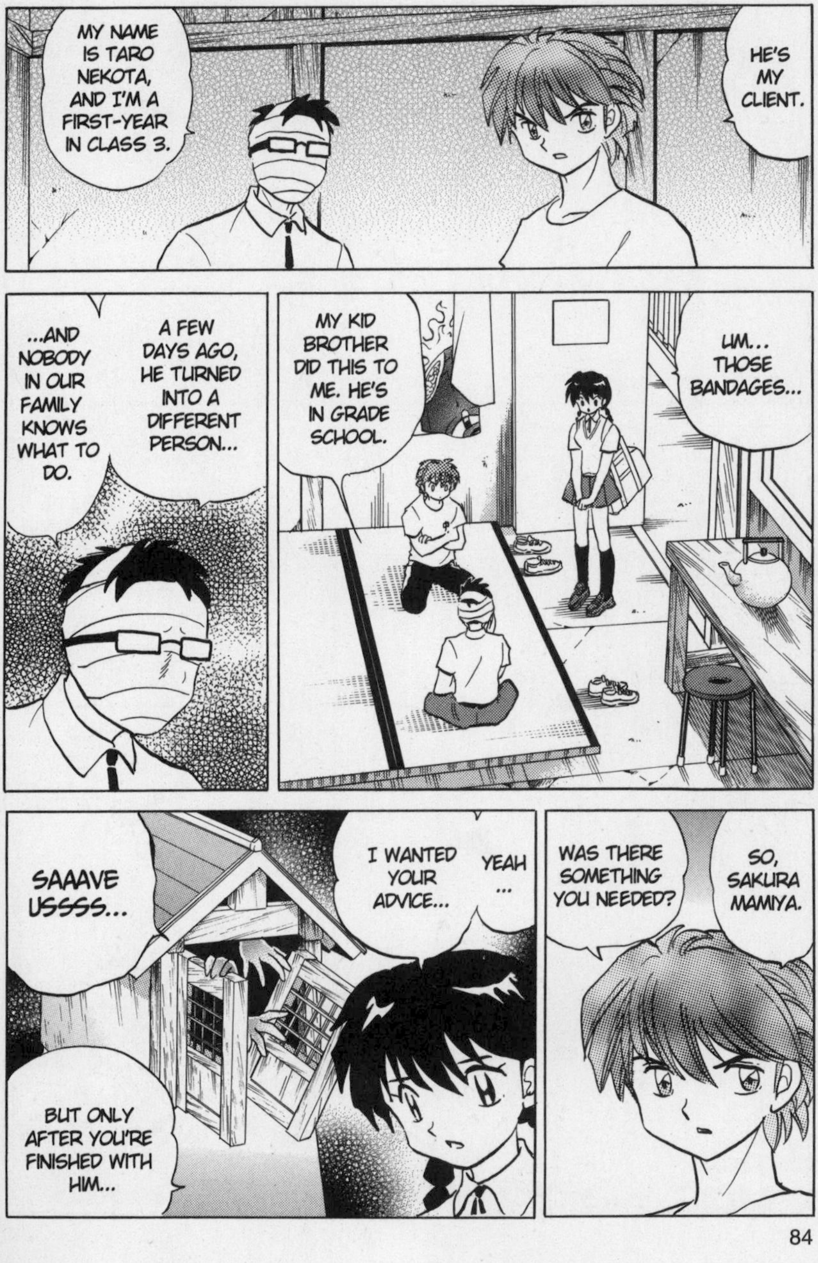
HE'S MY CLIENT.
MY NAME IS TARO NEKOTA, AND I'M A FIRST-YEAR IN CLASS 3.
UM... THOSE BANDAGES...
MY KID BROTHER DID THIS TO ME. HE'S IN GRADE SCHOOL.
A FEW DAYS AGO, HE TURNED INTO A DIFFERENT PERSON...
...AND NOBODY IN OUR FAMILY KNOWS WHAT TO DO.
SO, SAKURA MAMIYA.
WAS THERE SOMETHING YOU NEEDED?
YEAH ...
I WANTED YOUR ADVICE...
SAAAVE USSSS...
BUT ONLY AFTER YOU'RE FINISHED WITH HIM...

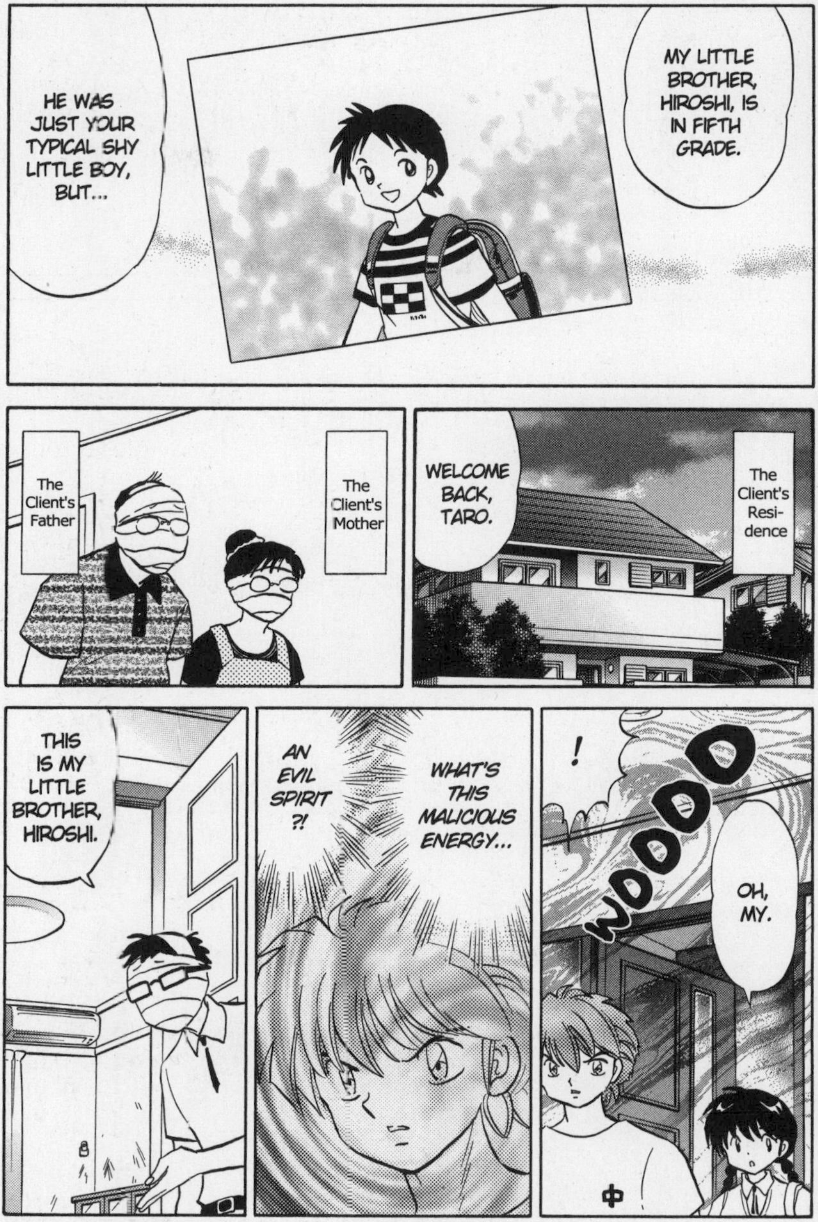
MY LITTLE BROTHER, HIROSHI, IS IN FIFTH GRADE.
HE WAS JUST YOUR TYPICAL SHY LITTLE BOY, BUT...
The Client's Residence
WELCOME BACK, TARO.
The Client's Mother
The Client's Father
!
WOOOO
OH, MY.
WHAT'S THIS MALICIOUS ENERGY...
AN EVIL SPIRIT ?!
THIS IS MY LITTLE BROTHER, HIROSHI.

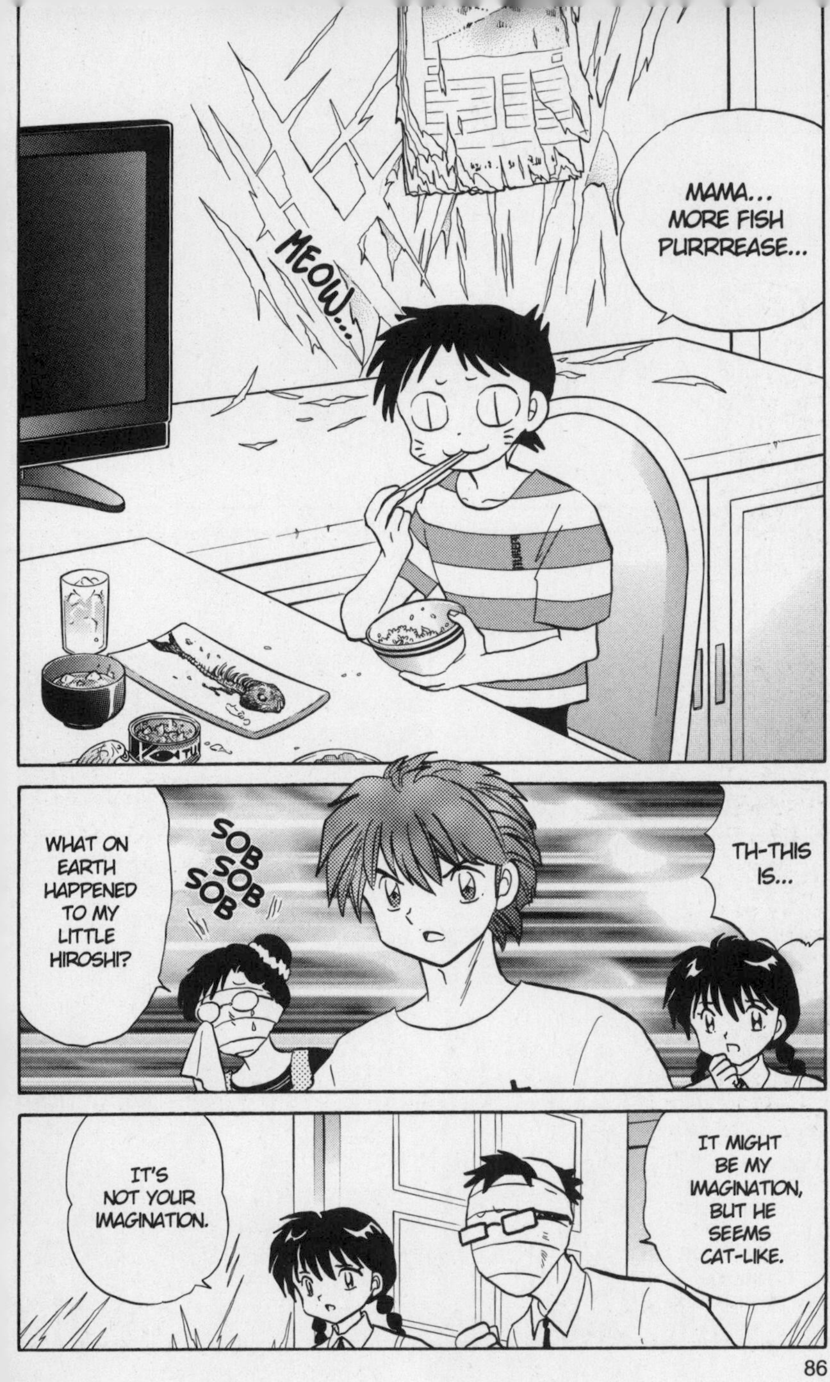
MAMA... MORE FISH PURRREASE...
MEOW...
TH-THIS IS...
SOB SOB SOB
WHAT ON EARTH HAPPENED TO MY LITTLE HIROSHI?
IT MIGHT BE MY IMAGINATION, BUT HE SEEMS CAT-LIKE.
IT'S NOT YOUR IMAGINATION.

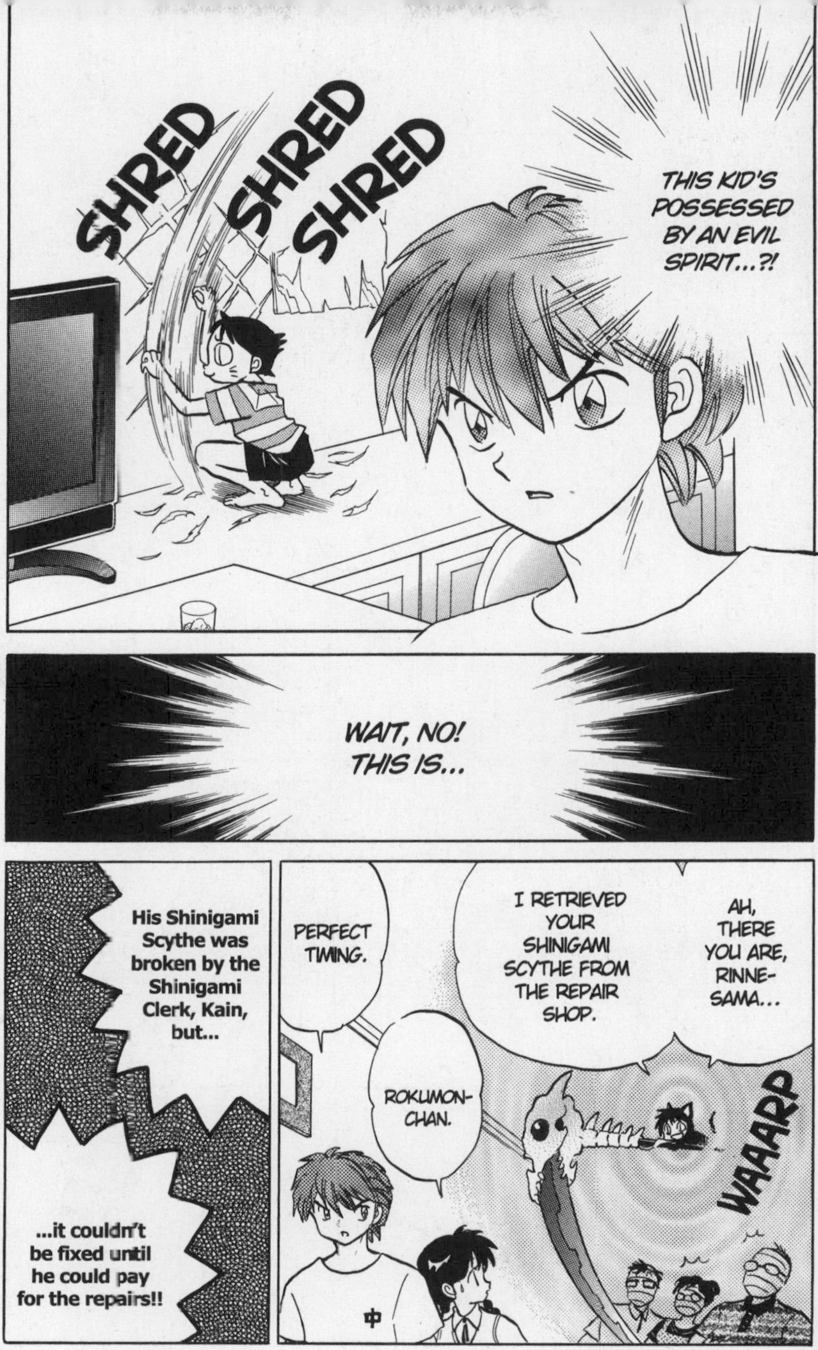
THIS KID'S POSSESSED BY AN EVIL SPIRIT...?!
SHRED
SHRED
SHRED
WAIT, NO! THIS IS...
AH, THERE YOU ARE, RINNE-SAMA...
I RETRIEVED YOUR SHINIGAMI SCYTHE FROM THE REPAIR SHOP.
PERFECT TIMING.
ROKUMON-CHAN.
WAAARP
His Shinigami Scythe was broken by the Shinigami Clerk, Kain, but...
...it couldn't be fixed until he could pay for the repairs!!

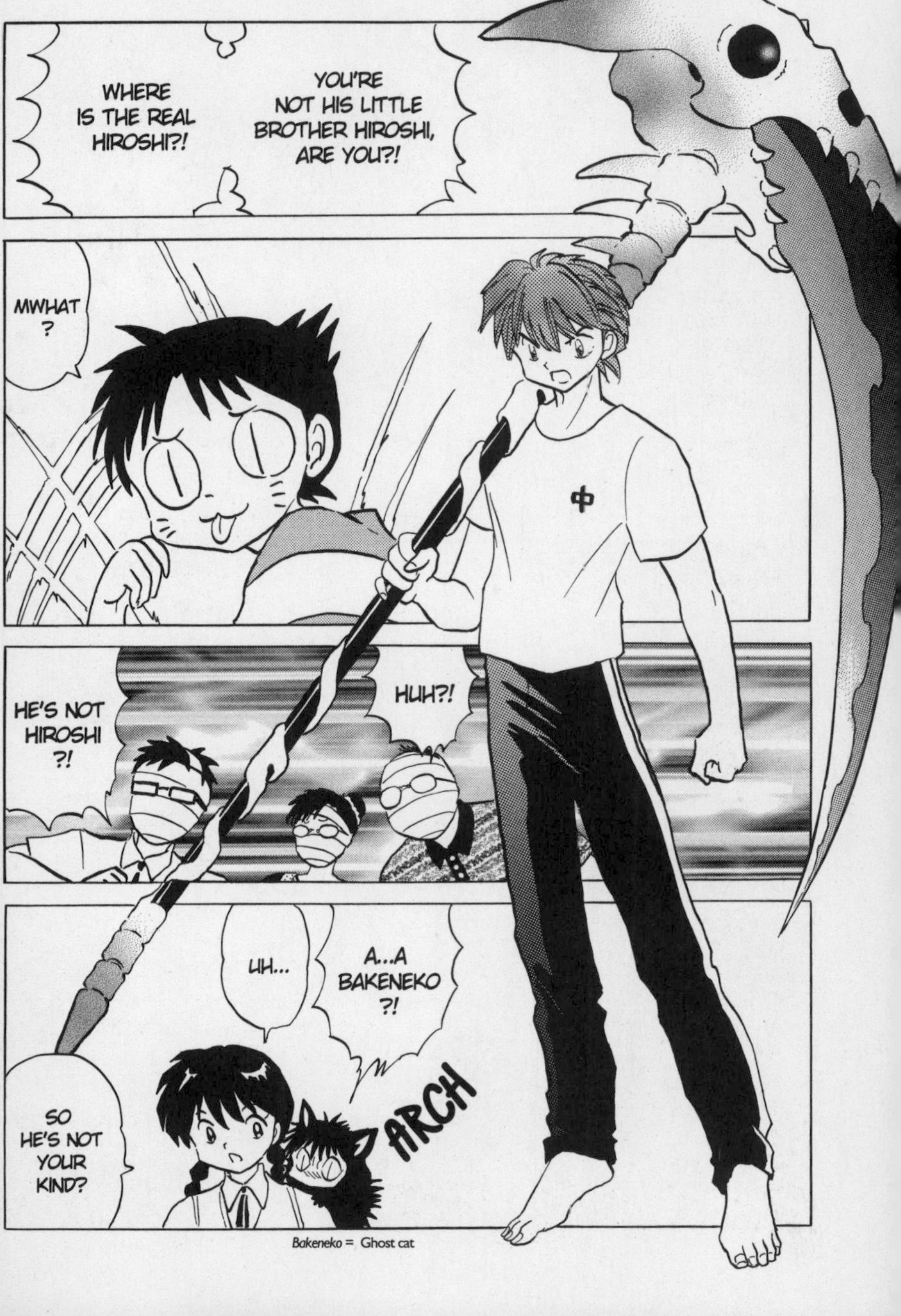
YOU'RE NOT HIS LITTLE BROTHER HIROSHI, ARE YOU?!
WHERE IS THE REAL HIROSHI?!
MWHAT?
HUH?!
HE'S NOT HIROSHI?!
A...A BAKENEKO?!
UH...
ARCH
SO HE'S NOT YOUR KIND?

Bakeneko = Ghost cat

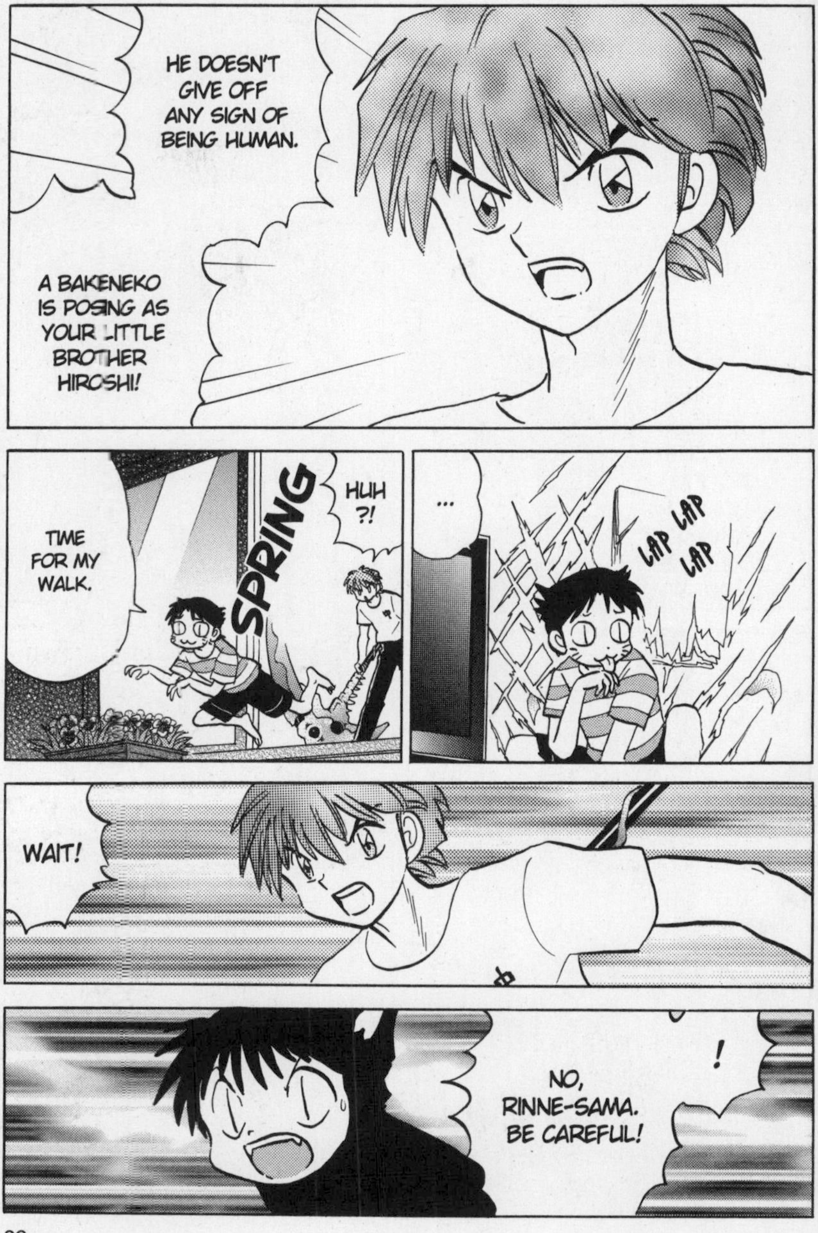
HE DOESN'T GIVE OFF ANY SIGN OF BEING HUMAN.
A BAKENEKO IS POSING AS YOUR LITTLE BROTHER HIROSHI!
...
LAP LAP LAP
HUH ?!
SPRING
TIME FOR MY WALK.
WAIT!
!
NO, RINNE-SAMA. BE CAREFUL!

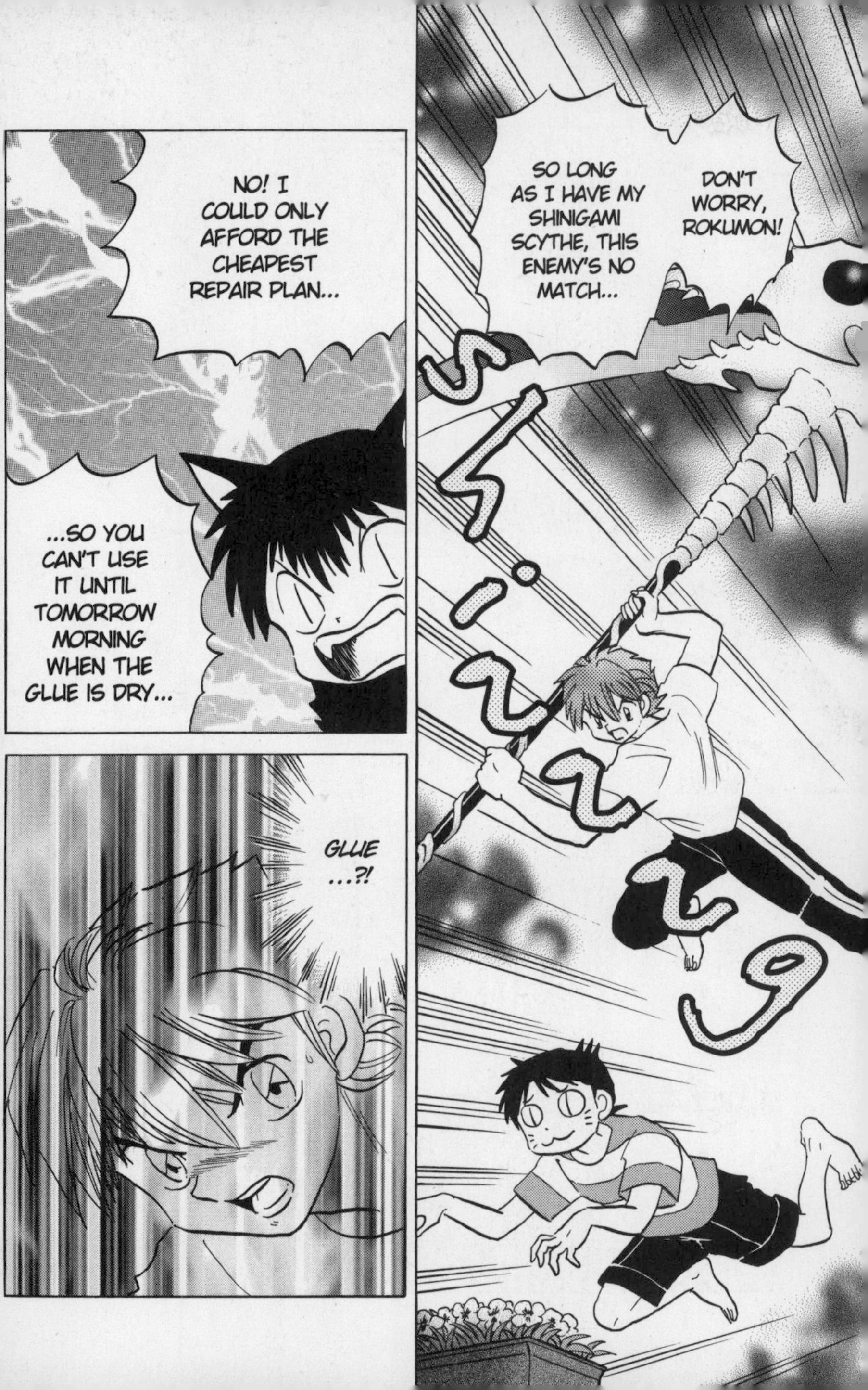
DON'T WORRY, ROKUMON!
SO LONG AS I HAVE MY SHINIGAMI SCYTHE, THIS ENEMY'S NO MATCH...
shinnng
NO! I COULD ONLY AFFORD THE CHEAPEST REPAIR PLAN...
...SO YOU CAN'T USE IT UNTIL TOMORROW MORNING WHEN THE GLUE IS DRY...
GLUE ...?!

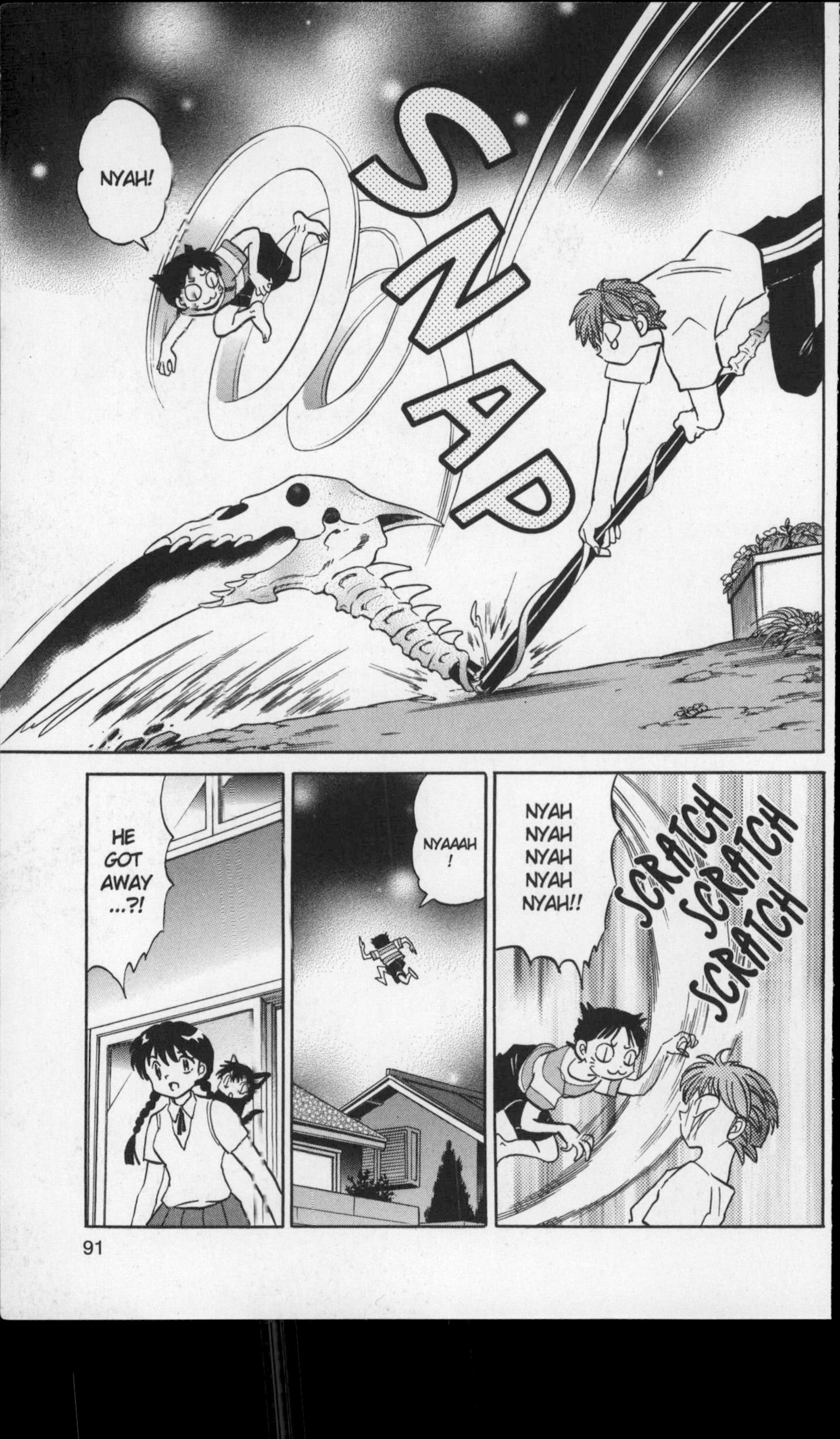
NYAH!
SNAP
NYAH NYAH NYAH NYAH NYAH!!
SCRATCH SCRATCH SCRATCH
NYAAAH!
HE GOT AWAY ...?!

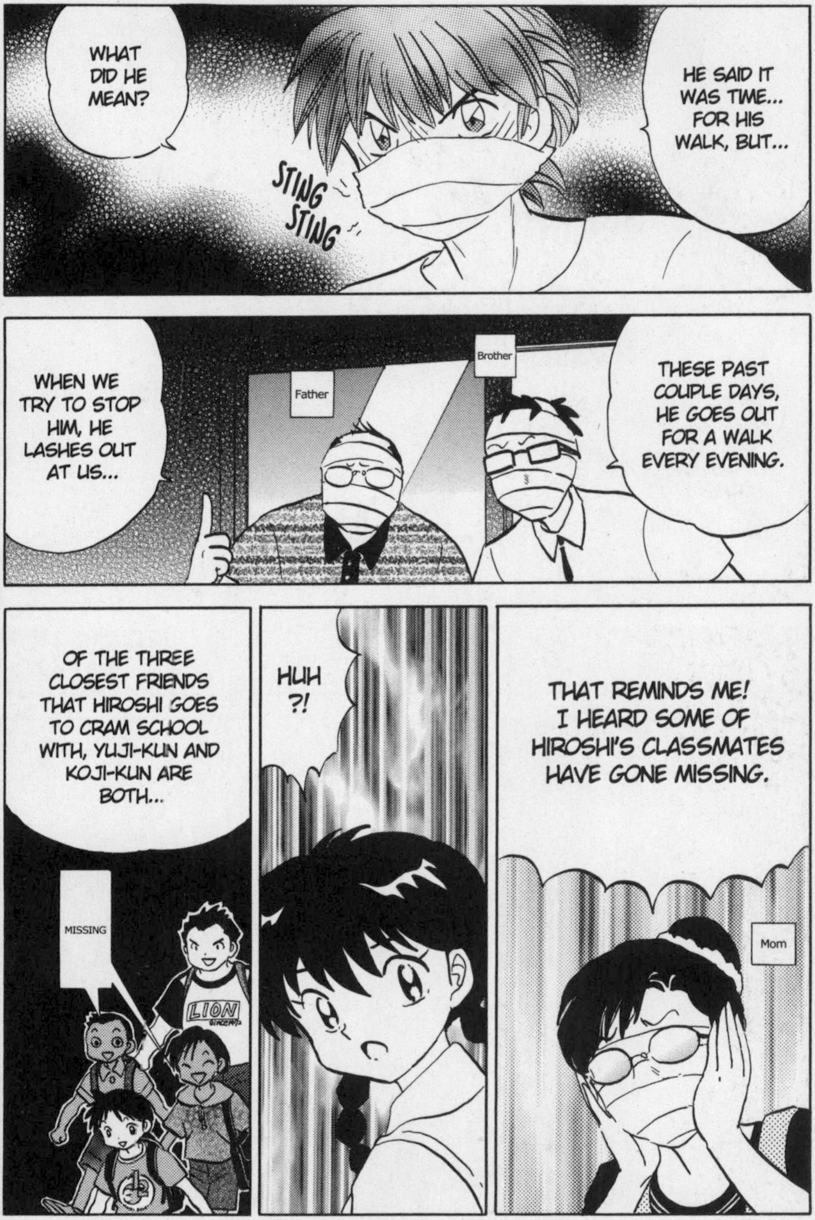
HE SAID IT WAS TIME... FOR HIS WALK, BUT...
STING STING
WHAT DID HE MEAN?
THESE PAST COUPLE DAYS, HE GOES OUT FOR A WALK EVERY EVENING.
Brother
Father
WHEN WE TRY TO STOP HIM, HE LASHES OUT AT US...
THAT REMINDS ME! I HEARD SOME OF HIROSHI'S CLASSMATES HAVE GONE MISSING.
Mom
HUH ?!
OF THE THREE CLOSEST FRIENDS THAT HIROSHI GOES TO CRAM SCHOOL WITH, YUJI-KUN AND KOJI-KUN ARE BOTH...
MISSING

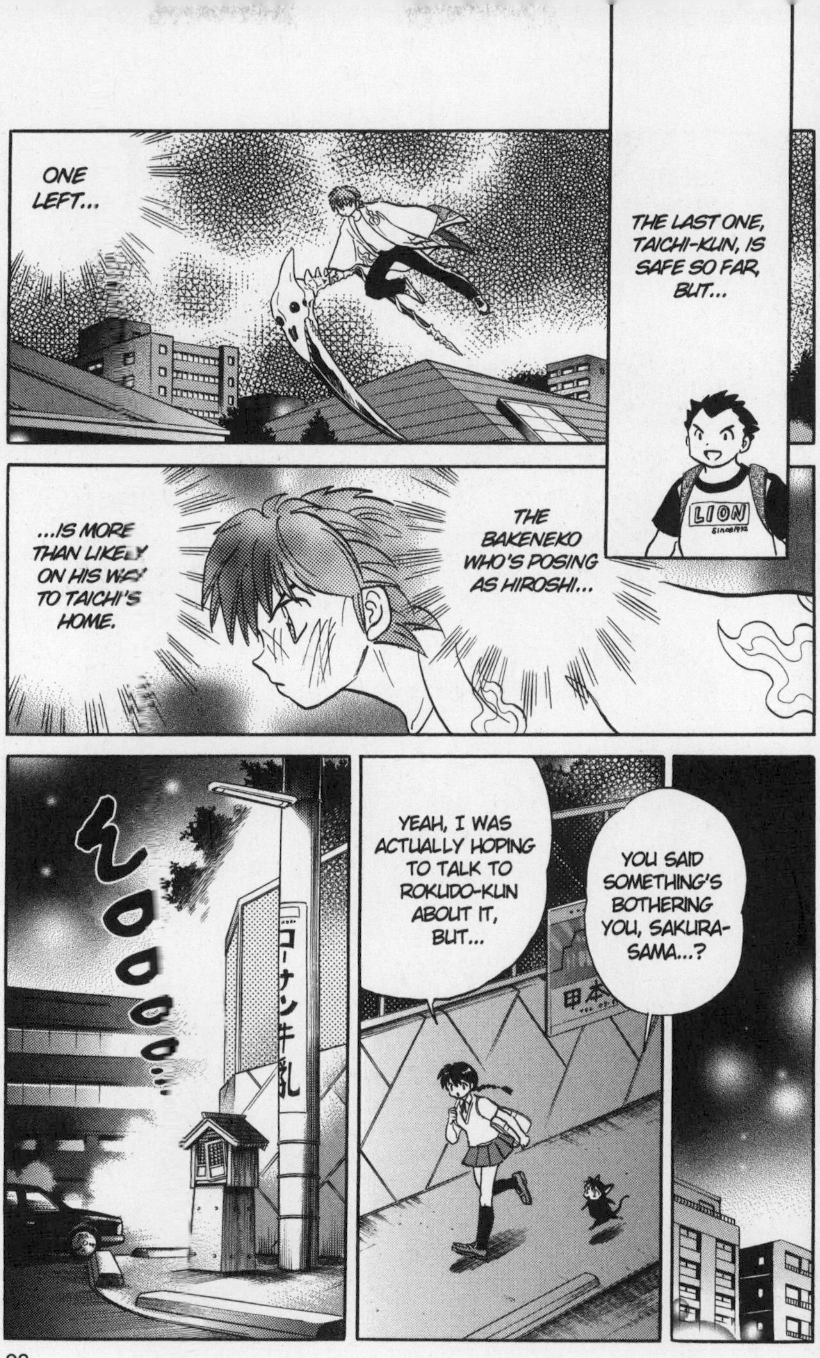
THE LAST ONE, TAICHI-KUN, IS SAFE SO FAR, BUT...
LION
ONE LEFT...
THE BAKENEKO WHO'S POSING AS HIROSHI...
...IS MORE THAN LIKELY ON HIS WAY TO TAICHI'S HOME.
YOU SAID SOMETHING'S BOTHERING YOU, SAKURA-SAMA...?
YEAH, I WAS ACTUALLY HOPING TO TALK TO ROKUDO-KUN ABOUT IT, BUT...
コーナン牛乳

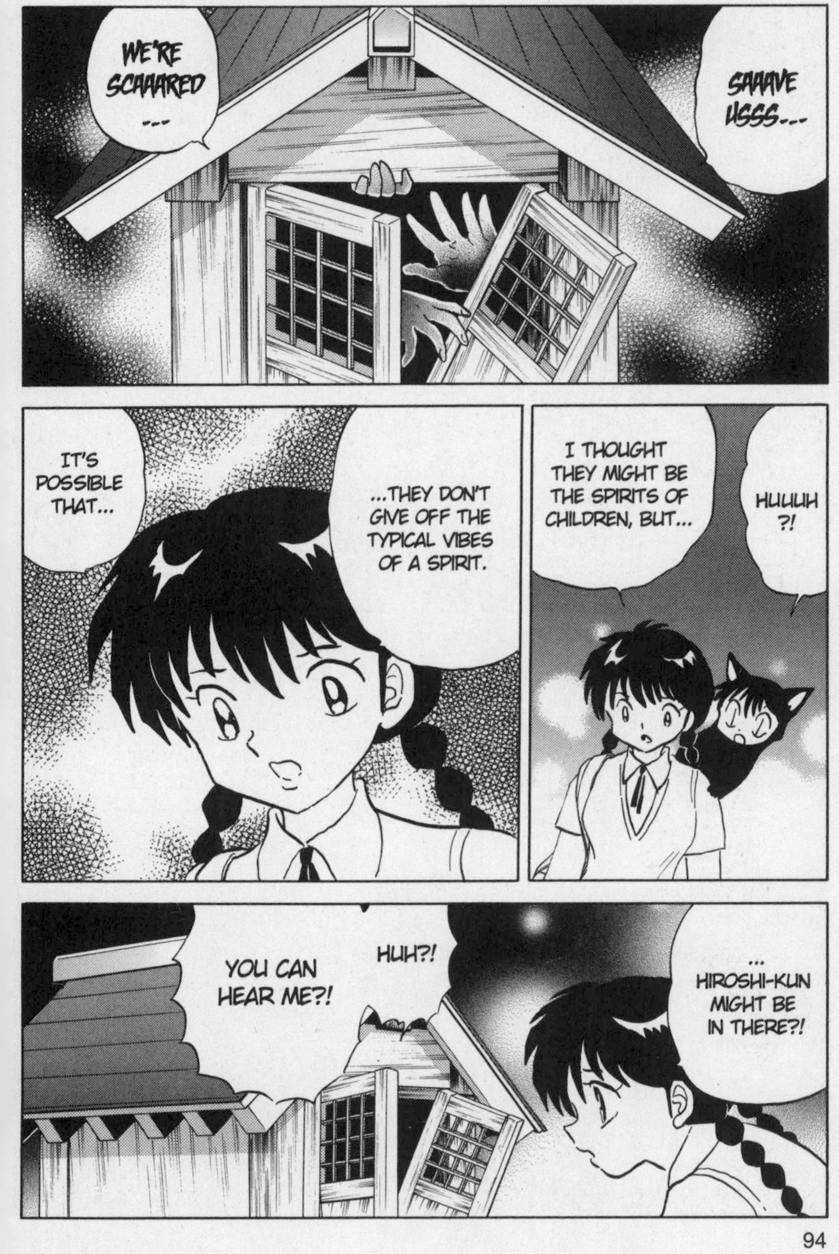
SAAAVE USSS...
WE'RE SCAAARED ...
I THOUGHT THEY MIGHT BE THE SPIRITS OF CHILDREN, BUT...
HUUUH ?!
...THEY DON'T GIVE OFF THE TYPICAL VIBES OF A SPIRIT.
IT'S POSSIBLE THAT...
... HIROSHI-KUN MIGHT BE IN THERE?!
HUH?!
YOU CAN HEAR ME?!

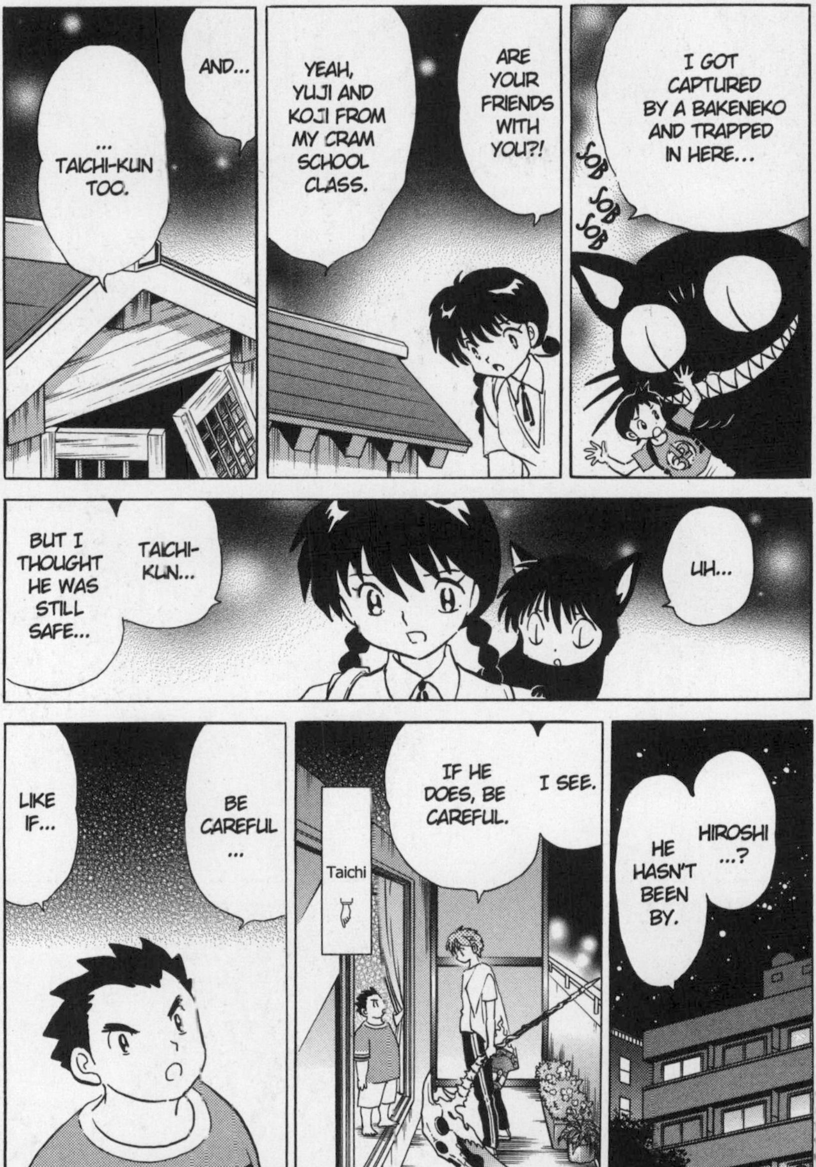
I GOT CAPTURED BY A BAKENEKO AND TRAPPED IN HERE...
SOB SOB SOB
ARE YOUR FRIENDS WITH YOU?!
YEAH, YUJI AND KOJI FROM MY CRAM SCHOOL CLASS.
AND...
... TAICHI-KUN TOO.
UH...
TAICHI-KUN...
BUT I THOUGHT HE WAS STILL SAFE...
HIROSHI ...?
HE HASN'T BEEN BY.
I SEE.
IF HE DOES, BE CAREFUL.
Taichi
BE CAREFUL ...
LIKE IF...

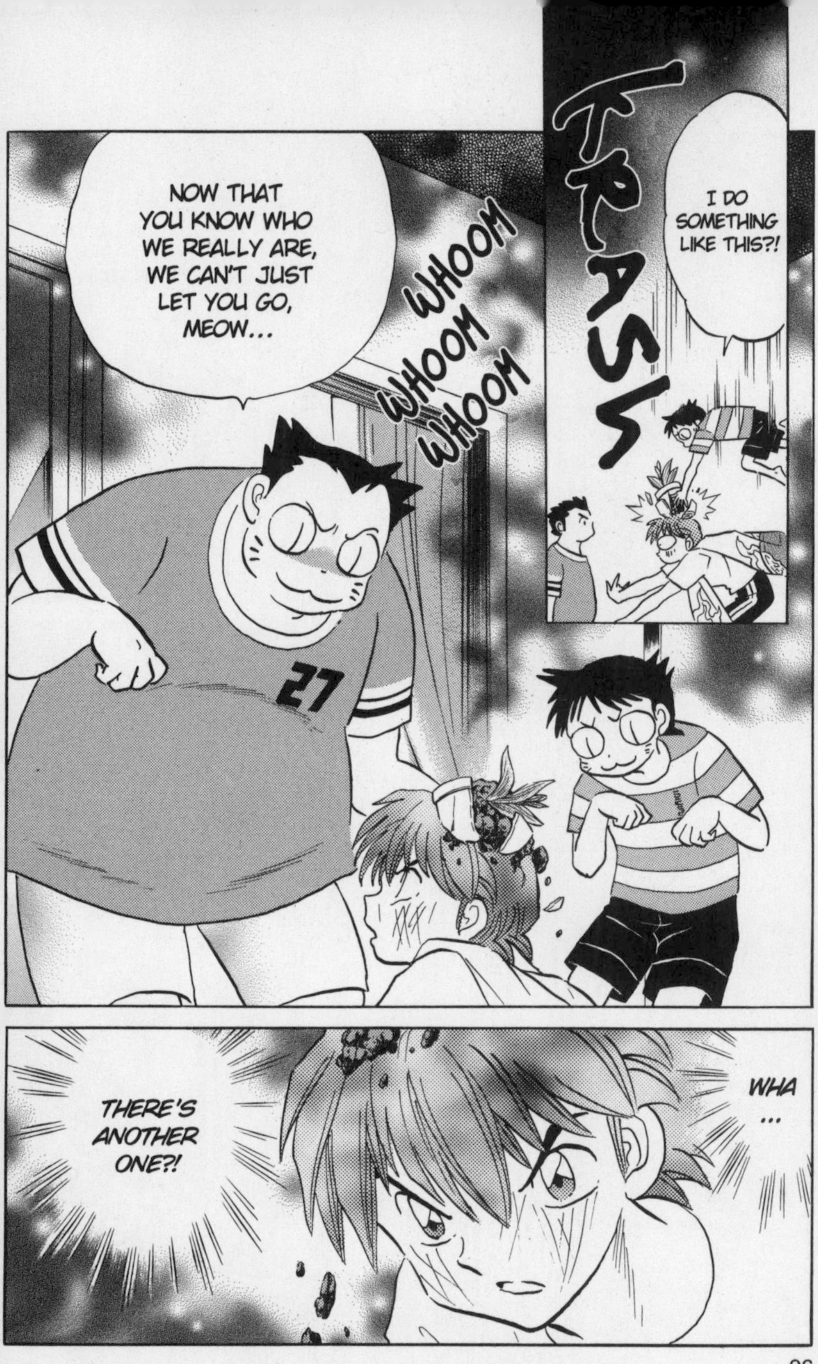
I DO SOMETHING LIKE THIS?!
NOW THAT YOU KNOW WHO WE REALLY ARE, WE CAN'T JUST LET YOU GO, MEOW...
WHOOM WHOOM WHOOM
WHA ...
THERE'S ANOTHER ONE?!

りんね
RIN-NE

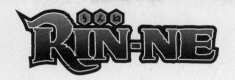

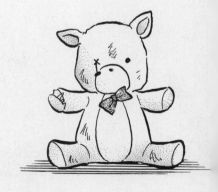

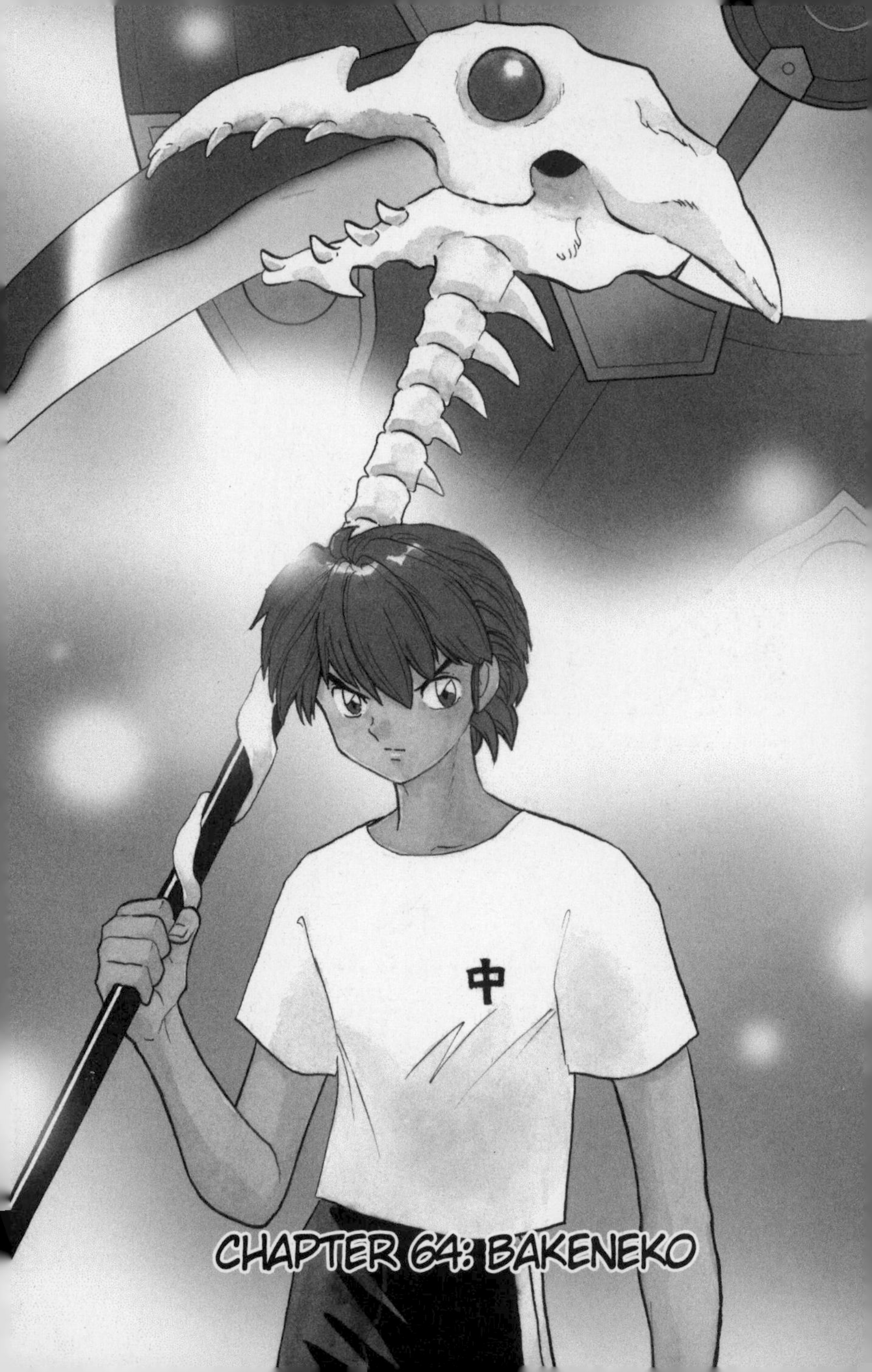
中
CHAPTER 64: BAKENEKO

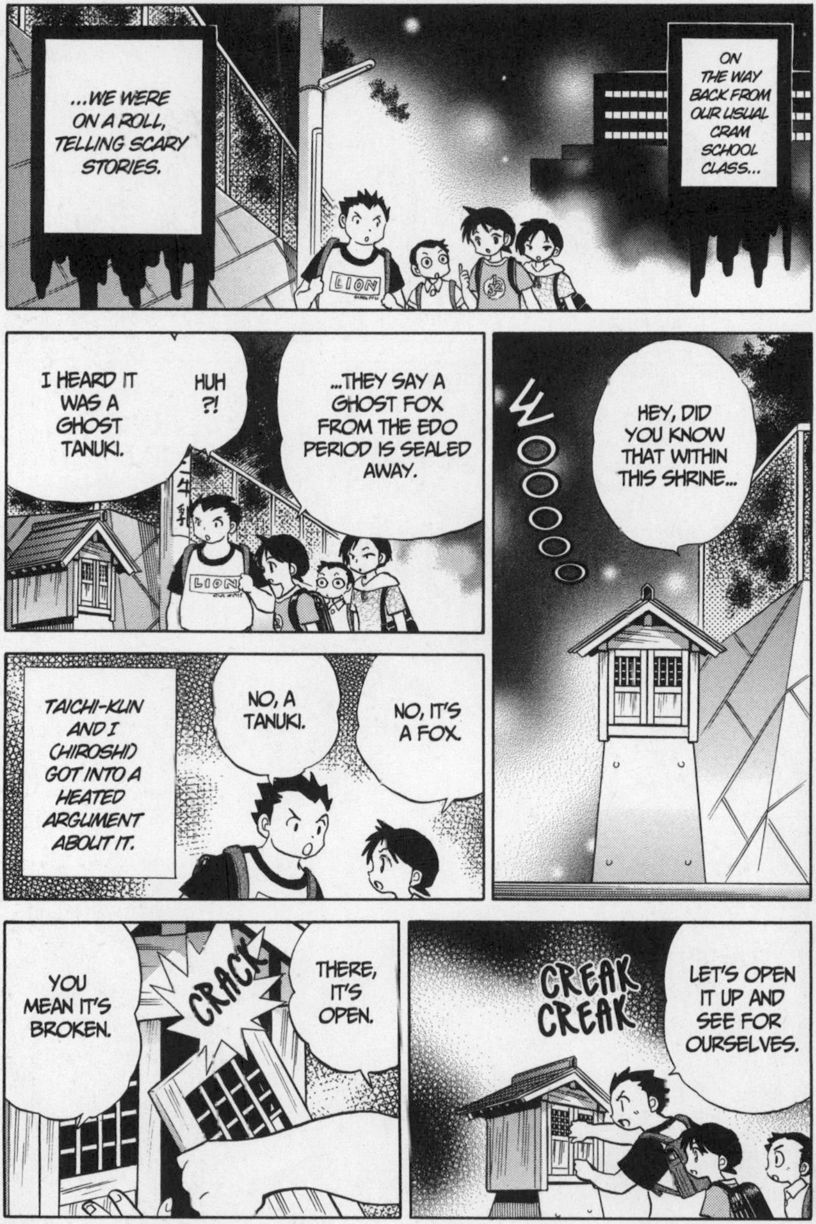
ON THE WAY BACK FROM OUR USUAL CRAM SCHOOL CLASS...
...WE WERE ON A ROLL, TELLING SCARY STORIES.
WOOOOOO
HEY, DID YOU KNOW THAT WITHIN THIS SHRINE...
...THEY SAY A GHOST FOX FROM THE EDO PERIOD IS SEALED AWAY.
HUH ?!
I HEARD IT WAS A GHOST TANUKI.
NO, IT'S A FOX.
NO, A TANUKI.
TAICHI-KUN AND I (HIROSHI) GOT INTO A HEATED ARGUMENT ABOUT IT.
LET'S OPEN IT UP AND SEE FOR OURSELVES.
CREAK CREAK
THERE, IT'S OPEN.
CRACK
YOU MEAN IT'S BROKEN.

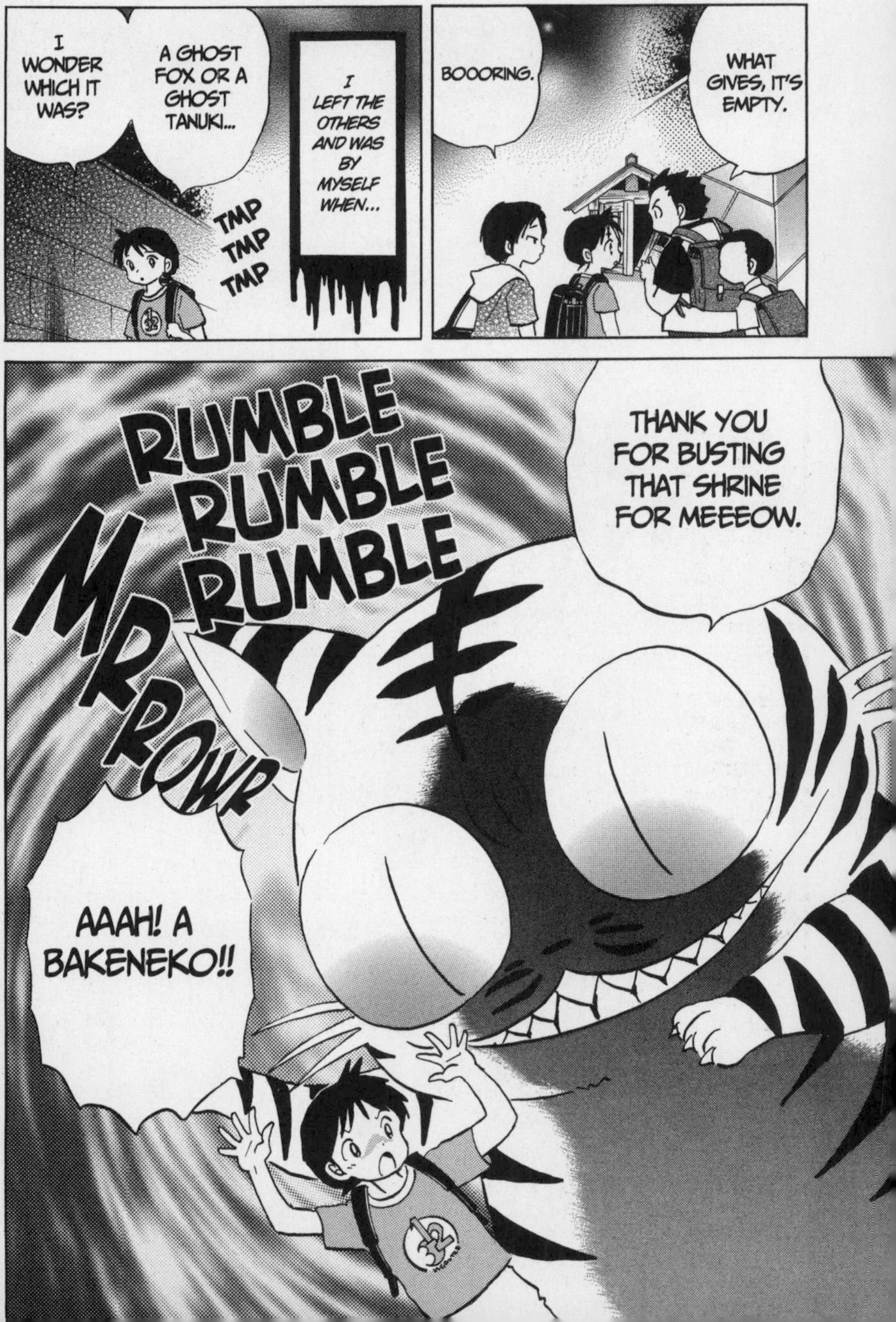
WHAT GIVES, IT'S EMPTY.
BOOORING.
I LEFT THE OTHERS AND WAS BY MYSELF WHEN...
A GHOST FOX OR A GHOST TANUKI...
I WONDER WHICH IT WAS?
TMP TMP TMP
THANK YOU FOR BUSTING THAT SHRINE FOR MEEEOW.
RUMBLE RUMBLE RUMBLE
MRROWR
AAAH! A BAKENEKO!!

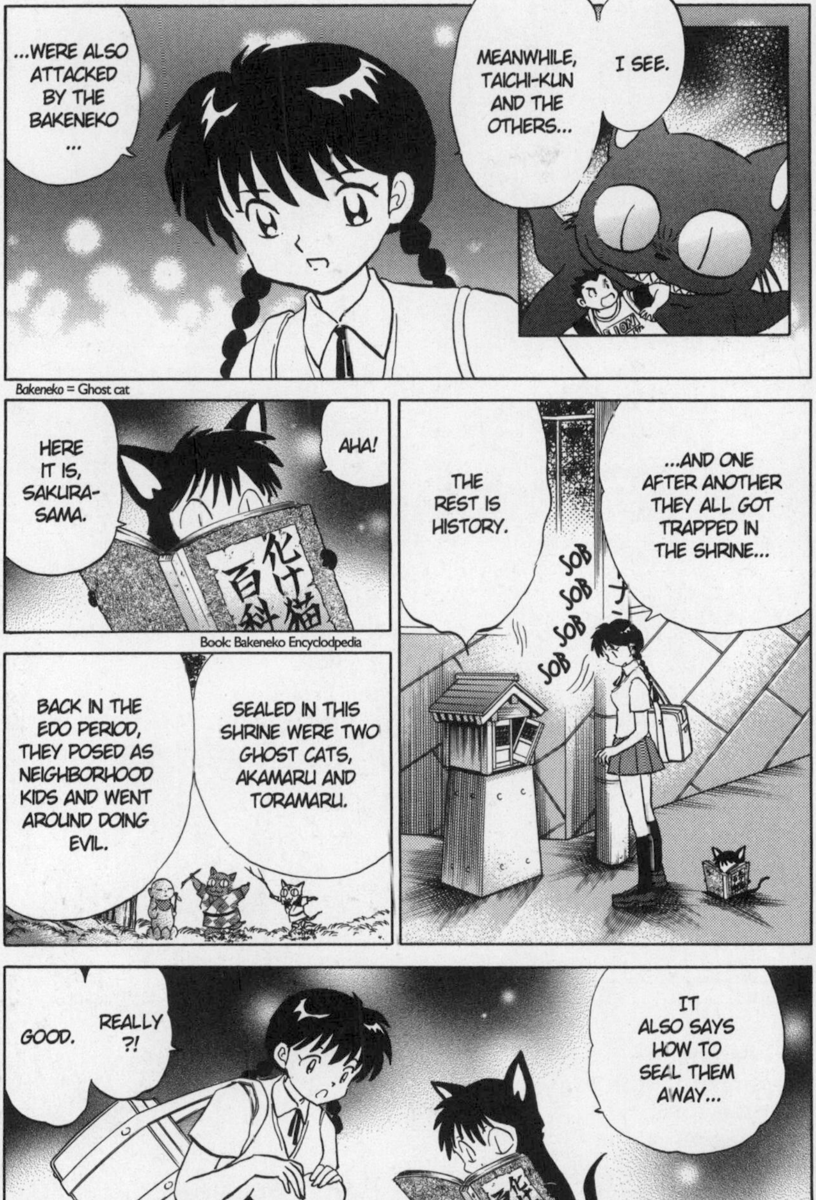
I SEE.
MEANWHILE, TAICHI-KUN AND THE OTHERS...
...WERE ALSO ATTACKED BY THE BAKENEKO ...
AHA!
HERE IT IS, SAKURA-SAMA.
化け猫百科
SEALED IN THIS SHRINE WERE TWO GHOST CATS, AKAMARU AND TORAMARU.
BACK IN THE EDO PERIOD, THEY POSED AS NEIGHBORHOOD KIDS AND WENT AROUND DOING EVIL.
...AND ONE AFTER ANOTHER THEY ALL GOT TRAPPED IN THE SHRINE...
THE REST IS HISTORY.
SOB SOB SOB SOB
IT ALSO SAYS HOW TO SEAL THEM AWAY...
REALLY ?!
GOOD.

Bakeneko = Ghost cat

Book: Bakeneko Encyclodpedia

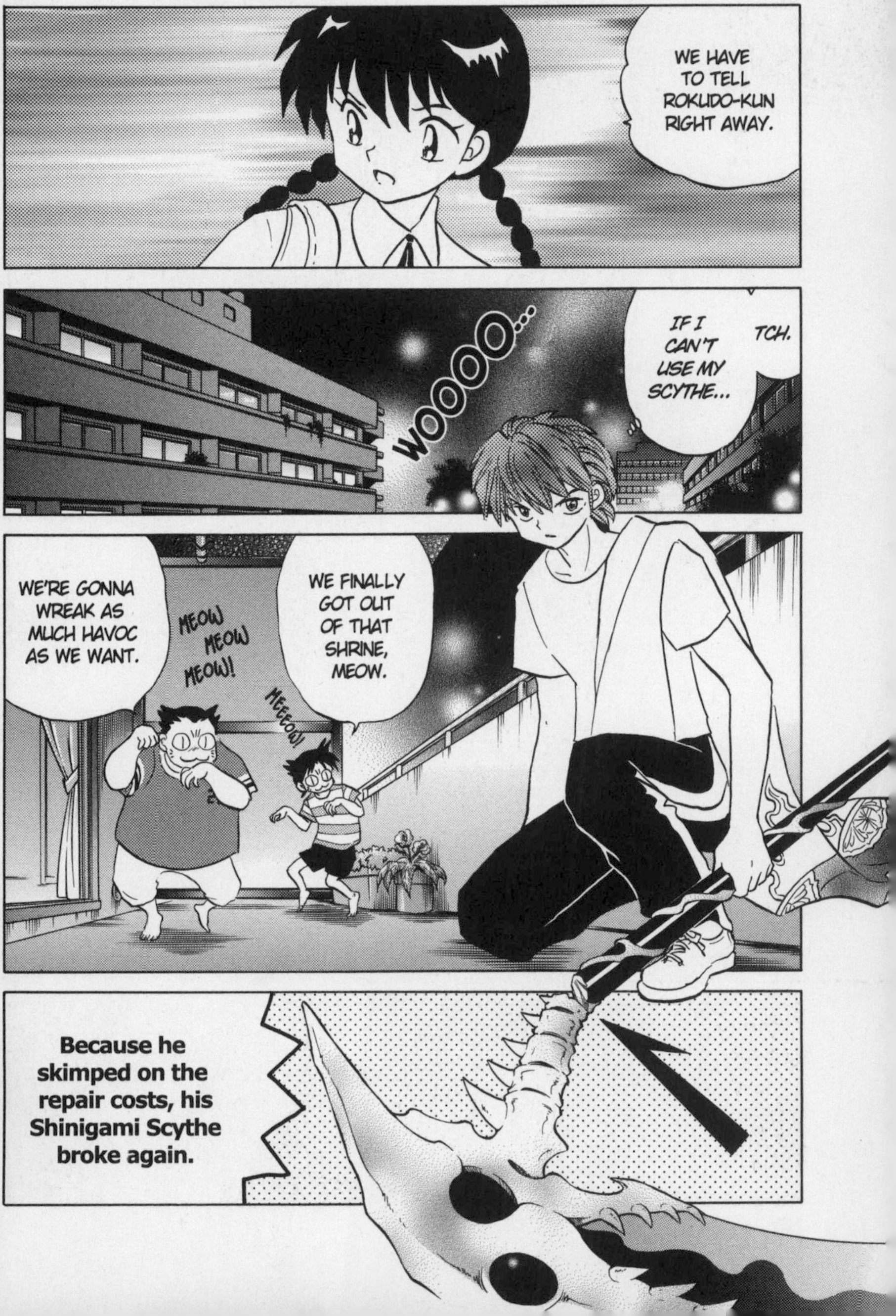
WE HAVE TO TELL ROKUDO-KUN RIGHT AWAY.
TCH.
IF I CAN'T USE MY SCYTHE...
WOOOO...
WE FINALLY GOT OUT OF THAT SHRINE, MEOW.
MEEEOW!
MEOW MEOW MEOW!
WE'RE GONNA WREAK AS MUCH HAVOC AS WE WANT.
Because he skimped on the repair costs, his Shinigami Scythe broke again.

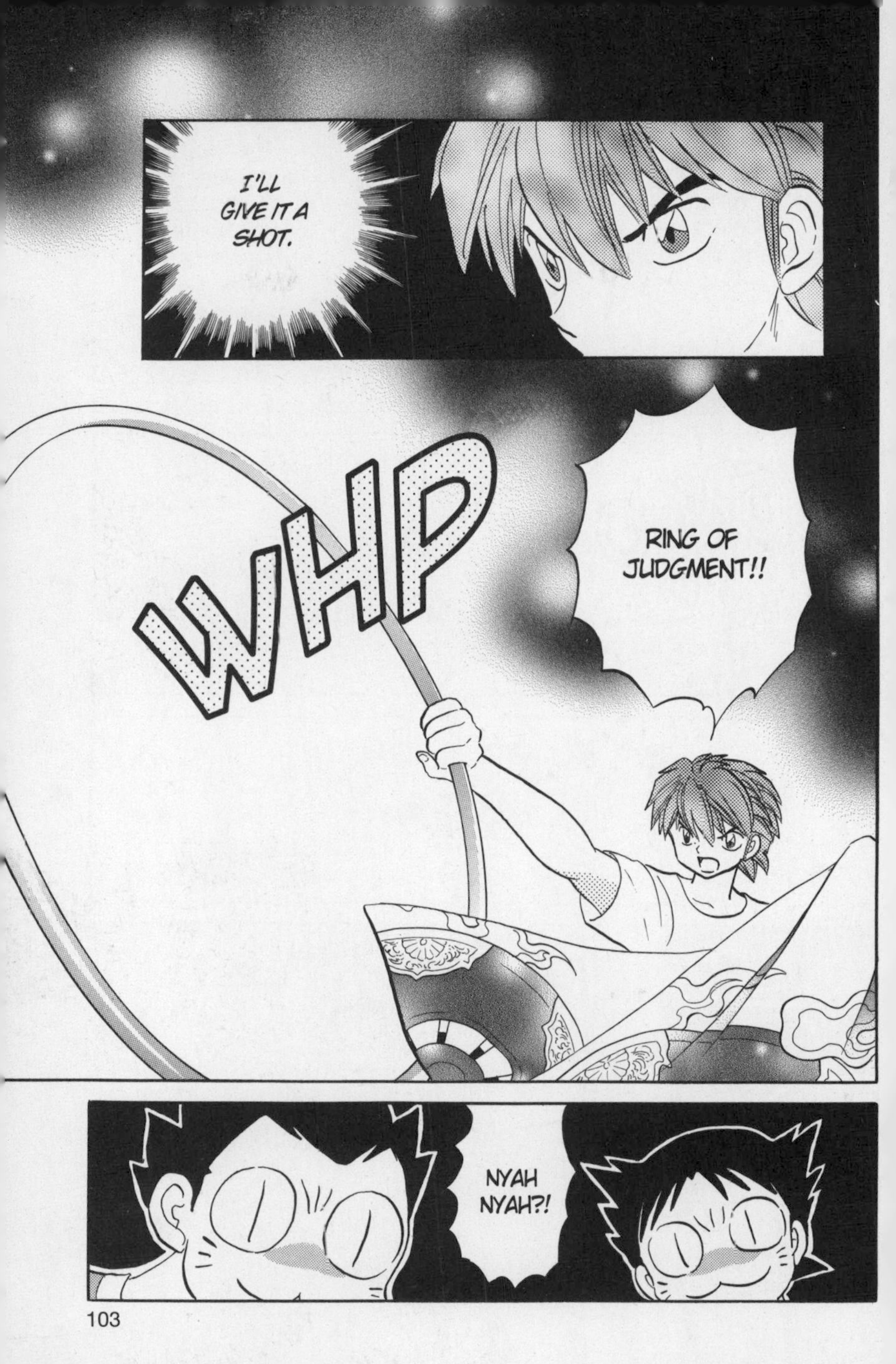
I'LL GIVE IT A SHOT.
RING OF JUDGMENT!!
WHP
NYAH NYAH?!

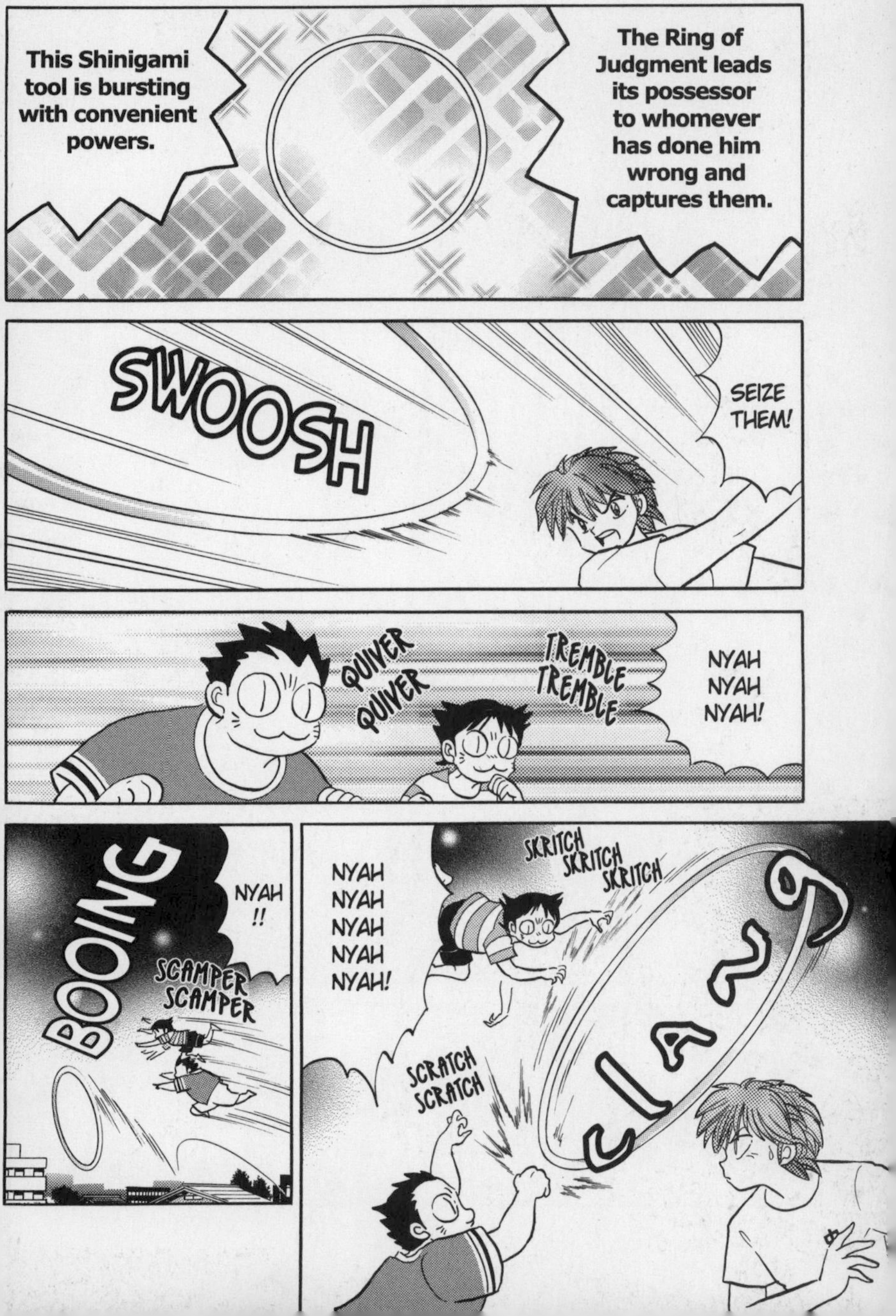
The Ring of Judgment leads its possessor to whomever has done him wrong and captures them.
This Shinigami tool is bursting with convenient powers.
SEIZE THEM!
SWOOSH
NYAH NYAH NYAH!
TREMBLE TREMBLE
QUIVER QUIVER
CLANG
SKRITCH SKRITCH SKRITCH
NYAH NYAH NYAH NYAH NYAH!
SCRATCH SCRATCH
NYAH !!
BOOING
SCAMPER SCAMPER

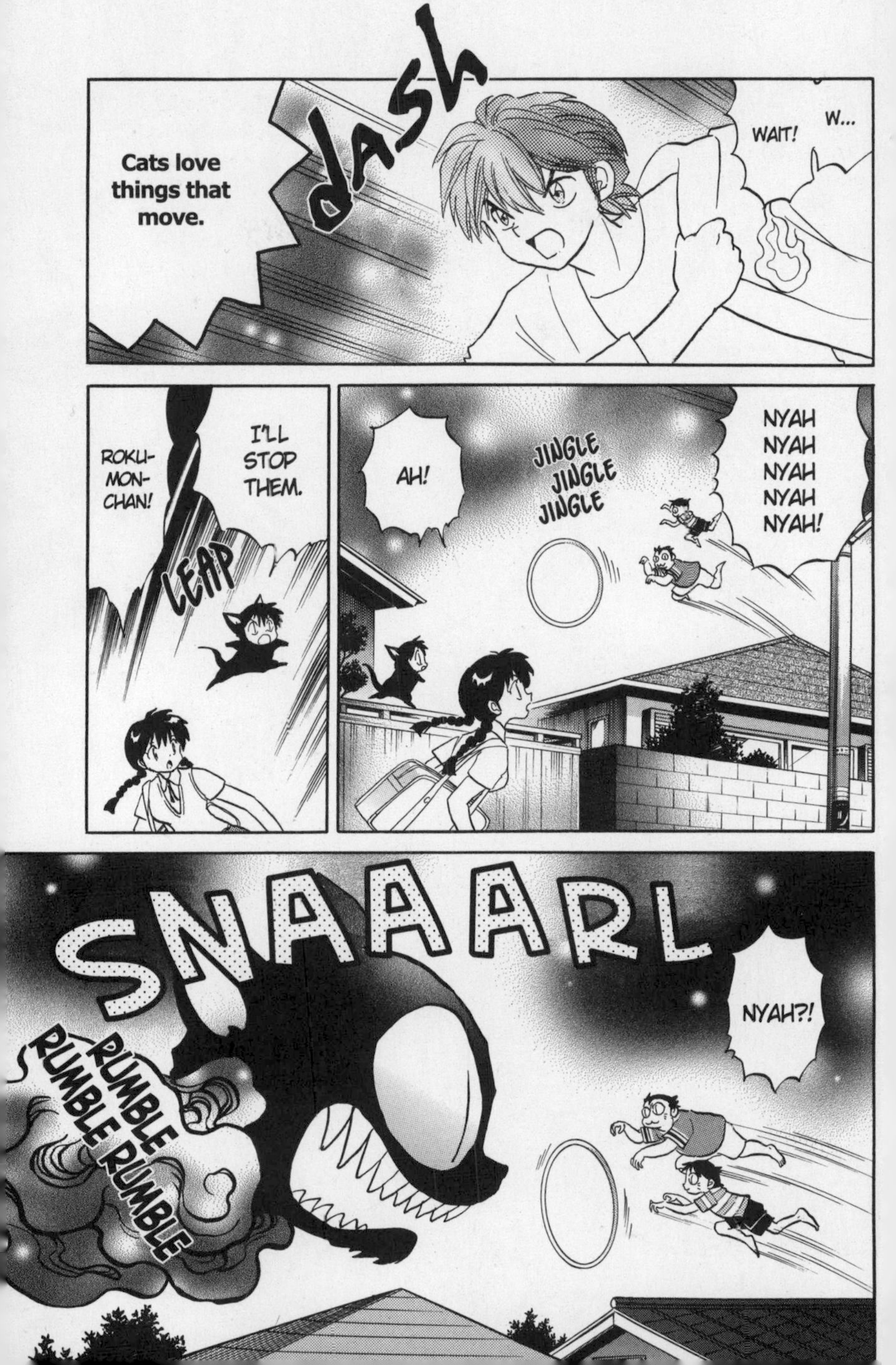
W...
WAIT!
dash
Cats love things that move.
NYAH NYAH NYAH NYAH NYAH!
JINGLE JINGLE JINGLE
AH!
I'LL STOP THEM.
ROKU-MON-CHAN!
LEAP
NYAH?!
SNAAARL
RUMBLE RUMBLE RUMBLE RUMBLE

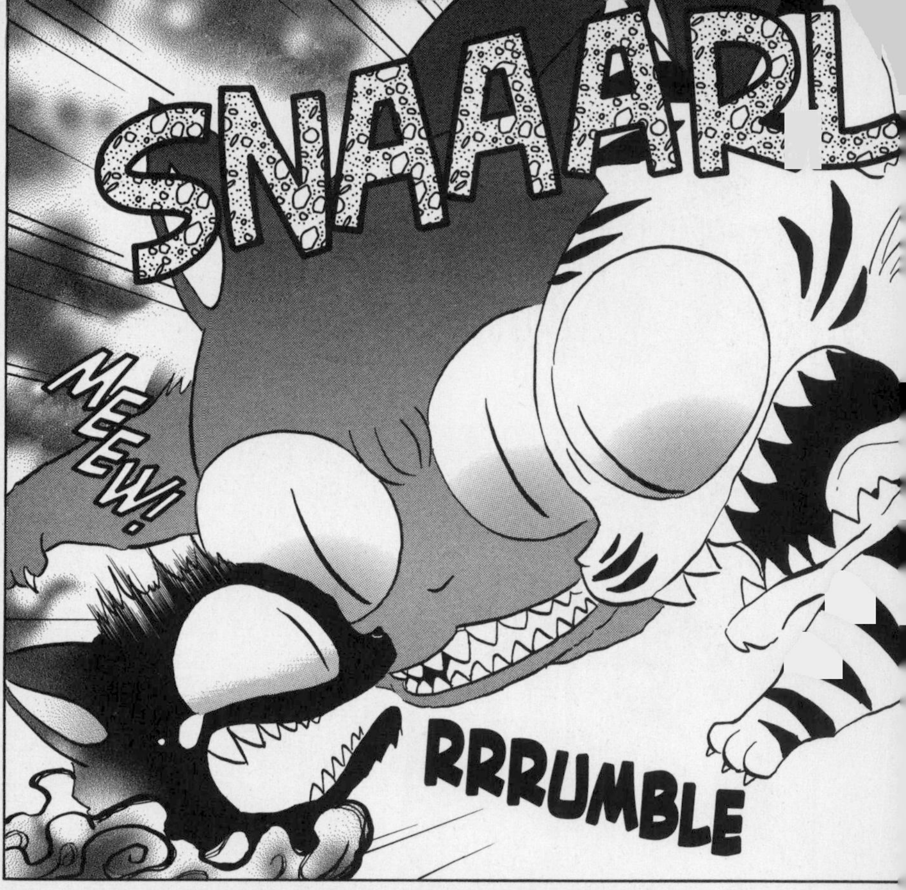
SNAAARL
MEEEW!
RRRUMBLE
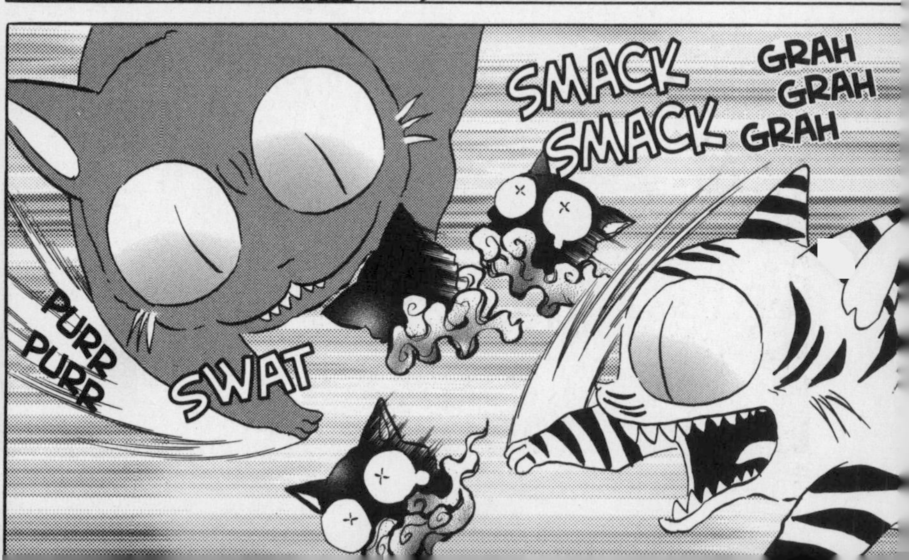
GRAH GRAH GRAH
SMACK SMACK
SWAT
PURR PURR

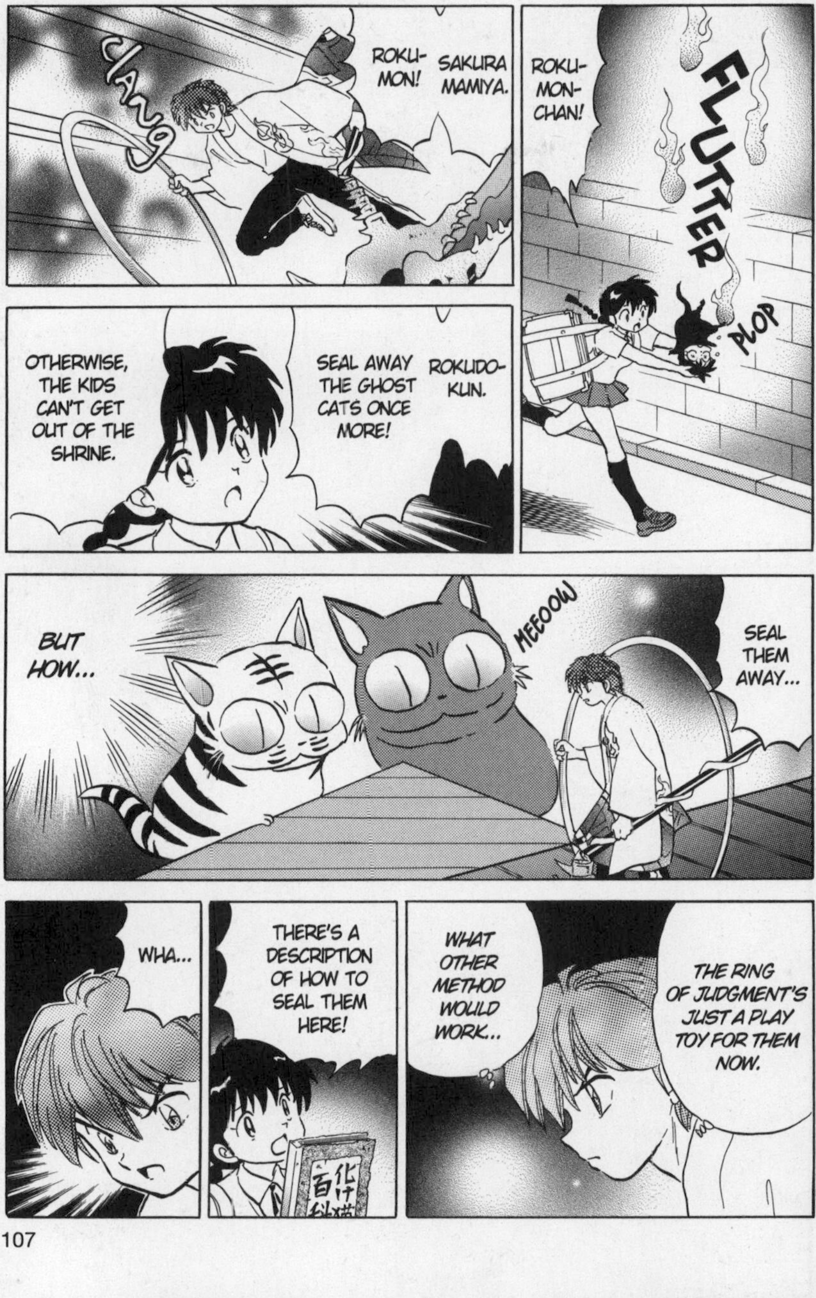
ROKU-MON-CHAN!
FLUTTER
PLOP
SAKURA MAMIYA.
ROKU-MON!
CLANG
ROKUDO-KUN.
SEAL AWAY THE GHOST CATS ONCE MORE!
OTHERWISE, THE KIDS CAN'T GET OUT OF THE SHRINE.
SEAL THEM AWAY...
MEEOOW
BUT HOW...
THE RING OF JUDGMENT'S JUST A PLAY TOY FOR THEM NOW.
WHAT OTHER METHOD WOULD WORK...
THERE'S A DESCRIPTION OF HOW TO SEAL THEM HERE!
WHA...

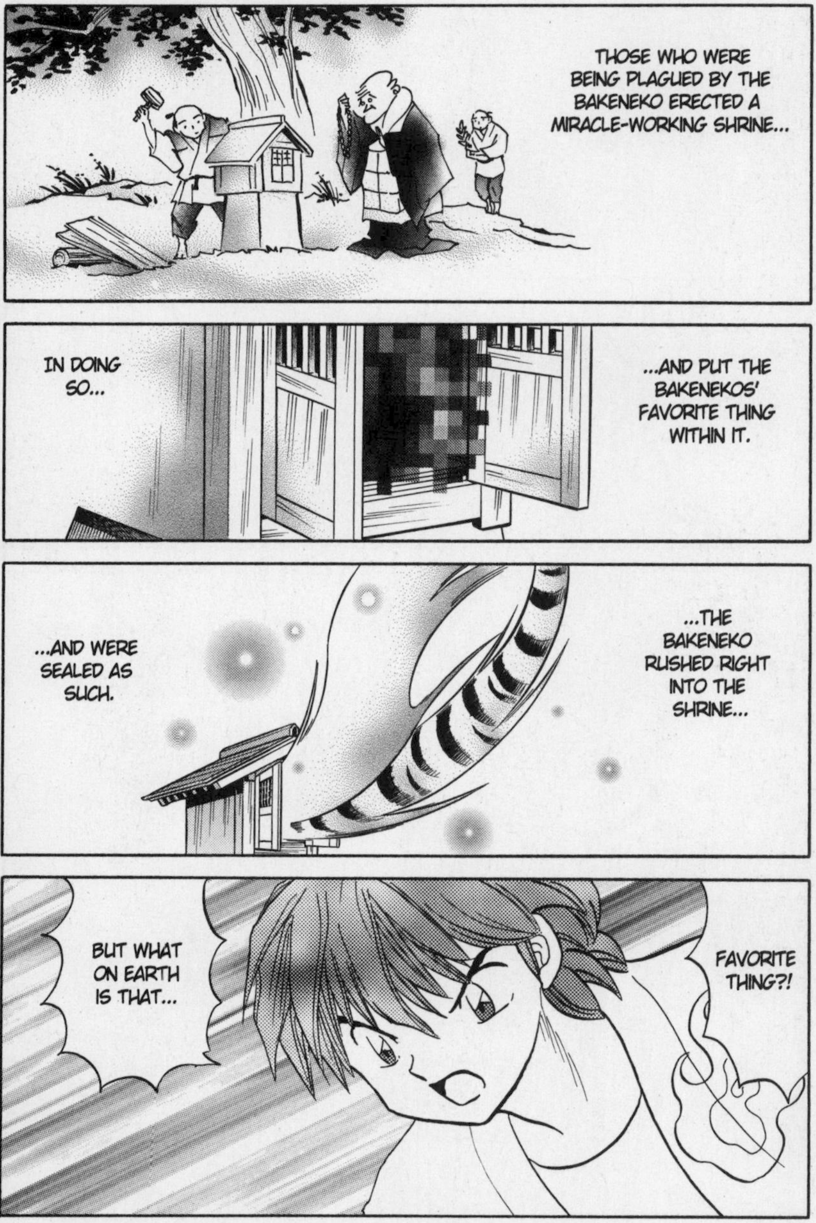
THOSE WHO WERE BEING PLAGUED BY THE BAKENEKO ERECTED A MIRACLE-WORKING SHRINE...
...AND PUT THE BAKENEKOS' FAVORITE THING WITHIN IT.
IN DOING SO...
...THE BAKENEKO RUSHED RIGHT INTO THE SHRINE...
...AND WERE SEALED AS SUCH.
FAVORITE THING?!
BUT WHAT ON EARTH IS THAT...

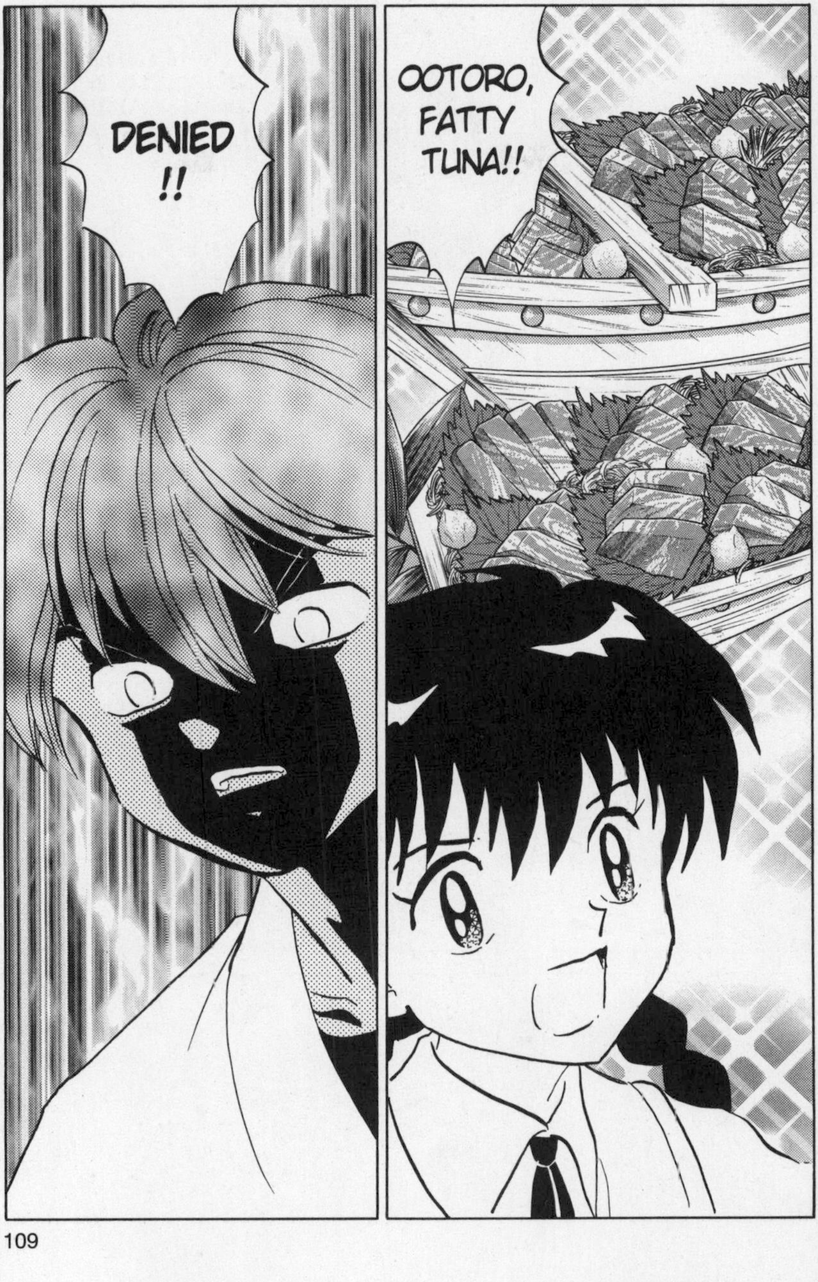
OOTORO, FATTY TUNA!!
DENIED !!

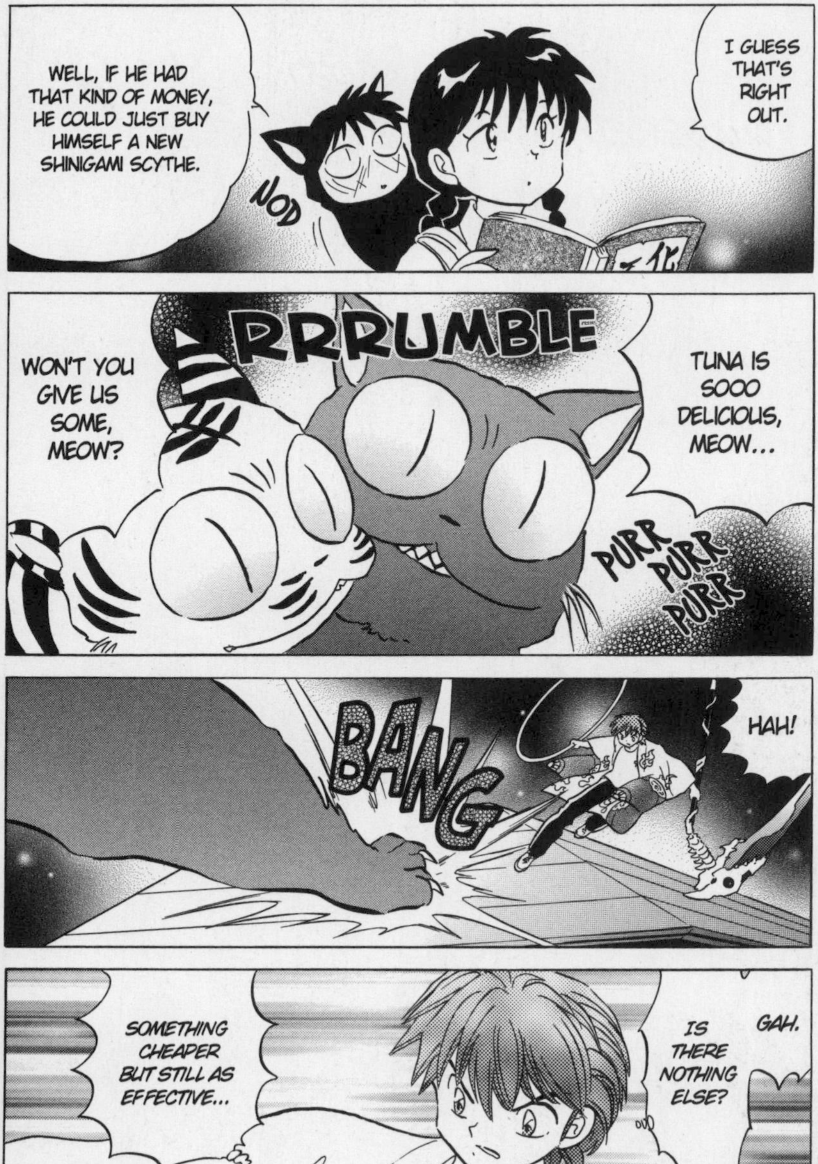
I GUESS THAT'S RIGHT OUT.
WELL, IF HE HAD THAT KIND OF MONEY, HE COULD JUST BUY HIMSELF A NEW SHINIGAMI SCYTHE.
NOD
RRRUMBLE
TUNA IS SOOO DELICIOUS, MEOW...
PURR PURR PURR
WON'T YOU GIVE US SOME, MEOW?
HAH!
BANG
GAH.
IS THERE NOTHING ELSE?
SOMETHING CHEAPER BUT STILL AS EFFECTIVE...

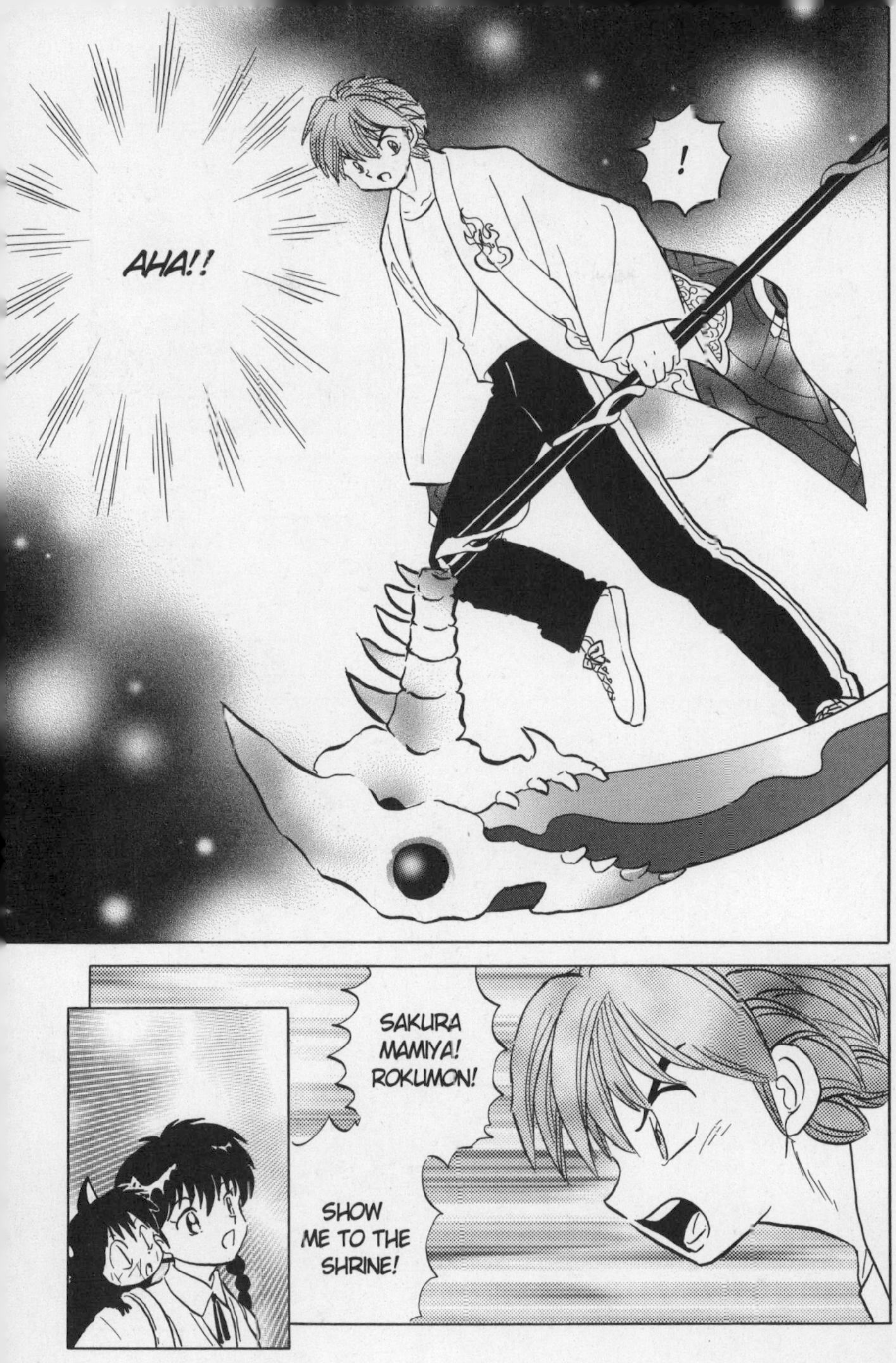
!
AHA!!
SAKURA MAMIYA! ROKUMON!
SHOW ME TO THE SHRINE!

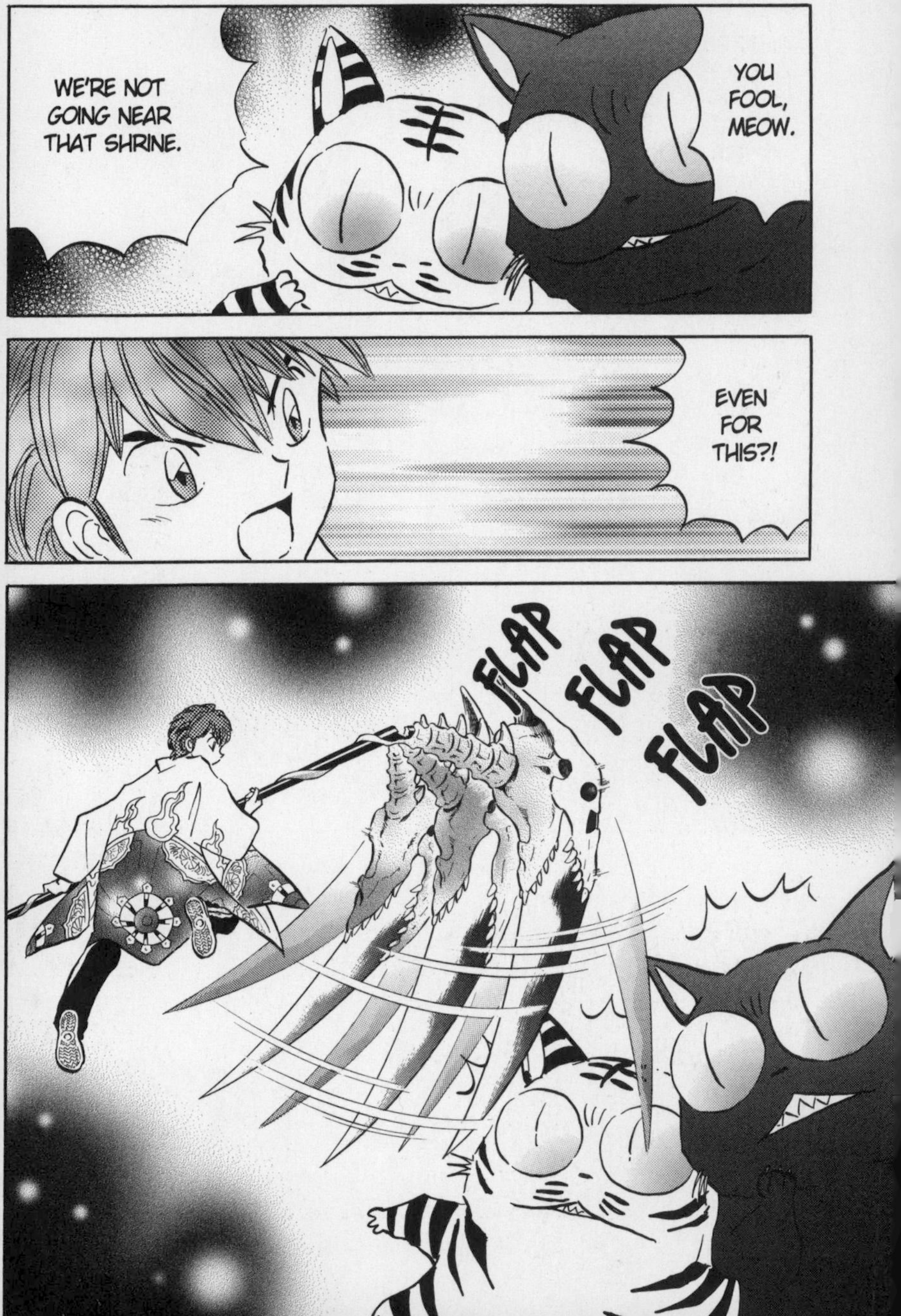
YOU FOOL, MEOW.
WE'RE NOT GOING NEAR THAT SHRINE.
EVEN FOR THIS?!
FLAP
FLAP
FLAP

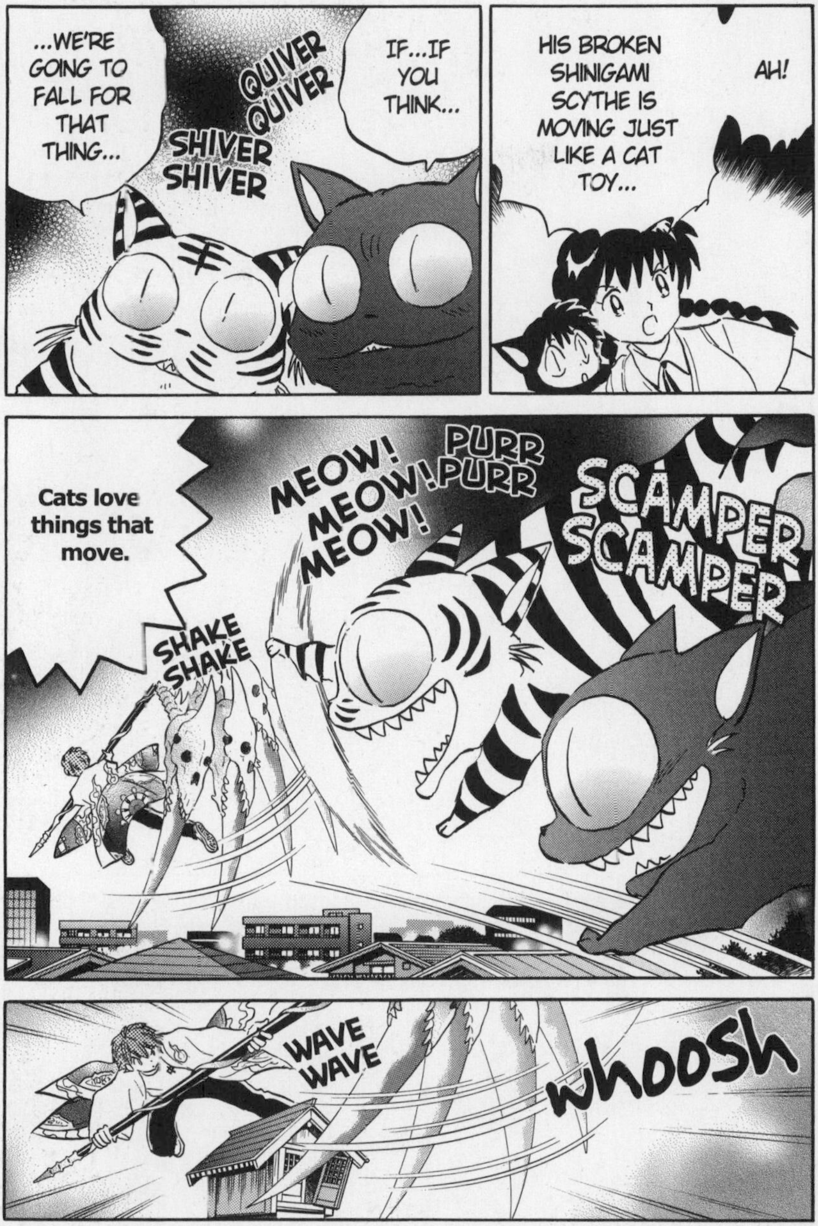
AH!
HIS BROKEN SHINIGAMI SCYTHE IS MOVING JUST LIKE A CAT TOY...
IF...IF YOU THINK...
QUIVER QUIVER
...WE'RE GOING TO FALL FOR THAT THING...
SHIVER SHIVER
SCAMPER SCAMPER
PURR PURR
MEOW! MEOW! MEOW!
Cats love things that move.
SHAKE SHAKE
whoosh
WAVE WAVE

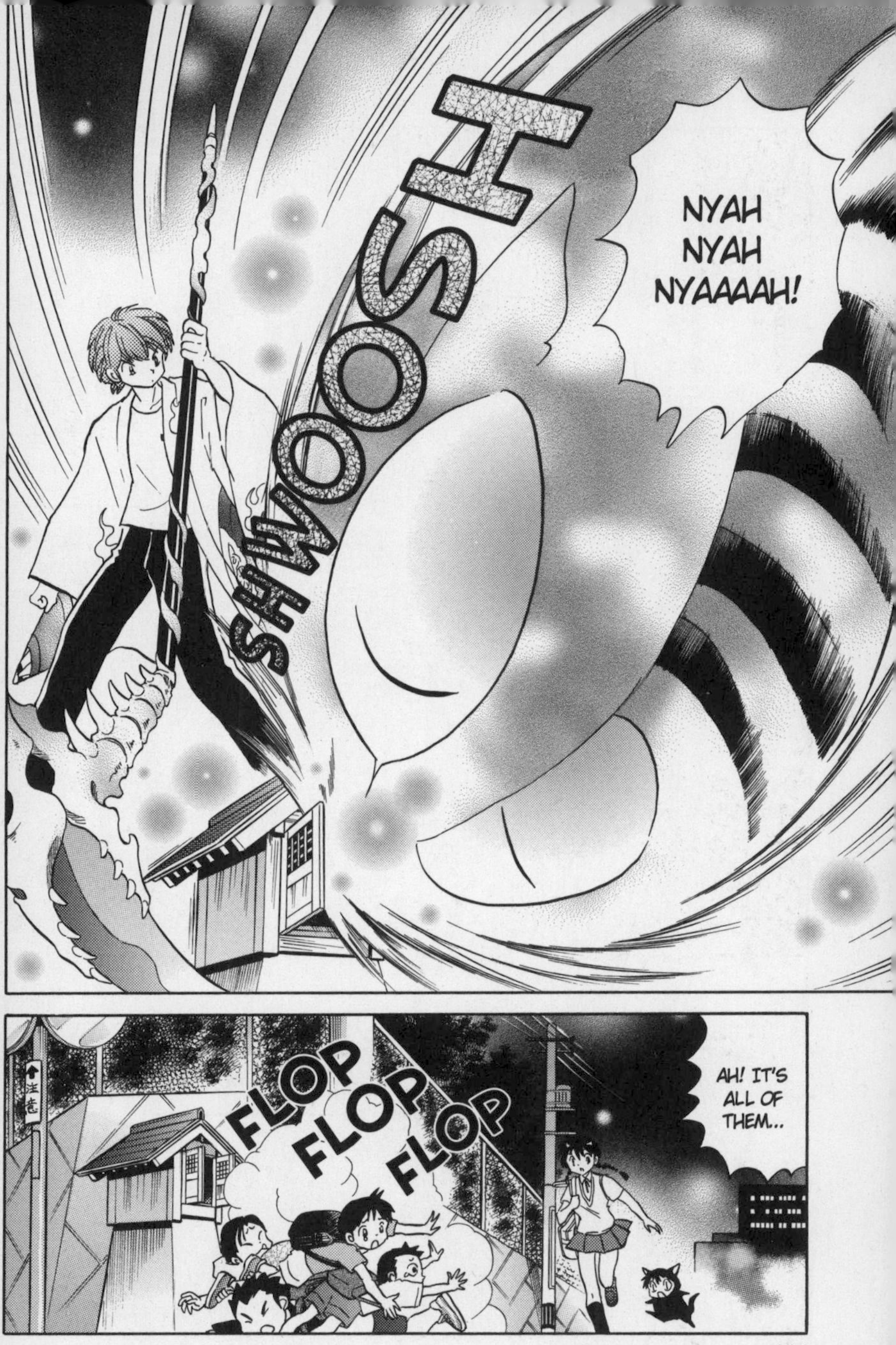
NYAH NYAH NYAAAAH!
SHWOOSH
AH! IT'S ALL OF THEM...
FLOP FLOP FLOP
注意

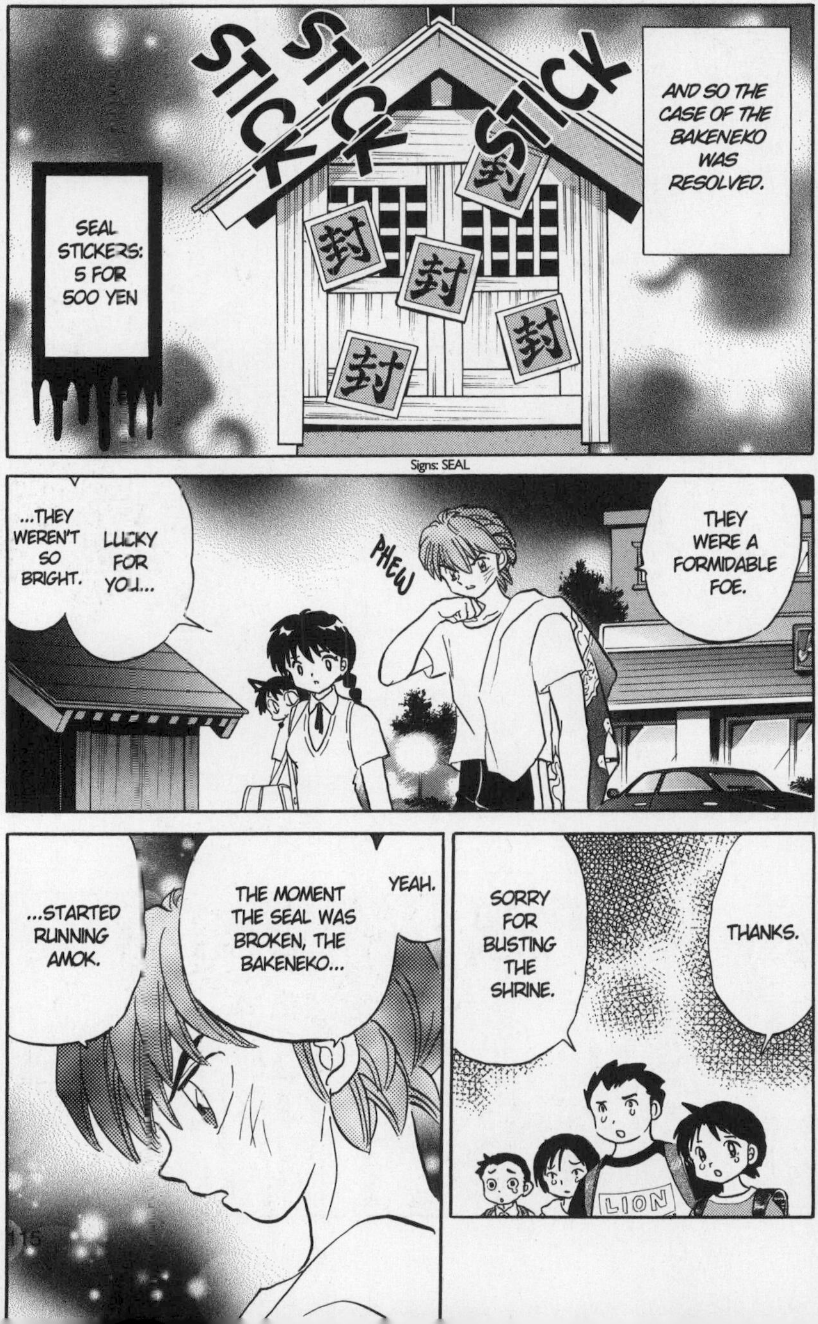
AND SO THE CASE OF THE BAKENEKO WAS RESOLVED.
STICK
STICK
STICK
SEAL STICKERS: 5 FOR 500 YEN
Signs: SEAL
THEY WERE A FORMIDABLE FOE.
PHEW
LUCKY FOR YOU...
...THEY WEREN'T SO BRIGHT.
THANKS.
SORRY FOR BUSTING THE SHRINE.
YEAH.
THE MOMENT THE SEAL WAS BROKEN, THE BAKENEKO...
...STARTED RUNNING AMOK.
LION

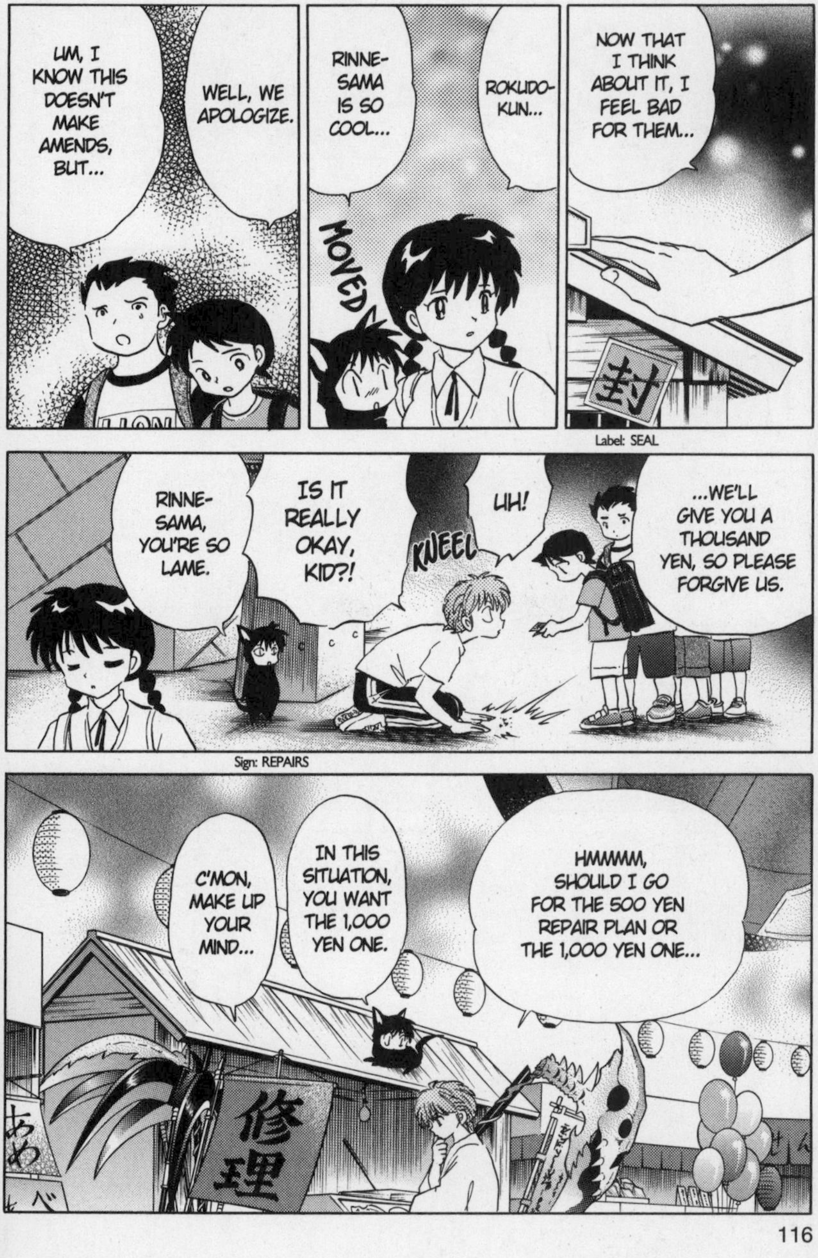
NOW THAT I THINK ABOUT IT, I FEEL BAD FOR THEM...
ROKUDO-KUN...
RINNE-SAMA IS SO COOL...
MOVED
WELL, WE APOLOGIZE.
UM, I KNOW THIS DOESN'T MAKE AMENDS, BUT...
...WE'LL GIVE YOU A THOUSAND YEN, SO PLEASE FORGIVE US.
UH!
KNEEL
IS IT REALLY OKAY, KID?!
RINNE-SAMA, YOU'RE SO LAME.
HMMMMM, SHOULD I GO FOR THE 500 YEN REPAIR PLAN OR THE 1,000 YEN ONE...
IN THIS SITUATION, YOU WANT THE 1,000 YEN ONE.
C'MON, MAKE UP YOUR MIND...
Label: SEAL

Sign: REPAIRS

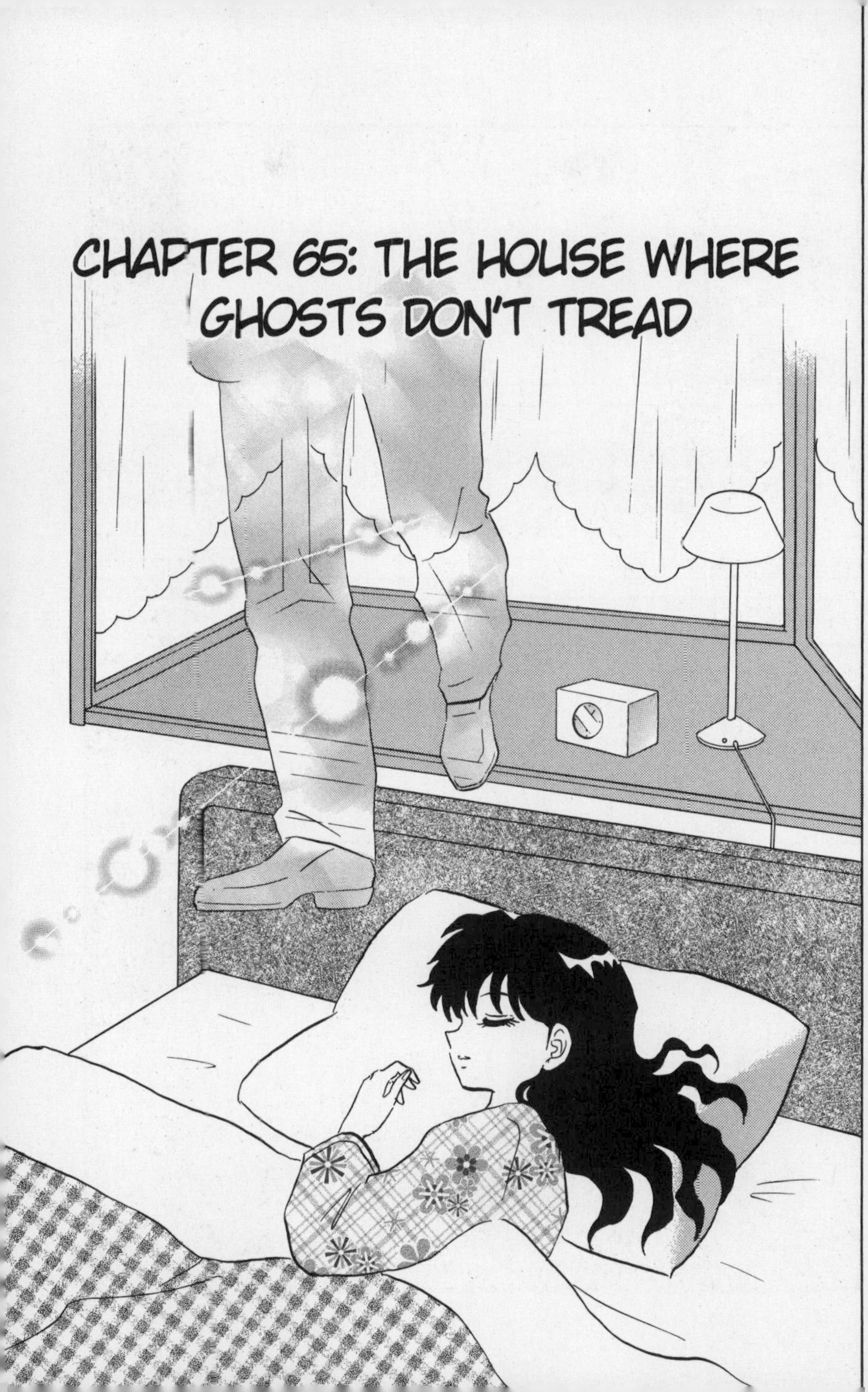
CHAPTER 65: THE HOUSE WHERE GHOSTS DON'T TREAD

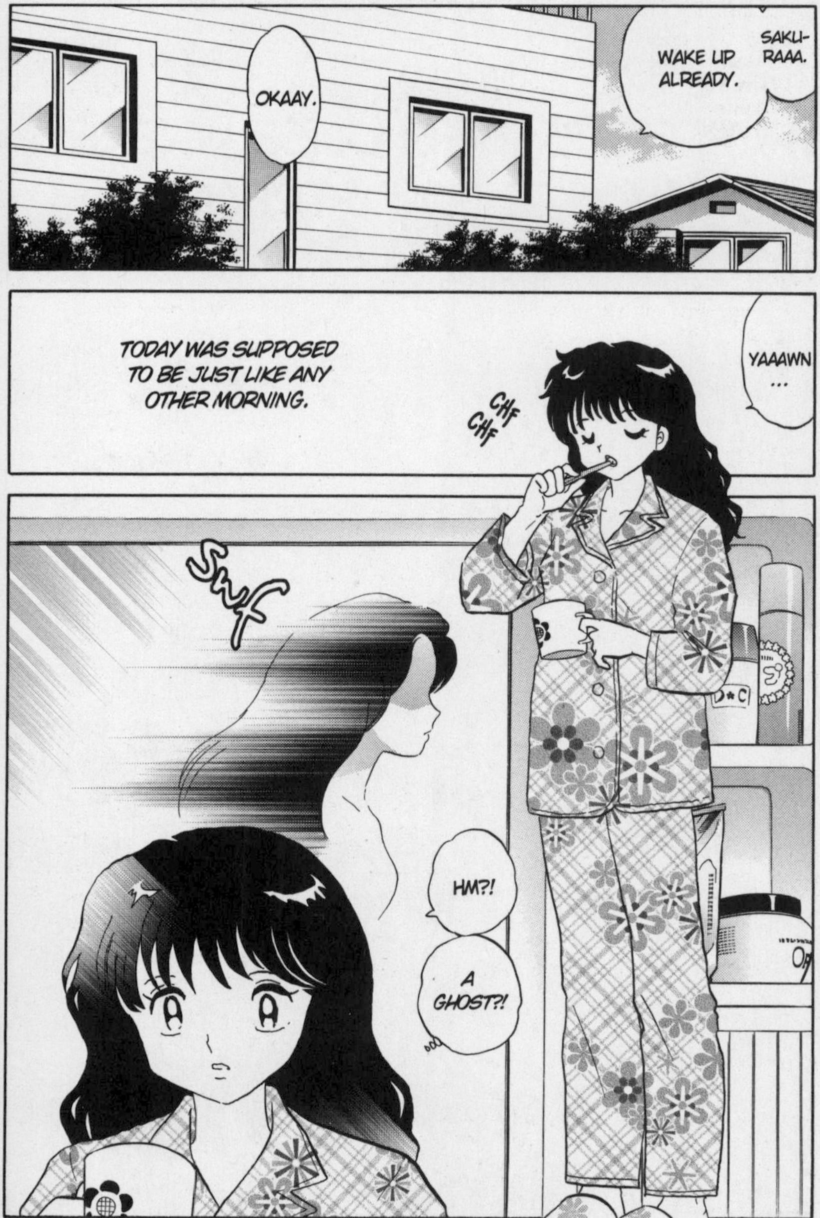
SAKU-RAAA. WAKE UP ALREADY.
OKAAY.
YAAAWN...
TODAY WAS SUPPOSED TO BE JUST LIKE ANY OTHER MORNING.
CHF CHF
HM?!
A GHOST?!
SNF

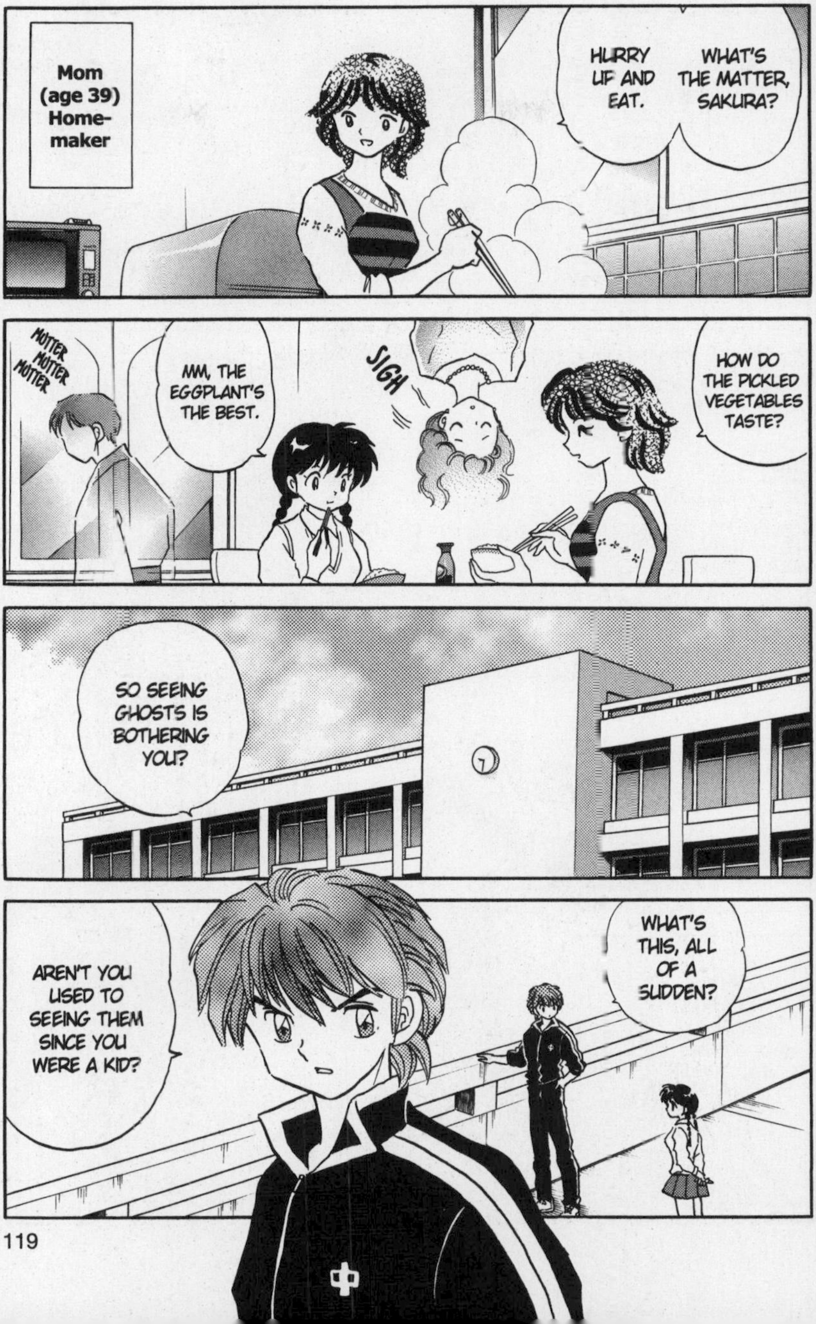
WHAT'S THE MATTER, SAKURA?
HURRY UP AND EAT.
Mom (age 39) Homemaker
HOW DO THE PICKLED VEGETABLES TASTE?
SIGH
MM, THE EGGPLANT'S THE BEST.
MUTTER MUTTER MUTTER
SO SEEING GHOSTS IS BOTHERING YOU?
WHAT'S THIS, ALL OF A SUDDEN?
AREN'T YOU USED TO SEEING THEM SINCE YOU WERE A KID?

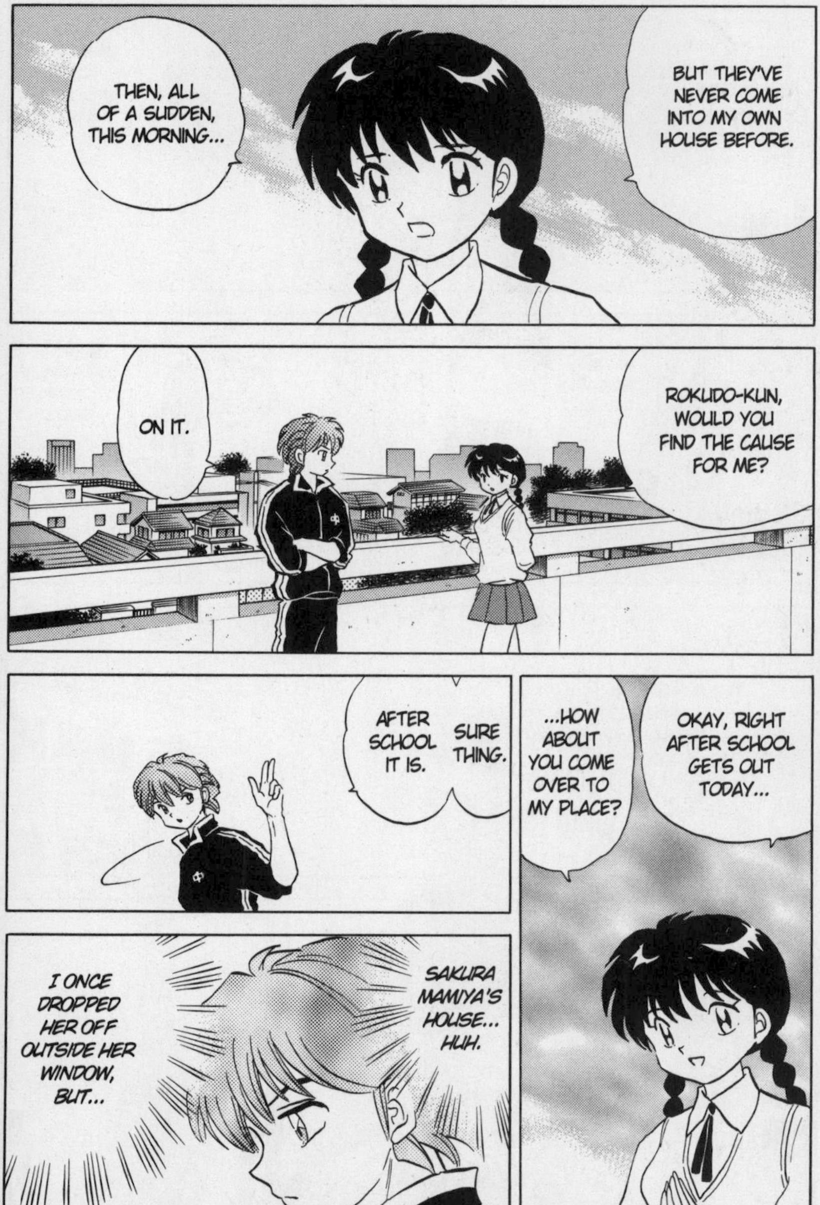
BUT THEY'VE NEVER COME INTO MY OWN HOUSE BEFORE.
THEN, ALL OF A SUDDEN, THIS MORNING...
ROKUDO-KUN, WOULD YOU FIND THE CAUSE FOR ME?
ON IT.
OKAY, RIGHT AFTER SCHOOL GETS OUT TODAY...
...HOW ABOUT YOU COME OVER TO MY PLACE?
SURE THING.
AFTER SCHOOL IT IS.
SAKURA MAMIYA'S HOUSE... HUH.
I ONCE DROPPED HER OFF OUTSIDE HER WINDOW, BUT...

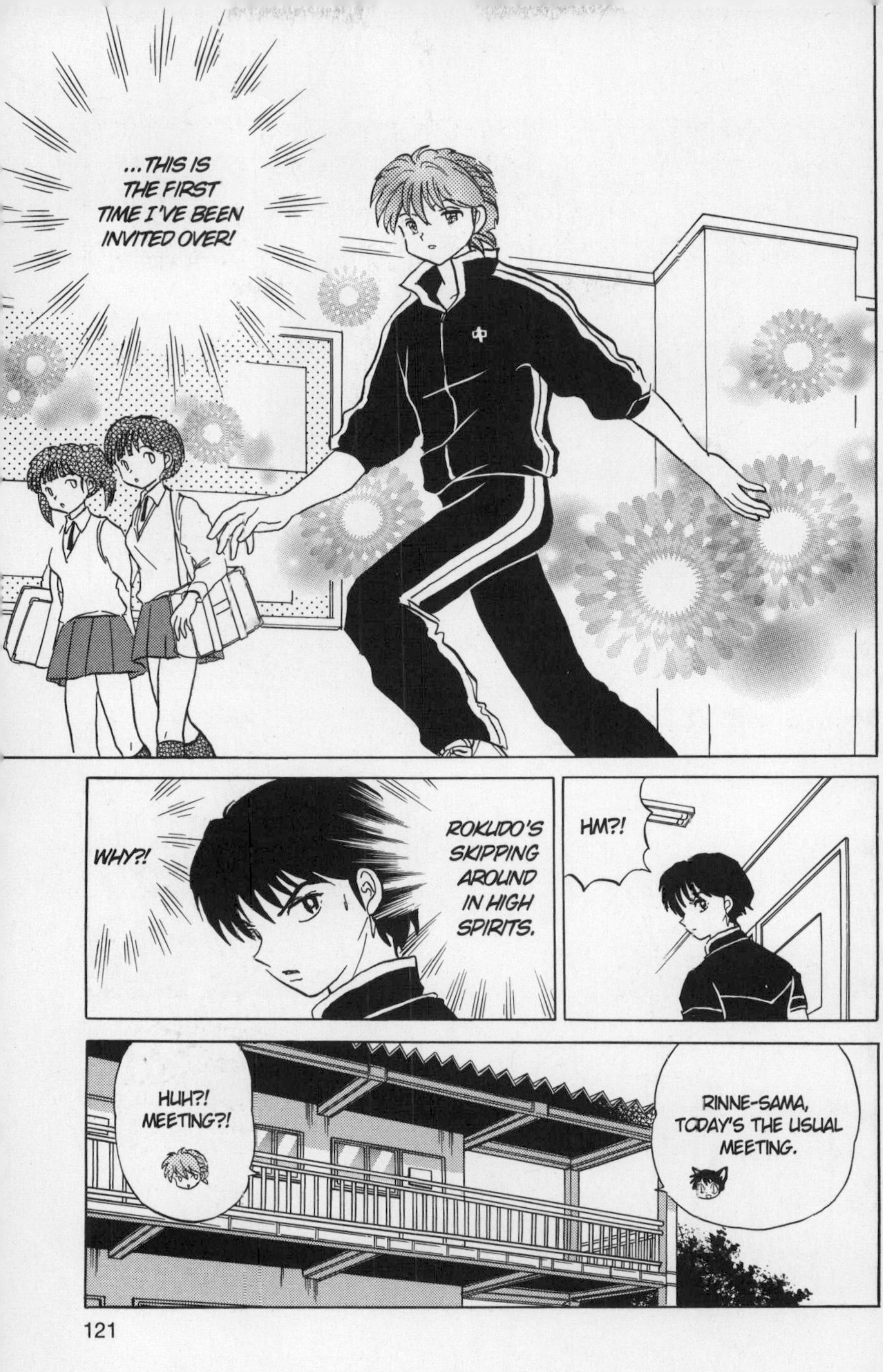
...THIS IS THE FIRST TIME I'VE BEEN INVITED OVER!
HM?!
ROKUDO'S SKIPPING AROUND IN HIGH SPIRITS.
WHY?!
RINNE-SAMA, TODAY'S THE USUAL MEETING.
HUH?! MEETING?!

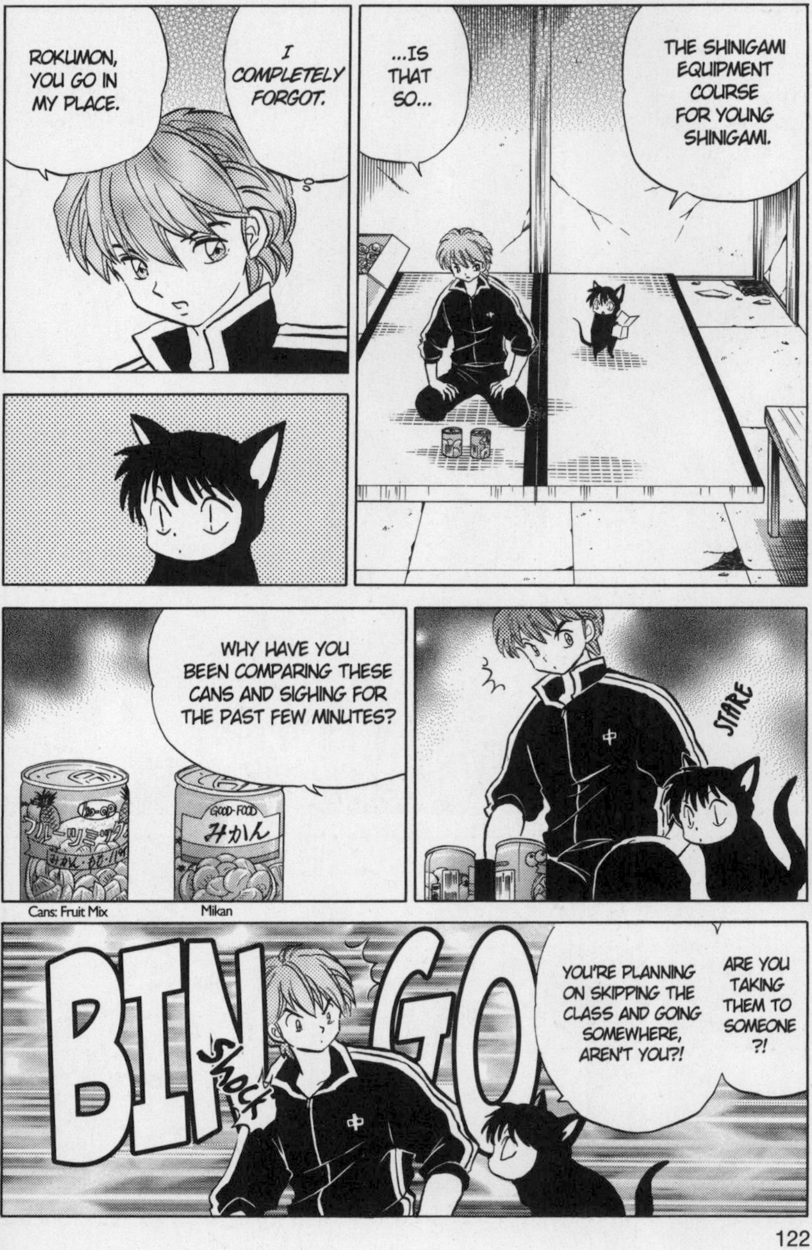
THE SHINIGAMI EQUIPMENT COURSE FOR YOUNG SHINIGAMI.
...IS THAT SO...
I COMPLETELY FORGOT.
ROKUMON, YOU GO IN MY PLACE.
STARE
WHY HAVE YOU BEEN COMPARING THESE CANS AND SIGHING FOR THE PAST FEW MINUTES?
GOOD-FOOD
みかん
ARE YOU TAKING THEM TO SOMEONE?!
YOU'RE PLANNING ON SKIPPING THE CLASS AND GOING SOMEWHERE, AREN'T YOU?!
BINGO
SHOCK
Cans: Fruit Mix
Mikan

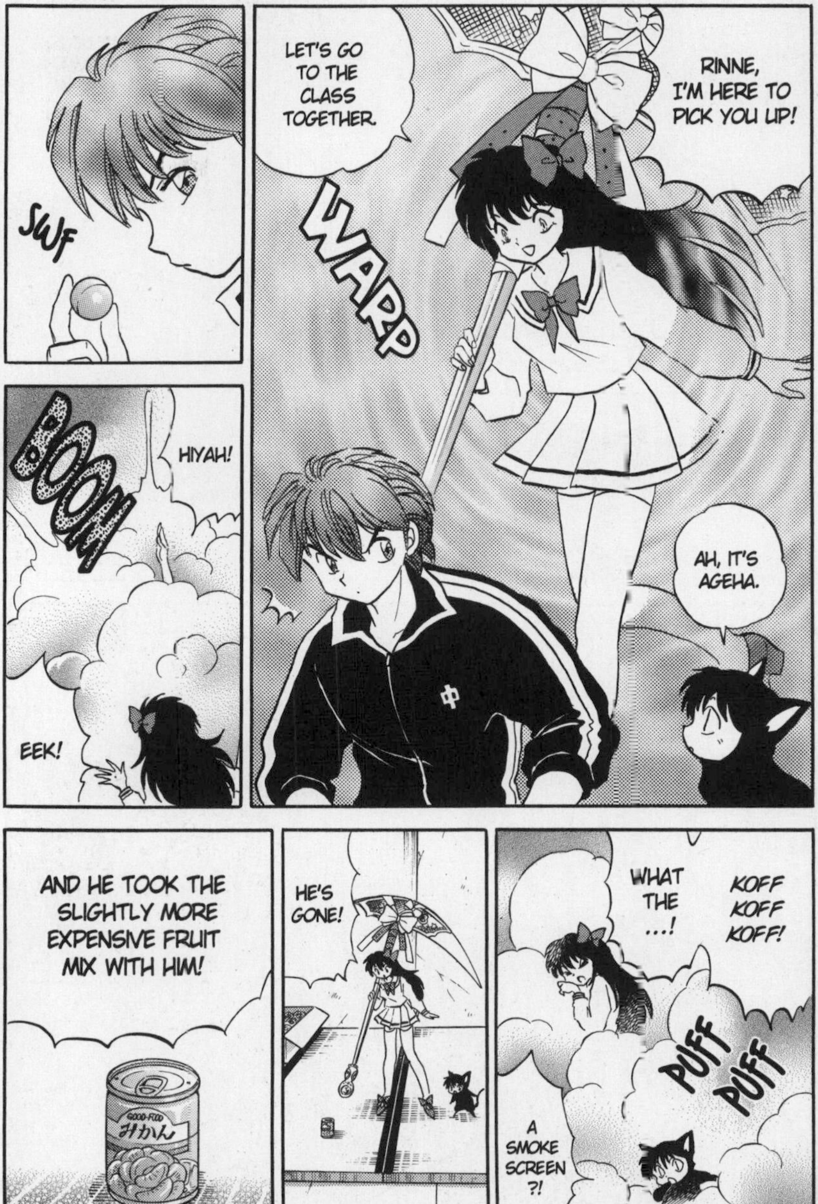
RINNE, I'M HERE TO PICK YOU UP!
LET'S GO TO THE CLASS TOGETHER.
WARP
AH, IT'S AGEHA.
SWF
BOOM
HIYAH!
EEK!
KOFF KOFF KOFF!
WHAT THE ...!
PUFF PUFF
A SMOKE SCREEN ?!
HE'S GONE!
AND HE TOOK THE SLIGHTLY MORE EXPENSIVE FRUIT MIX WITH HIM!
GOOD-FOOD
みかん

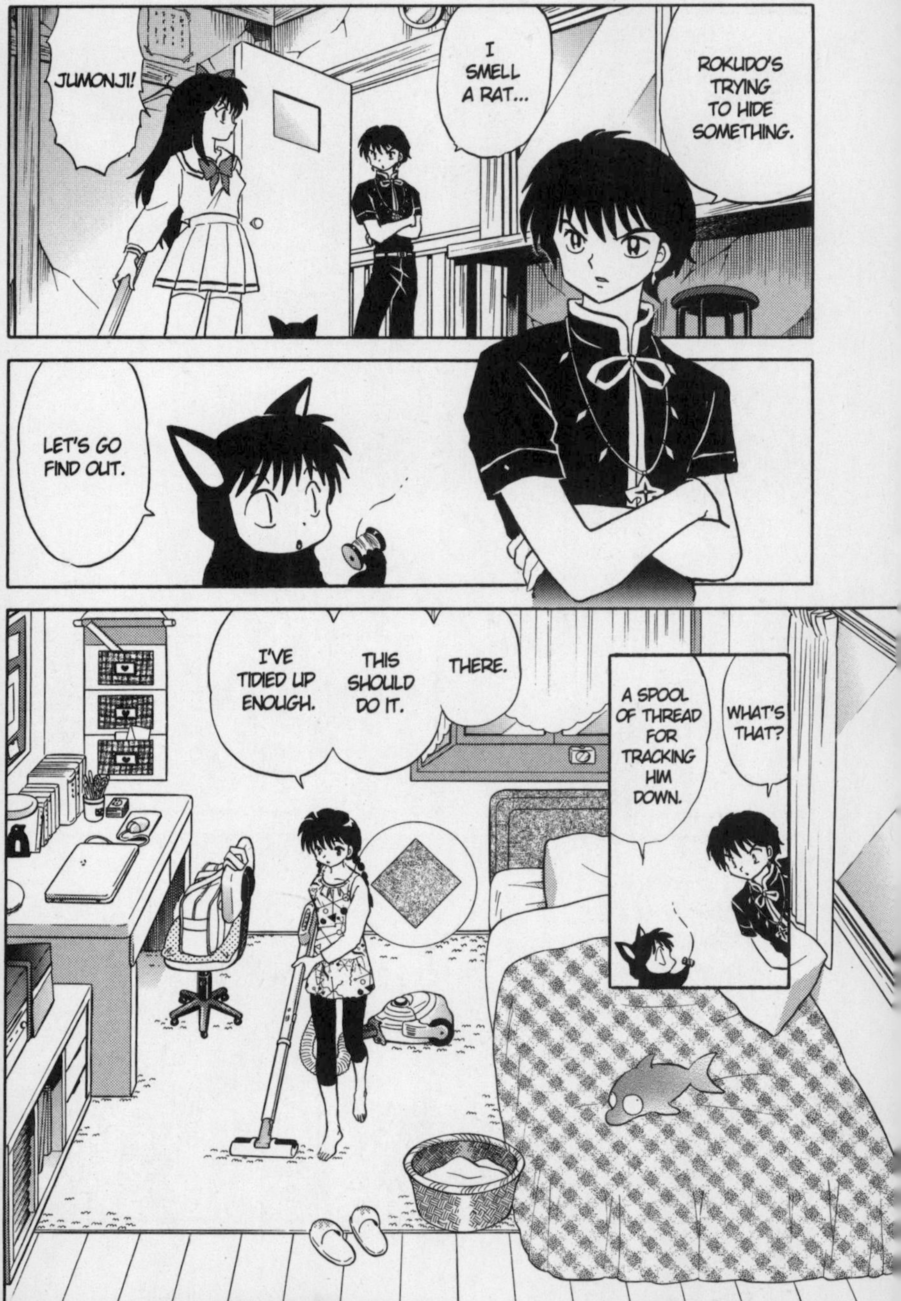
ROKUDO'S TRYING TO HIDE SOMETHING.
I SMELL A RAT...
JUMONJI!
LET'S GO FIND OUT.
WHAT'S THAT?
A SPOOL OF THREAD FOR TRACKING HIM DOWN.
THERE.
THIS SHOULD DO IT.
I'VE TIDIED UP ENOUGH.

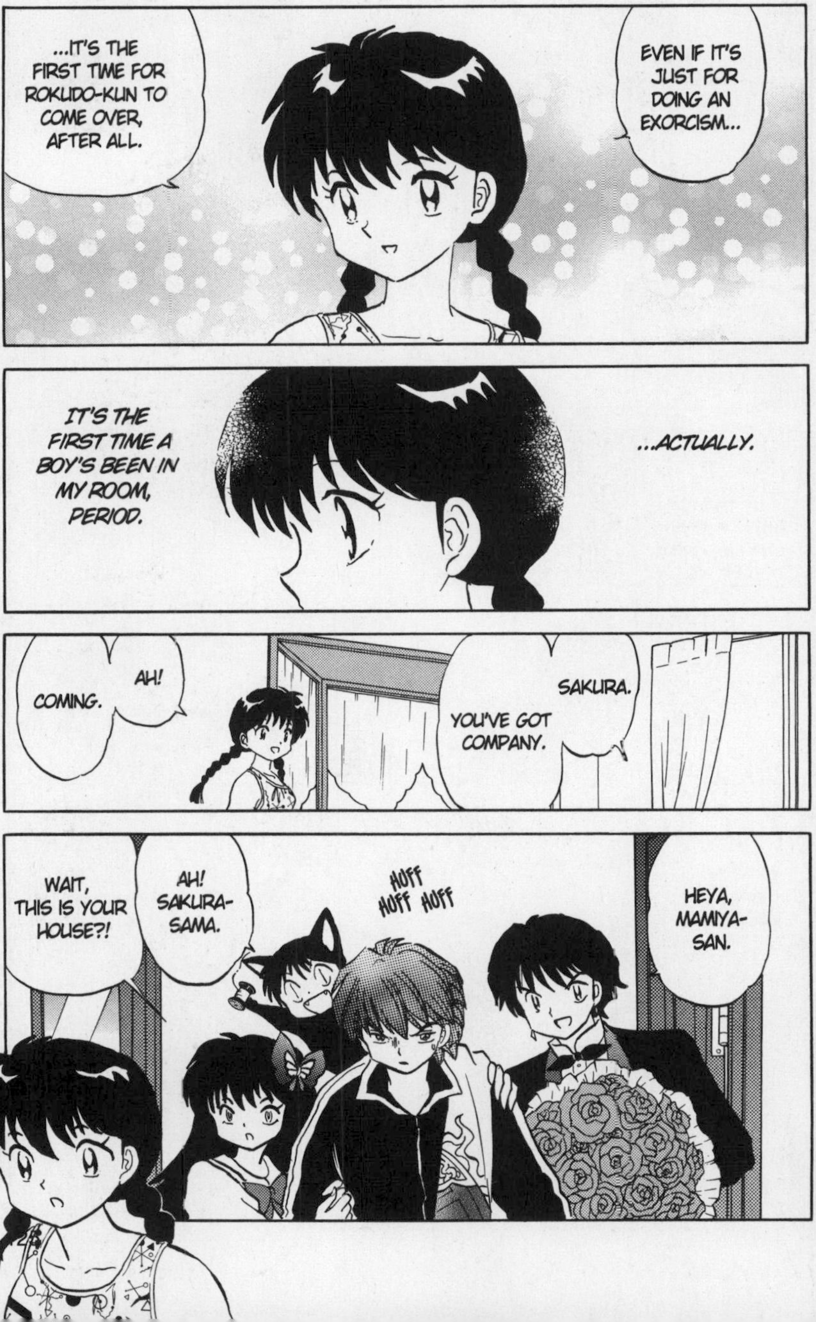
EVEN IF IT'S JUST FOR DOING AN EXORCISM...
...IT'S THE FIRST TIME FOR ROKUDO-KUN TO COME OVER, AFTER ALL.
IT'S THE FIRST TIME A BOY'S BEEN IN MY ROOM, PERIOD.
...ACTUALLY.
SAKURA.
YOU'VE GOT COMPANY.
AH!
COMING.
HEYA, MAMIYA-SAN.
HUFF HUFF HUFF
AH! SAKURA-SAMA.
WAIT, THIS IS YOUR HOUSE?!

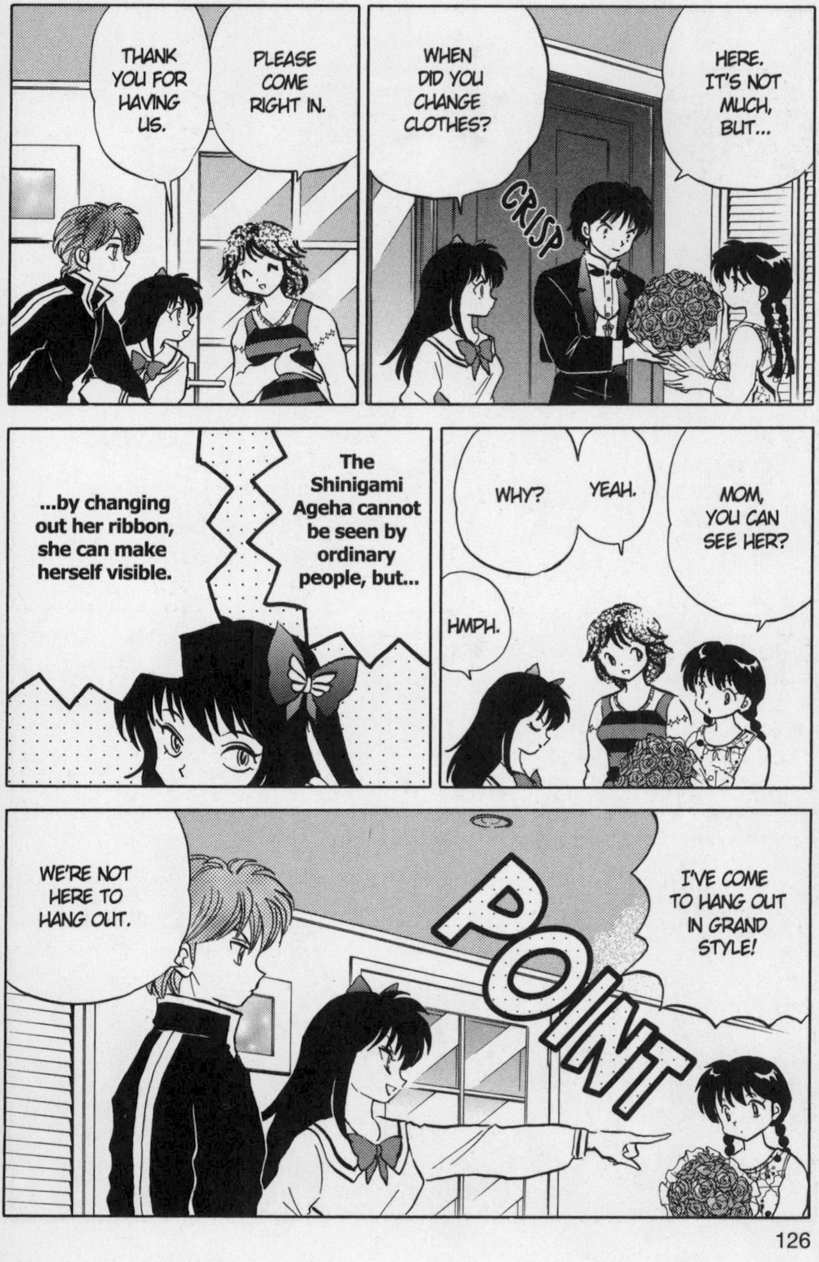
HERE. IT'S NOT MUCH, BUT...
WHEN DID YOU CHANGE CLOTHES?
CRISP
PLEASE COME RIGHT IN.
THANK YOU FOR HAVING US.
MOM, YOU CAN SEE HER?
YEAH.
WHY?
HMPH.
The Shinigami Ageha cannot be seen by ordinary people, but...
...by changing out her ribbon, she can make herself visible.
I'VE COME TO HANG OUT IN GRAND STYLE!
POINT
WE'RE NOT HERE TO HANG OUT.

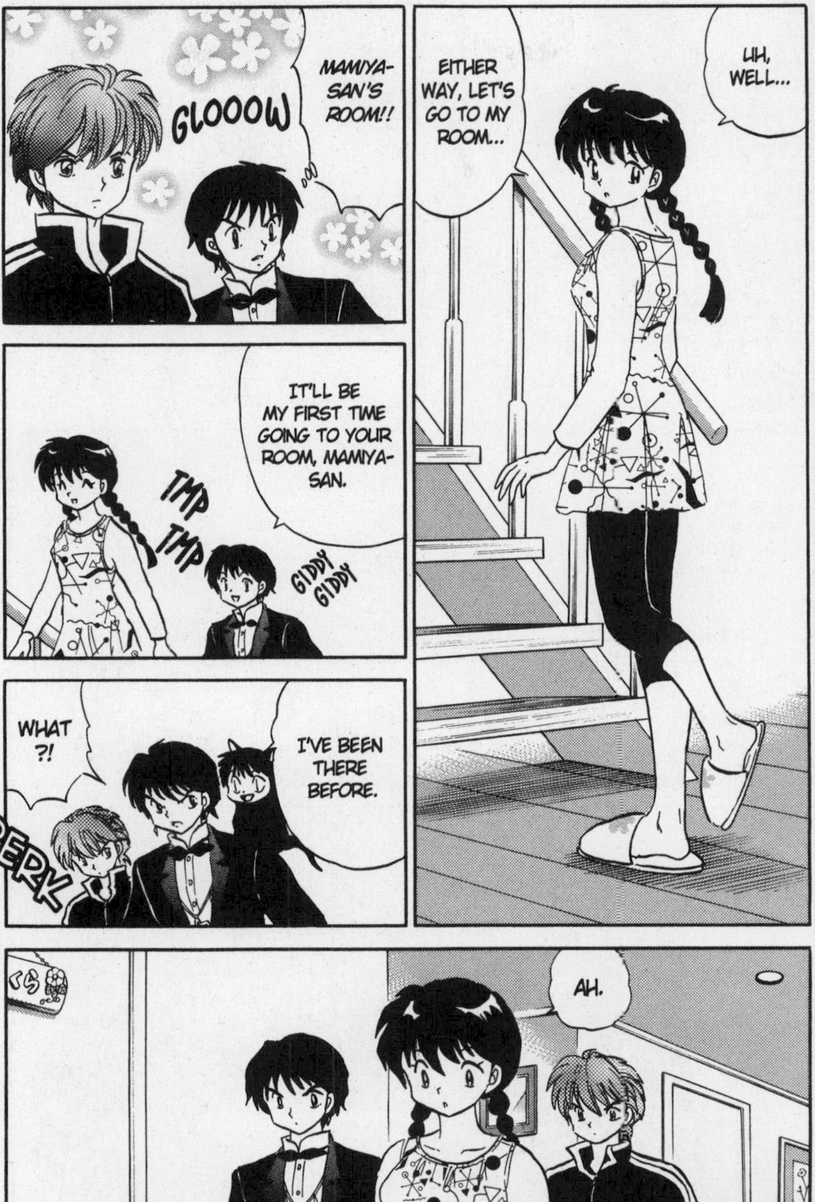
UH, WELL...
EITHER WAY, LET'S GO TO MY ROOM...
MAMIYA-SAN'S ROOM!!
GLOOOW
IT'LL BE MY FIRST TIME GOING TO YOUR ROOM, MAMIYA-SAN.
GIDDY GIDDY
TMP TMP
I'VE BEEN THERE BEFORE.
WHAT?!
PERK
AH.
くら

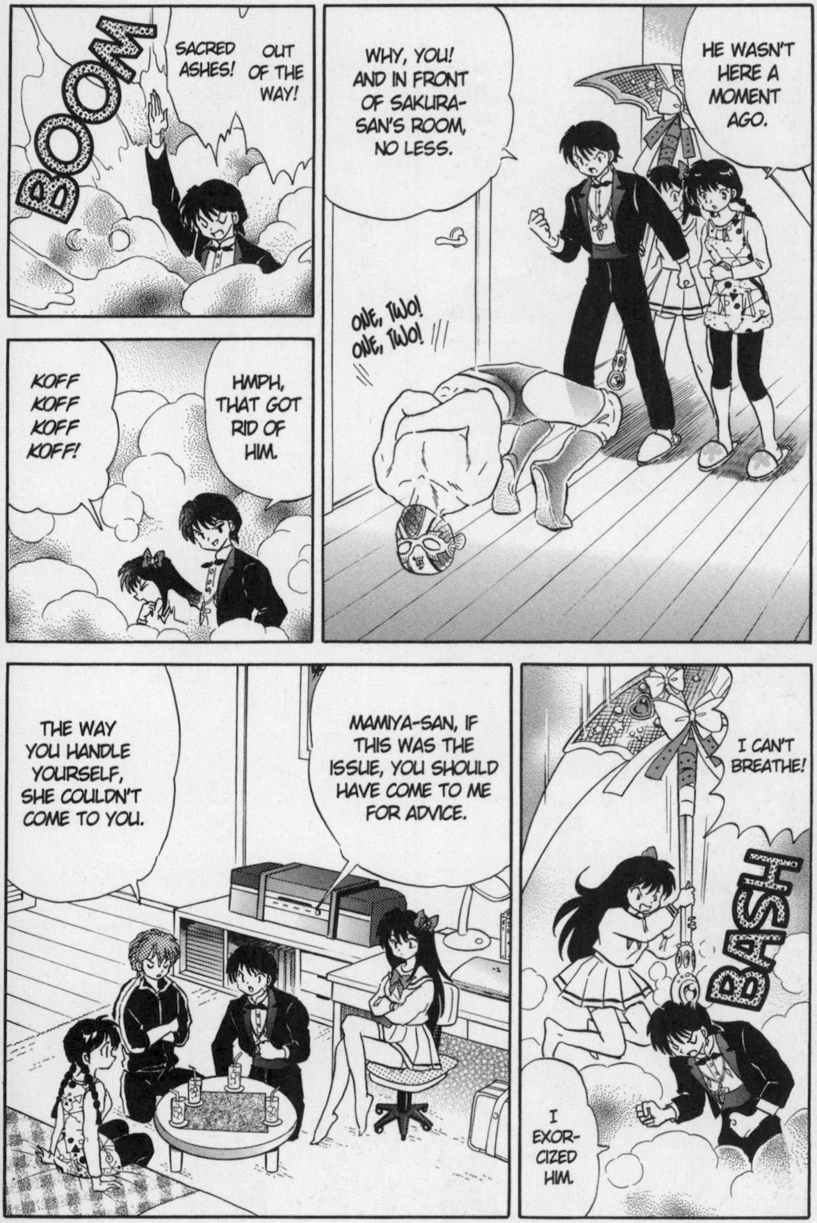
HE WASN'T HERE A MOMENT AGO.
WHY, YOU! AND IN FRONT OF SAKURA-SAN'S ROOM, NO LESS.
ONE, TWO! ONE, TWO!
OUT OF THE WAY!
SACRED ASHES!
BOOM
HMPH, THAT GOT RID OF HIM.
KOFF KOFF KOFF KOFF!
I CAN'T BREATHE!
BASH
I EXOR-CIZED HIM.
MAMIYA-SAN, IF THIS WAS THE ISSUE, YOU SHOULD HAVE COME TO ME FOR ADVICE.
THE WAY YOU HANDLE YOURSELF, SHE COULDN'T COME TO YOU.

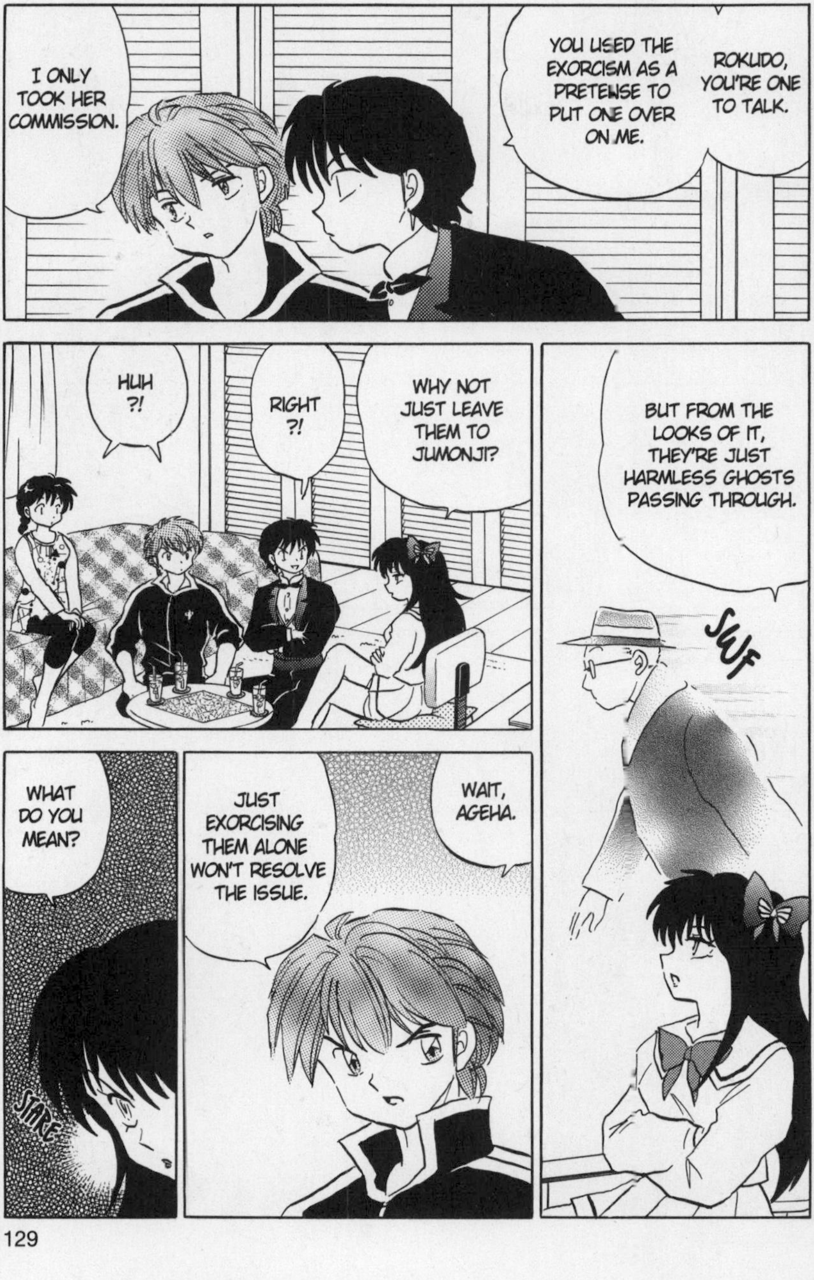
ROKUDO, YOU'RE ONE TO TALK.
YOU USED THE EXORCISM AS A PRETENSE TO PUT ONE OVER ON ME.
I ONLY TOOK HER COMMISSION.
BUT FROM THE LOOKS OF IT, THEY'RE JUST HARMLESS GHOSTS PASSING THROUGH.
SWF
WHY NOT JUST LEAVE THEM TO JUMONJI?
RIGHT ?!
HUH ?!
WAIT, AGEHA.
JUST EXORCISING THEM ALONE WON'T RESOLVE THE ISSUE.
WHAT DO YOU MEAN?
STARE

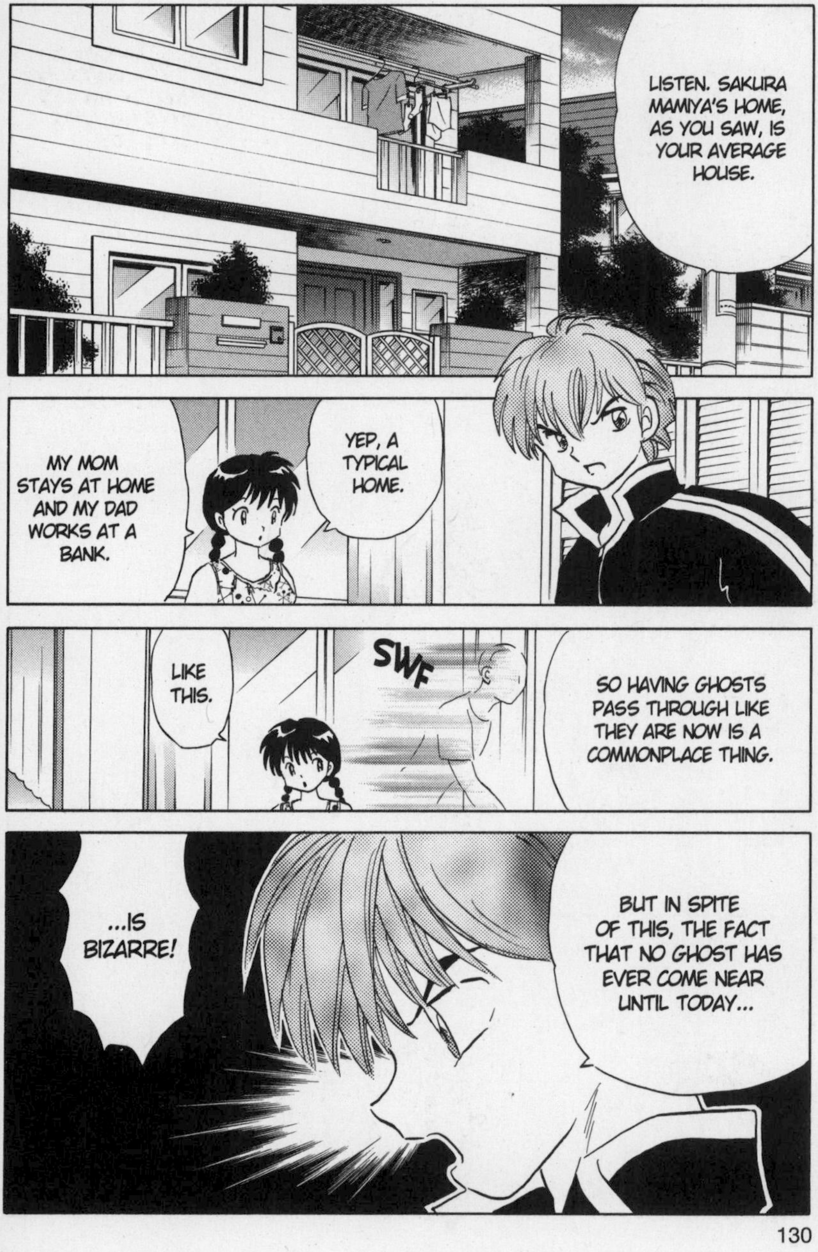
LISTEN. SAKURA MAMIYA'S HOME, AS YOU SAW, IS YOUR AVERAGE HOUSE.
YEP, A TYPICAL HOME.
MY MOM STAYS AT HOME AND MY DAD WORKS AT A BANK.
SO HAVING GHOSTS PASS THROUGH LIKE THEY ARE NOW IS A COMMONPLACE THING.
SWF
LIKE THIS.
BUT IN SPITE OF THIS, THE FACT THAT NO GHOST HAS EVER COME NEAR UNTIL TODAY...
...IS BIZARRE!

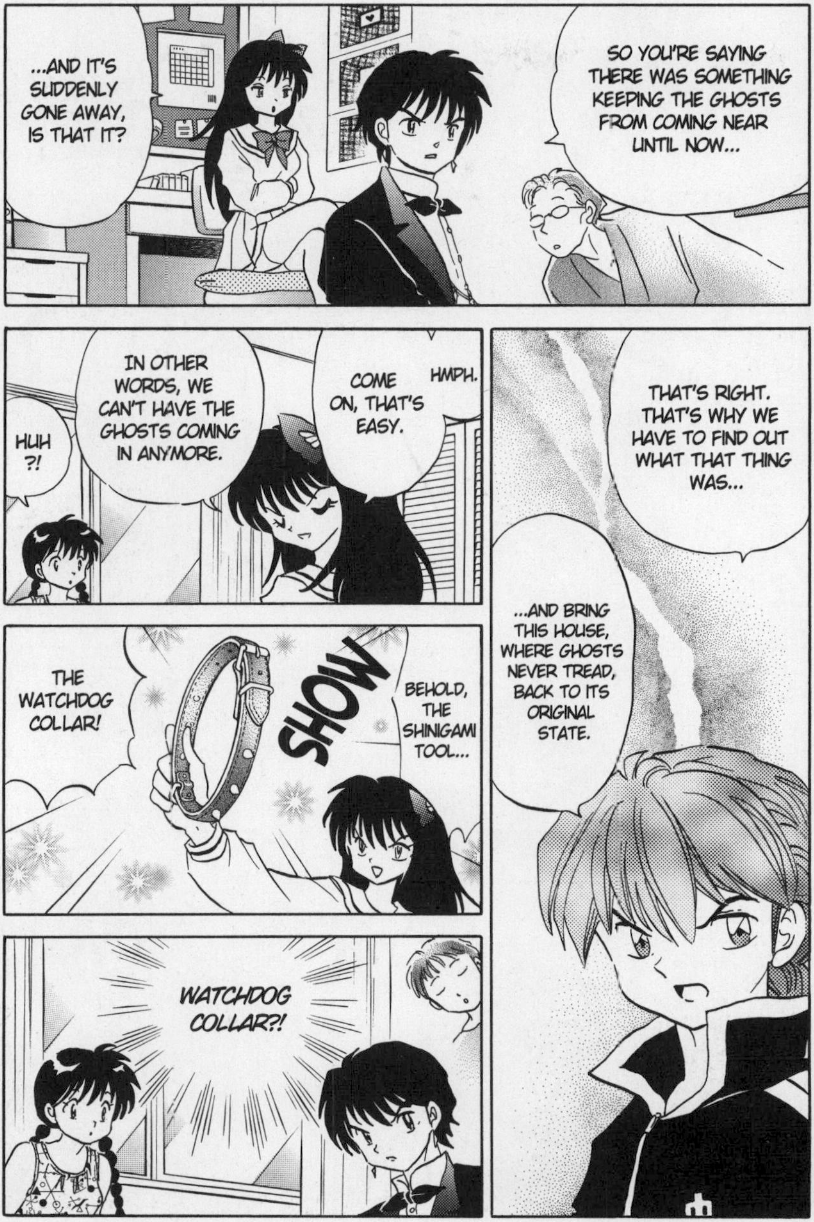
SO YOU'RE SAYING THERE WAS SOMETHING KEEPING THE GHOSTS FROM COMING NEAR UNTIL NOW...
...AND IT'S SUDDENLY GONE AWAY, IS THAT IT?
THAT'S RIGHT. THAT'S WHY WE HAVE TO FIND OUT WHAT THAT THING WAS...
...AND BRING THIS HOUSE, WHERE GHOSTS NEVER TREAD, BACK TO ITS ORIGINAL STATE.
HMPH.
COME ON, THAT'S EASY.
IN OTHER WORDS, WE CAN'T HAVE THE GHOSTS COMING IN ANYMORE.
HUH ?!
BEHOLD, THE SHINIGAMI TOOL...
SHOW
THE WATCHDOG COLLAR!
WATCHDOG COLLAR?!

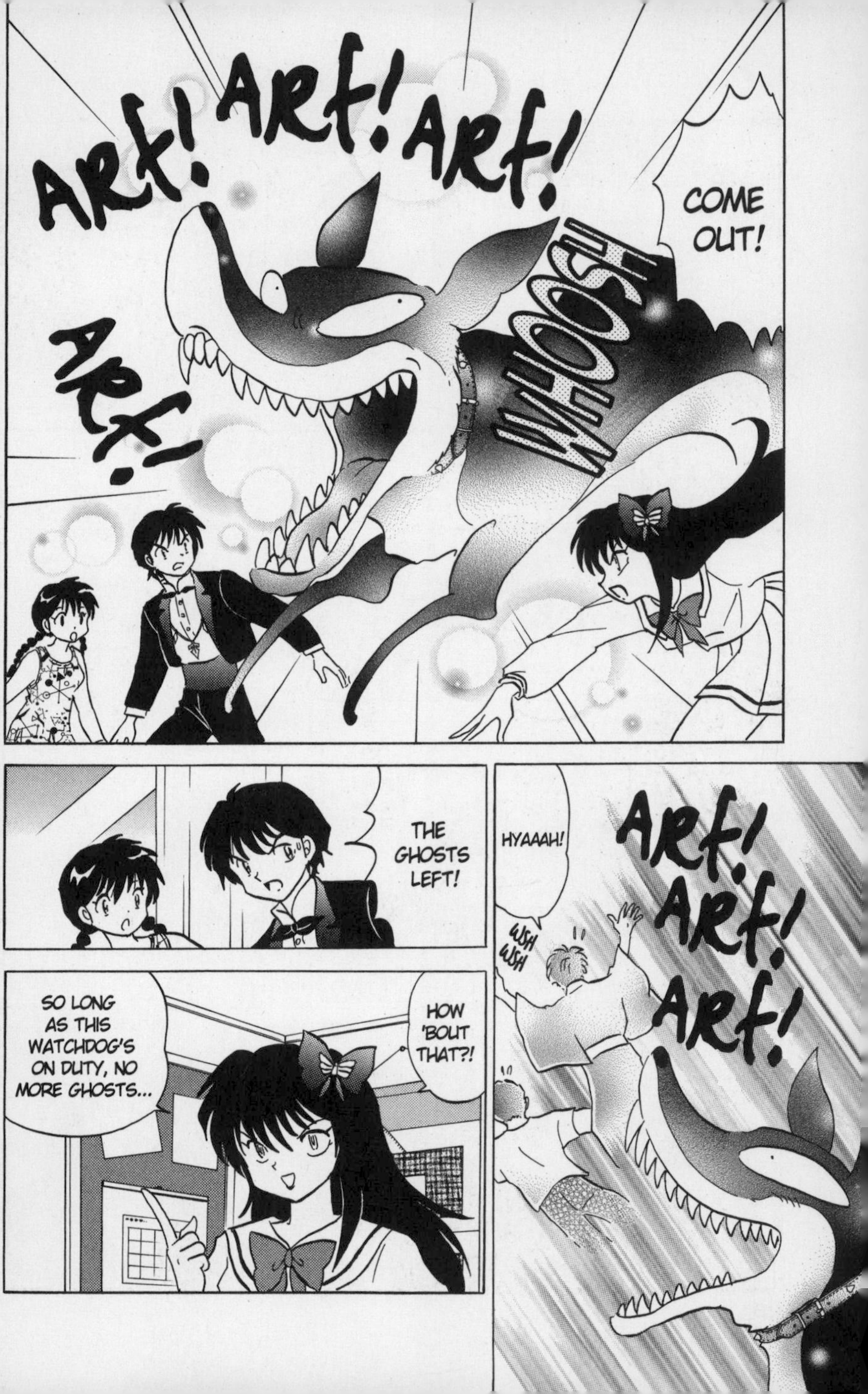
ARF! ARF! ARF!
COME OUT!
WHOOSH
ARF!
ARF! ARF! ARF!
HYAAAH!
WSH WSH
THE GHOSTS LEFT!
HOW 'BOUT THAT?!
SO LONG AS THIS WATCHDOG'S ON DUTY, NO MORE GHOSTS...

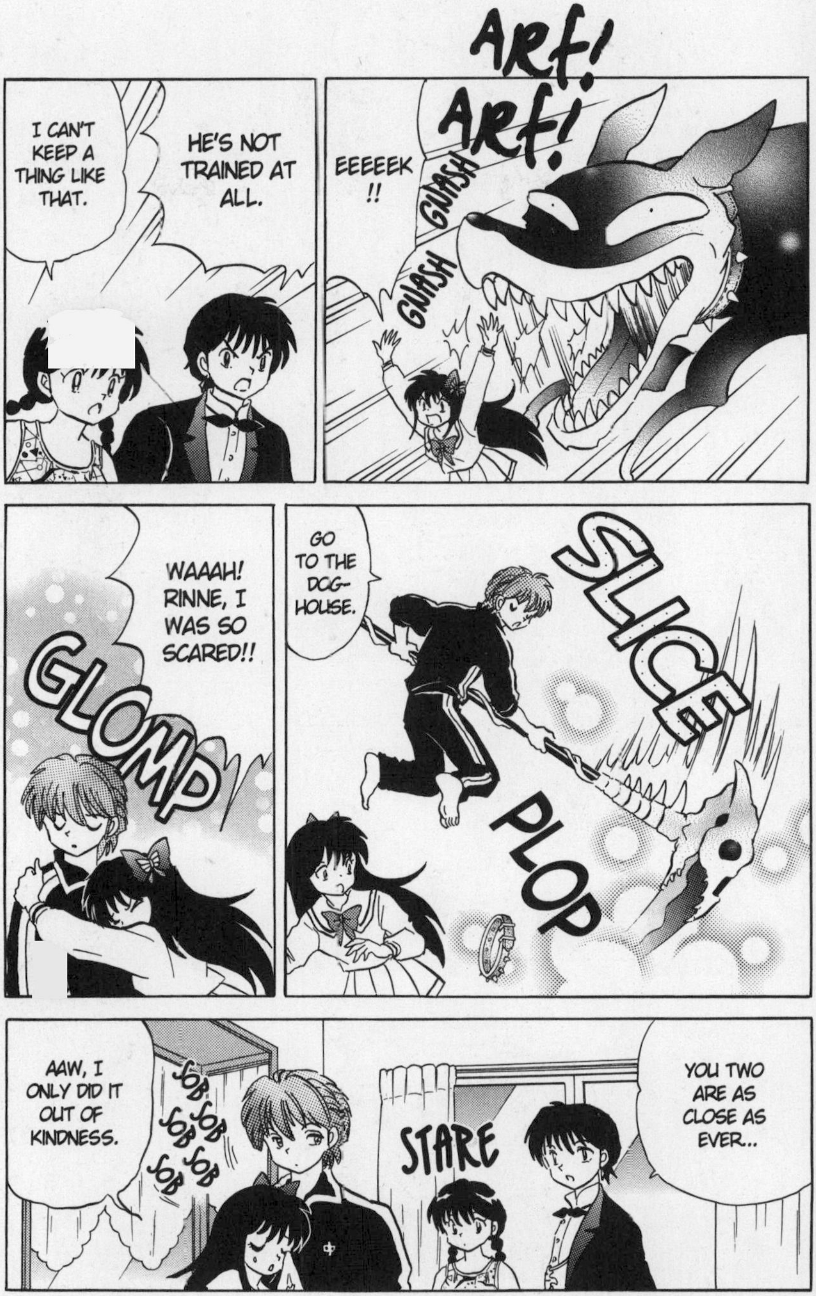
Arf! Arf!
EEEEEK !!
GUASH
GUASH
HE'S NOT TRAINED AT ALL.
I CAN'T KEEP A THING LIKE THAT.
GO TO THE DOG-HOUSE.
SLICE
PLOP
WAAAH! RINNE, I WAS SO SCARED!!
GLOMP
YOU TWO ARE AS CLOSE AS EVER...
STARE
SOB SOB SOB SOB SOB
AAW, I ONLY DID IT OUT OF KINDNESS.

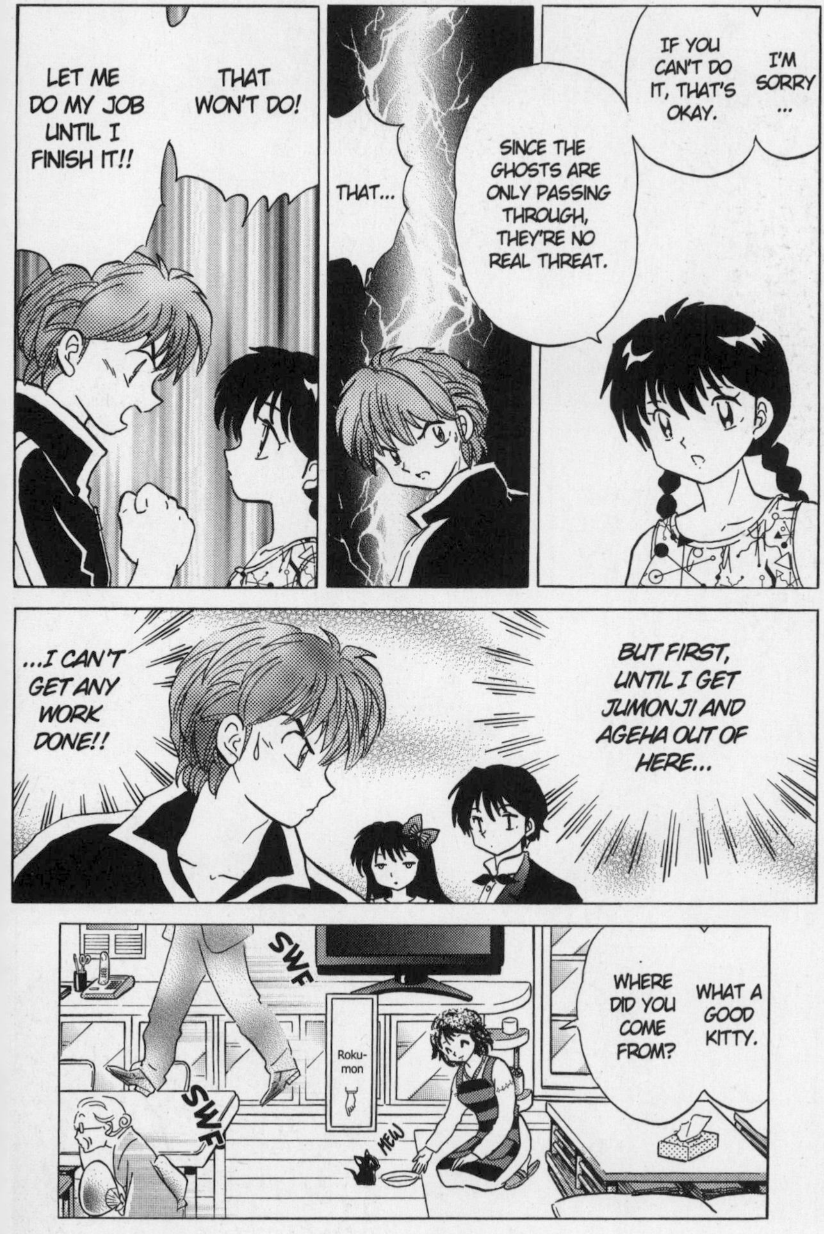
I'M SORRY ...
IF YOU CAN'T DO IT, THAT'S OKAY.
SINCE THE GHOSTS ARE ONLY PASSING THROUGH, THEY'RE NO REAL THREAT.
THAT...
THAT WON'T DO!
LET ME DO MY JOB UNTIL I FINISH IT!!
BUT FIRST, UNTIL I GET JUMONJI AND AGEHA OUT OF HERE...
...I CAN'T GET ANY WORK DONE!!
WHAT A GOOD KITTY.
WHERE DID YOU COME FROM?
Roku-mon
SWF
SWF
MEW

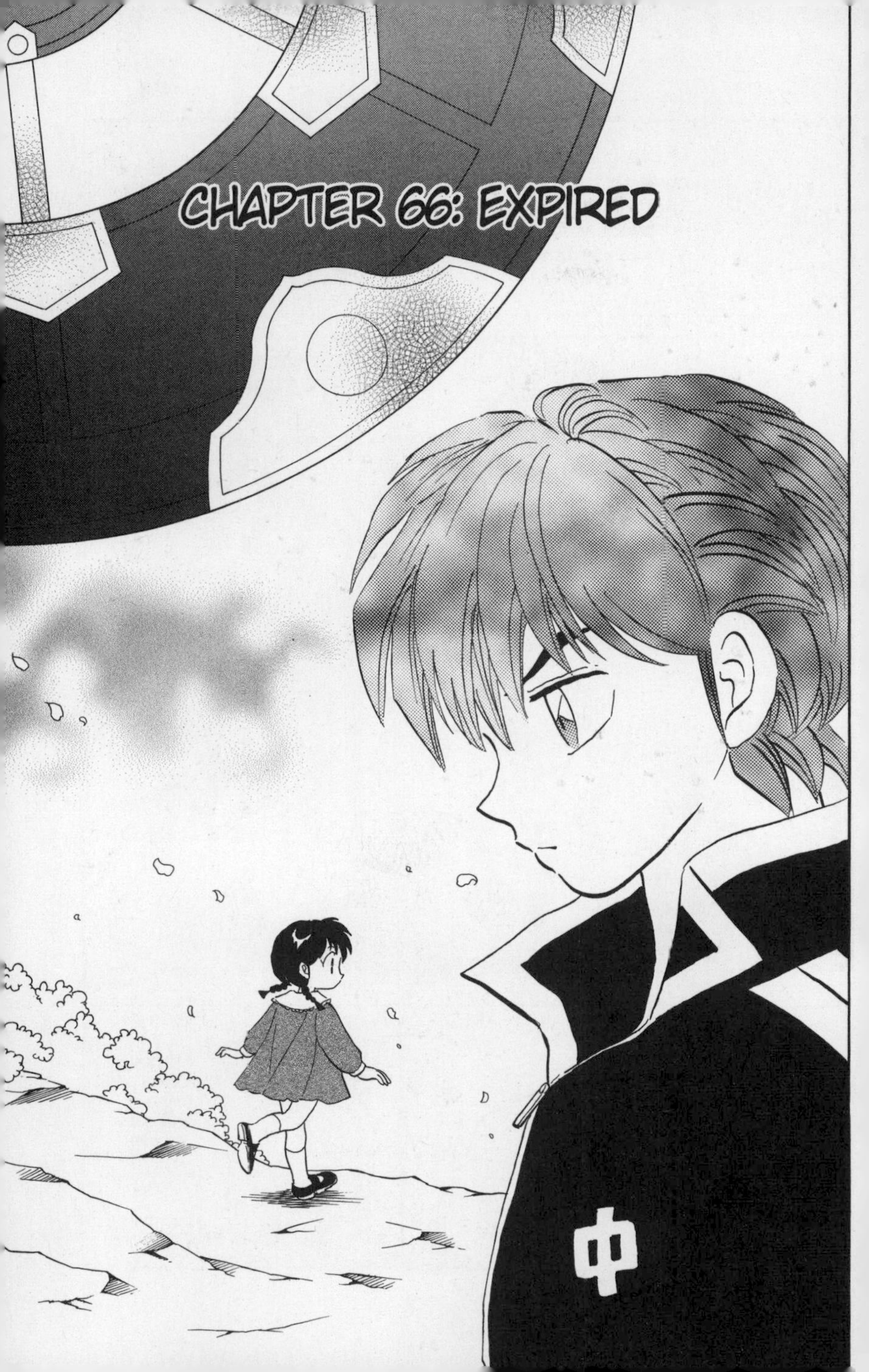
CHAPTER 66: EXPIRED
中

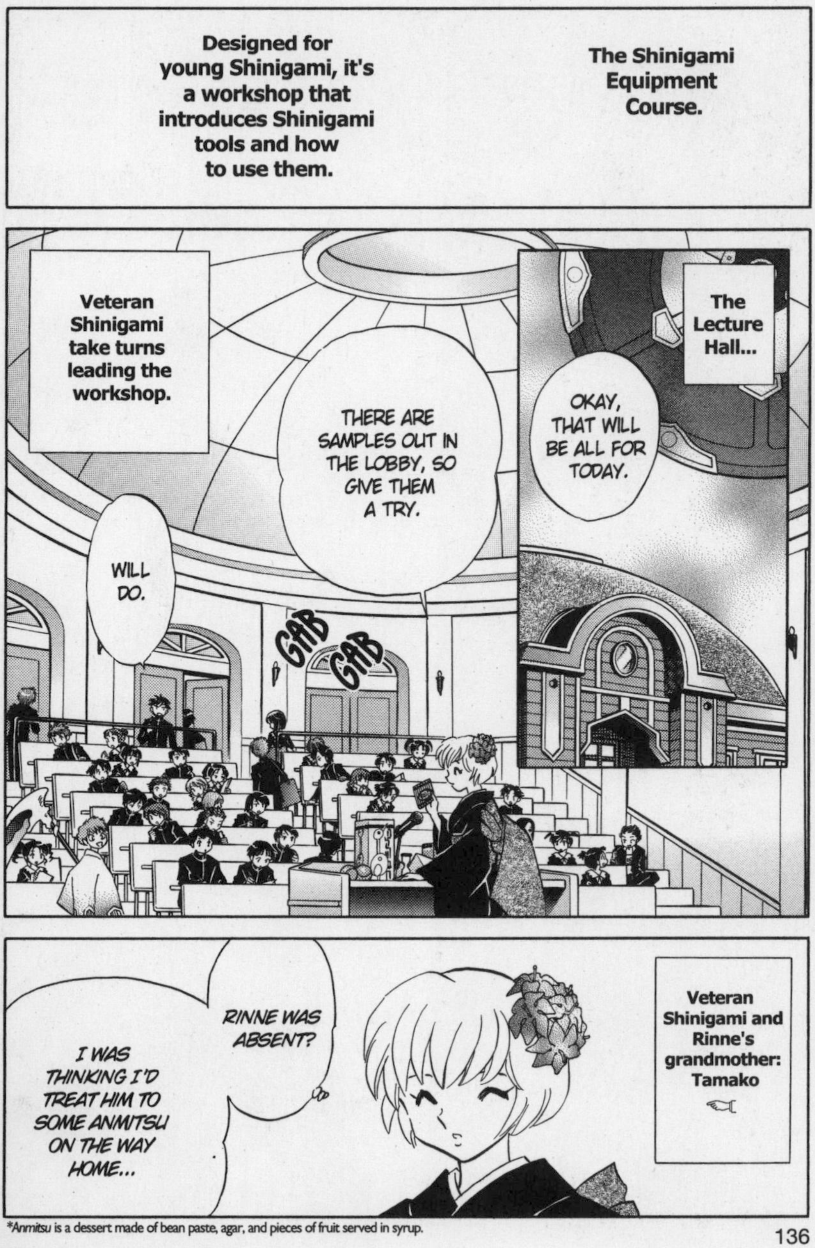
The Shinigami Equipment Course.
Designed for young Shinigami, it's a workshop that introduces Shinigami tools and how to use them.
The Lecture Hall...
OKAY, THAT WILL BE ALL FOR TODAY.
THERE ARE SAMPLES OUT IN THE LOBBY, SO GIVE THEM A TRY.
Veteran Shinigami take turns leading the workshop.
WILL DO.
GAB GAB
Veteran Shinigami and Rinne's grandmother: Tamako
RINNE WAS ABSENT?
I WAS THINKING I'D TREAT HIM TO SOME ANMITSU ON THE WAY HOME...

**Anmitsu* is a dessert made of bean paste, agar, and pieces of fruit served in syrup.

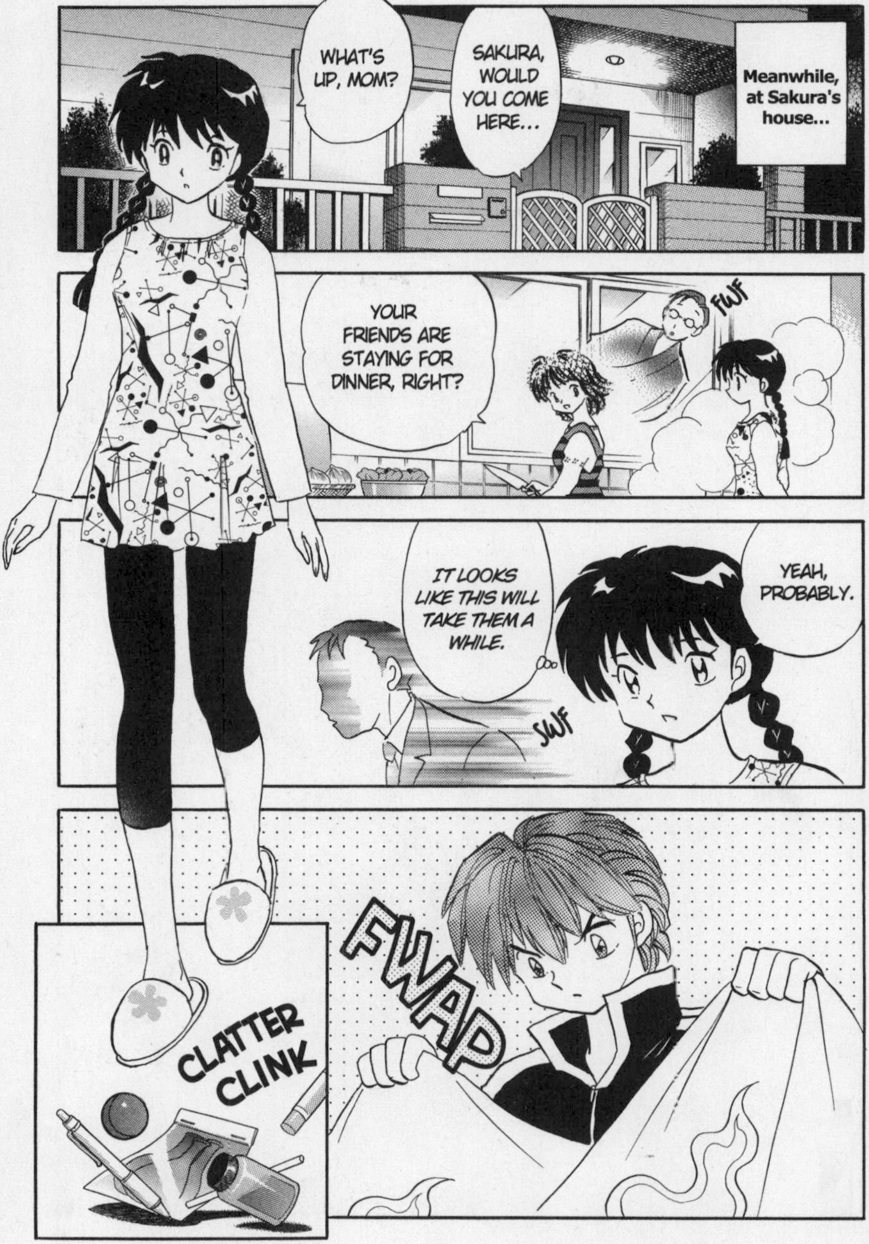
Meanwhile, at Sakura's house...
SAKURA, WOULD YOU COME HERE...
WHAT'S UP, MOM?
FWF
YOUR FRIENDS ARE STAYING FOR DINNER, RIGHT?
YEAH, PROBABLY.
IT LOOKS LIKE THIS WILL TAKE THEM A WHILE.
SWF
FWAP
CLATTER
CLINK

RINNE-SAMA, THESE ARE...

...THE FREE SAMPLES YOU GOT AT THE SHINIGAMI EQUIPMENT WORKSHOP.

THESE ARE THEIR EXTRA STOCK.

HUH.

LOUNGE LOUNGE

FLIP FLIP

YOU'LL BE ABLE TO CHASE THE GHOSTS FROM THIS HOUSE USING THOSE THINGS?

YEP.

BUT WHAT I HAVE TO CHASE OUT FIRST IS...

HM?!

FWOOOO

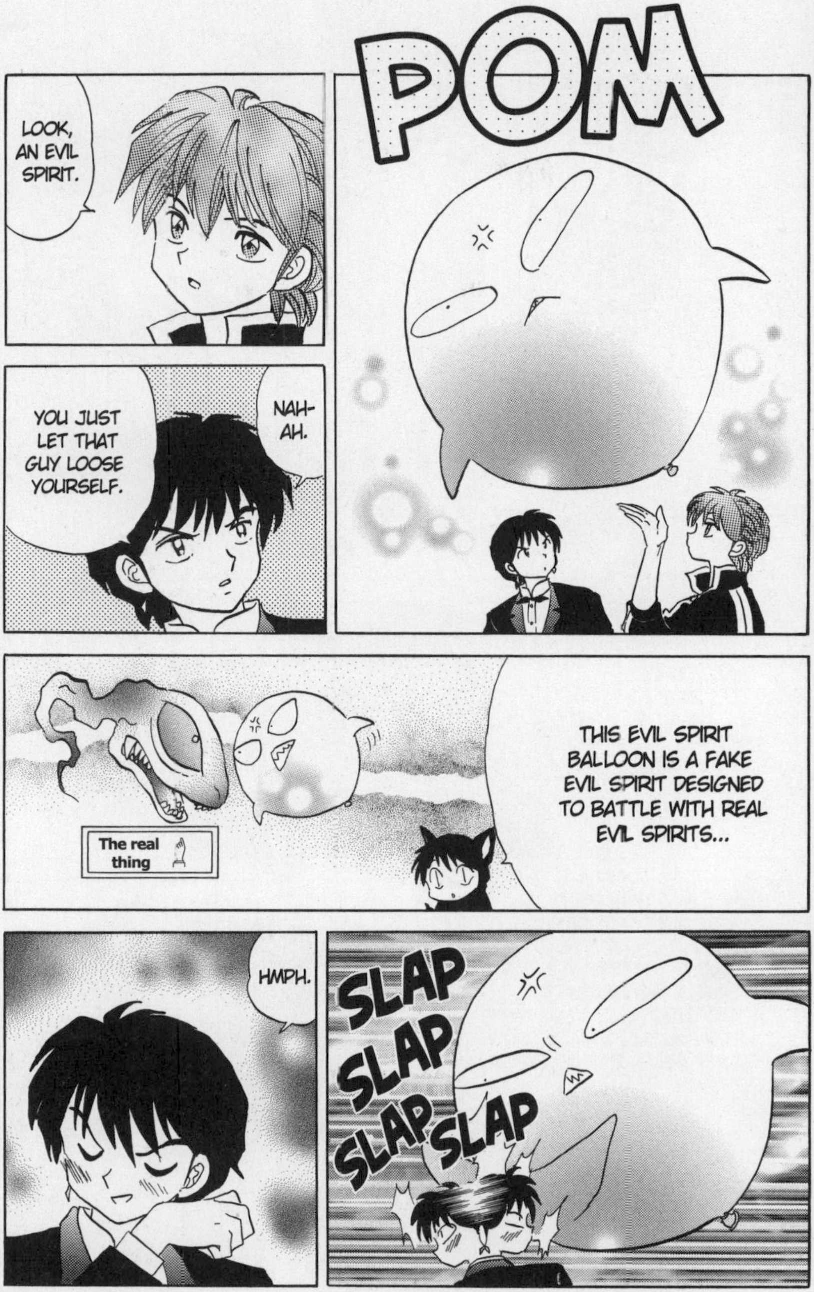
POM
LOOK, AN EVIL SPIRIT.
NAH-AH.
YOU JUST LET THAT GUY LOOSE YOURSELF.
THIS EVIL SPIRIT BALLOON IS A FAKE EVIL SPIRIT DESIGNED TO BATTLE WITH REAL EVIL SPIRITS...
The real thing
SLAP SLAP SLAP SLAP
HMPH.

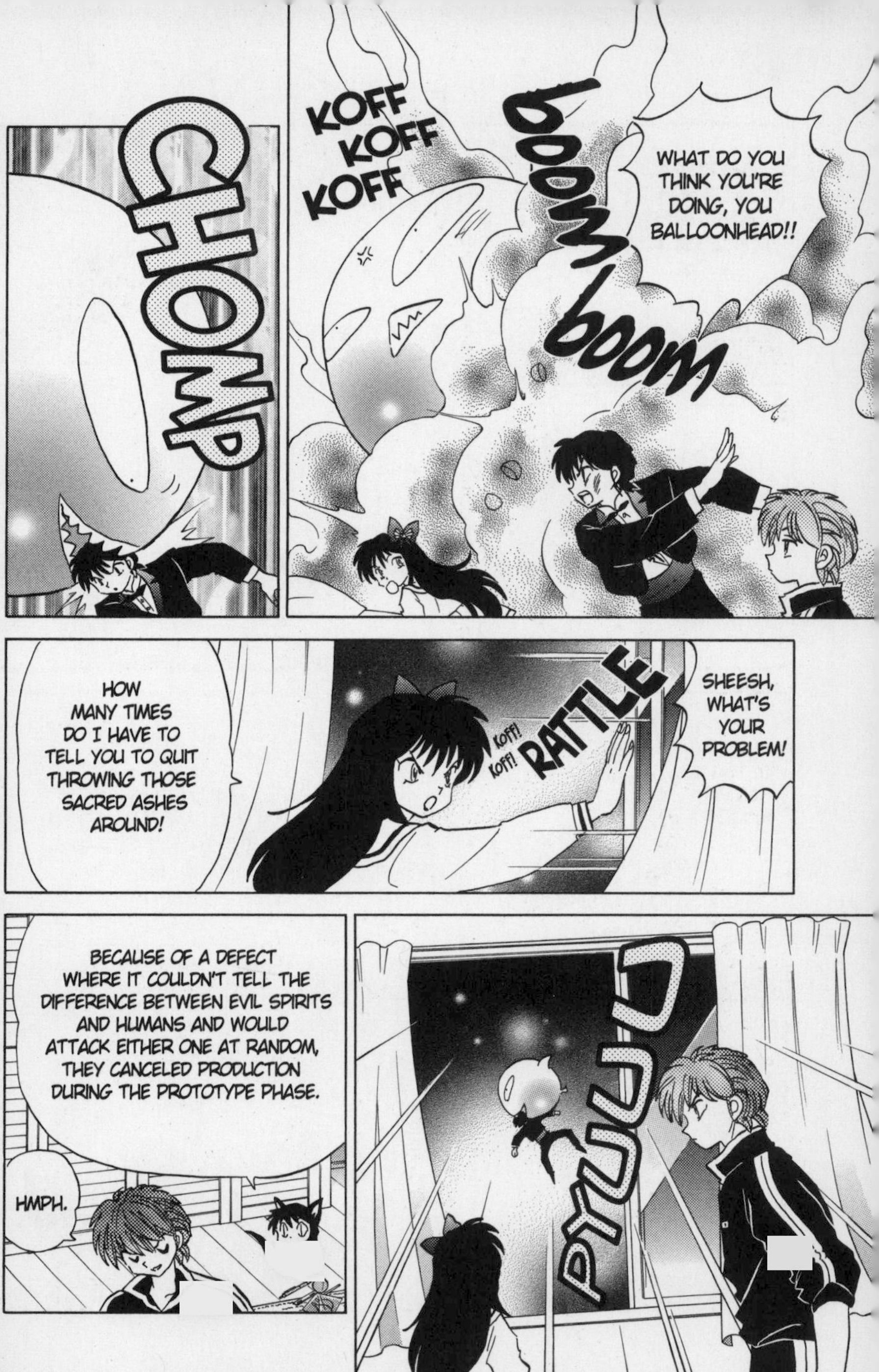
WHAT DO YOU THINK YOU'RE DOING, YOU BALLOONHEAD!!
boom boom
KOFF KOFF KOFF
CHOMP
SHEESH, WHAT'S YOUR PROBLEM!
RATTLE
Koff! Koff!
HOW MANY TIMES DO I HAVE TO TELL YOU TO QUIT THROWING THOSE SACRED ASHES AROUND!
PYUUU
BECAUSE OF A DEFECT WHERE IT COULDN'T TELL THE DIFFERENCE BETWEEN EVIL SPIRITS AND HUMANS AND WOULD ATTACK EITHER ONE AT RANDOM, THEY CANCELED PRODUCTION DURING THE PROTOTYPE PHASE.
HMPH.

GETTING RID OF JUMONJI FIRST WAS A SUCCESS. NEXT UP IS...
WE'RE ALONE NOW, RINNE.
HUG
KLATCH
...WHAT'RE YOU DOING?
STAAARE
SHE'S BACK SO SOON.
SAKURA MAMIYA, IT'S NOT WHAT YOU THINK...
YOU GOT CAUGHT RED-HANDED, DIDN'T YOU, RINNE-SAMA. AND IN SAKURA-SAMA'S ROOM, OF ALL PLACES!
I'D APPRECIATE IT IF YOU DID THAT ELSEWHERE.

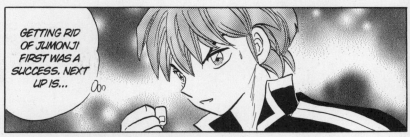

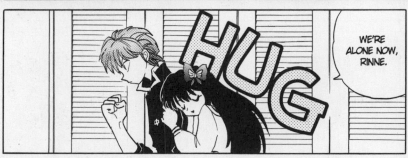

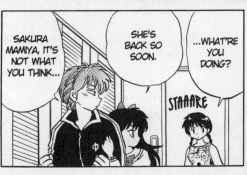

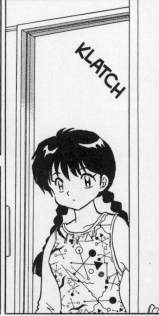

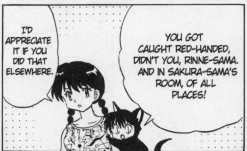

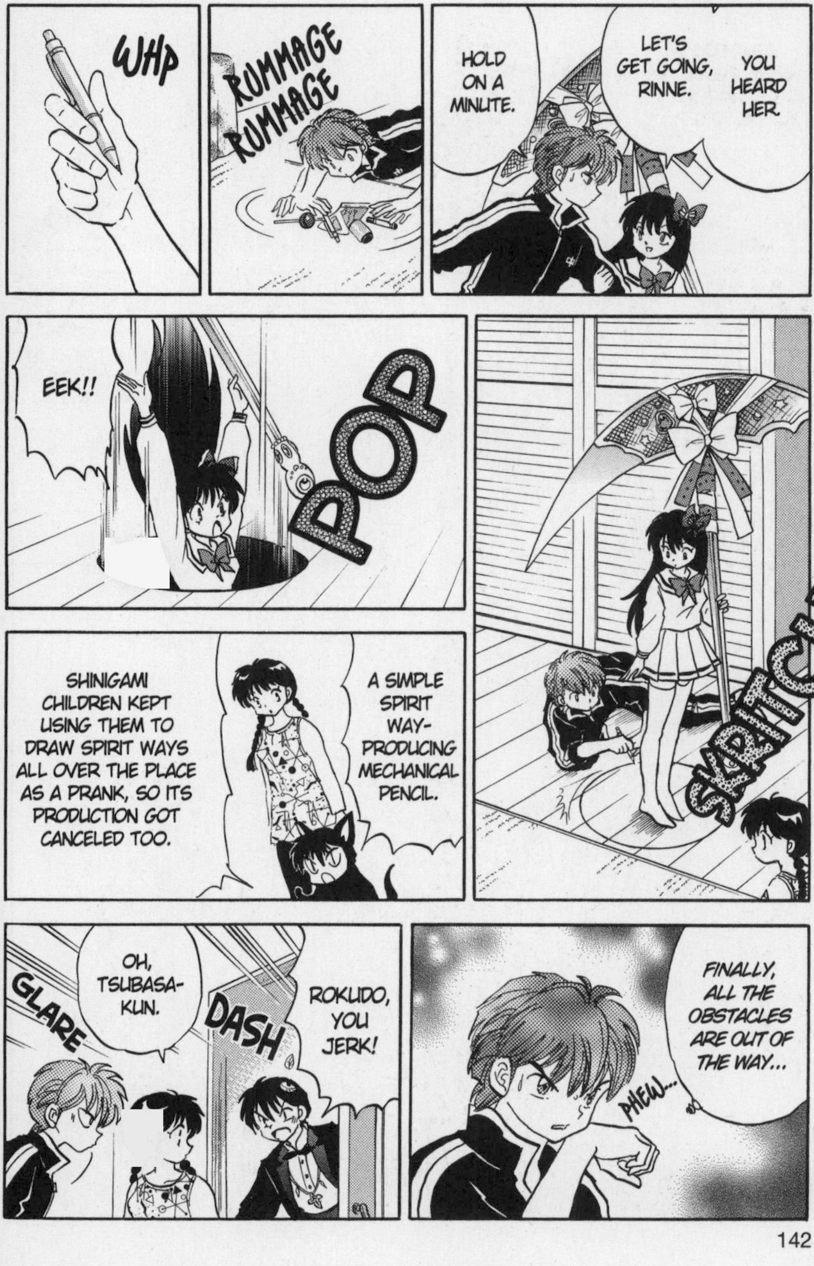
LET'S GET GOING, RINNE. YOU HEARD HER.
HOLD ON A MINUTE.
RUMMAGE RUMMAGE
WHP
SKRITCH
EEK!!
POP
A SIMPLE SPIRIT WAY-PRODUCING MECHANICAL PENCIL.
SHINIGAMI CHILDREN KEPT USING THEM TO DRAW SPIRIT WAYS ALL OVER THE PLACE AS A PRANK, SO ITS PRODUCTION GOT CANCELED TOO.
FINALLY, ALL THE OBSTACLES ARE OUT OF THE WAY...
PHEW...
ROKUDO, YOU JERK!
DASH
OH, TSUBASA-KUN.
GLARE

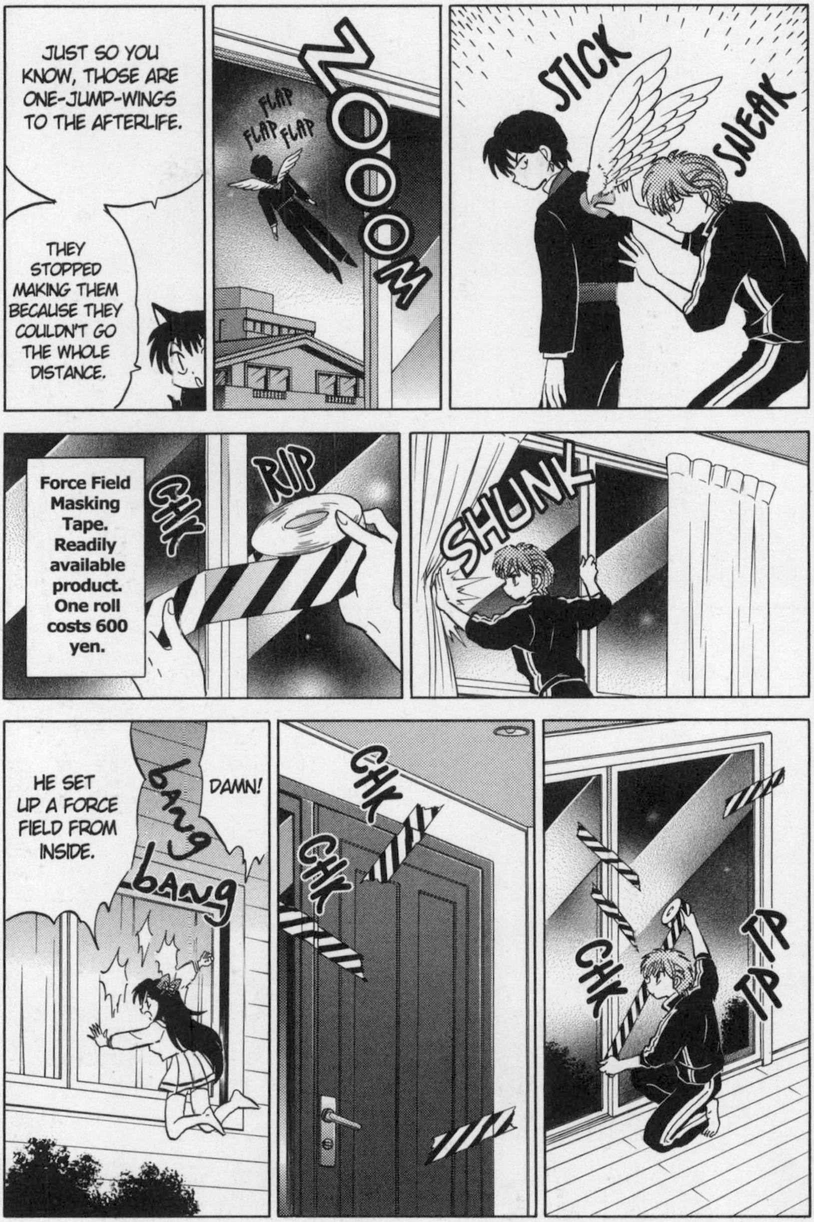
STICK
SNEAK
ZOOOM
FLAP FLAP FLAP
JUST SO YOU KNOW, THOSE ARE ONE-JUMP-WINGS TO THE AFTERLIFE.
THEY STOPPED MAKING THEM BECAUSE THEY COULDN'T GO THE WHOLE DISTANCE.
SHUNK
RIP
CHK
Force Field Masking Tape. Readily available product. One roll costs 600 yen.
TP TP
CHK
CHK
CHK
DAMN!
bang bang bang
HE SET UP A FORCE FIELD FROM INSIDE.

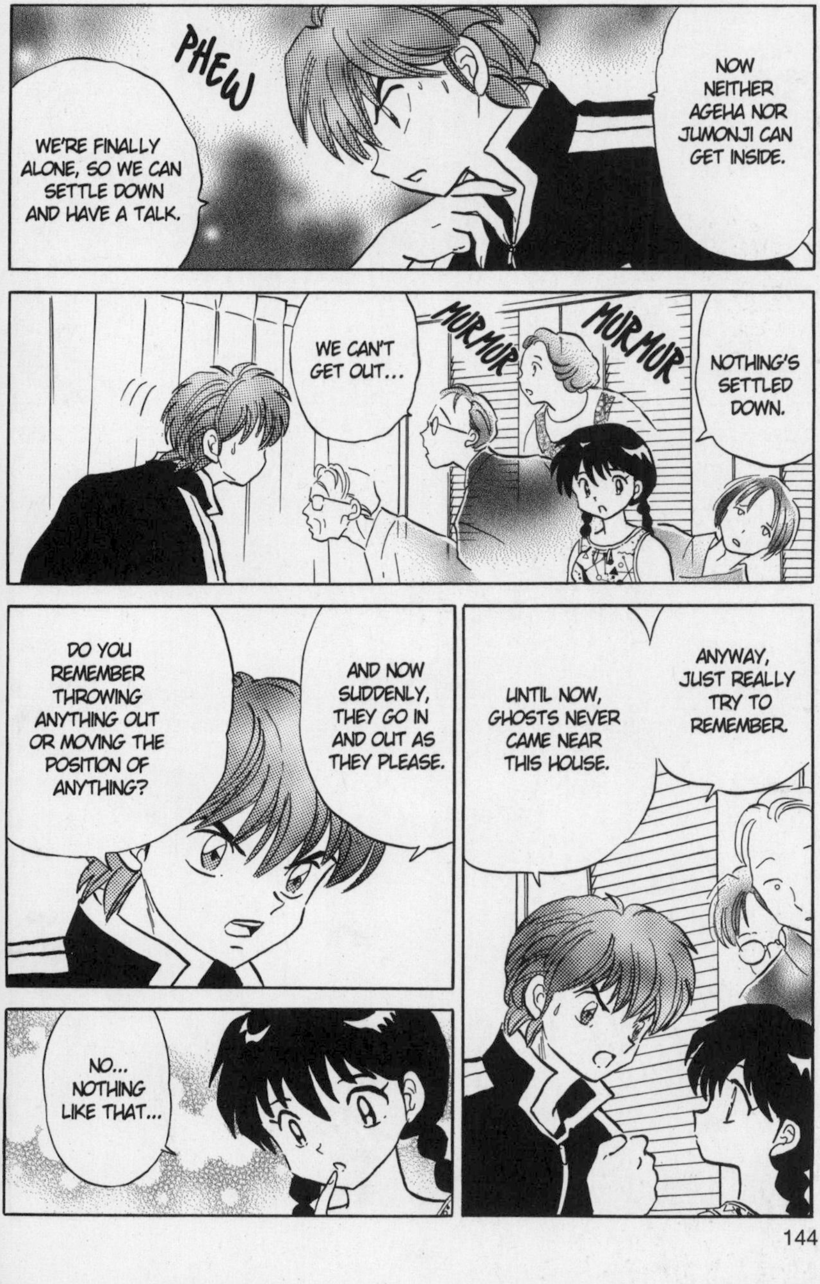
NOW NEITHER AGEHA NOR JUMONJI CAN GET INSIDE.
PHEW
WE'RE FINALLY ALONE, SO WE CAN SETTLE DOWN AND HAVE A TALK.
NOTHING'S SETTLED DOWN.
MURMUR
MURMUR
WE CAN'T GET OUT...
ANYWAY, JUST REALLY TRY TO REMEMBER.
UNTIL NOW, GHOSTS NEVER CAME NEAR THIS HOUSE.
AND NOW SUDDENLY, THEY GO IN AND OUT AS THEY PLEASE.
DO YOU REMEMBER THROWING ANYTHING OUT OR MOVING THE POSITION OF ANYTHING?
NO... NOTHING LIKE THAT...

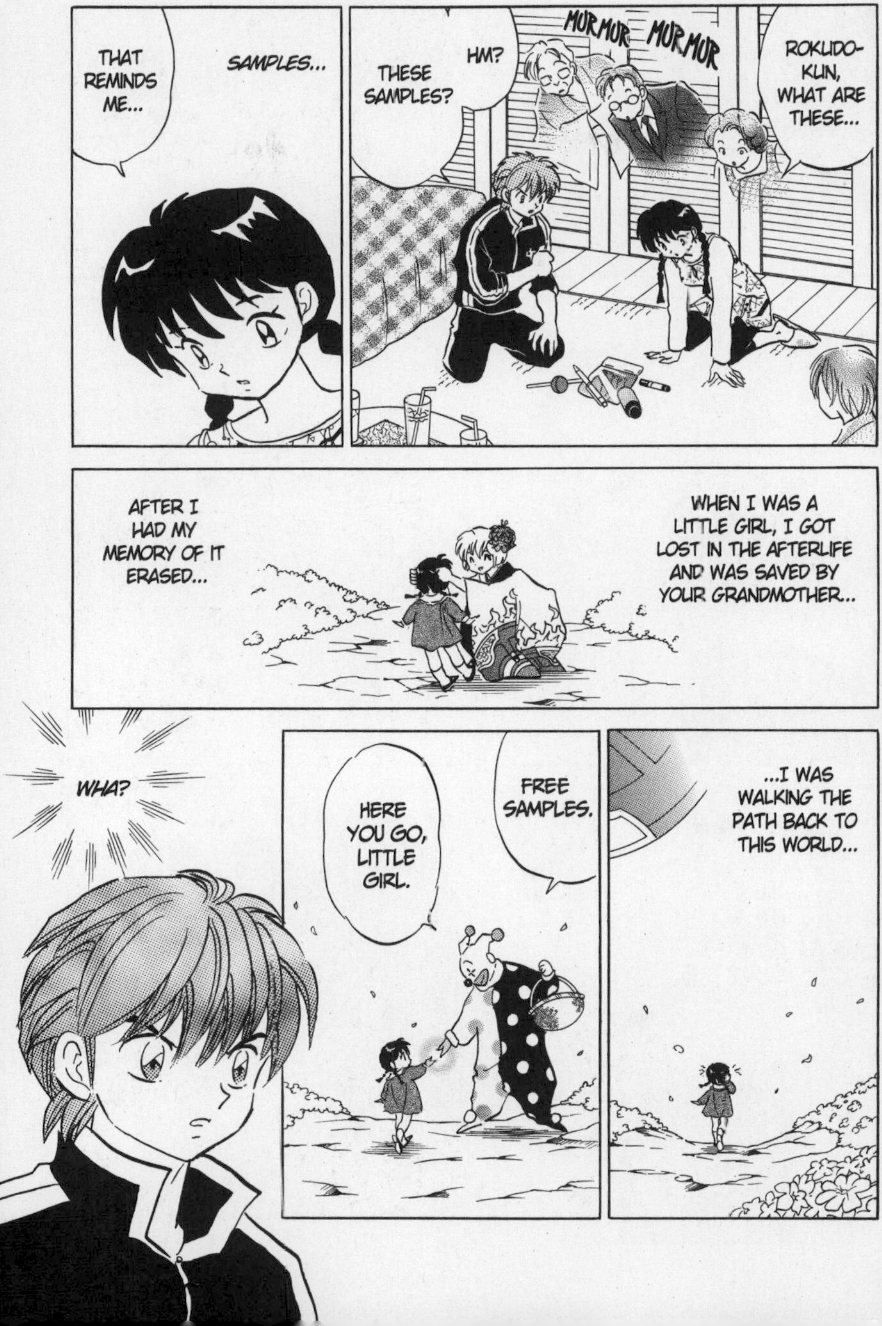
MURMUR MURMUR
ROKUDO-KUN, WHAT ARE THESE...
HM?
THESE SAMPLES?
SAMPLES...
THAT REMINDS ME...
WHEN I WAS A LITTLE GIRL, I GOT LOST IN THE AFTERLIFE AND WAS SAVED BY YOUR GRANDMOTHER...
AFTER I HAD MY MEMORY OF IT ERASED...
...I WAS WALKING THE PATH BACK TO THIS WORLD...
FREE SAMPLES.
HERE YOU GO, LITTLE GIRL.
WHA?

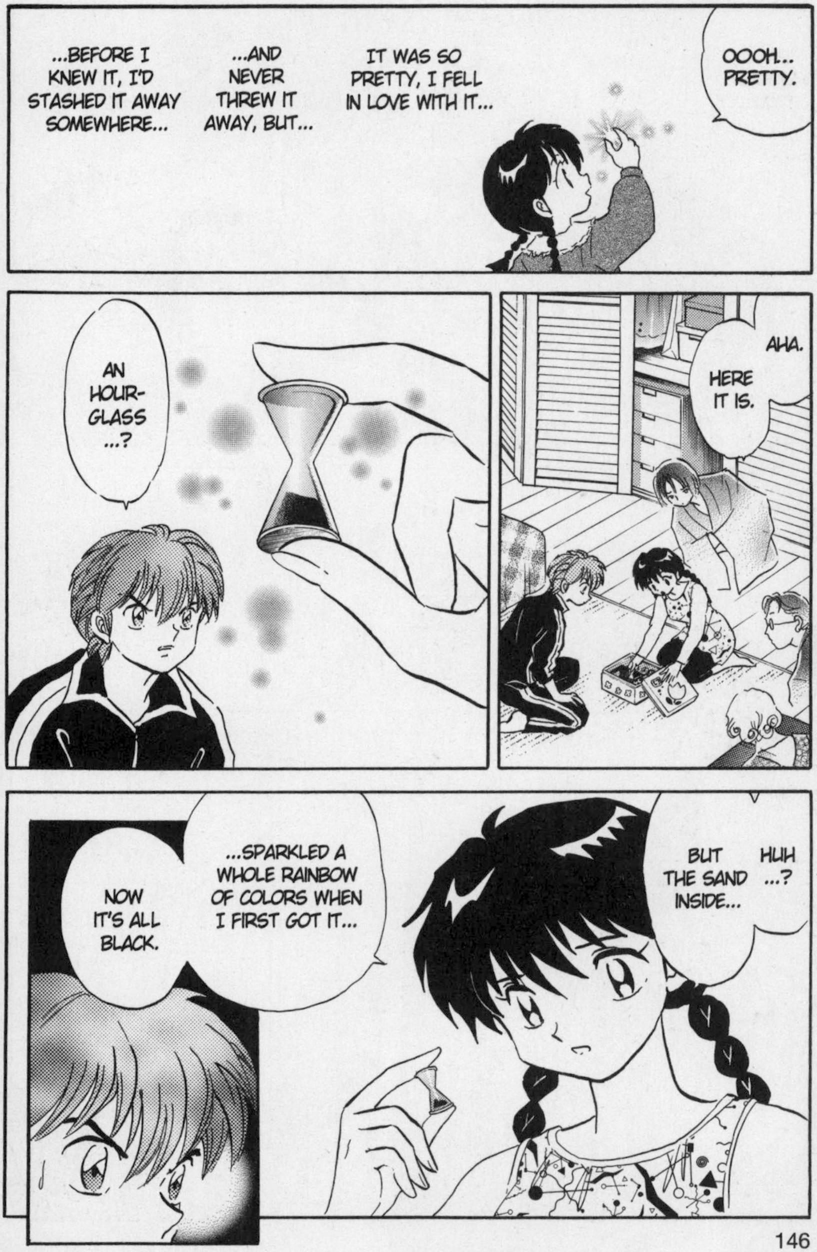
OOOH... PRETTY.
IT WAS SO PRETTY, I FELL IN LOVE WITH IT...
...AND NEVER THREW IT AWAY, BUT...
...BEFORE I KNEW IT, I'D STASHED IT AWAY SOMEWHERE...
AHA.
HERE IT IS.
AN HOUR-GLASS ...?
HUH ...?
BUT THE SAND INSIDE...
...SPARKLED A WHOLE RAINBOW OF COLORS WHEN I FIRST GOT IT...
NOW IT'S ALL BLACK.

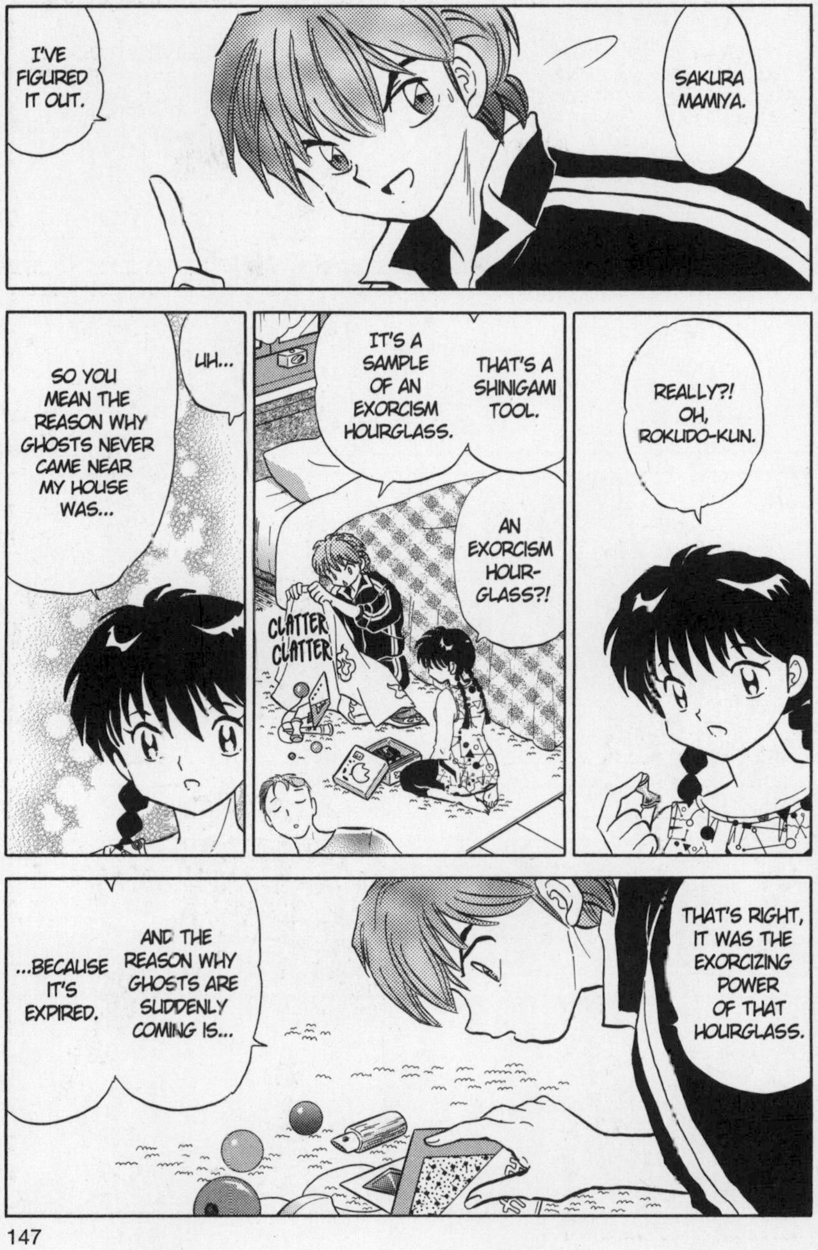
SAKURA MAMIYA.
I'VE FIGURED IT OUT.
REALLY?! OH, ROKUDO-KUN.
THAT'S A SHINIGAMI TOOL.
IT'S A SAMPLE OF AN EXORCISM HOURGLASS.
AN EXORCISM HOUR-GLASS?!
CLATTER CLATTER
UH...
SO YOU MEAN THE REASON WHY GHOSTS NEVER CAME NEAR MY HOUSE WAS...
THAT'S RIGHT, IT WAS THE EXORCIZING POWER OF THAT HOURGLASS.
AND THE REASON WHY GHOSTS ARE SUDDENLY COMING IS...
...BECAUSE IT'S EXPIRED.

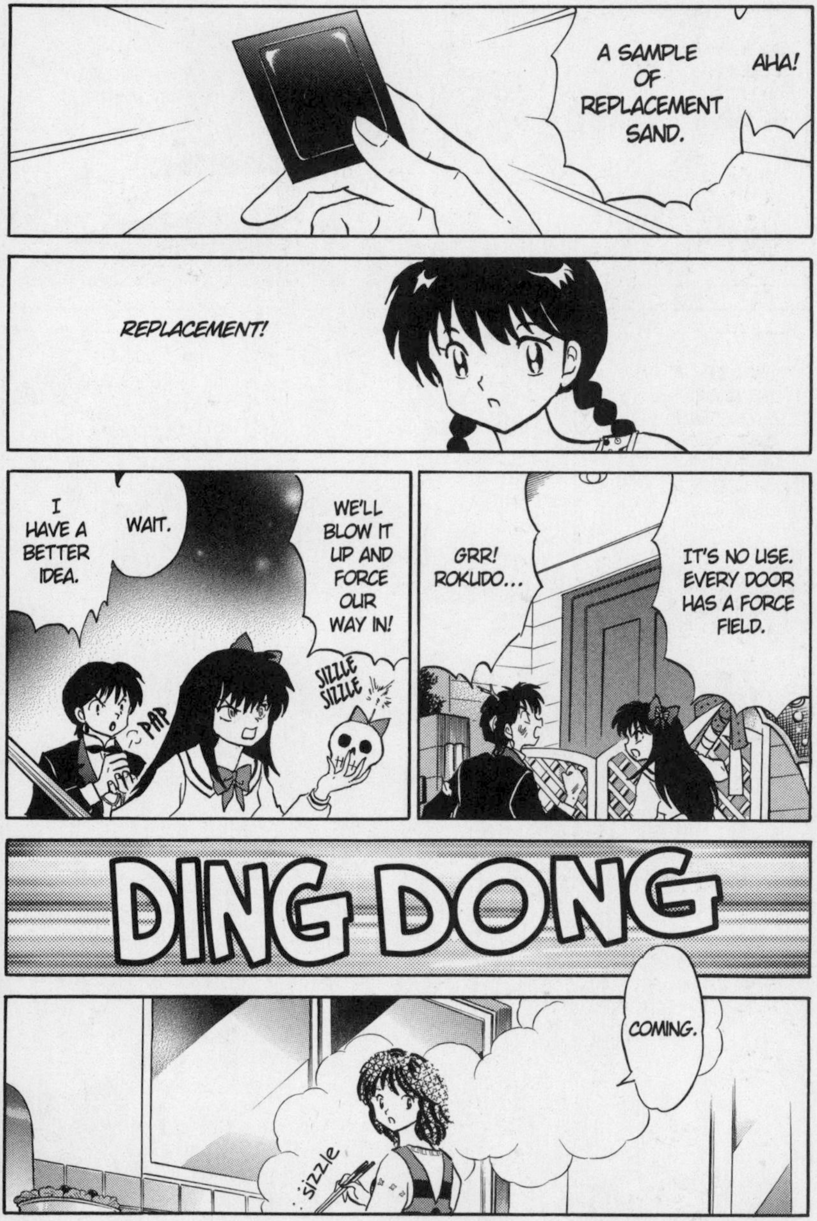
AHA!
A SAMPLE OF REPLACEMENT SAND.
REPLACEMENT!
IT'S NO USE. EVERY DOOR HAS A FORCE FIELD.
GRR! ROKUDO...
WE'LL BLOW IT UP AND FORCE OUR WAY IN!
SIZZLE SIZZLE
WAIT.
I HAVE A BETTER IDEA.
PAP
DING DONG
COMING.
sizzle

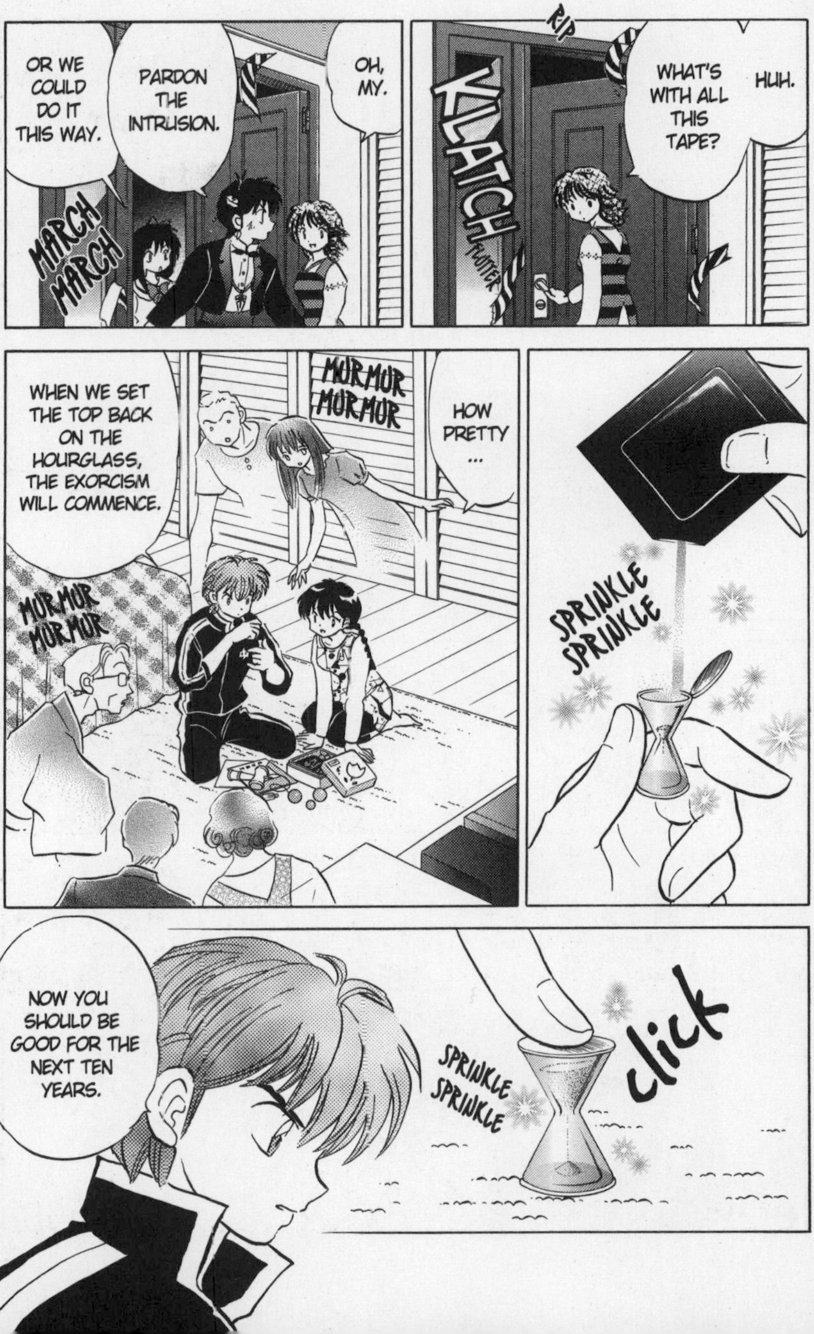
HUH.
WHAT'S WITH ALL THIS TAPE?
RIP
KLATCH
FLUTTER
OH, MY.
PARDON THE INTRUSION.
OR WE COULD DO IT THIS WAY.
MARCH MARCH
SPRINKLE SPRINKLE
HOW PRETTY ...
MURMUR MURMUR
WHEN WE SET THE TOP BACK ON THE HOURGLASS, THE EXORCISM WILL COMMENCE.
MURMUR MURMUR
click
SPRINKLE SPRINKLE
NOW YOU SHOULD BE GOOD FOR THE NEXT TEN YEARS.

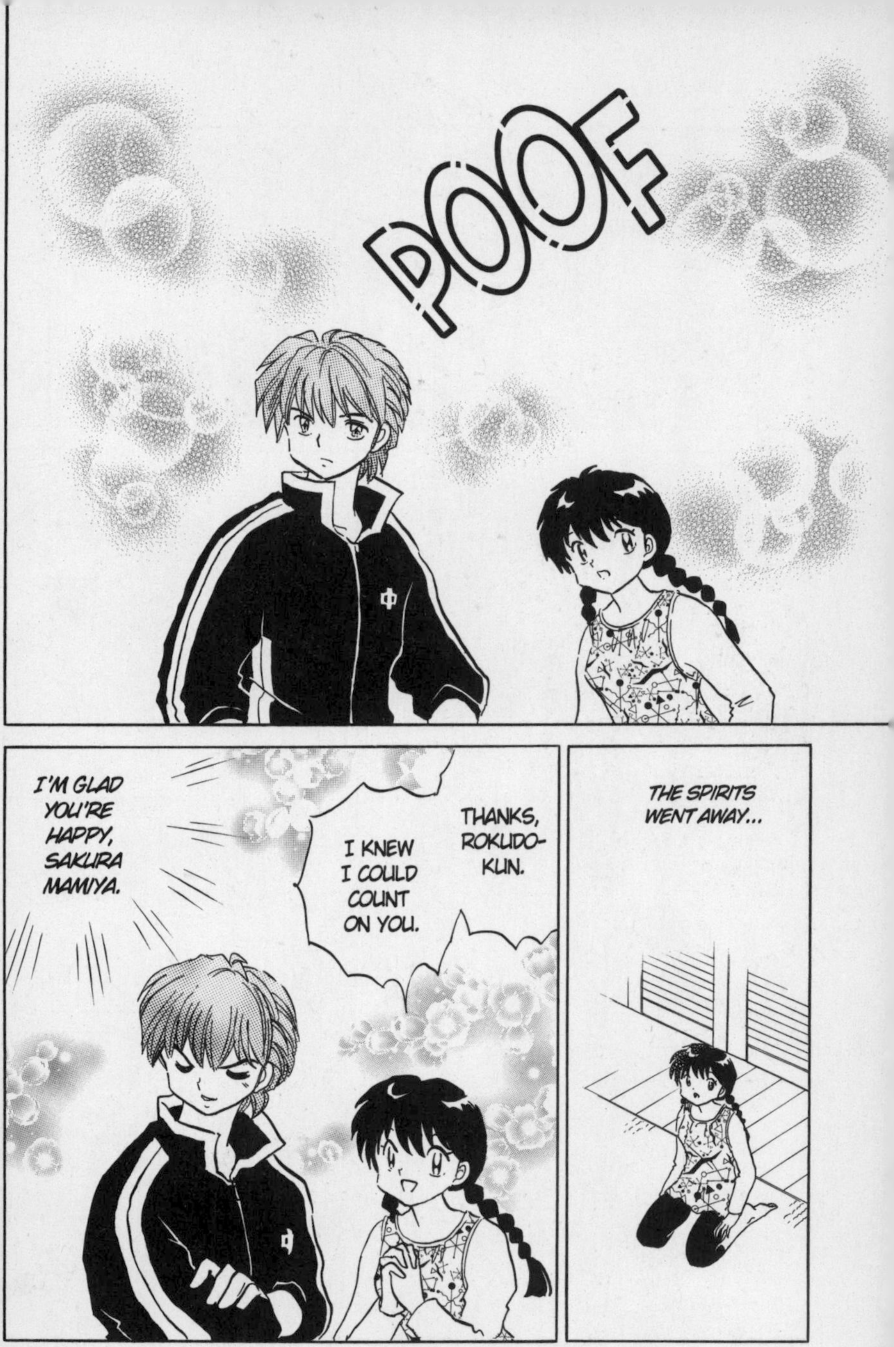
POOF
THE SPIRITS WENT AWAY...
THANKS, ROKUDO-KUN.
I KNEW I COULD COUNT ON YOU.
I'M GLAD YOU'RE HAPPY, SAKURA MAMIYA.

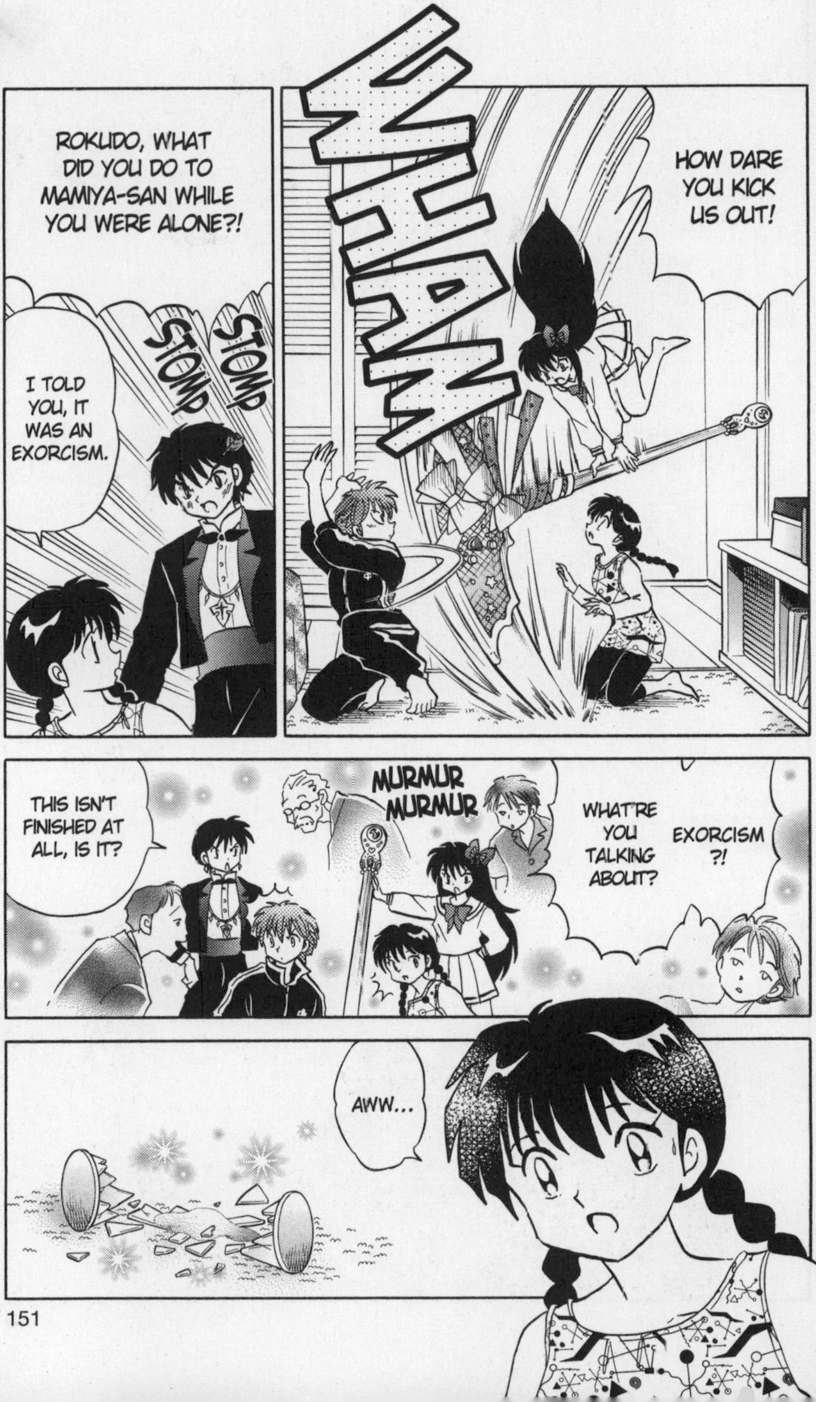
WHAM
HOW DARE YOU KICK US OUT!
ROKUDO, WHAT DID YOU DO TO MAMIYA-SAN WHILE YOU WERE ALONE?!
STOMP STOMP
I TOLD YOU, IT WAS AN EXORCISM.
EXORCISM ?!
WHAT'RE YOU TALKING ABOUT?
MURMUR MURMUR
THIS ISN'T FINISHED AT ALL, IS IT?
AWW...

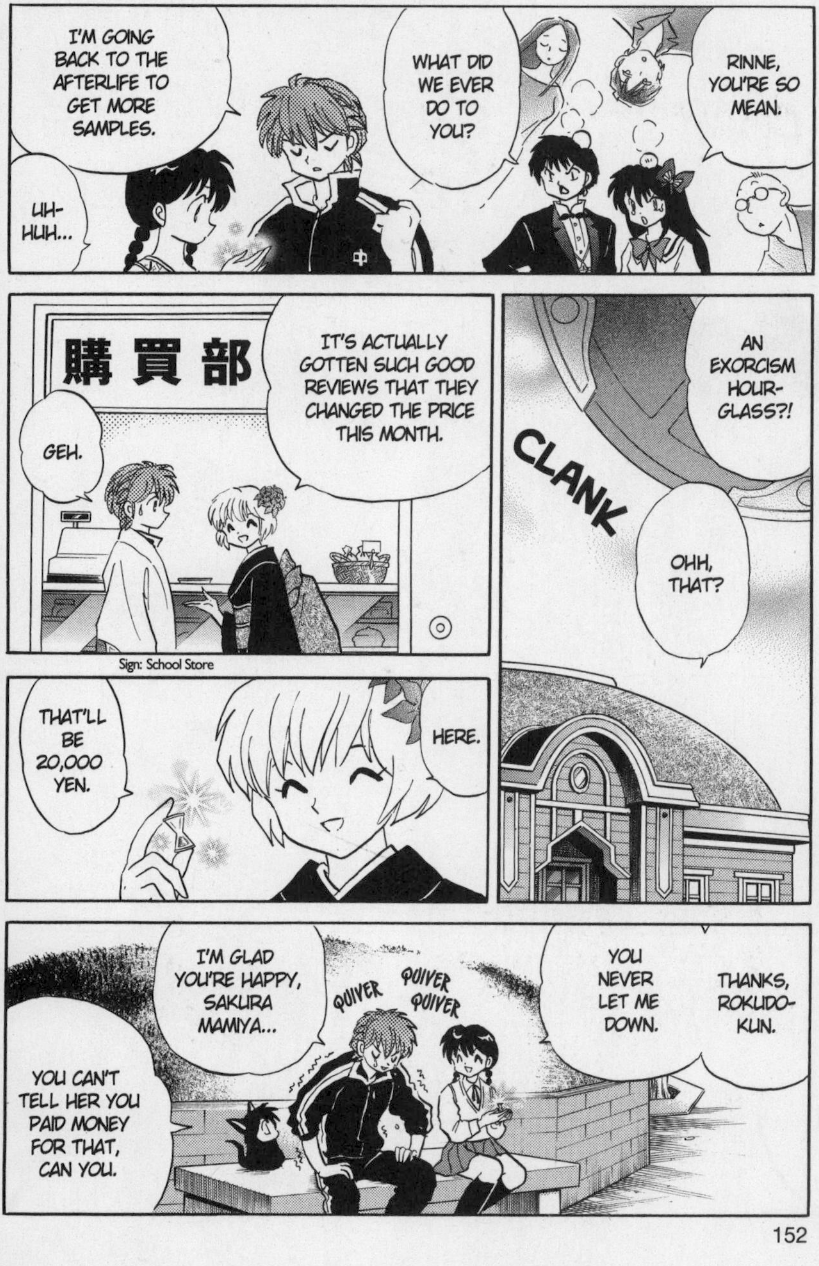

RINNE, YOU'RE SO MEAN.
WHAT DID WE EVER DO TO YOU?
I'M GOING BACK TO THE AFTERLIFE TO GET MORE SAMPLES.
UH-HUH...
AN EXORCISM HOUR-GLASS?!
CLANK
OHH, THAT?
IT'S ACTUALLY GOTTEN SUCH GOOD REVIEWS THAT THEY CHANGED THE PRICE THIS MONTH.
購買部
GEH.
Sign: School Store
HERE.
THAT'LL BE 20,000 YEN.
THANKS, ROKUDO-KUN.
YOU NEVER LET ME DOWN.
QUIVER QUIVER
QUIVER
I'M GLAD YOU'RE HAPPY, SAKURA MAMIYA...
YOU CAN'T TELL HER YOU PAID MONEY FOR THAT, CAN YOU.

CHAPTER 67: THE HORTICULTURE CLUB INCIDENT

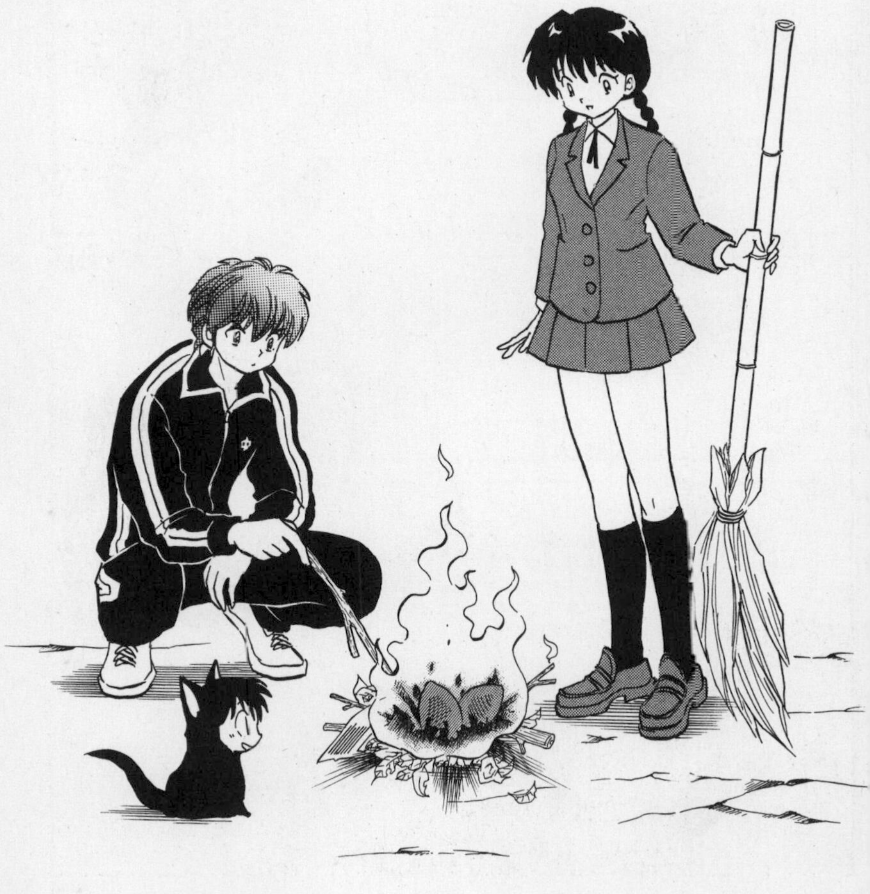

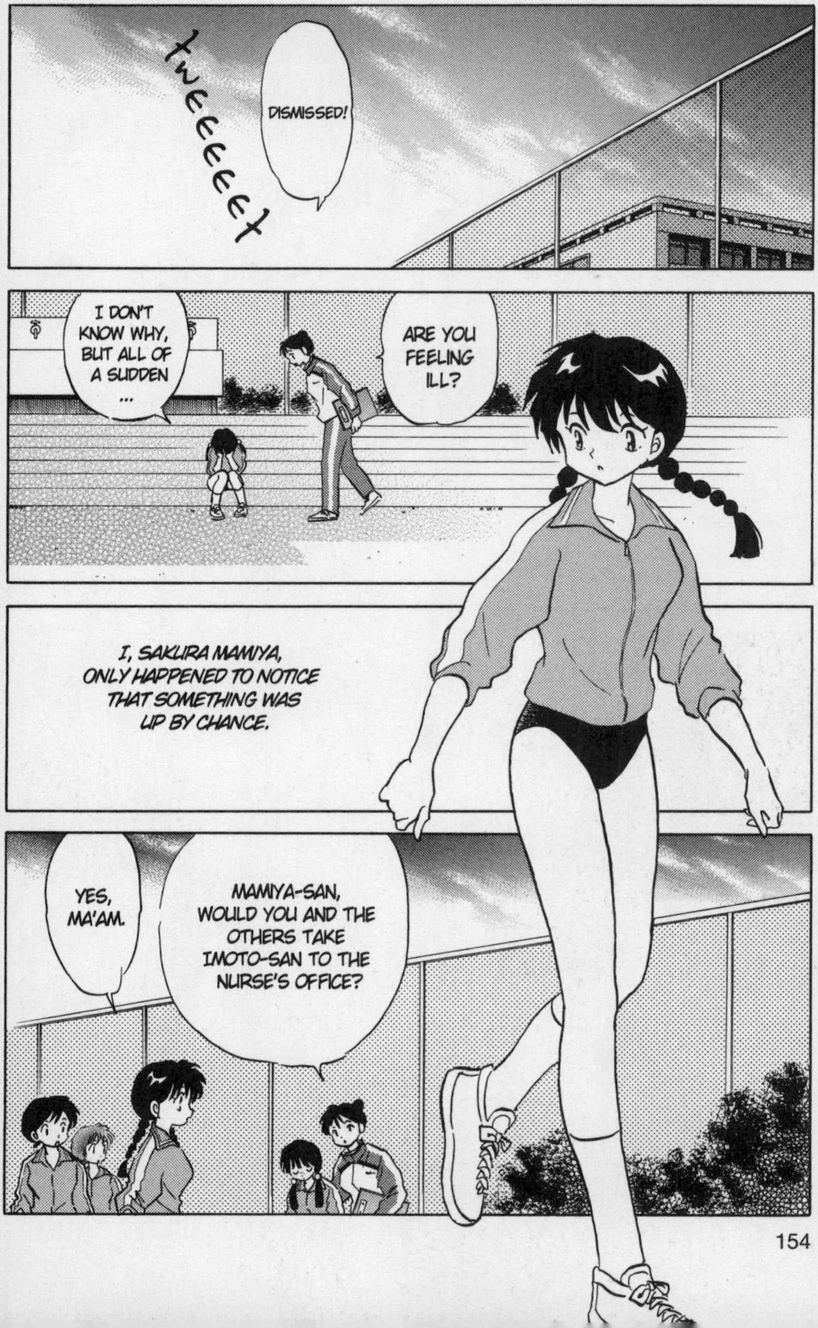
DISMISSED!
tweeeeet
ARE YOU FEELING ILL?
I DON'T KNOW WHY, BUT ALL OF A SUDDEN ...
I, SAKURA MAMIYA, ONLY HAPPENED TO NOTICE THAT SOMETHING WAS UP BY CHANCE.
MAMIYA-SAN, WOULD YOU AND THE OTHERS TAKE IMOTO-SAN TO THE NURSE'S OFFICE?
YES, MA'AM.

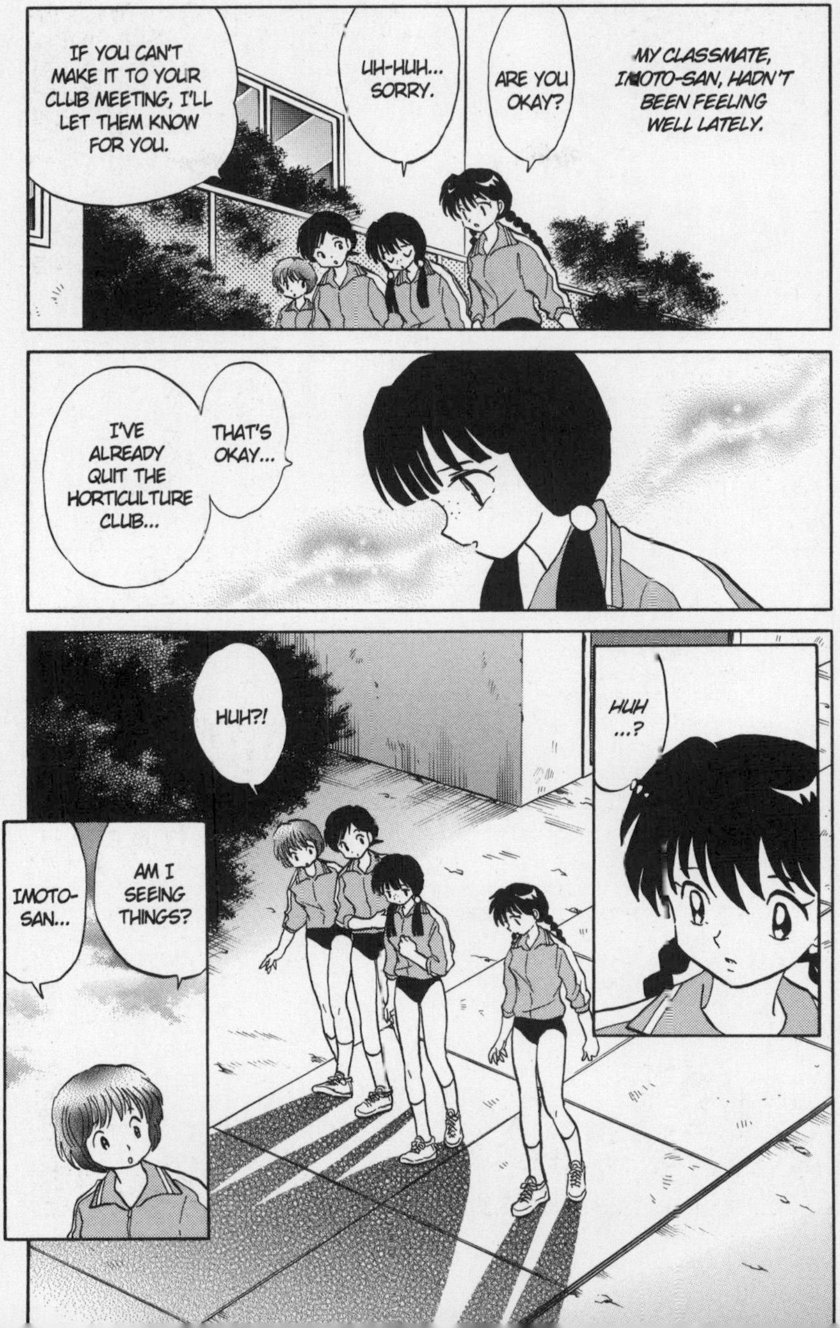
MY CLASSMATE, IMOTO-SAN, HADN'T BEEN FEELING WELL LATELY.
ARE YOU OKAY?
UH-HUH... SORRY.
IF YOU CAN'T MAKE IT TO YOUR CLUB MEETING, I'LL LET THEM KNOW FOR YOU.
THAT'S OKAY...
I'VE ALREADY QUIT THE HORTICULTURE CLUB...
HUH ...?
HUH?!
AM I SEEING THINGS?
IMOTO-SAN...

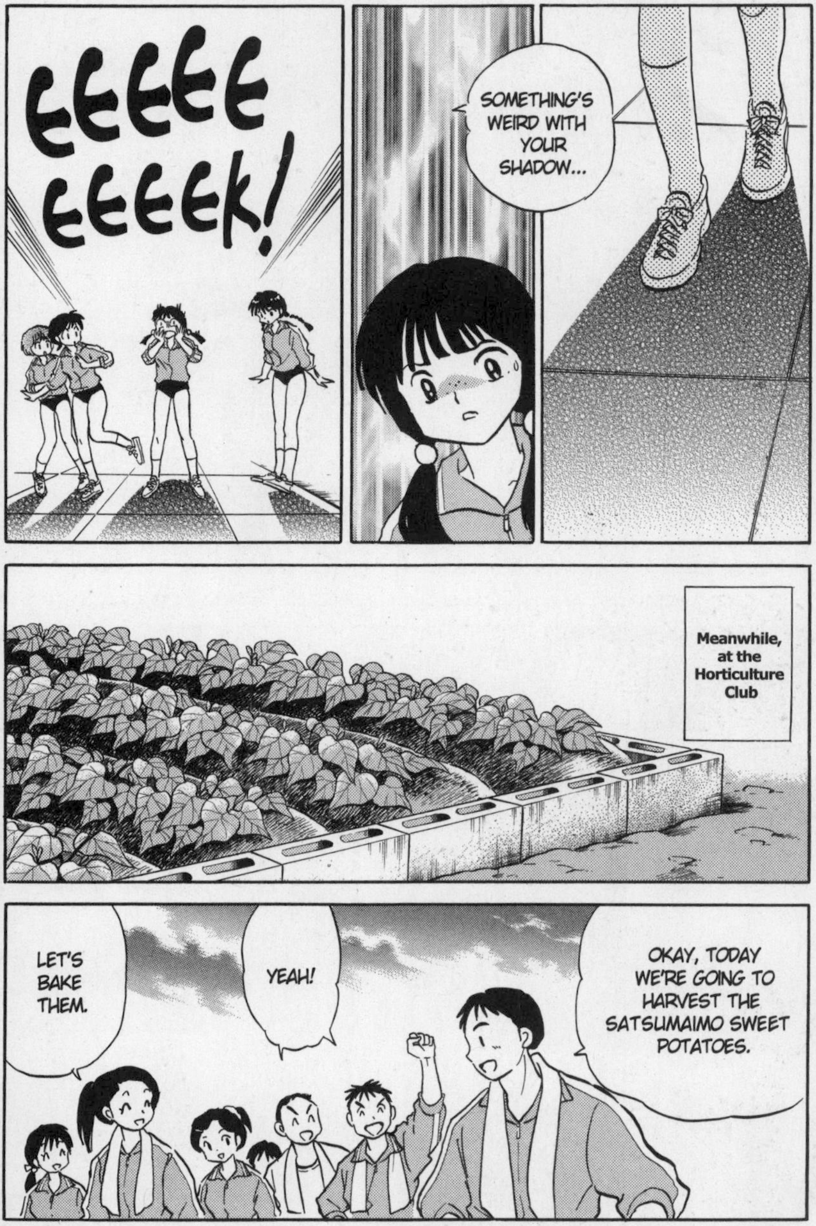
SOMETHING'S WEIRD WITH YOUR SHADOW...
EEEEEE EEEEEK!
Meanwhile, at the Horticulture Club
OKAY, TODAY WE'RE GOING TO HARVEST THE SATSUMAIMO SWEET POTATOES.
YEAH!
LET'S BAKE THEM.

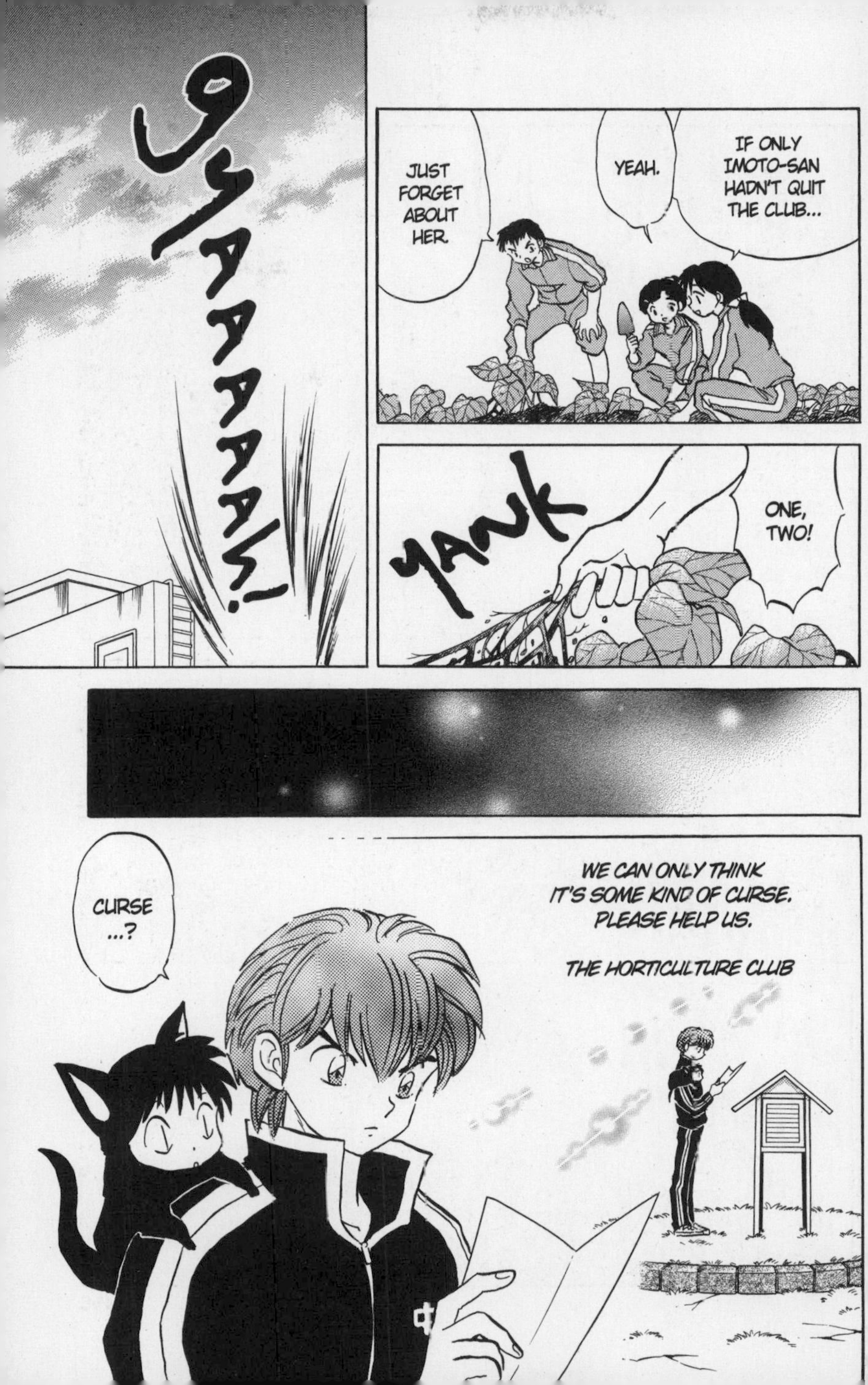
IF ONLY IMOTO-SAN HADN'T QUIT THE CLUB...
YEAH.
JUST FORGET ABOUT HER.
ONE, TWO!
YANK
GYAAAAAH!
WE CAN ONLY THINK IT'S SOME KIND OF CURSE. PLEASE HELP US.
THE HORTICULTURE CLUB
CURSE ...?

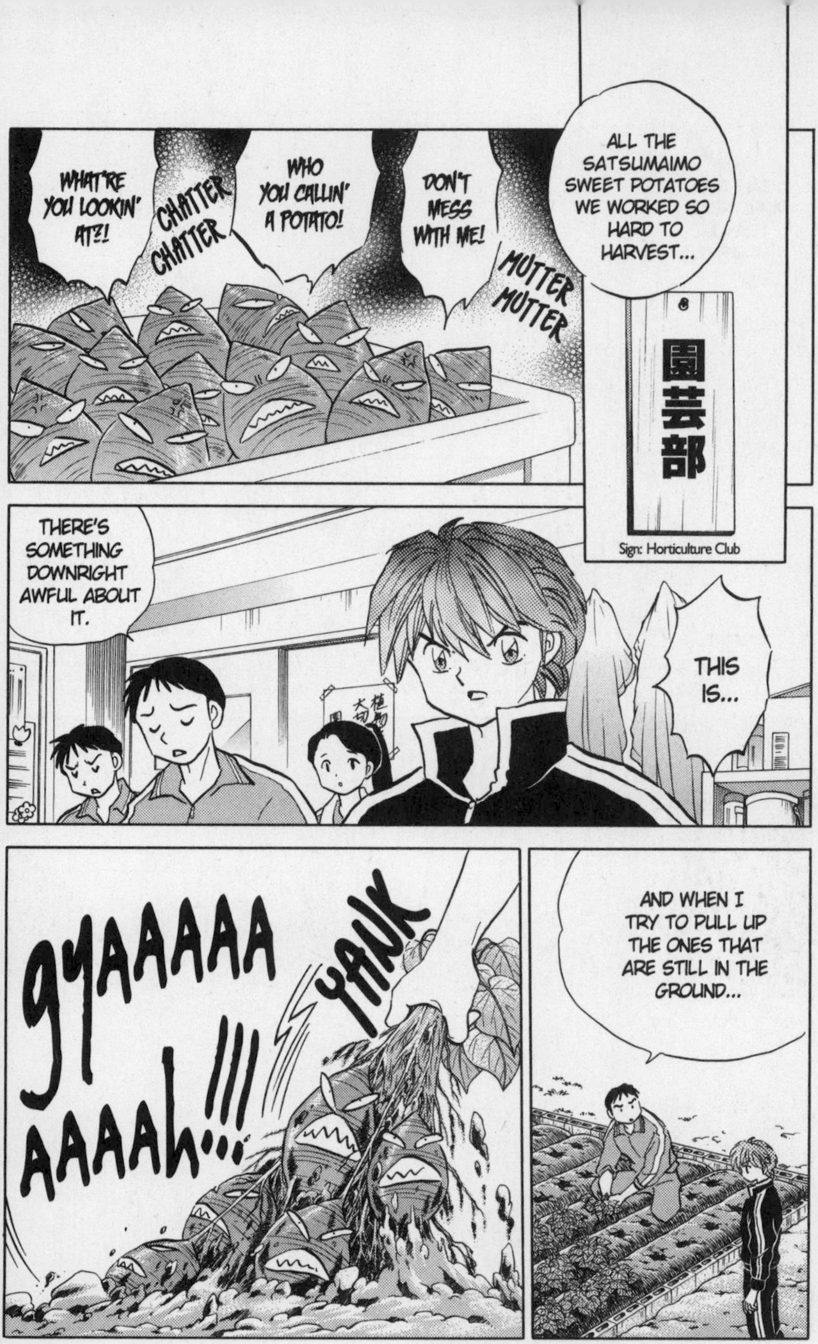
ALL THE SATSUMAIMO SWEET POTATOES WE WORKED SO HARD TO HARVEST...
園芸部
Sign: Horticulture Club
MUTTER MUTTER
DON'T MESS WITH ME!
WHO YOU CALLIN' A POTATO!
CHATTER CHATTER
WHAT'RE YOU LOOKIN' AT?!
THIS IS...
THERE'S SOMETHING DOWNRIGHT AWFUL ABOUT IT.
AND WHEN I TRY TO PULL UP THE ONES THAT ARE STILL IN THE GROUND...
YANK
GYAAAAAAAAAAH!!!

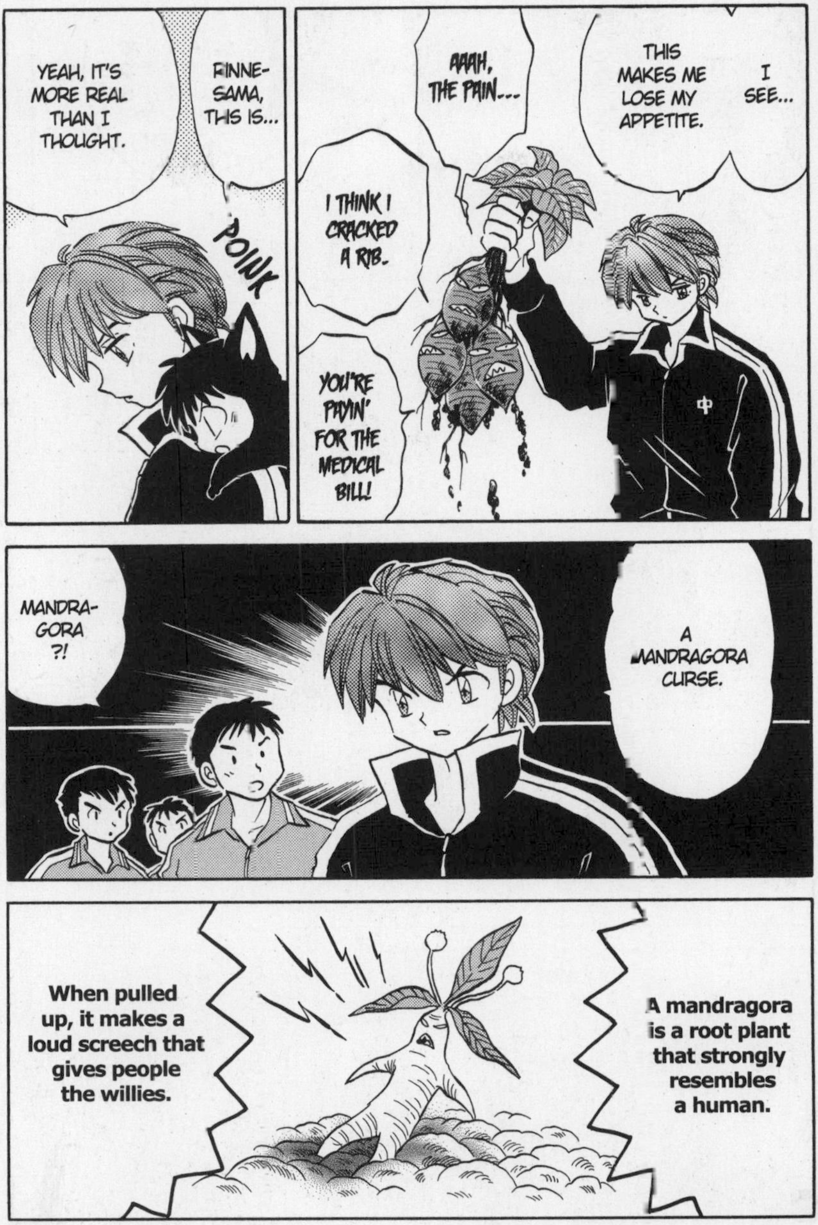
I SEE...
THIS MAKES ME LOSE MY APPETITE.
AAAH, THE PAIN...
I THINK I CRACKED A RIB.
YOU'RE PAYIN' FOR THE MEDICAL BILL!
RINNE-SAMA, THIS IS...
POINK
YEAH, IT'S MORE REAL THAN I THOUGHT.
A MANDRAGORA CURSE.
MANDRA-GORA?!
A mandragora is a root plant that strongly resembles a human.
When pulled up, it makes a loud screech that gives people the willies.

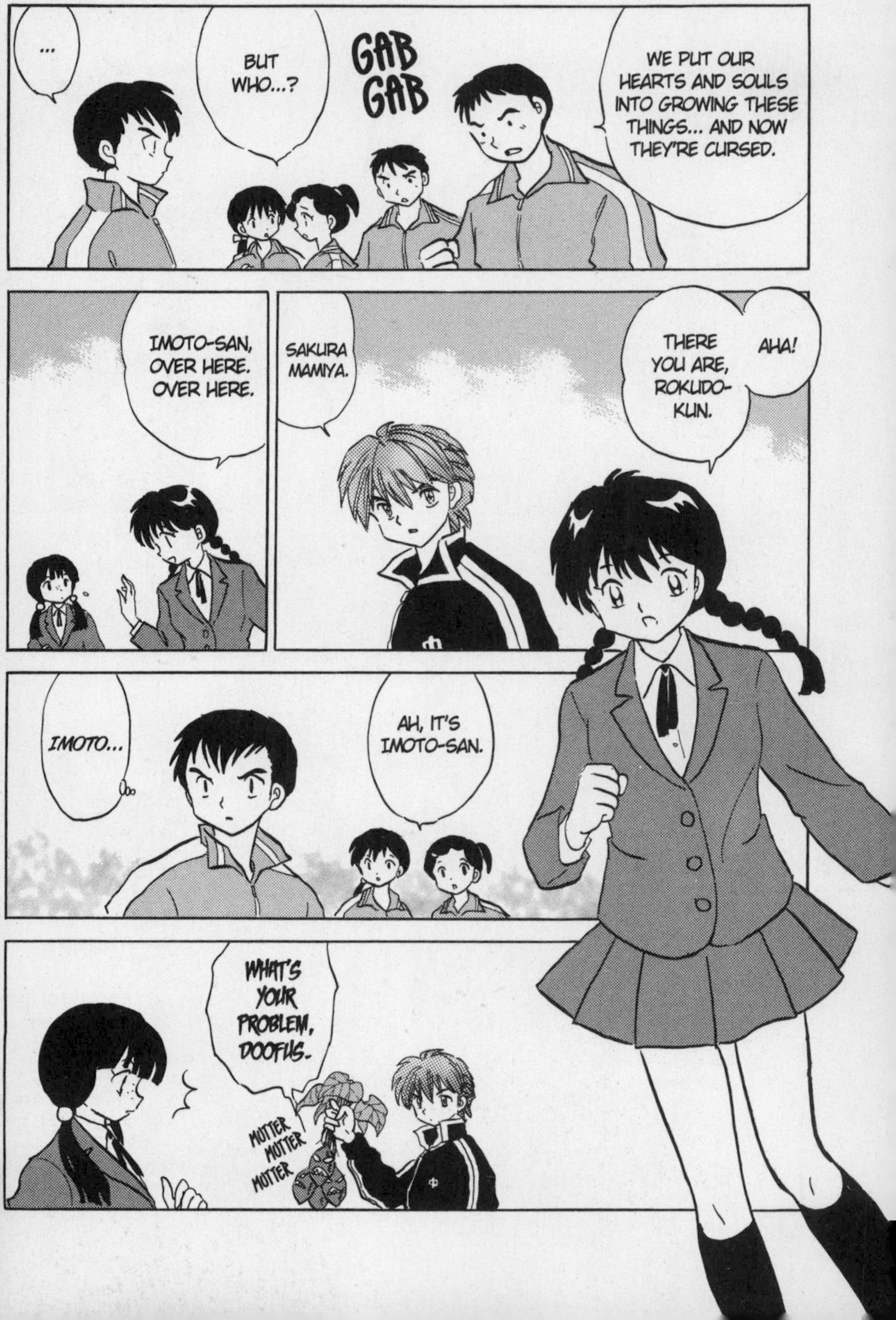
WE PUT OUR HEARTS AND SOULS INTO GROWING THESE THINGS... AND NOW THEY'RE CURSED.
GAB GAB
BUT WHO...?
...
AHA!
THERE YOU ARE, ROKUDO-KUN.
SAKURA MAMIYA.
IMOTO-SAN, OVER HERE. OVER HERE.
AH, IT'S IMOTO-SAN.
IMOTO...
WHAT'S YOUR PROBLEM, DOOFUS.
MOTTER MOTTER MOTTER

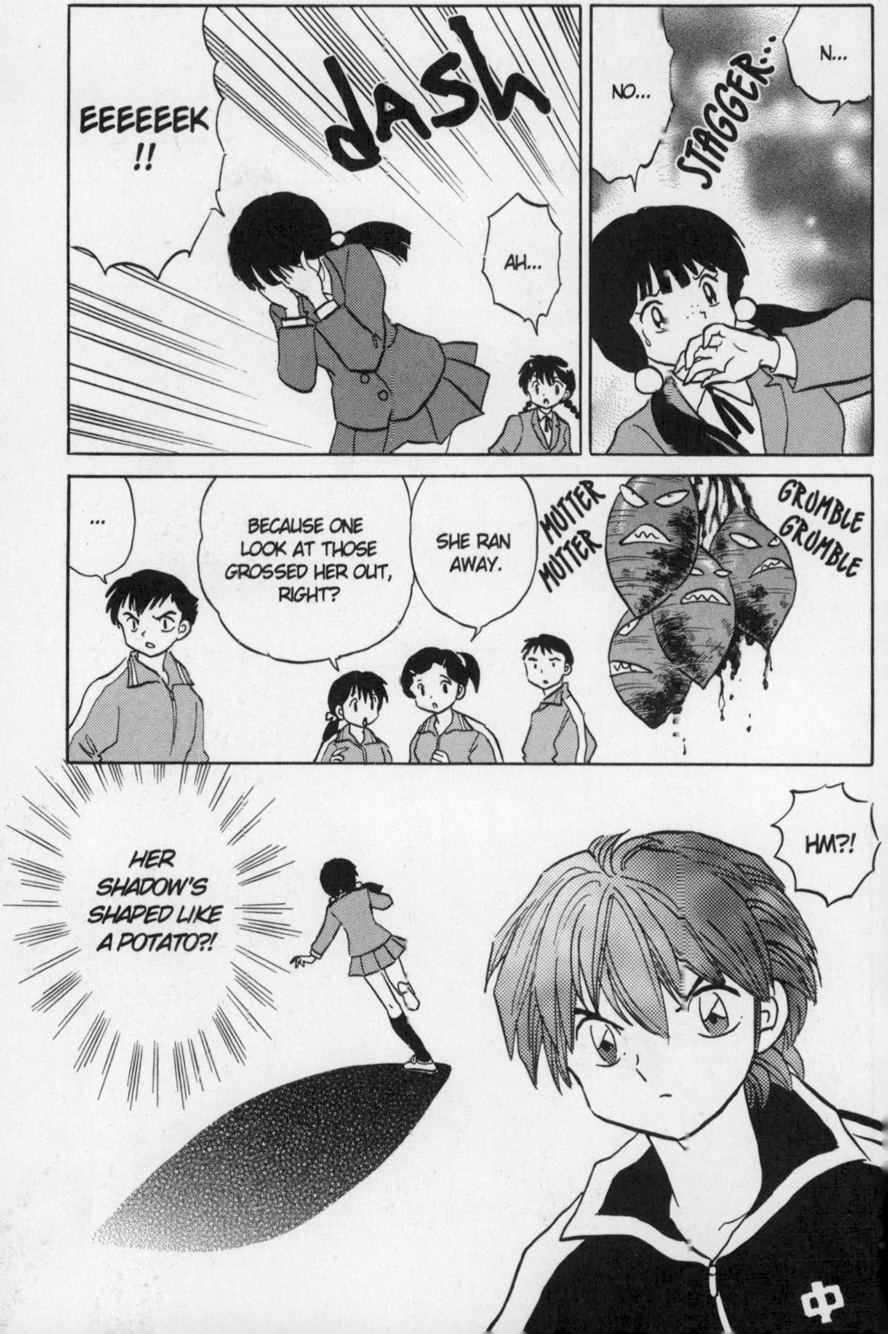
N...
STAGGER...
NO...
EEEEEEK !!
dash
AH...
GRUMBLE GRUMBLE
MUTTER MUTTER
SHE RAN AWAY.
BECAUSE ONE LOOK AT THOSE GROSSED HER OUT, RIGHT?
...
HM?!
HER SHADOW'S SHAPED LIKE A POTATO?!

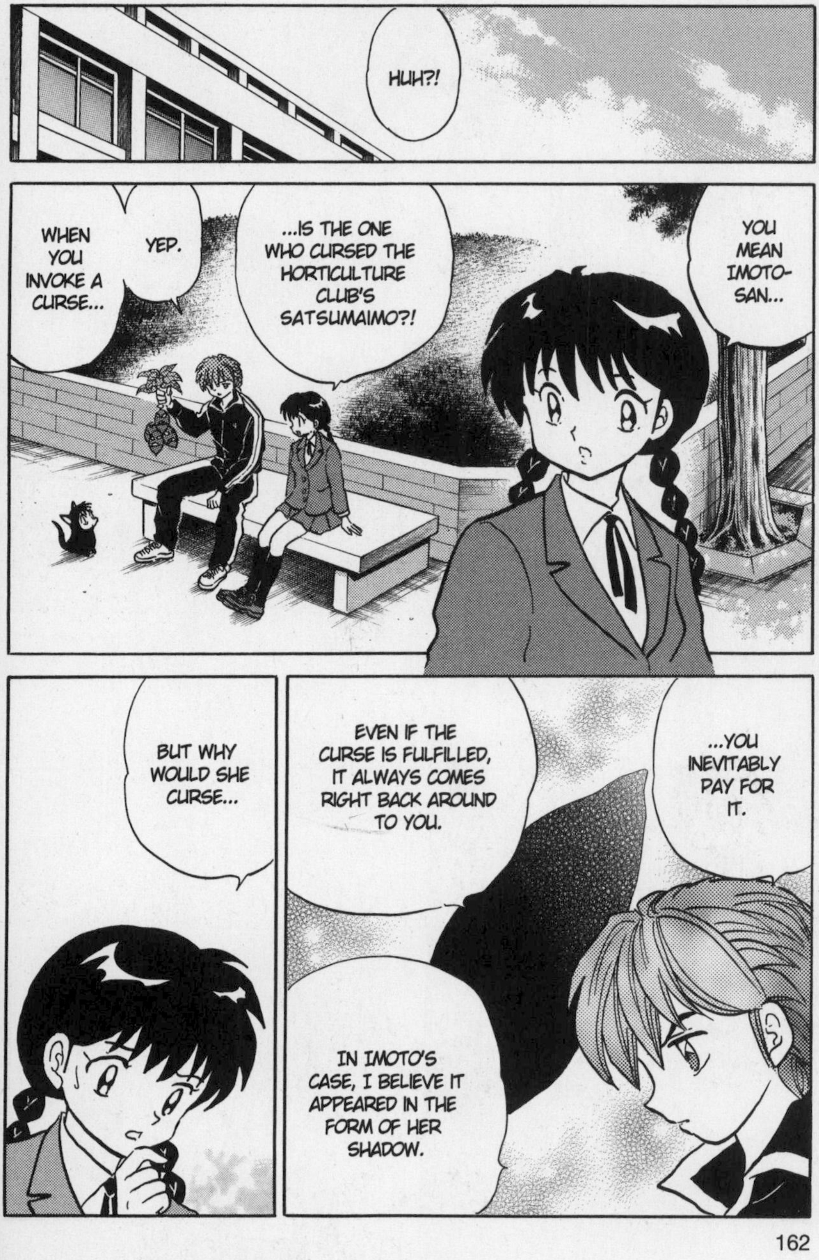
HUH?!
YOU MEAN IMOTO-SAN...
...IS THE ONE WHO CURSED THE HORTICULTURE CLUB'S SATSUMAIMO?!
YEP.
WHEN YOU INVOKE A CURSE...
...YOU INEVITABLY PAY FOR IT.
EVEN IF THE CURSE IS FULFILLED, IT ALWAYS COMES RIGHT BACK AROUND TO YOU.
IN IMOTO'S CASE, I BELIEVE IT APPEARED IN THE FORM OF HER SHADOW.
BUT WHY WOULD SHE CURSE...

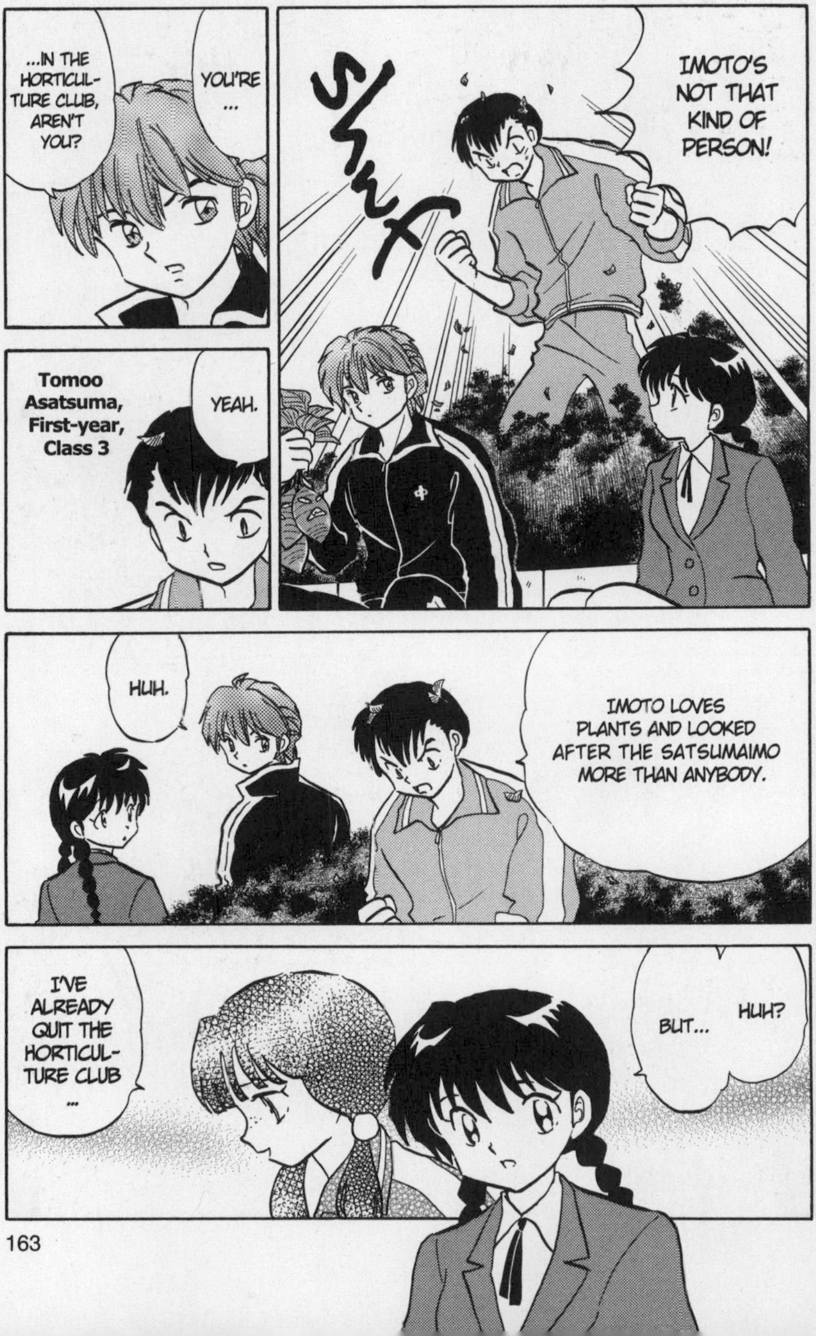
IMOTO'S NOT THAT KIND OF PERSON!
YOU'RE ...
...IN THE HORTICUL-TURE CLUB, AREN'T YOU?
YEAH.
Tomoo Asatsuma, First-year, Class 3
IMOTO LOVES PLANTS AND LOOKED AFTER THE SATSUMAIMO MORE THAN ANYBODY.
HUH.
HUH?
BUT...
I'VE ALREADY QUIT THE HORTICUL-TURE CLUB ...

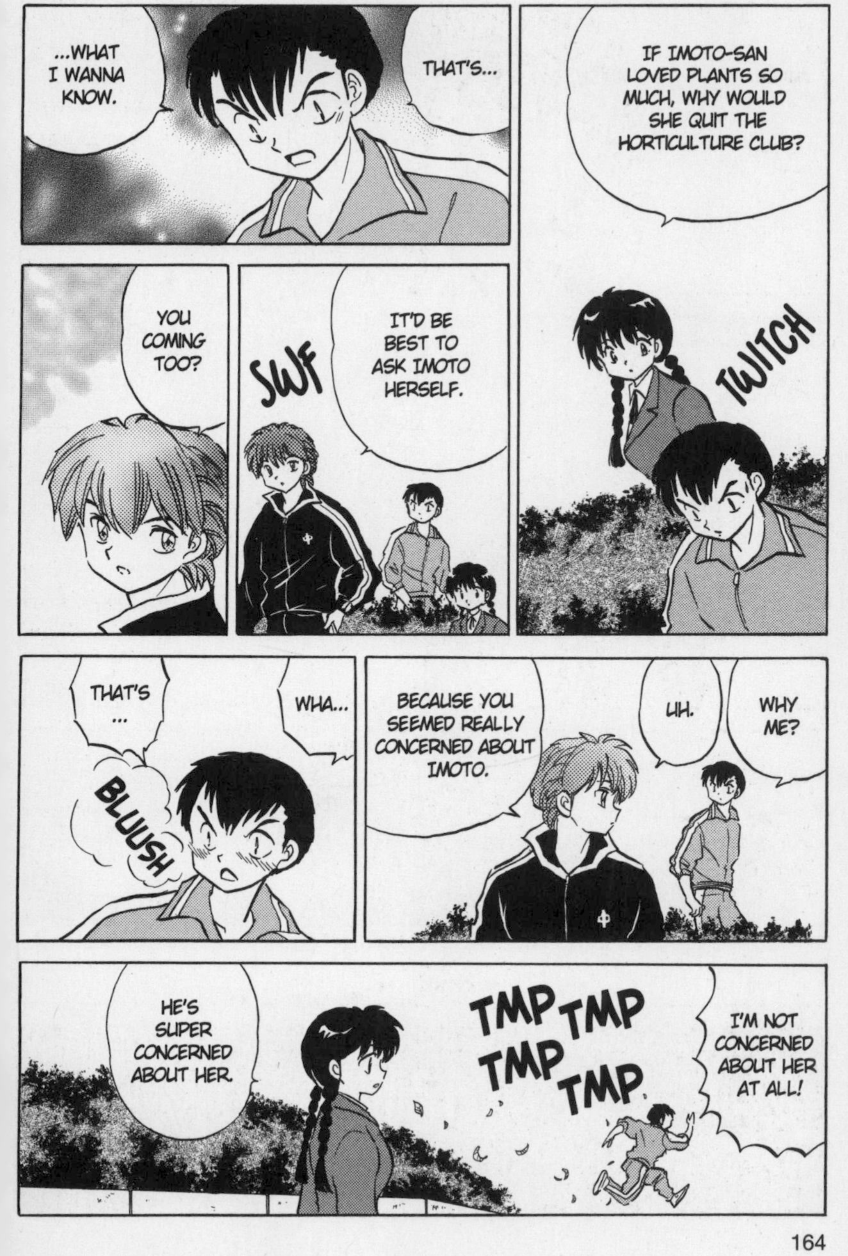
IF IMOTO-SAN LOVED PLANTS SO MUCH, WHY WOULD SHE QUIT THE HORTICULTURE CLUB?
TWITCH
THAT'S...
...WHAT I WANNA KNOW.
IT'D BE BEST TO ASK IMOTO HERSELF.
SWF
YOU COMING TOO?
WHY ME?
UH.
BECAUSE YOU SEEMED REALLY CONCERNED ABOUT IMOTO.
WHA...
THAT'S ...
BLUUSH
I'M NOT CONCERNED ABOUT HER AT ALL!
TMP TMP TMP TMP
HE'S SUPER CONCERNED ABOUT HER.

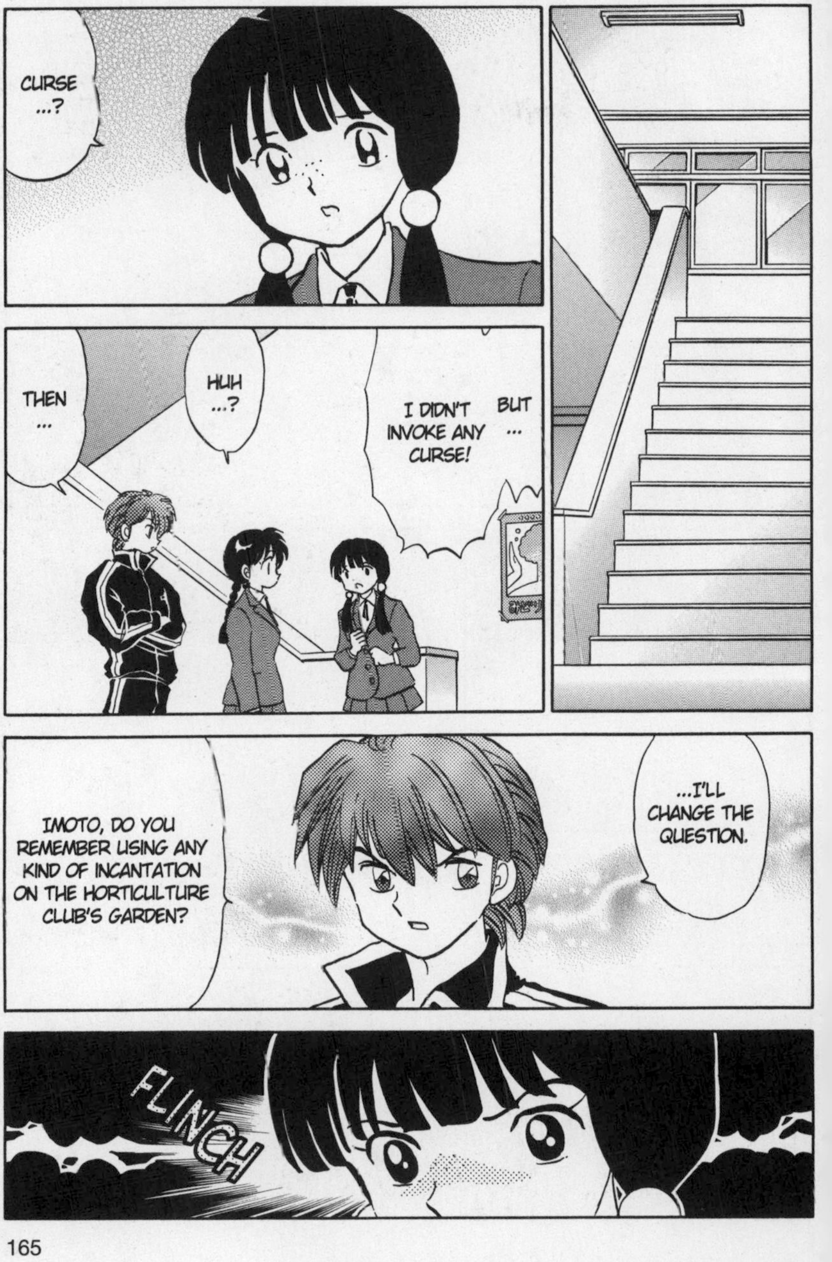
CURSE ...?
BUT ...
I DIDN'T INVOKE ANY CURSE!
HUH ...?
THEN ...
...I'LL CHANGE THE QUESTION.
IMOTO, DO YOU REMEMBER USING ANY KIND OF INCANTATION ON THE HORTICULTURE CLUB'S GARDEN?
FLINCH

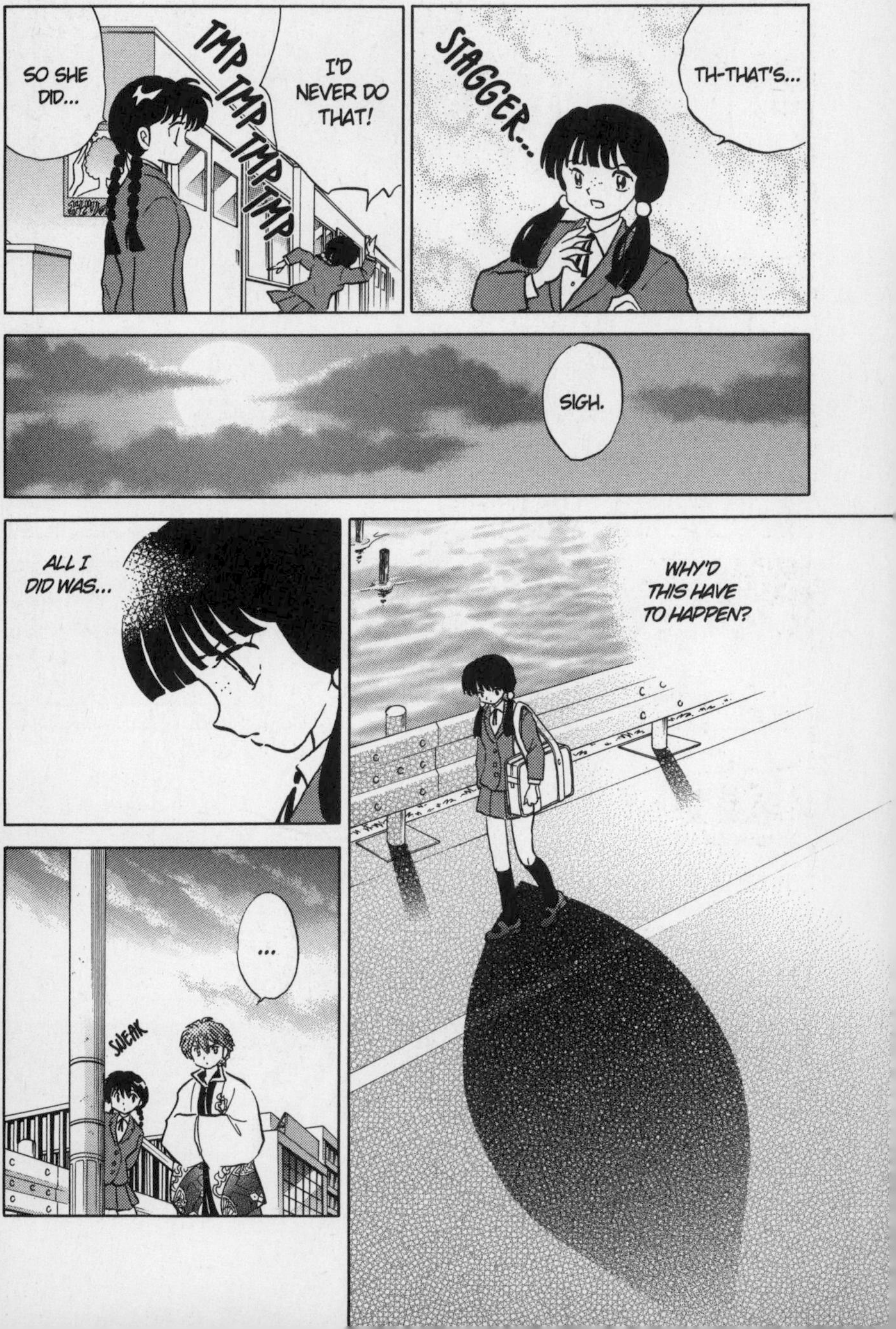
STAGGER...
TH-THAT'S...
I'D NEVER DO THAT!
TMP TMP TMP TMP
SO SHE DID...
SIGH.
WHY'D THIS HAVE TO HAPPEN?
ALL I DID WAS...
...
SNEAK

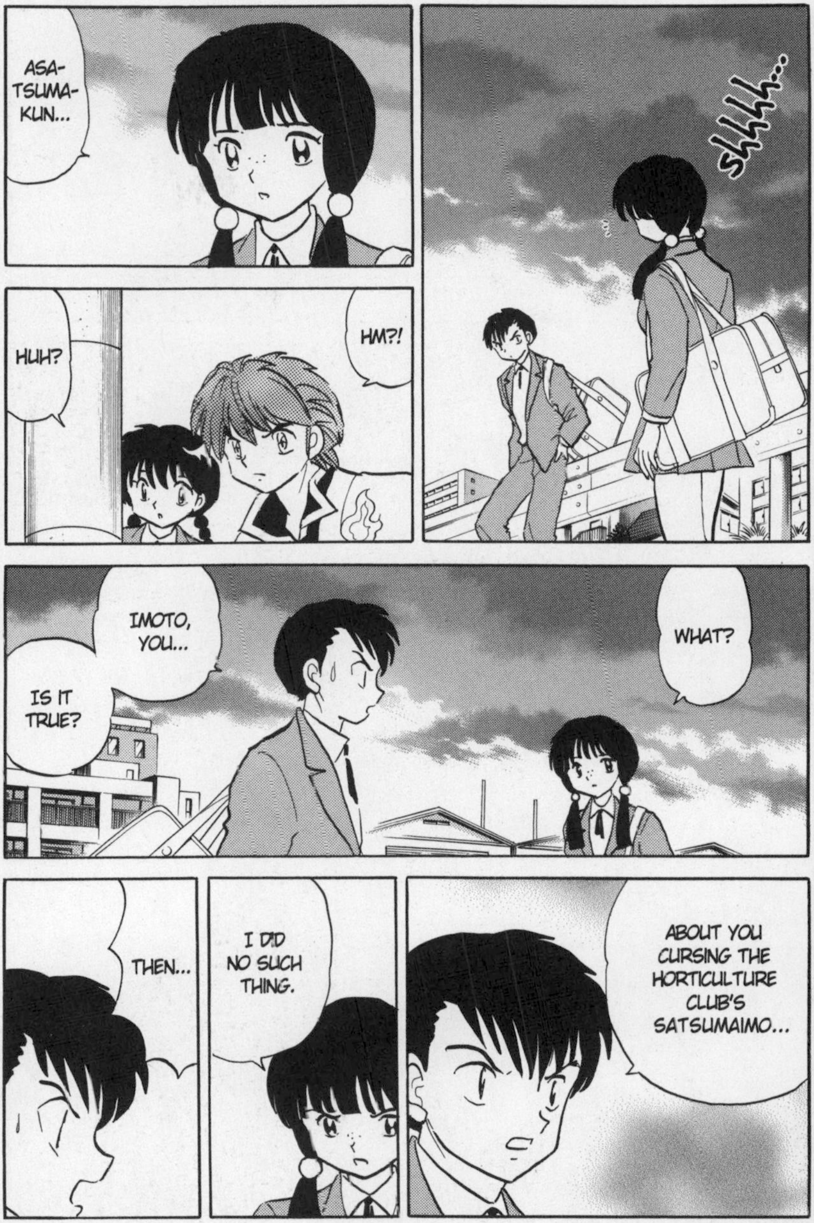
SHHHH...
ASA-TSUMA-KUN...
HM?!
HUH?
WHAT?
IMOTO, YOU...
IS IT TRUE?
ABOUT YOU CURSING THE HORTICULTURE CLUB'S SATSUMAIMO...
I DID NO SUCH THING.
THEN...

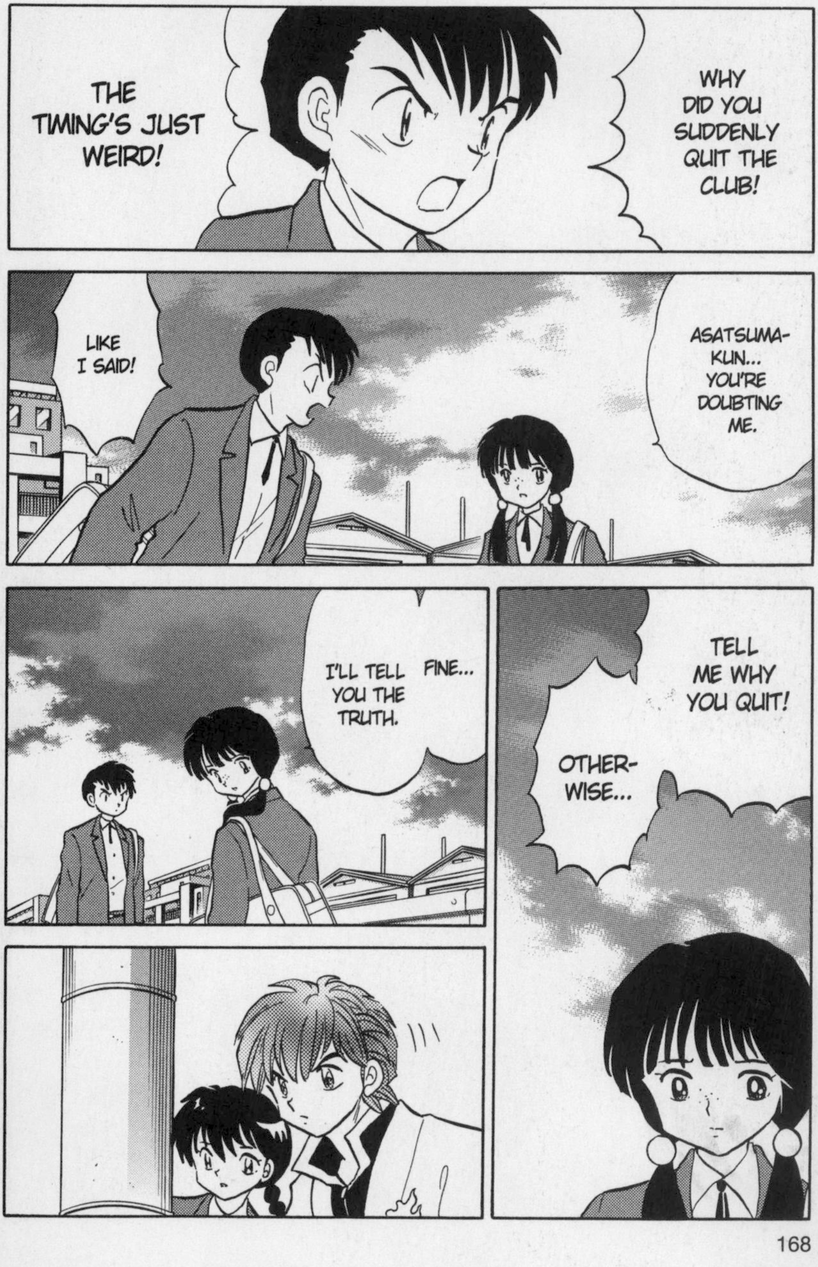
WHY DID YOU SUDDENLY QUIT THE CLUB!
THE TIMING'S JUST WEIRD!
ASATSUMA-KUN... YOU'RE DOUBTING ME.
LIKE I SAID!
TELL ME WHY YOU QUIT!
OTHER-WISE...
FINE...
I'LL TELL YOU THE TRUTH.

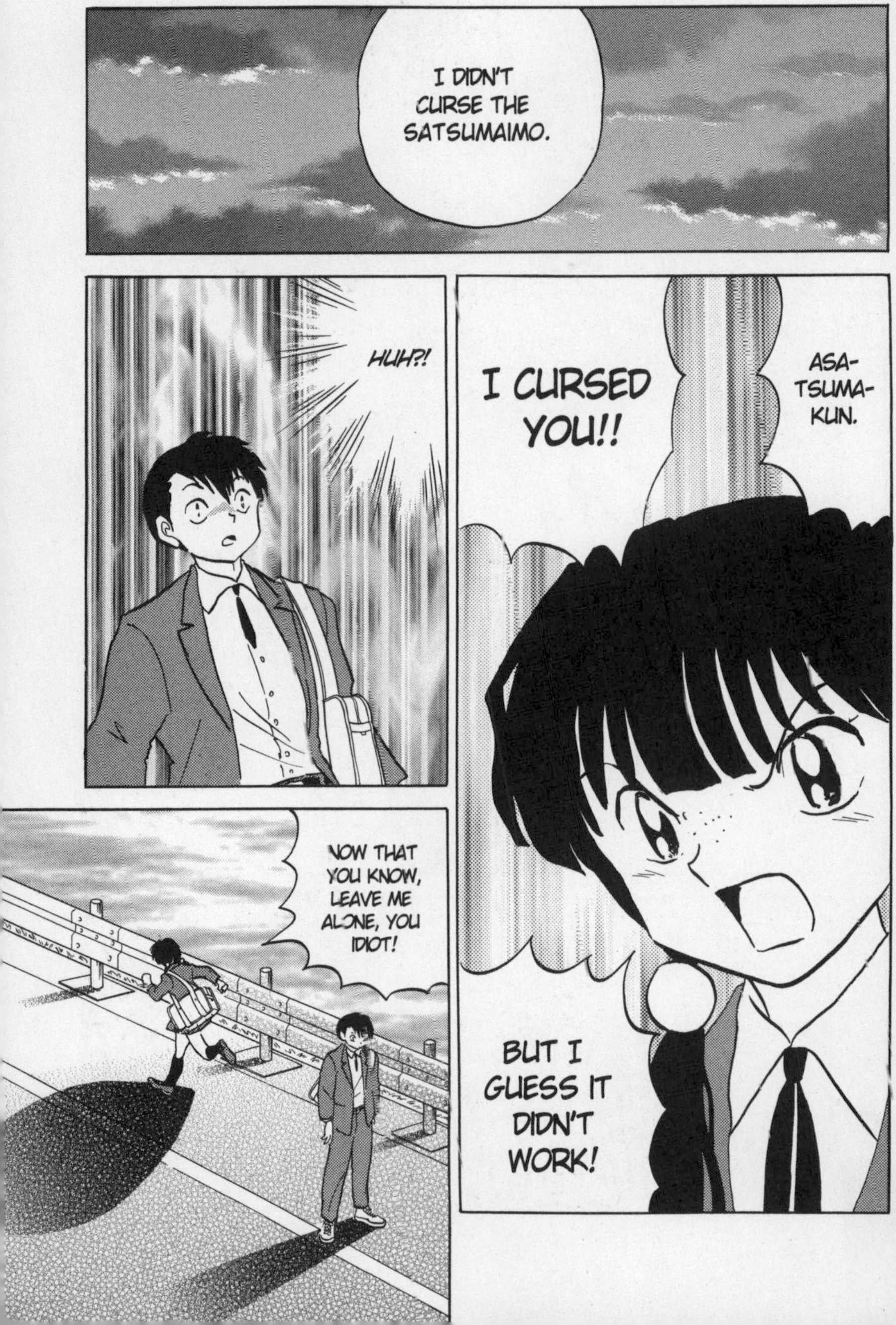
I DIDN'T CURSE THE SATSUMAIMO.
ASA-TSUMA-KUN.
I CURSED YOU!!
BUT I GUESS IT DIDN'T WORK!
HUH?!
NOW THAT YOU KNOW, LEAVE ME ALONE, YOU IDIOT!

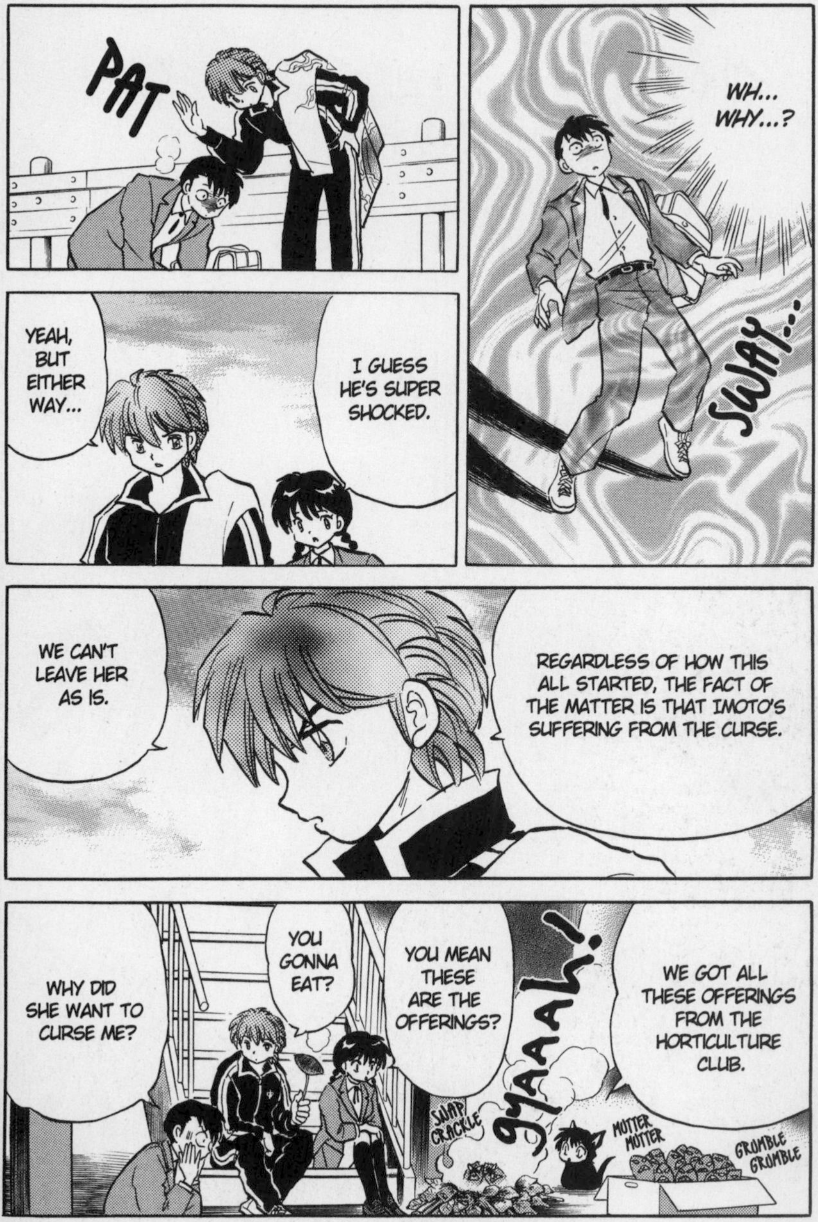

WH... WHY...?
SWAY...
PAT
I GUESS HE'S SUPER SHOCKED.
YEAH, BUT EITHER WAY...
REGARDLESS OF HOW THIS ALL STARTED, THE FACT OF THE MATTER IS THAT IMOTO'S SUFFERING FROM THE CURSE.
WE CAN'T LEAVE HER AS IS.
WE GOT ALL THESE OFFERINGS FROM THE HORTICULTURE CLUB.
GRUMBLE GRUMBLE
MUTTER MUTTER
GYAAAA!
YOU MEAN THESE ARE THE OFFERINGS?
SNAP CRACKLE
YOU GONNA EAT?
WHY DID SHE WANT TO CURSE ME?

CHAPTER 68: HOW THE CURSE WAS CAST

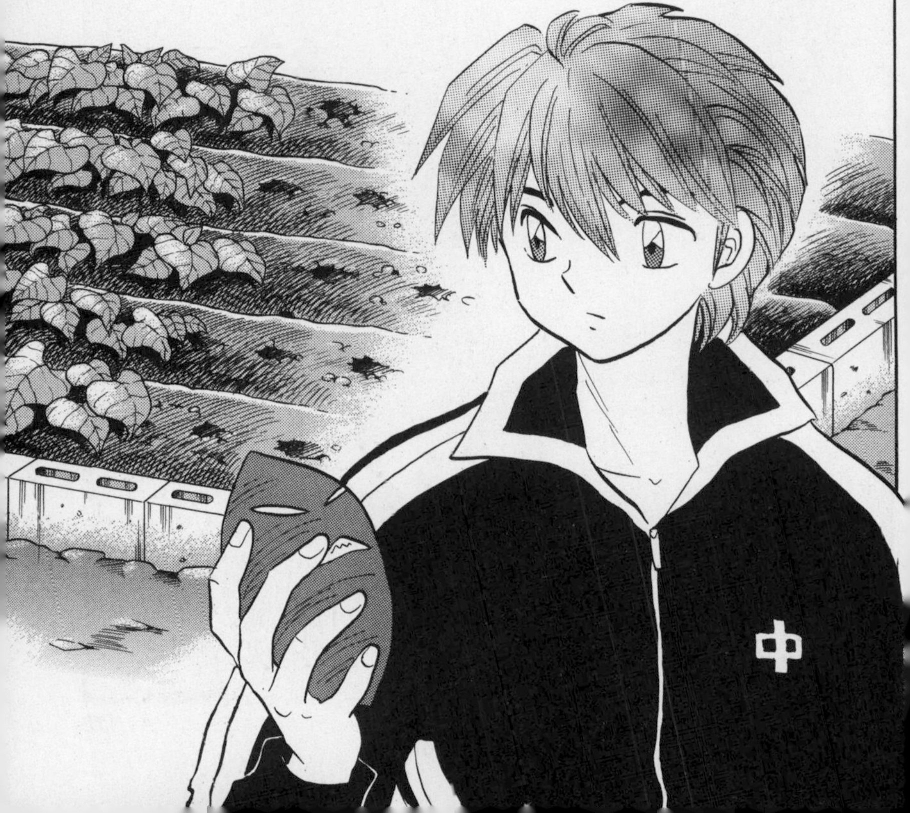

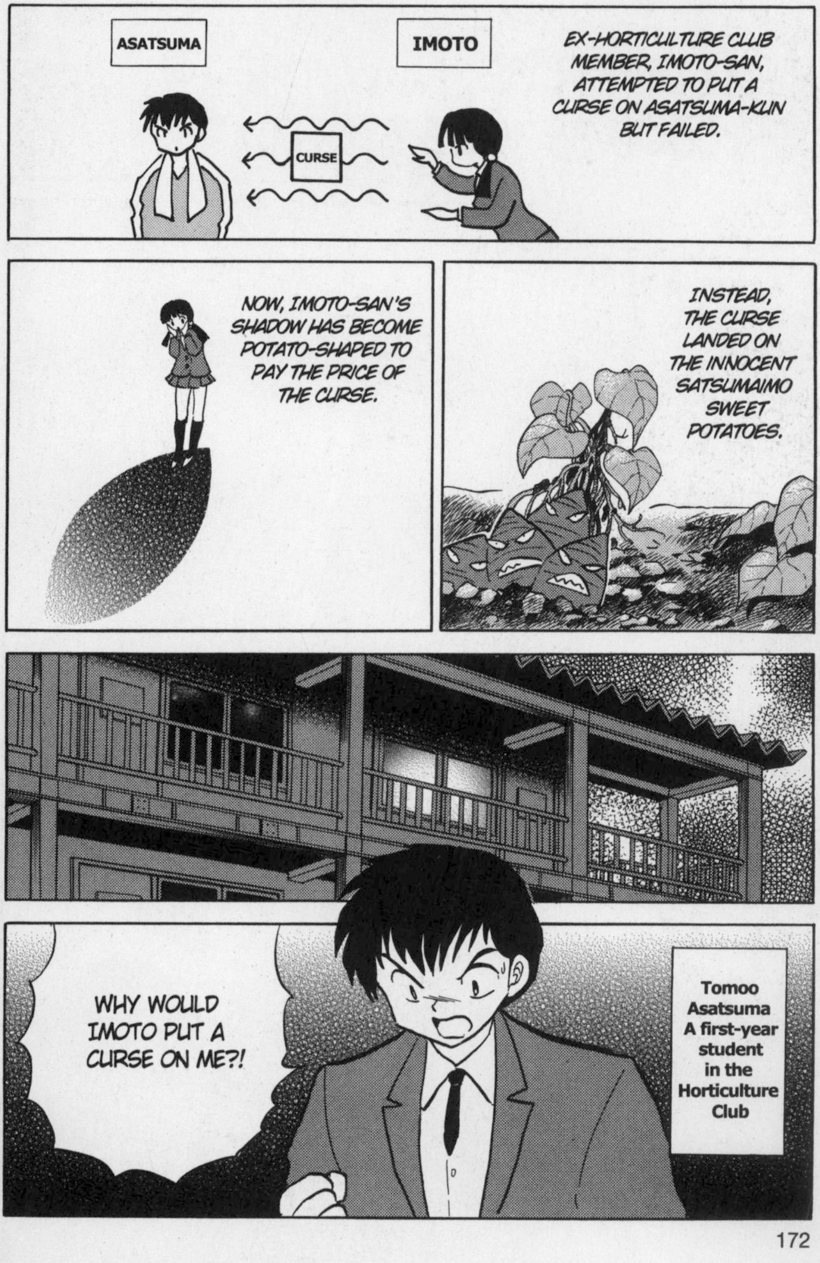
EX-HORTICULTURE CLUB MEMBER, IMOTO-SAN, ATTEMPTED TO PUT A CURSE ON ASATSUMA-KUN BUT FAILED.
IMOTO
ASATSUMA
CURSE
INSTEAD, THE CURSE LANDED ON THE INNOCENT SATSUMAIMO SWEET POTATOES.
NOW, IMOTO-SAN'S SHADOW HAS BECOME POTATO-SHAPED TO PAY THE PRICE OF THE CURSE.
Tomoo Asatsuma A first-year student in the Horticulture Club
WHY WOULD IMOTO PUT A CURSE ON ME?!

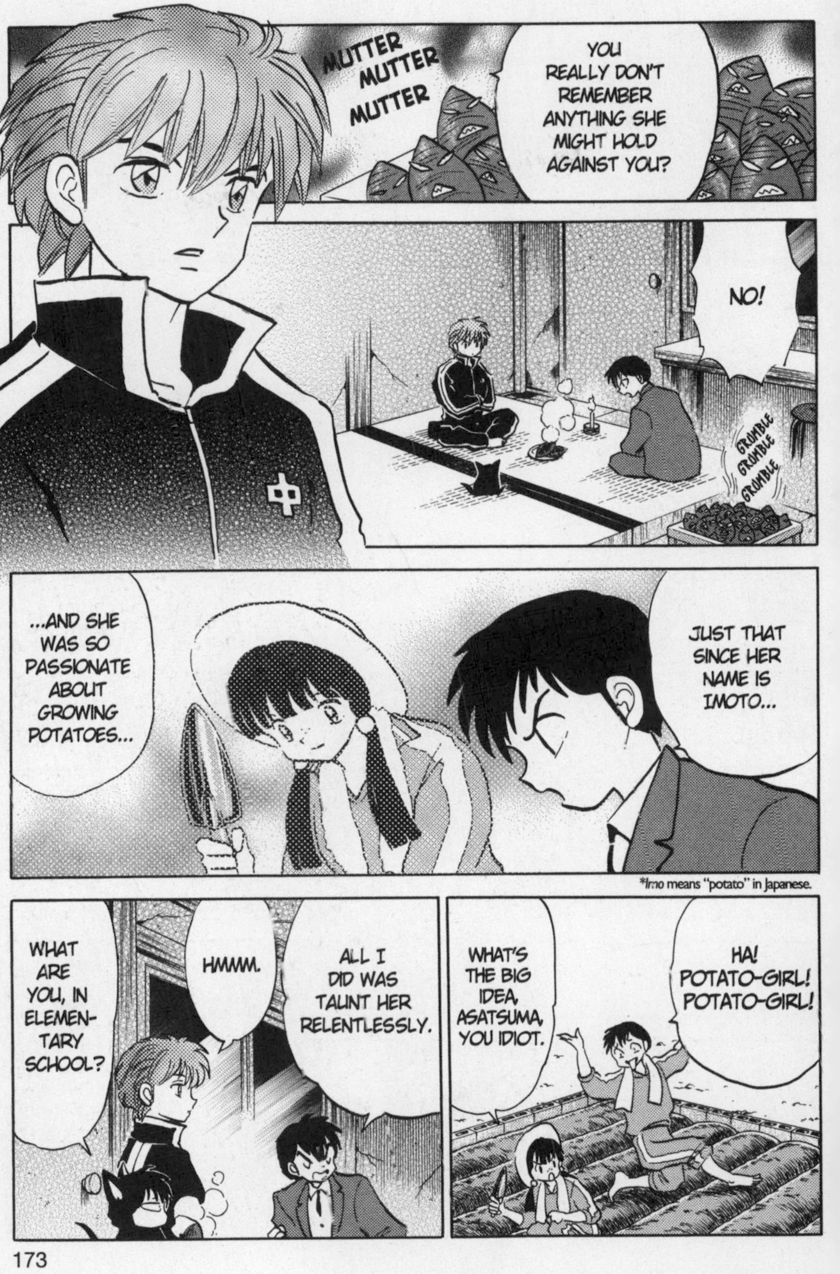
YOU REALLY DON'T REMEMBER ANYTHING SHE MIGHT HOLD AGAINST YOU?
MUTTER MUTTER MUTTER
NO!
GRUMBLE GRUMBLE GRUMBLE
JUST THAT SINCE HER NAME IS IMOTO...
...AND SHE WAS SO PASSIONATE ABOUT GROWING POTATOES...
HA! POTATO-GIRL! POTATO-GIRL!
WHAT'S THE BIG IDEA, ASATSUMA, YOU IDIOT.
ALL I DID WAS TAUNT HER RELENTLESSLY.
HMMM.
WHAT ARE YOU, IN ELEMENTARY SCHOOL?

*Imo means "potato" in Japanese.

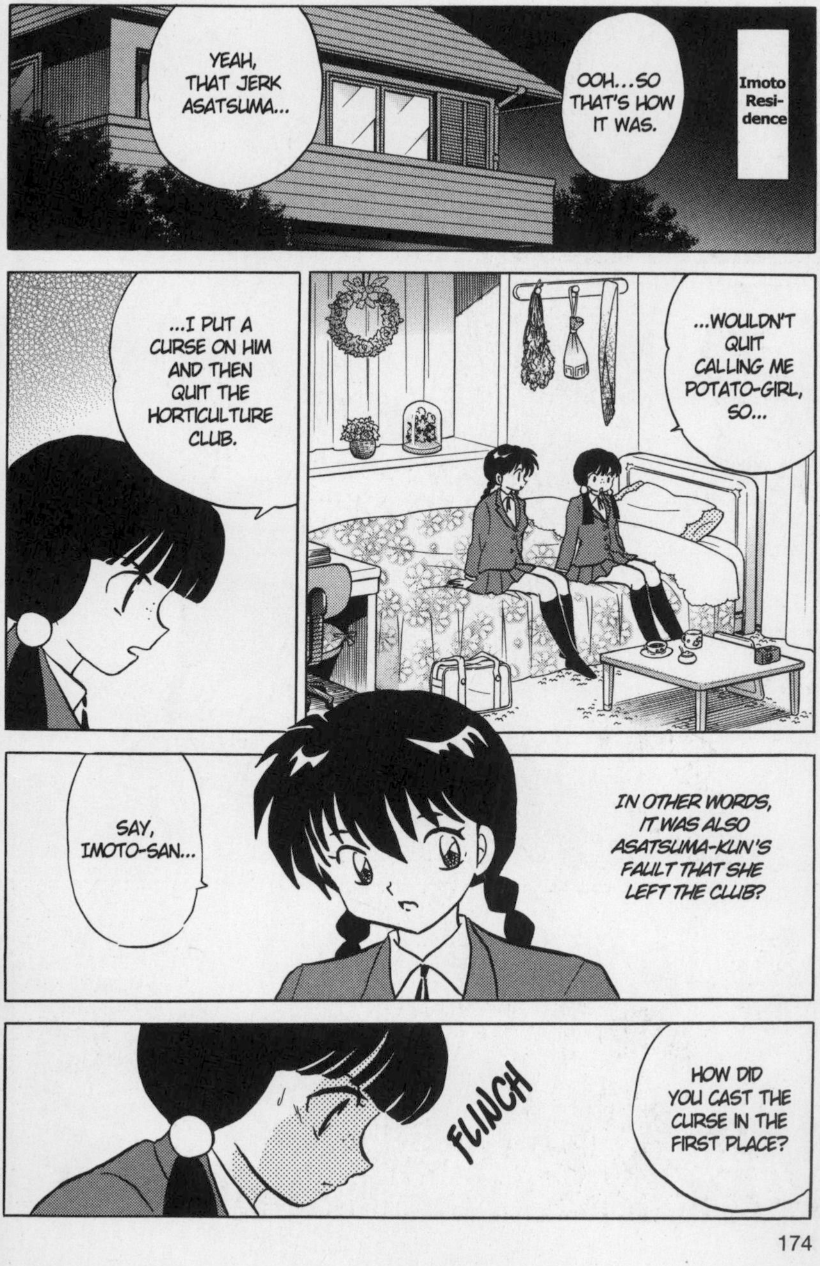
Imoto Residence
OOH...SO THAT'S HOW IT WAS.
YEAH, THAT JERK ASATSUMA...
...WOULDN'T QUIT CALLING ME POTATO-GIRL, SO...
...I PUT A CURSE ON HIM AND THEN QUIT THE HORTICULTURE CLUB.
IN OTHER WORDS, IT WAS ALSO ASATSUMA-KUN'S FAULT THAT SHE LEFT THE CLUB?
SAY, IMOTO-SAN...
HOW DID YOU CAST THE CURSE IN THE FIRST PLACE?
FLINCH

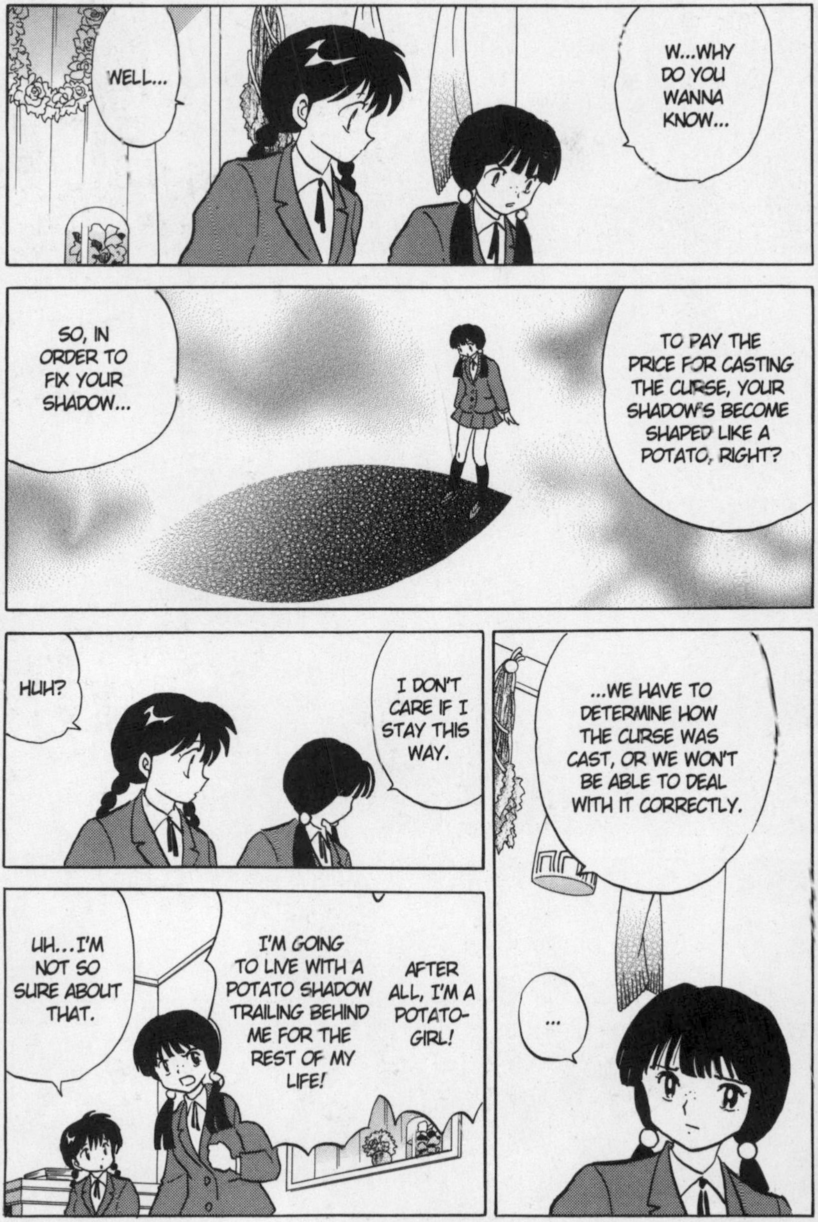
W...WHY DO YOU WANNA KNOW...
WELL...
TO PAY THE PRICE FOR CASTING THE CURSE, YOUR SHADOW'S BECOME SHAPED LIKE A POTATO, RIGHT?
SO, IN ORDER TO FIX YOUR SHADOW...
...WE HAVE TO DETERMINE HOW THE CURSE WAS CAST, OR WE WON'T BE ABLE TO DEAL WITH IT CORRECTLY.
...
I DON'T CARE IF I STAY THIS WAY.
HUH?
AFTER ALL, I'M A POTATO-GIRL!
I'M GOING TO LIVE WITH A POTATO SHADOW TRAILING BEHIND ME FOR THE REST OF MY LIFE!
UH...I'M NOT SO SURE ABOUT THAT.

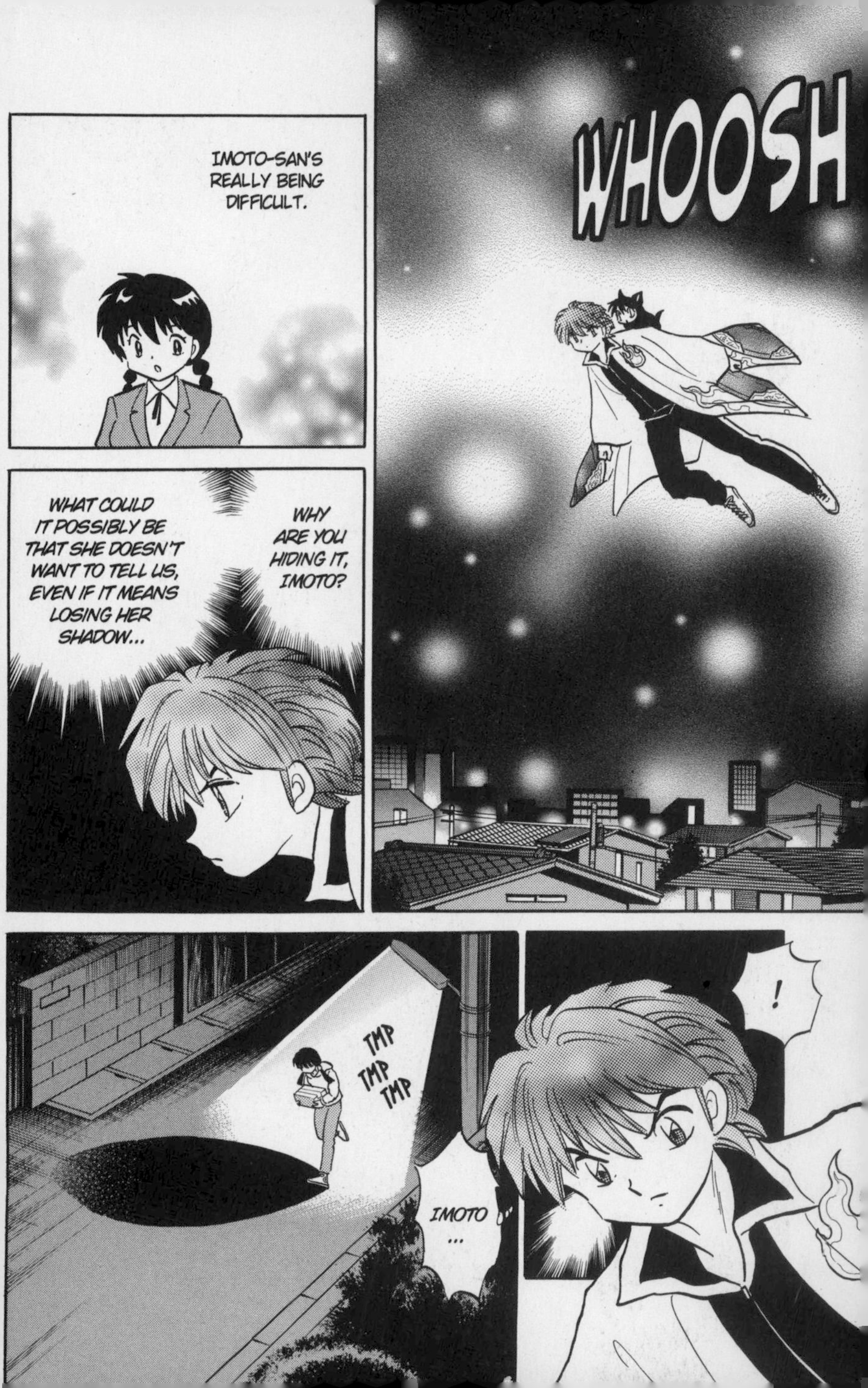
WHOOSH
IMOTO-SAN'S REALLY BEING DIFFICULT.
WHY ARE YOU HIDING IT, IMOTO?
WHAT COULD IT POSSIBLY BE THAT SHE DOESN'T WANT TO TELL US, EVEN IF IT MEANS LOSING HER SHADOW...
!
TMP TMP TMP
IMOTO ...

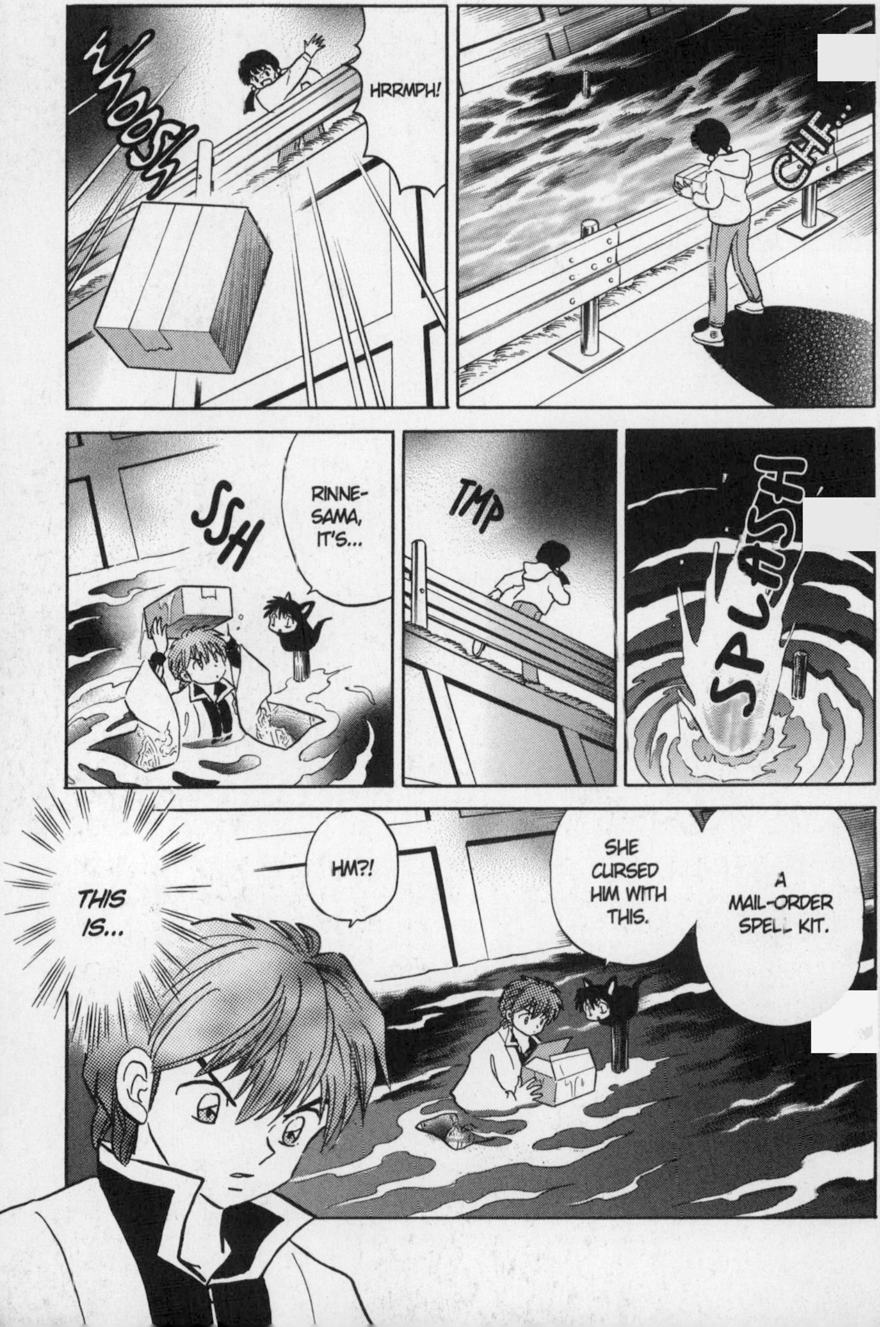
CHF...
WHOOSH
HRRMPH!
SPLASH
TMP
SSH
RINNE-SAMA, IT'S...
A MAIL-ORDER SPELL KIT.
SHE CURSED HIM WITH THIS.
HM?!
THIS IS...

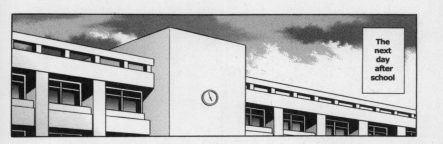

The next day after school

DEAR IMOTO, I REALLY WANT TO APOLOGIZE TO YOU.

COME TO THE HORTICULTURE CLUB'S SWEET POTATO PATCH AFTER SCHOOL.

ASATSUMA

RUSTLE....

AH.

AH.

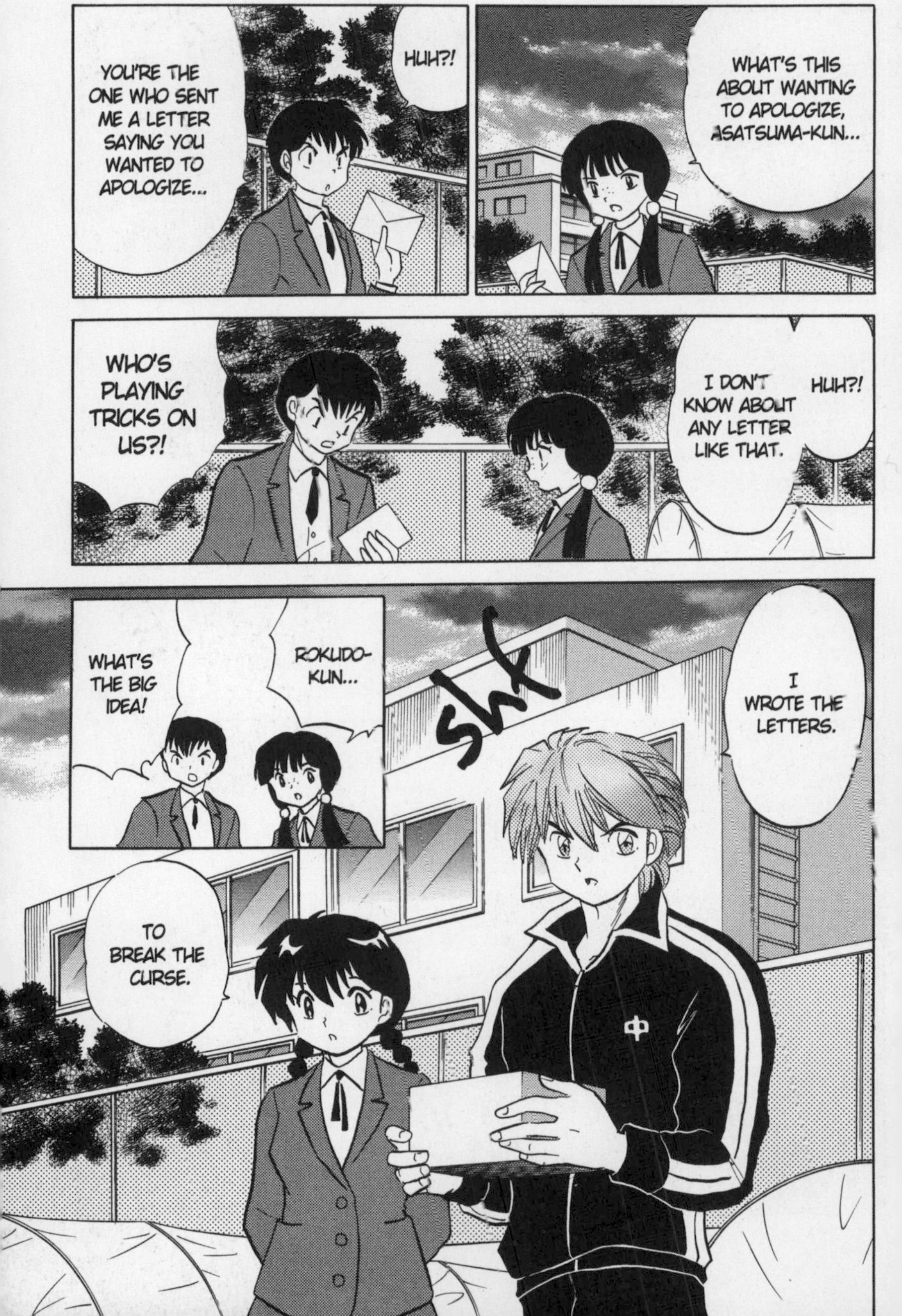
WHAT'S THIS ABOUT WANTING TO APOLOGIZE, ASATSUMA-KUN...
HUH?!
YOU'RE THE ONE WHO SENT ME A LETTER SAYING YOU WANTED TO APOLOGIZE...
HUH?!
I DON'T KNOW ABOUT ANY LETTER LIKE THAT.
WHO'S PLAYING TRICKS ON US?!
SHK
I WROTE THE LETTERS.
ROKUDO-KUN...
WHAT'S THE BIG IDEA!
TO BREAK THE CURSE.

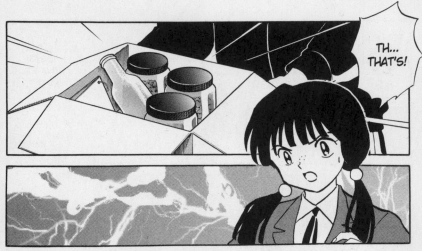

TH... THAT'S!
IMOTO, IT'S THE CURSE GOODS YOU THREW OUT.
SPELL FERTILIZER AND MAGIC FIXATIVE WATER.
YOU SAID YOU CURSED ASATSUMA, BUT...
...IN THE END, WHAT GOT CURSED WAS THE SATSUMAIMO SWEET POTATO PATCH.
FEH!
MUTTER MUTTER
THAT'S WHY YOUR SHADOW TOOK ON A SATSUMAIMO SWEET POTATO SHAPE.

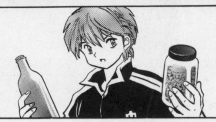

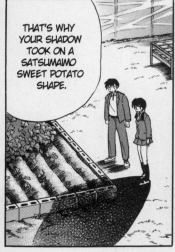

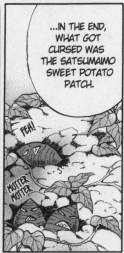

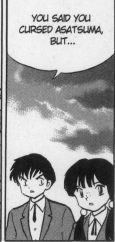

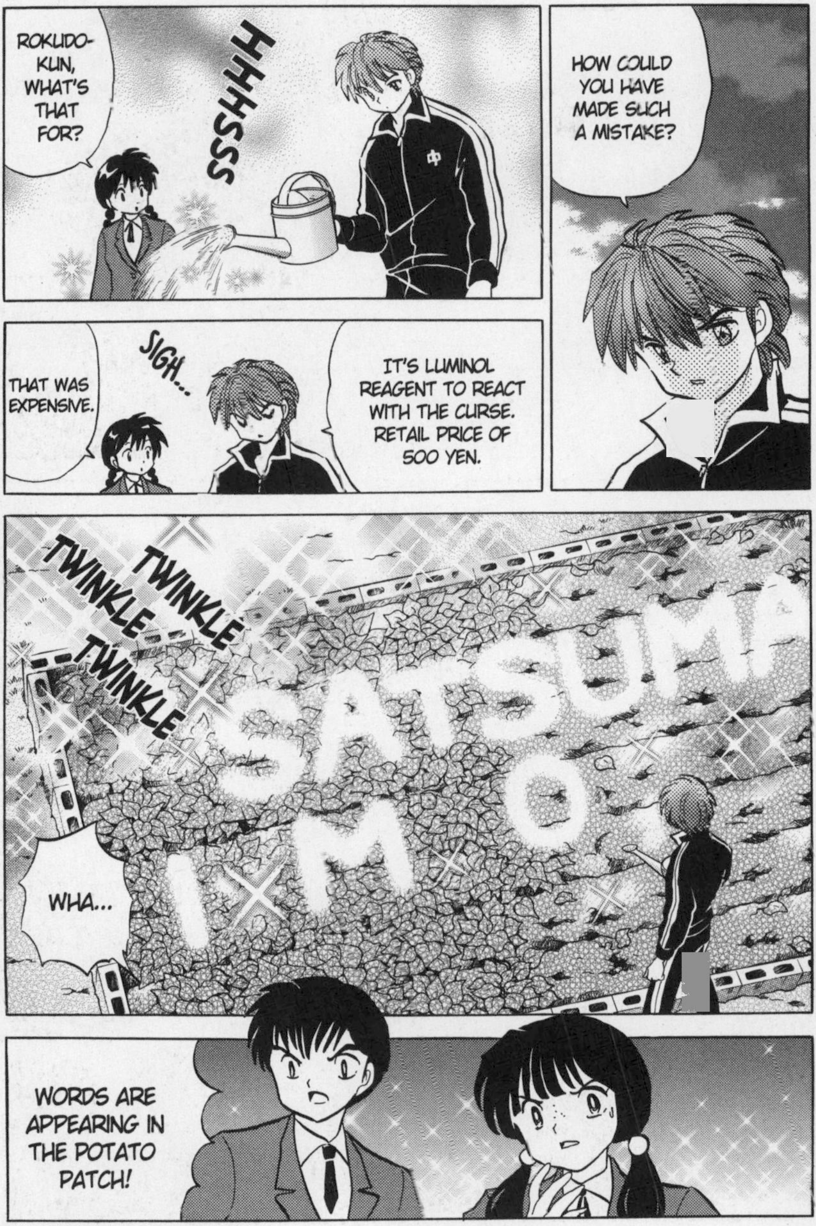
HOW COULD YOU HAVE MADE SUCH A MISTAKE?
ROKUDO-KUN, WHAT'S THAT FOR?
HHHHSSSS
IT'S LUMINOL REAGENT TO REACT WITH THE CURSE. RETAIL PRICE OF 500 YEN.
SIGH...
THAT WAS EXPENSIVE.
TWINKLE
TWINKLE
TWINKLE
SATSUMA IMO
WHA...
WORDS ARE APPEARING IN THE POTATO PATCH!

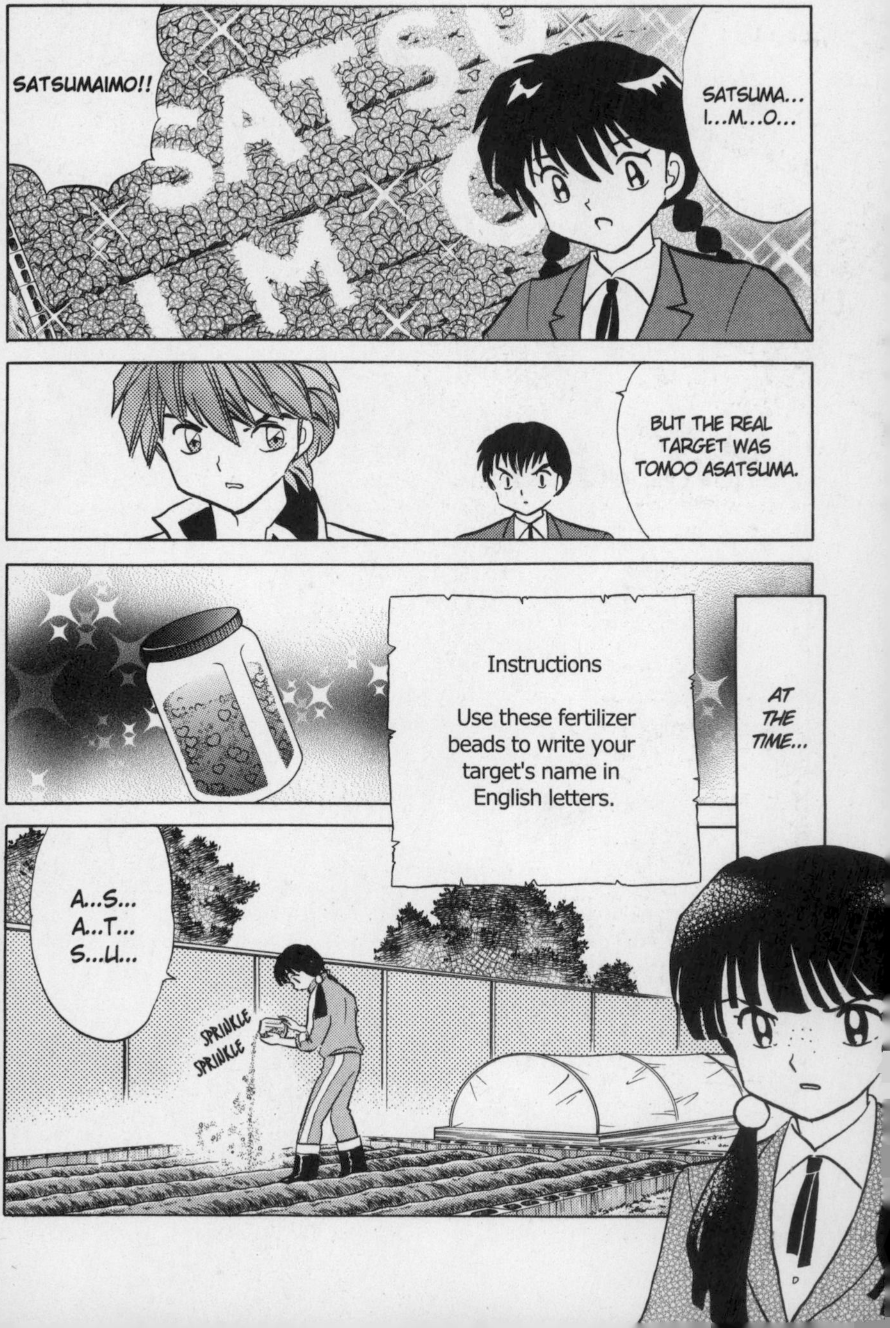
SATSUMA... I...M...O...
SATSUMAIMO!!
BUT THE REAL TARGET WAS TOMOO ASATSUMA.
AT THE TIME...
Instructions
Use these fertilizer beads to write your target's name in English letters.
A...S... A...T... S...U...
SPRINKLE SPRINKLE

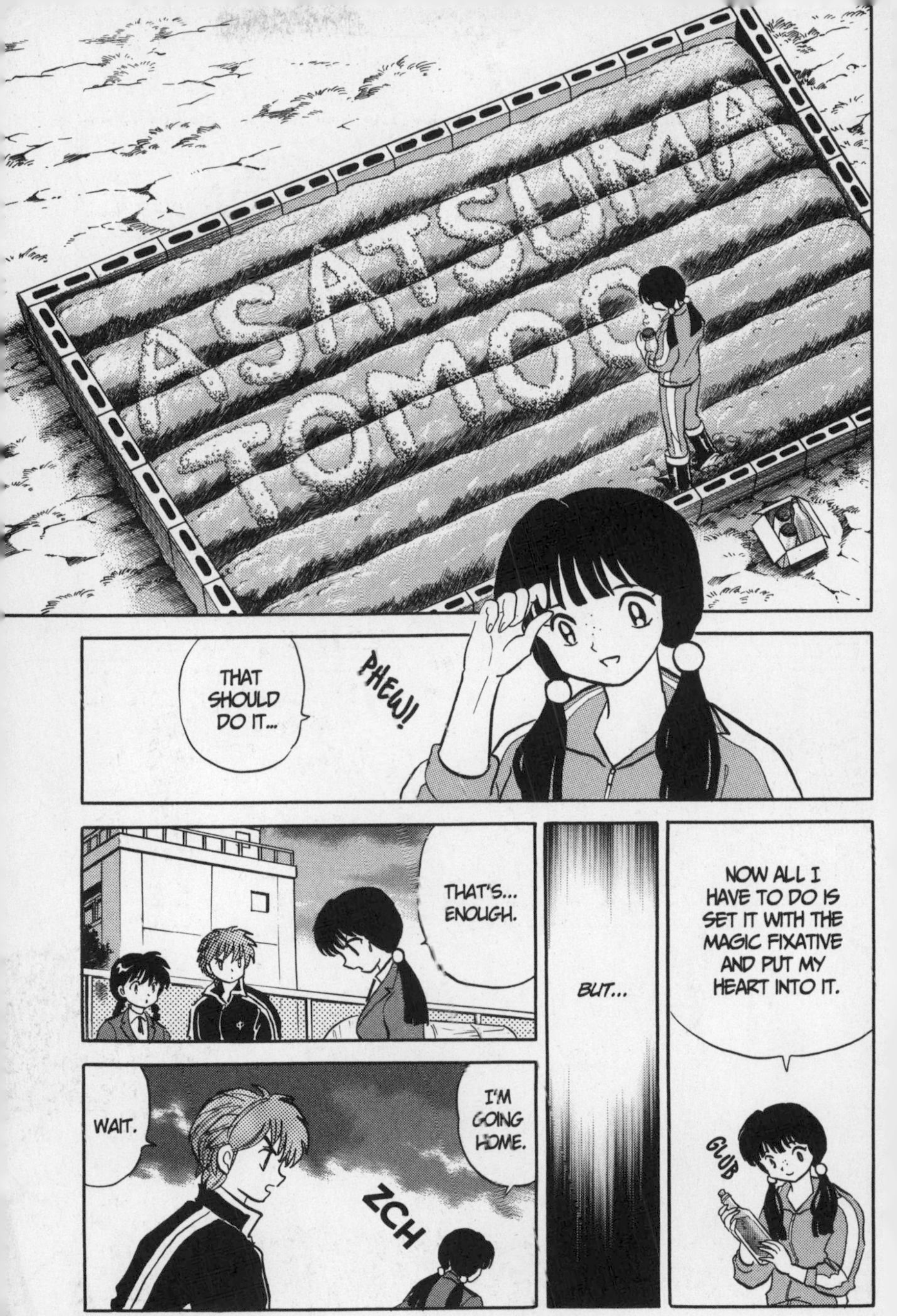
ASATSUMA
TOMOO
PHEW!
THAT SHOULD DO IT...
NOW ALL I HAVE TO DO IS SET IT WITH THE MAGIC FIXATIVE AND PUT MY HEART INTO IT.
GLUB
BUT...
THAT'S... ENOUGH.
I'M GOING HOME.
ZCH
WAIT.

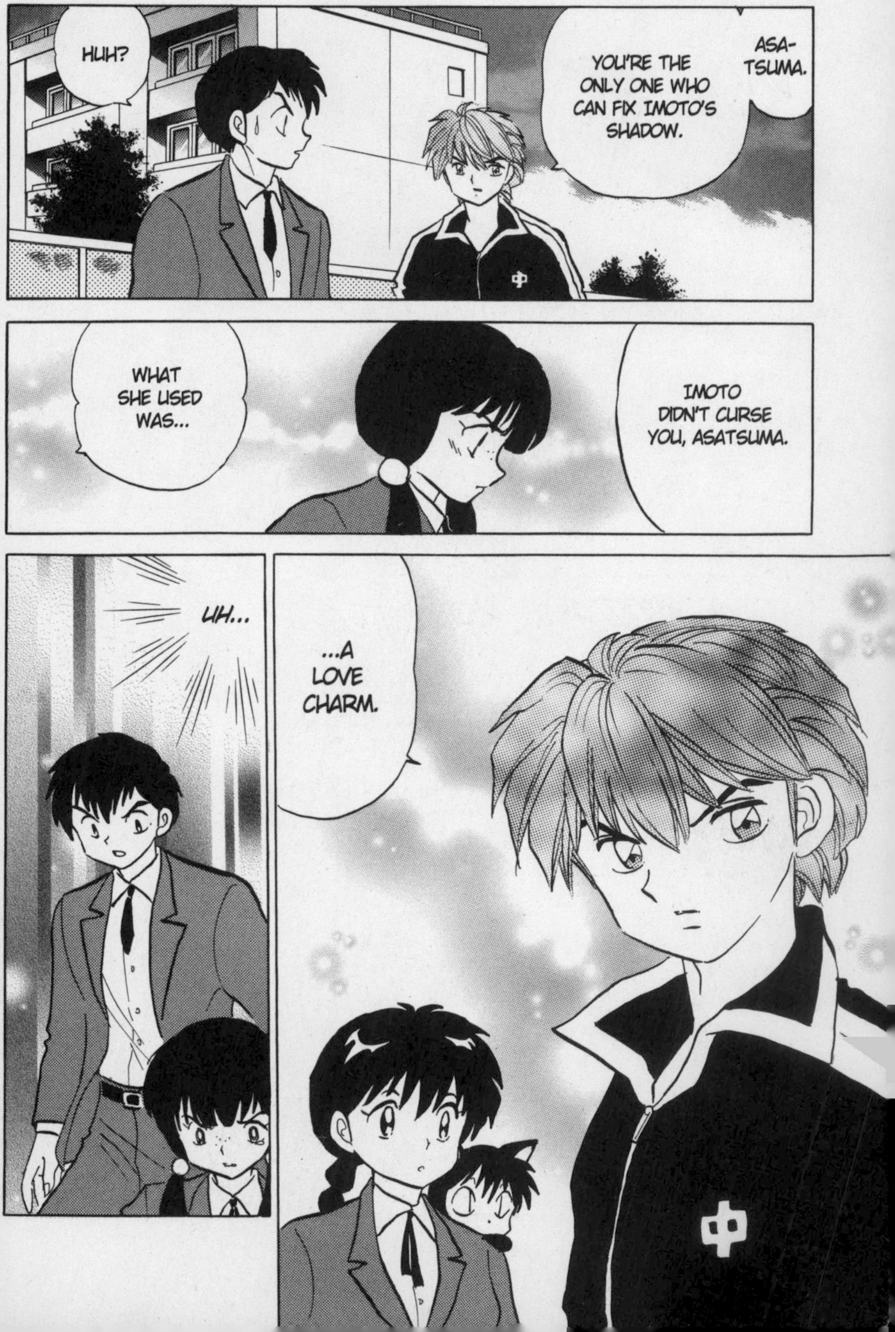
ASA-TSUMA.
YOU'RE THE ONLY ONE WHO CAN FIX IMOTO'S SHADOW.
HUH?
IMOTO DIDN'T CURSE YOU, ASATSUMA.
WHAT SHE USED WAS...
...A LOVE CHARM.
UH...

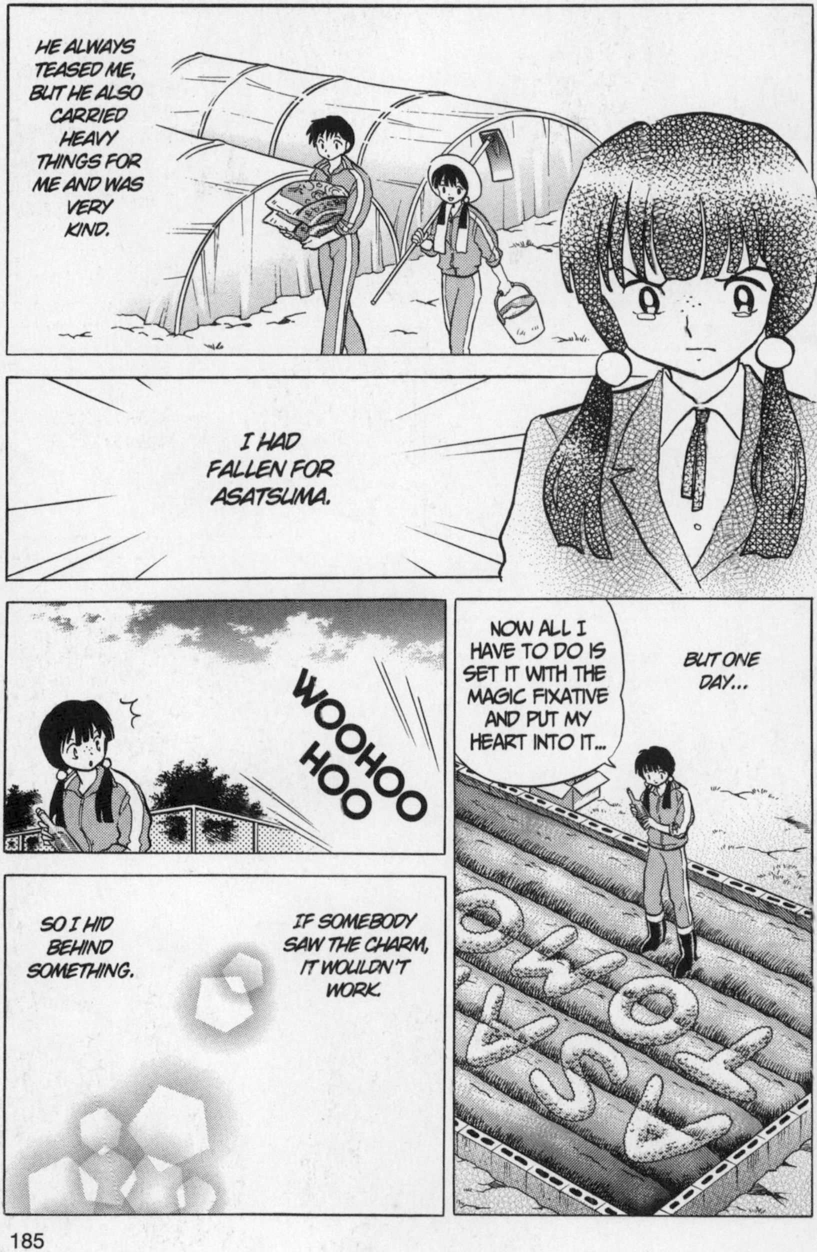
HE ALWAYS TEASED ME, BUT HE ALSO CARRIED HEAVY THINGS FOR ME AND WAS VERY KIND.
I HAD FALLEN FOR ASATSUMA.
BUT ONE DAY...
NOW ALL I HAVE TO DO IS SET IT WITH THE MAGIC FIXATIVE AND PUT MY HEART INTO IT...
WOOHOO HOO
IF SOMEBODY SAW THE CHARM, IT WOULDN'T WORK.
SO I HID BEHIND SOMETHING.

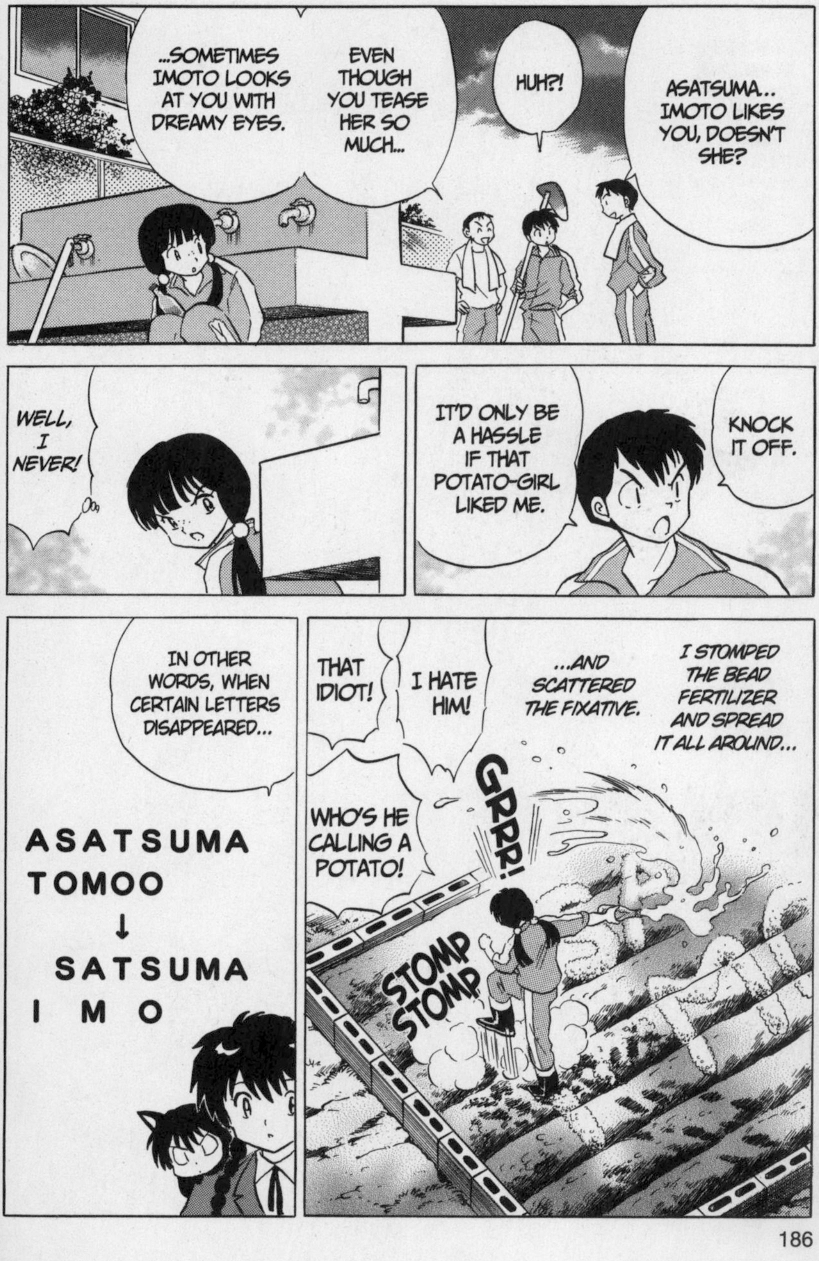
ASATSUMA... IMOTO LIKES YOU, DOESN'T SHE?
HUH?!
EVEN THOUGH YOU TEASE HER SO MUCH...
...SOMETIMES IMOTO LOOKS AT YOU WITH DREAMY EYES.
KNOCK IT OFF.
IT'D ONLY BE A HASSLE IF THAT POTATO-GIRL LIKED ME.
WELL, I NEVER!
I STOMPED THE BEAD FERTILIZER AND SPREAD IT ALL AROUND...
...AND SCATTERED THE FIXATIVE.
I HATE HIM!
THAT IDIOT!
GRRR!
WHO'S HE CALLING A POTATO!
STOMP STOMP
IN OTHER WORDS, WHEN CERTAIN LETTERS DISAPPEARED...
ASATSUMA TOMOO
↓
SATSUMA IMO

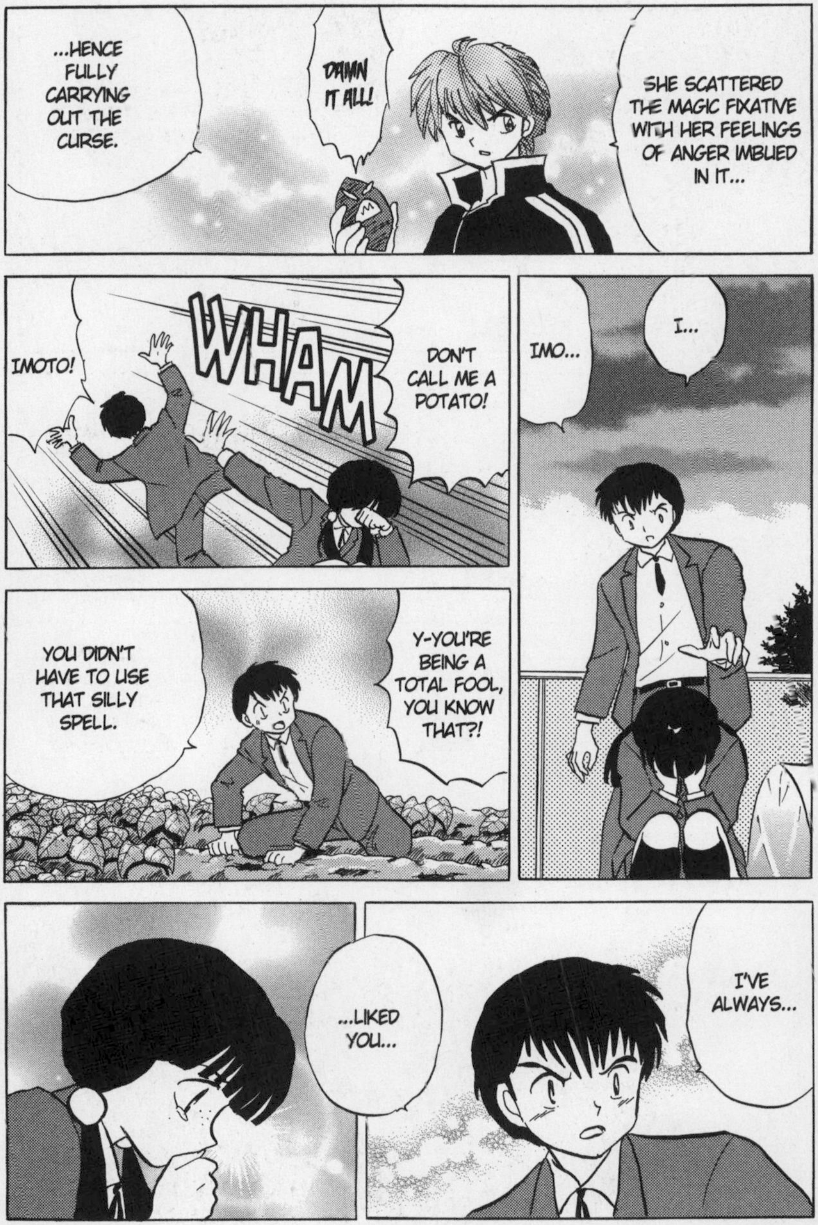
SHE SCATTERED THE MAGIC FIXATIVE WITH HER FEELINGS OF ANGER IMBUED IN IT...
DAMN IT ALL!
...HENCE FULLY CARRYING OUT THE CURSE.
I...
IMO...
DON'T CALL ME A POTATO!
WHAM
IMOTO!
Y-YOU'RE BEING A TOTAL FOOL, YOU KNOW THAT?!
YOU DIDN'T HAVE TO USE THAT SILLY SPELL.
I'VE ALWAYS...
...LIKED YOU...

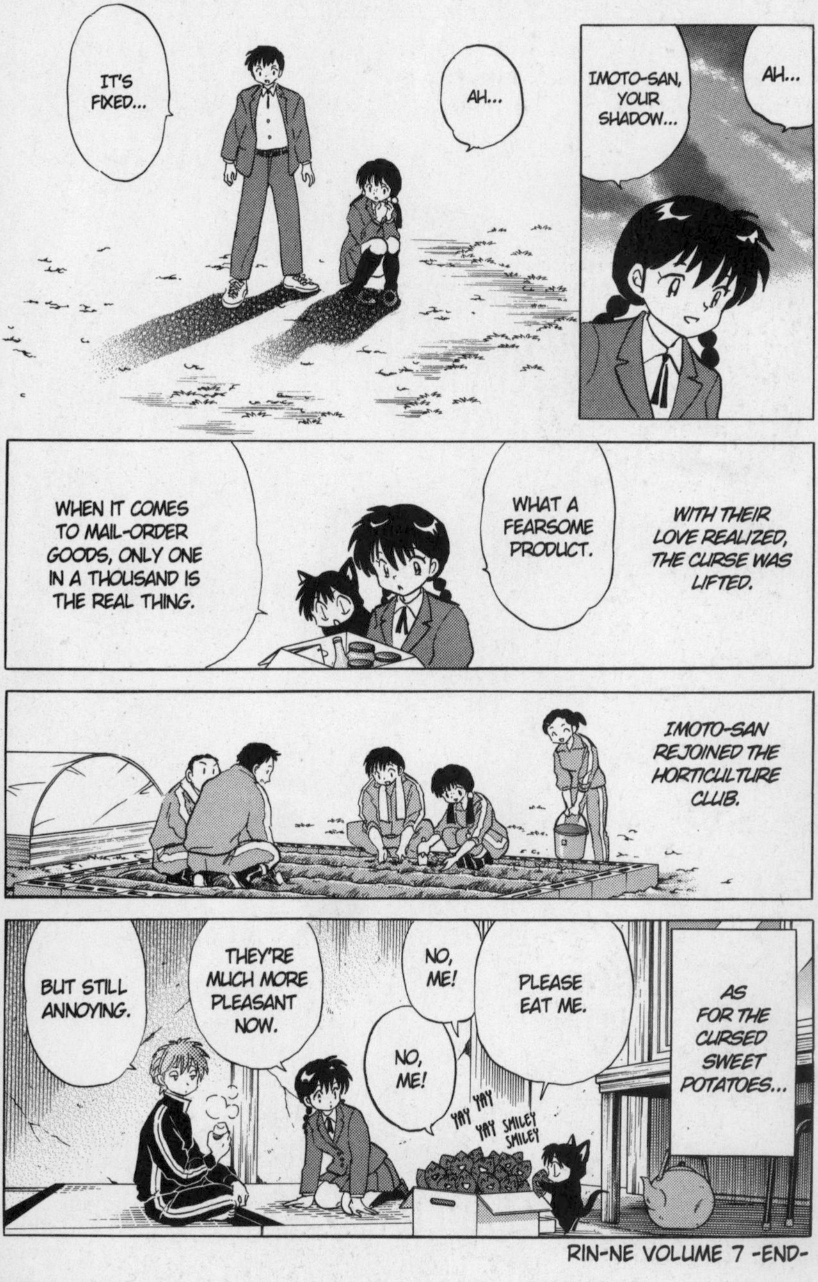
AH...
IMOTO-SAN, YOUR SHADOW...
AH...
IT'S FIXED...
WITH THEIR LOVE REALIZED, THE CURSE WAS LIFTED.
WHAT A FEARSOME PRODUCT.
WHEN IT COMES TO MAIL-ORDER GOODS, ONLY ONE IN A THOUSAND IS THE REAL THING.
IMOTO-SAN REJOINED THE HORTICULTURE CLUB.
AS FOR THE CURSED SWEET POTATOES...
PLEASE EAT ME.
NO, ME!
NO, ME!
YAY YAY YAY SMILEY SMILEY
THEY'RE MUCH MORE PLEASANT NOW.
BUT STILL ANNOYING.

RIN-NE VOLUME 7 -END-

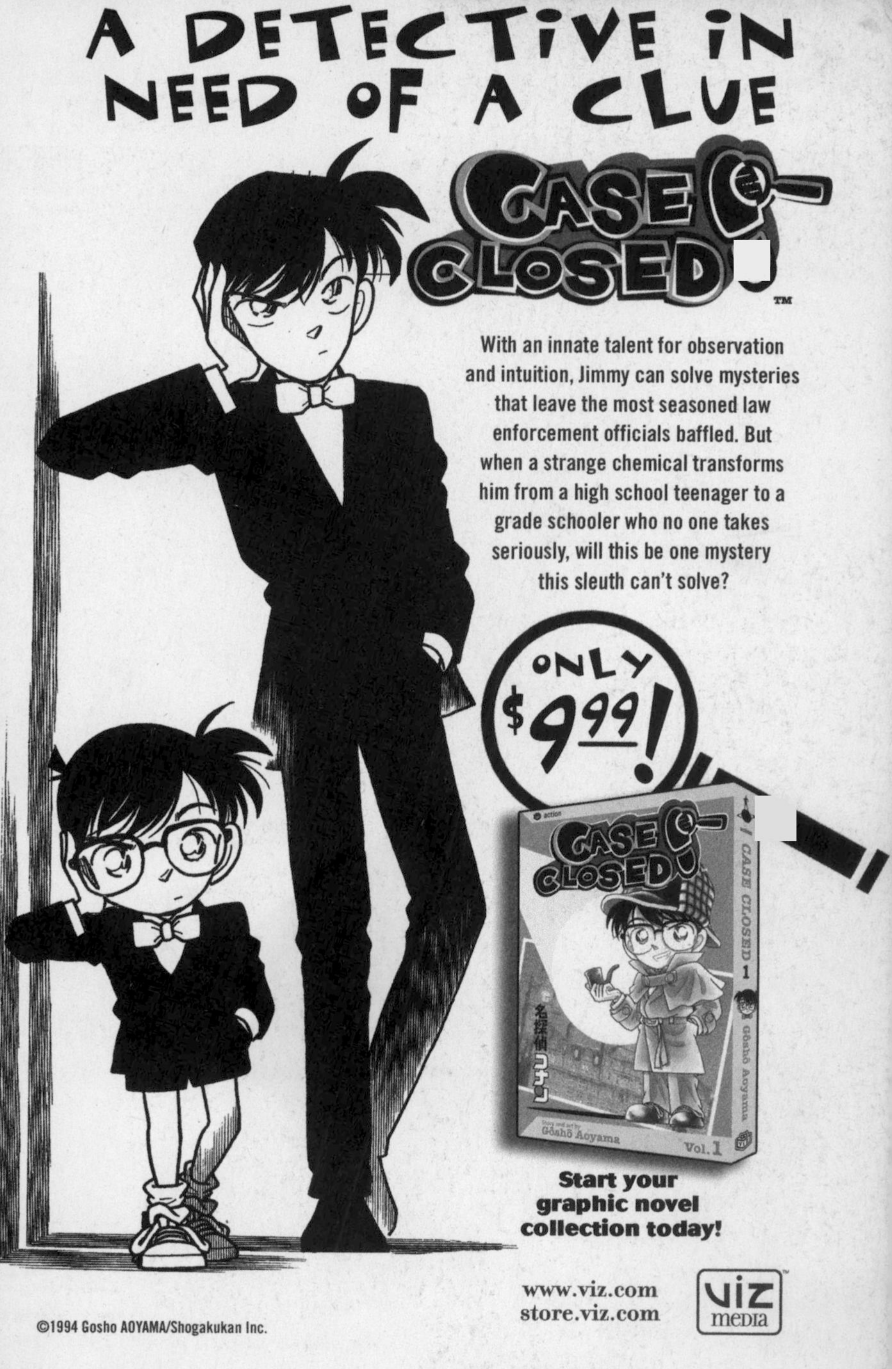
A DETECTIVE IN NEED OF A CLUE
CASE CLOSED
™
With an innate talent for observation and intuition, Jimmy can solve mysteries that leave the most seasoned law enforcement officials baffled. But when a strange chemical transforms him from a high school teenager to a grade schooler who no one takes seriously, will this be one mystery this sleuth can't solve?
ONLY $9.99!
action
CASE CLOSED
CASE CLOSED 1
名探偵コナン
Gōshō Aoyama
Vol. 1
Start your graphic novel collection today!
www.viz.com
store.viz.com
VIZ MEDIA
©1994 Gosho AOYAMA/Shogakukan Inc.

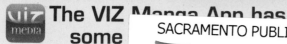

The VIZ Manga App has some ...

**The world's best manga is now on
the iPad,™ iPhone™ and iPod touch™**

To learn more, visit viz.com/25years

From legendary manga like *Death Note* to
Absolute Boyfriend, the best manga in the
world is now available on multiple devices
through the official VIZ Manga app.

- **Hundreds of volumes available**
- **Free App**
- **New content weekly**
- **Free chapter 1 previews**